Projections of Memory

Projections of Memory

ROMANTICISM, MODERNISM, AND THE AESTHETICS OF FILM

Richard I. Suchenski

OXFORD
UNIVERSITY PRESS

Oxford University Press is a department of the University of Oxford. It furthers
the University's objective of excellence in research, scholarship, and education
by publishing worldwide. Oxford is a registered trade mark of Oxford University
Press in the UK and certain other countries.

Published in the United States of America by Oxford University Press
198 Madison Avenue, New York, NY 10016, United States of America.

Cover still from *Scénario du film Passion*, a film by Jean-Luc Godard © 1982 Gaumont.

CIP data is on file at the Library of Congress
ISBN 978–0–19–027410–8 (hbk.); 978–0–19–027411–5 (pbk.)

1 3 5 7 9 8 6 4 2
Printed by Sheridan Books, Inc., United States of America

{ CONTENTS }

{ ACKNOWLEDGMENTS }

In writing this book, I have benefited greatly from conversations with many people. My debt to Dudley Andrew, John MacKay, Alexander Nemerov, P. Adams Sitney, and Jeffrey Stout is deep and, I hope, reflected inside. I am fortunate to have an editor as supportive and responsive as Brendan O'Neill, and I am very grateful for the efforts of Stephen Bradley, Leslie Johnson, Nancy Rebecca, Suvesh Subramanian, Richard Isomaki, and Oxford's production team. The insightful comments of the outside reviewers helped me strengthen key arguments. Jim and Mary Ottaway deserve special thanks for their enthusiasm, counsel, and invaluable editorial assistance. For their thoughtful feedback on earlier versions of this project, I would also like to thank Ashish Avikunthak, Tim Barringer, David Bromwich, Scott Bukatman, Francesco Casetti, Katerina Clark, the late Richard Maxwell, Charlie Musser, Rob Nelson, Brigitte Peucker, Tony Pipolo, James Quandt, Noa Steimatsky, and Katie Trumpener.

A range of international institutions have provided generous research and material support. My first thanks must go to the Mrs. Giles Whiting Foundation, the Stavros S. Niarchos Foundation, and Yale University's Department of the History of Art, which provided fellowships at critical junctures. For making archival materials available and facilitating my research, many thanks are due to Robert Beavers; Kevin Brownlow; Charles Silver and the staff of the Celeste Bartos Film Study Center of the Museum of Modern Art; John Mhiripiri, Jonas Mekas, and Robert Haller of Anthology Film Archives; Georg Wasner, Markus Wessolowski, and the staff of the Österreichisches Filmmuseum; Éric Le Roy, Caroline Patte, Fereidoun Mahboubi, and the staff of the Archives françaises du film, Centre national du cinéma et de l'image animée (CNC); Monique Faulhaber, Samantha Leroy, and Émilie Cauquy of the Cinémathèque française; Sue Jones and the staff of the British Film Institute; Elena Rossi-Snook and the staff of the New York Public Library; and all of the museums that provided high-resolution stills. I am also grateful to the Association for Studies in French Cinema for the award of a research bursary enabling me to cover part of the costs of image reproduction.

During the countless hours of work needed to see this through to completion, I have been encouraged and inspired by my wife Christina (my *belle noiseuse*). Our daughter Pia was born in the later stages of writing, and she has kept me laughing since then. I dedicate this book to them.

Projections of Memory

{ Introduction }

A work of art is an attempt to express something that is unique, it is
an affirmation of something that is whole, complete, absolute. But it is
likewise an integral part of a system of highly complex relationships.
A work of art results from an altogether independent activity; it is the
translation of a free and exalted dream. But flowing within it the
energies of many civilizations may be plainly discerned.

—HENRI FOCILLON, *THE LIFE OF FORMS IN ART* (1934)[1]

And all my creating and striving amounts to this, that I create and
piece together into one, what is now fragment and riddle and grisly
accident.

—FRIEDRICH NIETZSCHE, *THUS SPOKE ZARATHUSTRA* (1885)[2]

Nostalghia *(Andrei Tarkovsky, 1983).*

At the 1983 Telluride Film Festival, Stan Brakhage presented a medal to Andrei Tarkovsky, declaring that he was the world's greatest living narrative filmmaker because he deeply understood the three essential tasks for cinema in the twentieth century. Brakhage defined these as "make the epic . . . keep it personal, because only in the eccentricities of our personal lives do we have any chance at the truth . . . [and] do the dream work."[3] The film that Tarkovsky had brought with him to the festival, *Nostalghia* (1983), does all of these things, bringing itself firmly within the Western cultural tradition through open citations of landmarks of painting (Piero della Francesca's *Madonna del Parto*, 1460), sculpture (the *Equestrian Statue of Marcus Aurelius* in the center of Rome, 176), architecture (Michelangelo's Piazza del Campidoglio, 1538–1650), and music (Beethoven's Ninth Symphony, Opus 125, 1824). All of these are filtered through the perspective of an outsider, the protagonist Andrei Gorchakov, a Russian scholar and a surrogate for the Soviet filmmaker, who elected to remain in exile while shooting in Italy. The film culminates in a final image that is saturated with multiple levels of nostalgia—for the homeland that has been abandoned (signified by a Russian dacha), for the values attached to the artworks included in the film, and for an elevated conception of art-making that is at odds with the priorities of modern life—all mediated by a treatment of the natural sublime derived from German Romanticism and framed by the ruins of a cathedral (figures I.1–I.2).

FIGURE I.1 Ruins of the Monastery Eldena near Greifswald *(Caspar David Friedrich, 1824–1825; photograph © bpk, Berlin / Nationalgalerie, Berlin / Joerg P. Anders / Art Resource, NY).*

FIGURE I.2 Ulrich von Hutten's Grave *(Caspar David Friedrich, 1823–1824, Staatliche Kunstsammlungen, Weimar, courtesy Klassik Stiftung Weimar).*

With this ambivalent ending, Tarkovsky implicitly portrays cinema as a medium uniquely capable of containing the essences of all the other arts. It is therefore highly appropriate that the protagonist is shown resting inside the exposed nave of a cathedral, a central Romantic motif whose literary locus is Victor Hugo's 1831 novel, *Notre-Dame de Paris.* In a long section entitled "This Will Kill That," Hugo's narrator describes the process by which the collective energies and symbolic forms incarnated by the cathedral in the Middle Ages were supplanted by the democratic power of the Gutenberg press:

> The genius distributed amongst the masses was everywhere compressed under feudalism, as if under a testudo of bronze shields; architecture was its one outlet, it was released through that art and its Iliads took the form of cathedrals. The other arts all submitted to the allegiance and discipline of architecture. They were the workmen in the great work. . . . And even poor poetry, properly so called, still stubbornly vegetating in manuscripts, was obliged, if it wanted to be something, to enter within the framework of the building in the form of a hymn or of *prose*; the self-same role, after

all, which the tragedies of Aeschylus had played in the priestly festivals of Greece, or the book of Genesis in the Temple of Solomon. . . . Thus, up until Gutenberg, architecture was the chief, the universal form of writing. . . . In the fifteenth century, everything changed. The human mind discovered a means of perpetuating itself which was not only more lasting and resistant than architecture, but also simpler and easier. Architecture was dethroned. The lead characters of Gutenberg succeeded the stone characters of Orpheus. . . . *The book was to kill the building.* . . . It was the total renewal of man's mode of expression, the human mind sloughing off one form to put on another, a complete and definite change of skin by that symbolic serpent which, ever since Adam, has represented the intelligence.[4]

In the twentieth century, these functions were largely taken on by the cinema, which absorbed elements from the earlier arts and incorporated them into an even more universal means of communication. As a mode of expression predicated (like a press) on mass reproduction, the cinema has been seen as several degrees removed from the "aura" Walter Benjamin ascribed to singular art objects.[5] Films like *Nostalghia*, however, attempt to retrieve some of the properties Hugo aligns with the cathedral, redefining the terms by which film art and film artists are to be understood. In its most extreme forms, this supremely Romantic impulse has driven certain filmmakers to create extraordinarily ambitious films that also use duration to resist the industrial structures cinema is normally dependent upon. These films actively participate in a modernist interrogation of the relationship between form and content, often taking their innovations to what seem to be their limits, simultaneously establishing and exhausting their own paradigms.

Since the mid-1910s, the length of commercially distributed feature films has remained relatively standardized, usually ranging between four and eight reels or approximately 70 and 140 minutes. Nevertheless, a parallel corpus of much longer films, which break the chains of conventional exhibition, has played an important role throughout film history. During the first great period of cinematic experimentation, the 1920s, temporal magnitude connoted seriousness of purpose, and filmmakers made brazenly extravagant claims about the meaning of their outsized running times. Erich von Stroheim announced that his eight-hour *Greed* (1924) would effect a revival of classical theater, while Abel Gance insisted that, when showing works like his *Napoléon vu par Abel Gance* (1927), movie theaters would become "Cathedrals of Light."[6] These beliefs were suppressed after the arrival of sound—which ensured the dominance of tightly integrated, factory-like production studios—and for more than thirty years there would be few attempts to produce films of comparable scope. When the widespread adoption of less cumbersome 16mm equipment, the disintegration of studio-controlled monopolies, and the emergence of a young postwar audience opened up new possibilities for adventurous filmmaking, a group of even more challenging long-form works appeared, all created by directors who idealized the "lost paradise" of the silent era.

What the filmmakers producing these inordinately long works share is a combination of audacity, intensity, and absolute commitment, as well as a willingness to court anachronism. Uniting all of these is a striving for sublimity, for a mode of experience that excites the mind to outrun its own capacities. The sublime has long been connected to questions of scale: the Greek rhetorician Longinus associated it with grandeur and strong emotion; in *A Philosophical Enquiry into the Origin of Our Ideas of the Sublime and Beautiful* (1757), Edmund Burke linked it directly to "greatness of dimension."[7] Hugo built upon this tradition in his manifesto for Romanticism, the "Preface to *Cromwell*" (1827), by asserting that "the modern spirit" has its origins in the "fertile union of the grotesque with the sublime" and calling for new equivalents to the organic fusion once embodied by the cathedral.[8] Acknowledging that *Cromwell*, a four-hundred-page theatrical behemoth, was unperformable "in its present proportions," he predicted that "people in France will soon become accustomed to devoting a whole evening to a single play . . . worth a multitude of others."[9]

Whether through open affirmation or ironized negation, the long-form films discussed in this book are heavily informed by the ideas and iconography of Romanticism, using them as part of an exploration of the function and meaning of cinema. Where genuine Romanticism in Hollywood has to enter via subterfuge (Alfred Hitchcock), a style of mad excess teetering on kitsch (King Vidor's *Duel in the Sun*, 1946), or a veil of irony bordering on camp (as in the jokey preface to James Whale's 1935 *Bride of Frankenstein*), films like *Napoléon vu par Abel Gance* or *Eniaios* (Gregory Markopoulos, 1947–1992) invite comparison with works like Richard Wagner's *Der Ring des Nibelungen* (1848–1876) or Percy Bysshe Shelley's *Prometheus Unbound* (1820).[10] More than anything else, it is the figure of Prometheus that symbolizes the conflation in these films of utopian idealism, formal invention, and creative independence. Longinus argued that "by some innate power the true sublime uplifts our souls; we are filled with a proud exaltation and a sense of vaunting joy, just as though we had ourselves produced [it]."[11] By eliciting this sensation, Promethean egoism can become generative. Goethe tellingly ends his "On German Architecture" (1773) by depicting a young artist inspired by the image of a cathedral to believe that "more than Prometheus, [he can] carry down the rapture of the gods to the earth."[12] Like the Titan who stole fire from the heavens and shared it with humanity, these filmmakers (whose degree of self-identification with Prometheus varies in significant ways) all strove to create their own cinematic cathedrals, monuments to the imagination that promise transformations of vision, selfhood, and experience.

The much more restrained Hollywood paradigm, at least during the period from the early 1930s through the 1970s, is epitomized by *Gone with the Wind* (Victor Fleming, 1939), a popular epic that addressed momentous historical events by focusing on the emotional dramas of a small group of well-defined characters played by charismatic stars. In Nicholas Ray's *In a Lonely Place* (1950), an aspiring ingénue tells the screenwriter protagonist that his screenplay is like an epic, defined as "a picture that's *real* long and has lots of things going on." For all their considerable differences in tone, style, and politics, *The Ten Commandments* (Cecil B. DeMille, 1923), *Ben-Hur* (William Wyler, 1959), and *Reds* (Warren Beatty, 1981) all follow this model, as do novelistic, multipart films released in other countries like Sergei Bondarchuk's *War and Peace* (1966–1967, four parts) and *The Human Condition* (Kobayashi Masaki, 1959–1961, three parts).[13] No matter where they are located or what the subject matter is, filmmakers creating this form of big-budget studio spectacle are operating by the same rules of the game. It is possible to make personal statements within this format, but doing so requires a director with a strong personality who is nevertheless able to adapt to the commercial dictates of the material at hand. *El Cid* (Anthony Mann, 1961) is an exemplary case, and part of Mann's achievement is to make this massive work resonate with his thematic obsessions and muscular style—built upon dynamic shifts in spatial configuration, a rigorous use of color, and the sudden alternation of close and distant framing—without losing its moorings as a narrative spectacle. As with other expensive films of this kind, however, there are certain expectations of pacing, casting, narrative transparency, and length (to enable as many daily shows as possible) that are inescapable. To do otherwise, as von Stroheim did, is to risk banishment and obloquy.

Hollywood epics rarely run for more than three hours, while the projects addressed in the chapters that follow are meant to be watched in barely interrupted blocks lasting as long as eight hours, sometimes over a period of days or weeks. These films are unusual in both their formal adventurousness and their presentation, utilizing their duration and the conditions of the film-screening situation to create a particularly intense form of spectatorial engagement that is related to a larger utopian program. There are many films that meet one or another of these criteria, but the long-form projects analyzed here are major limit cases around which other works of this kind can be oriented. The ecstatic tone of *Napoléon vu par Abel Gance*, for example, encapsulates the euphoric hopes of its period and the concomitant sense that cinema will go on without end. What made the *Napoléon* project unique was its fusion of the most advanced techniques of the first cinematic avant-garde of the 1920s with the most visually arresting forms of cinematic showmanship; its style and sensibility can be related, at one and the same time, to the work of Jean Epstein and David Lean. Conceived as the apex of silent era experimentation, the film offers the strongest possible link to Romantic aesthetics and ideas, particularly as they were understood by art historian Élie

Faure, whose biography of the French emperor was one of the sources for the film.

Although they have a shared investment in temporal scale, ritual, and a Promethean conception of the artist, filmmakers working in this manner after World War II proceeded with assumptions very different from their silent era predecessors. The war acted as a rupture, blocking access to a past onto which unrealized, and perhaps unrealizable, aspirations could be projected. If, as David Quint has argued, the generic counterpart to epic is romance—the one providing a "linear teleology" defined by the victors and the other marked by obsessive and seemingly disconnected meanderings whose "emblem" is "the wandering ship of Odysseus"—then these projects, interrelating both, incline toward the latter.[14] In his seven-and-a-half-hour *Hitler, a Film from Germany* (1977), Hans-Jürgen Syberberg transplants these ideas onto the war itself, examining the mutual co-option of both filmmaking and utopian Romantic rhetoric in the Nazi period and highlighting the difficulties intrinsic to post-1945 attempts to construct cinematic cathedrals. Syberberg's Brechtian distance and reliance on sound acts as a dialectical foil to the image-oriented paradigm advanced by Gance. By addressing their work together, the first chapter attempts to demonstrate the historically contingent nature, and implications, of this type of project. Like Syberberg, the central figures in subsequent chapters—Gregory Markopoulos, Jacques Rivette, and Jean-Luc Godard—instead take a yearning for artistic totality defined by particular myths and metaphors, what one could call an image of Romanticism, and refashion it to their own ends. Acutely aware of the power of Mary Shelley's creator-destroying "Modern Prometheus" and the dangers inherent in Byronic self-assertion, these filmmakers created long-form works that can best be understood in light of the self-conscious Romantic poetics described by Friedrich Schlegel in the *Athenaeum Fragments* (1798). Reflecting upon themselves in an "endless succession of mirrors," they precariously hover "on the wings of poetic reflection" while oscillating back and forth between creation and destruction.[15]

In his eighty-hour *Eniaios*, Markopoulos intensifies both the underlying Romanticism and the montage aesthetics of Gance, but does so by completely rejecting the ordinary networks of cinema, re-envisioning film as a medium capable of reconnecting the viewer to the sacred world of myth. With *L'Amour fou* (1968) and *Out 1* (1971), Rivette productively develops the tension between sharp, architectonic editing and seemingly improvisational long takes as far as it can go, in effect taking an approach to cinema associated with the French New Wave to the brink of madness. Finally, with the *Histoire(s) du cinéma* project, Godard takes the friction created by his matrix of cross-references to the threshold of legibility, reviving the strategies of superimposition used by earlier avant-gardists (like Gance and Markopoulos) to visually layer different periods and to make contrapuntal use of extracts from the histories of film, painting, music, and literature. A four-and-a-half-hour video work that is deeply concerned with the impact of the projected image and elegiacally posits the death of cinema, *Histoire(s) du cinéma* gives new meaning to an aesthetics of fragments, using a dense network of associations to meditate on the end of the twentieth century and its preeminent medium.

As the retrospective tenor of Godard's late work acutely demonstrates, the persistent influence of Romanticism on these filmmakers is also evident in their treatment of memory. Since the publication of John Locke's *An Essay Concerning Human Understanding* (1689), the impression of continuity established by and within memory has been understood to be the fundamental precondition of individual selfhood. Rebutting the mechanistic assumptions of the Enlightenment, the early Romantics emphasized the vitality of memory, drawing attention to its ability to both give coherence to and creatively transform discrete perceptions. Schlegel argued that the "concept of *unity* can by no means be deduced except out of *memory*; it can no more be explained through the senses than through reason."[16] Novalis described memory as "the element of individuation" and "the necessary preliminary to poetry," referring to it, in the fourth of his *Hymns to the Night* (1800), as a "moss-grown monument."[17] Like Schlegel, Novalis attempted to distinguish passive recollection from active memory, which he aligned with "productive imagination."[18] Samuel Taylor Coleridge developed a similar contrast between fancy and imagination in his *Biographia Literaria* (1817), connecting the former with the passivity of "ordinary memory," and arguing that the latter instead "dissolves, diffuses, dissipates, in order to recreate . . . at all events it struggles to idealize and to unify."[19] The fixed structure of film projection—with reels of printed film frames unspooling sequentially—is even more rigidly iterative than that of the mind. One of the goals of the projects discussed in this book is to involve the active memory of the viewer and encourage heightened engagement through structures of parallelism and contrast (von Stroheim/Markopoulos), the frequent mnemonic return to particular tropes or figures (Rivette), and the exploration of the complex interrelationship between subjective experience and collective histories (Godard).

These projects are all considered in conjunction with the evolving aesthetic programs of their directors, using a critical methodology that, combining the techniques of film and art history, is commensurate with the type of engagement the works themselves encourage or demand. Far too often, film studies and art history have spoken at cross purposes. The former has generally confined itself in recent years either to the study of national/transnational cinemas (and of filmmakers positioned within these cultural contexts) or to generalizing theoretical reflections largely disconnected from the interpretive and perceptual challenges of ambitious films. For its part, art history has rarely known what to do with cinema, especially with films that do not fit comfortably within the frameworks of contemporary art, are insufficiently popular to function as examples of a dominant visual culture, and cannot be positioned as direct extensions of canonical modern art movements (e.g., the Surrealist collaborations of Luis Buñuel and Salvador Dalí).

In one way or another, each of the filmmakers in this book tried to raise the artistic status of cinema, and close attention is paid to the way in which the relationship between utopian Romanticism and cinematic modernism is configured in and across the works. Modernism here has a double aspect, criticizing the strictures of consumer society while simultaneously reinvigorating tradition by engendering forms that extend their artistic heritage even as they challenge its basic parameters. Examining the creative strategies of these works in relation to one another and to the larger historical forces that shape them, tracing the shifts and permutations of their forms and aspirations, provides a new perspective on these kinds of long-form projects and also helps to clarify the stakes of cinema more broadly. Situated, on the one hand, between the Hollywood epic and television, and, on the other, between nineteenth-century (the panorama, opera) and twenty-first-century (video installations) modes of large-scale artistic presentation, this form of cinema acts as a nexus through which currents from the other arts can interpenetrate. Synthesizing their disparate influences into magisterial edifices, these projects treat cinema, like the oneiric sanctuary at the end of *Nostalghia*, as a space in which the most ancient forms can be made radically new.

"The Era of the Image Has Arrived"

I love the Art of today because I love
Light above all and all people
Love Light above all
They invented Fire.

—GUILLAUME APOLLINAIRE (1913)[1]

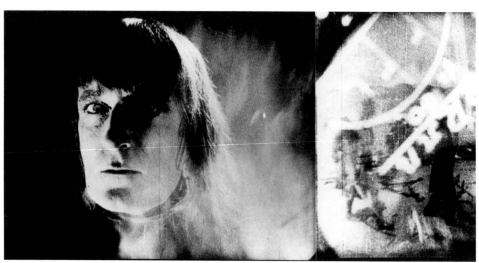

Napoléon vu par Abel Gance *(Abel Gance, 1927)*

(courtesy Photoplay Productions).

Several months after *The Birth of a Nation*'s premiere in February 1915, D. W. Griffith participated in an important interview that has been almost totally ignored by subsequent historians. After arguing that "the scope of the motion picture is absolutely boundless," he makes a very revealing claim:

> There will always be room for the one and two reel picture, just as there is always room for the short story in literature, but the day will come when, outside of the real gems among the shorter pieces, the long picture, so long that it cannot be shown in a day, will be regarded as the masterpiece.[2]

How exactly would audiences see such films? "Mark my words, we will soon see the day when it may take two or three days' time for a theatre to show a single picture, when a man will drop in early in the afternoon and stay until the theatre closes at night, and then come back the next day to see the rest of it," Griffith declares.[3] Although he claims that "people will see [the very long film] in installments, just as they read a book a chapter at a time," it is clear from his other statements (and from the increasingly complex structure of his narratives) that he is not referring to the serial presentation that had emerged only a few years before, and certainly not to the way films like Vitagraph's *The Life of Moses* (J. Stuart Blackton, 1909)—or, for that matter, his first two-reel film *Enoch Arden* (1911)—had been broken up into separately screened sections, but rather to the intensive experience of total, integrated works.[4]

These long films, which would be of such great depth and imaginative richness that audiences would want to commit massive amounts of time to view them, would warrant special, concentrated presentations like that accorded to Richard Wagner's *Der Ring des Nibelungen* (1848–1876).[5] This was certainly not the attitude of the producers, exhibitors, or audiences of the time, but it does reflect the scale of Griffith's ambitions (or rather his assumption that ambition was inexorably intertwined with scale) as well as his sense of the forward trajectory of cinema. It was Griffith's belief that if films of sufficient heft could be made, he could create "literature in motion picture form" and ensure cinema's place in the pantheon.[6] Cultural legitimation was certainly a major factor in his desire to commission an explicitly Wagnerian score synchronized with the onscreen action of *The Birth of a Nation* and to screen the film in regular theaters at roughly the same admission prices used for live performances. Yet even though his points of reference are to the established arts, Griffith also polemically acknowledges the ability of the cinema to smoothly interrelate a variety of perspectives, pointing out that the motion picture "can show anything from the feelings of a lettuce up to the growth and fall of a great empire."[7] He would try to do both in his next film, *Intolerance* (1916), the closest he would ever come to the expansive epic he called for.

Intolerance was one of three American epics released in 1916 against the backdrop of World War I, and like *Civilization* (Thomas Ince, 1916) and *Joan the Woman* (Cecil B. DeMille, 1916), it is unified through an overt allegory that frames the central narrative action. Whereas Ince's film includes elaborate "dream" sequences in which the protagonist is divinely instructed to renounce all forms of war, and the DeMille film narrates the life of Joan of Arc from the trenches, *Intolerance* moves between four different periods with increasing rapidity as the film goes on and is therefore more dependent on its pacifist superstructure. The repeated cuts to an image of Lillian Gish rocking a cradle help to anchor the different narrative streams, distilling human suffering into a single image designed to make the relationships between the various permutations of intolerance clear while also serving as evidence of the ultimately visionary nature of the film. *Intolerance* finally builds toward the sort of eschatological plea for peace and harmony that Griffith had used, more incongruously, at the end of *The Birth of a Nation*. Interestingly, the program notes distributed at the premiere quote Ralph Waldo Emerson:

> If we would not be marplots with our miserable interferences, the work, the society, letters, arts, science, religion of men would go on far better than now, and the heaven predicted from the beginning of the world, and still predicted from the bottom of the heart, would organize itself, as do now the rose and the air and the sun.[8]

The plot of the "modern" section of *Intolerance* is built around the misguided efforts of invasive, self-righteous reformers, but they are simply a foil to the film's larger utopian program. Like Emerson, Griffith suggests that genuine social progress can happen only through the awakening of individual conscience by the power of art.[9]

Many aspects of Griffith's visual repertoire remain anachronistically tied to nineteenth-century practices, and it has long been a commonplace to refer to his narrative debt to the Dickensian novel, especially since the publication of Sergei Eisenstein's essay "Griffith, Dickens, and the Film Today" in 1944. Griffith encouraged this when he explained that his most celebrated innovation, the "switch-back," was inspired by Dickens' technique of "switching off": "He introduces a multitude of characters and incidents, and breaks off abruptly to go from one to another, but at the end he cleverly gathers all the apparently loose-threads together again, and rounds off the whole."[10] This is certainly true of Griffith's work generally, but the pivot image of *Intolerance* is derived from another source, one much closer to Emerson: Walt Whitman's 1855 *Leaves of Grass* ("Out of the cradle endlessly rocking").[11] Griffith's cradle, like Whitman's, conveys a complex sense of eternal cyclicity. Although his overdetermined image lacks the subtle force of Whitman's poem, it does exert a sort of hieratic power, with the numerous repetitions creating the impression that it possesses a (cosmic) temporal logic markedly different from the interlocking narrative streams that it joins.

In his discussion of *Intolerance*, Vachel Lindsay called the cradle the "key hieroglyph" of the film, connecting it to the ideas about cinema in his pioneering book *The Art of the Motion Picture* (1915).[12] Lindsay, eager to claim that cinema was the equal of the rival arts, suggested that there were deep affinities between the pictorial language of ancient Egypt and the new medium, seeing in that the key to the art of the silent "photoplay." The correlation of artwork and hieroglyph had been a recurring trope in Symbolist writings, but its roots lie in the rhetoric of Romantics like Philipp Otto Runge, Novalis, and Eugène Delacroix, who wrote that his figures "are like a solid bridge by which the imagination penetrating them reaches the mysterious and profound sensation of which the forms are, in some way, the hieroglyph."[13] In this sense, the hieroglyph acts as an entry point into secret magical knowledge, a hermetic system of internal correspondences underlying surface reality to which the distinctive visual vocabulary of an artist can provide access. This priestly conception of the artist was revived by several early twentieth-century modernists whose work was exactly contemporary with Griffith's filmmaking: the Expressionist Ernst Ludwig Kirchner claimed to have "developed the hieroglyph and enriched modern art thereby," while Futurist painter Gino Severeni entitled an important canvas *Dynamic Hieroglyph of the Bal Tabarin* (1912).[14]

The hieroglyph was also an important metaphor for nineteenth-century historians like Leopold von Ranke (an influence on *The Birth of a Nation*), who urged scholars to look for the "holy hieroglyph, perceived only in its outline" that reflects the omnipresence of God in history.[15] John Irwin has argued that a similar notion of hieroglyphics permeated American Romantic literature in the middle to late nineteenth century, manifesting itself in the work of Henry David Thoreau and Emerson as well as Whitman's *Leaves of Grass*, which Irwin claims was conceived as "a kind of hieroglyphic Bible."[16] Lindsay's use of the term continues this tradition while purging it of both its obscurantist and religious connotations, focusing instead on its potential as a means of mass visual communication. With the advent of the cinema, he claims, "A tribe that has thought in words since the days that it worshipped Thor and told legends of the cunning of the tongue of Loki, suddenly begins to think in pictures."[17] Griffith would surely have subscribed to Lindsay's ideas, arguing in his own writings that cinema had an extraordinary psychological power and an unprecedented capacity to affect the viewer's understanding. He summed up his grandiose sense of the cinema when he claimed, "We have found a universal language, a power that can make men brothers and end war forever."[18] This shift from text to image is reinforced in *Intolerance* through the books and cuneiform tablets in the visual intertitles, emblems of the picture writing Griffith practiced throughout the film (figure 1.1).

In at least one crucial respect, Griffith's films were very different from the sort of "hieroglyphic" works developed by artists like Delacroix or Kirchner. It was not easy to decode images during viewing because they were neither

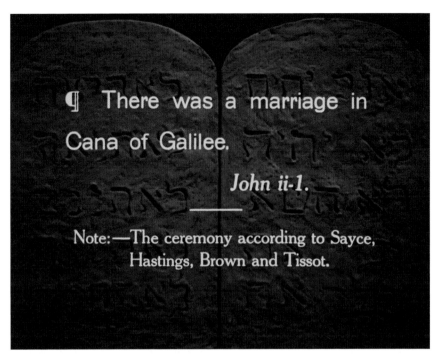

FIGURE 1.1 Intolerance *(D. W. Griffith, 1916).*

wholly autonomous nor simply juxtaposed like a visual script, but were instead inserted within an elaborate montage chain, remaining onscreen for a few seconds at most before the next link appeared. More than any film before it, *Intolerance* was fundamentally shaped by its editing. Over the course of two months, Griffith edited down the 300,000 feet of raw footage into an extremely dense film running, in its integral form, for 13,700 feet, or fourteen reels.[19] The four different periods were like "four currents, [flowing] side by side," and, wherever possible, Griffith attempted to link them through associations of movement, gesture, or spatial arrangement.[20] Although the final film possesses a polyphonic shape that holds up to sustained analysis, Griffith's method was improvisational, and the editing was largely intuitive, with some of it done in-camera during shooting. Hollywood, which barely existed at the time *Intolerance* was made, would try to tame and systematize Griffith's idiosyncratic editing patterns a few years later, while Soviet directors like Eisenstein would try to draw out their latent dialectical possibilities, but they were almost universally recognized as a major step forward for the cinema.[21]

Some people involved with the production of *Intolerance* have suggested that Griffith originally intended to make a film much longer than the one that was released to general audiences in 1916. Lillian Gish, who described herself as "closer to *Intolerance* than anyone else except [cameraman] Billy

Bitzer and Jimmy Smith, the cutter," argued that earlier cuts of *Intolerance* lasted for at least eight hours, split into two parts to be screened on consecutive days.[22] Griffith is said to have abandoned these plans when theater owners refused to accommodate a two-day film, and the prints released in 1916 generally ran for around three hours (the fourteen-reel premiere version would have run three and a half to four hours). Even in this form, *Intolerance* proved almost impossible for most spectators to digest. Anita Loos, who contributed to the intertitles and claims to have been the "first viewer to ever see *Intolerance*," later wrote: "I must be honest and say I thought D. W. had lost his mind."[23]

Griffith would never achieve a film on the scale he described in his 1915 essay, but two directors who saw themselves as his true heirs—Erich von Stroheim and Abel Gance—would try, repeatedly, throughout the 1920s. Both Gance and von Stroheim began their careers making pictures with ordinary running times, but, within a few short years, they would both struggle to create massive films that they hoped would stand shoulder to shoulder with the great masterpieces of literature, music, and painting. In this, they were extending the Griffith model of long-form filmmaking, and both directors frequently stressed their connection with the "master." Having "graduated from the cinematic school of D. W. Griffith," von Stroheim was determined to make the cinema into "an art encompassing all the arts."[24]

Realism Transcended

> We shall tell it at length, in precise and thorough detail—for when
> was a story short on diversion or long on boredom simply because of
> the time and space required for the telling? Unafraid of the odium of
> appearing too meticulous, we are much more inclined to the view that
> only thoroughness can be truly entertaining.
>
> —THOMAS MANN, FOREWORD TO *THE MAGIC MOUNTAIN* (1924)[25]

The entire career of von Stroheim, Hollywood's most iconic martyr, was founded upon myths. Son of a Jewish merchant and a failed member of the Austrian military, Erich Oswald "von" Stroheim strategically presented himself as a member of the Viennese aristocracy from the moment he arrived in the United States, and he promoted all of his films as part of an autobiographical construction.[26] Success at playing vicious Huns during World War I earned von Stroheim the right to direct, and key aspects of his style were established in his debut, *Blind Husbands* (1919)—a somber, almost ritualistic tempo, gestural precision, and an attempt to represent interior states through intricate spatial arrangements. From the early 1920s on, this was wedded to an extreme notion of length, which von Stroheim argued would allow him to revive ancient theater, now "taken in by the eye, not the ear."[27]

Von Stroheim's third film would mark a decisive shift in this direction. By the time shooting was completed for *Foolish Wives* (1922), von Stroheim had used an astonishing 320 reels of negative (partially due to the insistent retakes demanded by a director who was both a perfectionist and an experimenter). Once the individual shots had been assembled and edited, the December 1921 first cut ran for thirty-two reels, or approximately six hours of projection time, far more than any other film made up to that point (figure 1.2). Decades later, von Stroheim would try to justify the length of his films by claiming that he had "always wanted to make a great film, a good film and a long one, too, with an intermission—at a psychologically suitable moment—to give the audience time for dinner as the great Eugene O'Neill did in *Strange Interlude* (1928). He did it several years after me."[28] Von Stroheim repeated versions of this story on several occasions, in an understandable attempt to soften his reputation as a profligate filmmaker, but he seems to have misremembered the lengths of his initial cuts (with a dinner break, a full screening of *Foolish Wives* would have lasted from mid-afternoon to midnight). In the early 1920s, his statements reflected a very different attitude. Asked by a reporter how his thirty-two-reel film could be presented in an evening, von Stroheim responded, "That is a detail I hadn't time to bother about."[29]

FIGURE 1.2 *Erich von Stroheim editing (from the Kevin Brownlow Collection).*

Like Griffith, von Stroheim found inspiration in respected literary works, which he tried to adapt in wholly visual terms. The Cinémathèque française contains two heavily annotated copies of Frank Norris' *McTeague* (1899) that von Stroheim used as the basis for *Greed* (1924) and apparently kept with him on set.[30] Looking at the pages makes it clear that his interest lay in the novel's action rather than its many descriptive passages. Aside from rearranging a few scenes and toning down Norris' racially charged treatment of the "Polish Jew" Zerkow, the basic narrative structure of the original *Greed* screenplay is very similar to that of *McTeague*, but the details are treated in revealingly different ways. Both Norris and von Stroheim try to depict fundamental human drives, but where Norris does so by linking the particularities of his characters to the social milieu they inhabit, von Stroheim focuses on visual tropes and small details of performance. In *McTeague*, Norris inserts a handful of references to the protagonist's pet canary; in *Greed*, the canary becomes part of a visual network coursing through the film, with von Stroheim adding a wounded bird in the prologue as well as a second canary (given to Trina) and using both birds as stand-ins for the characters in a montage sequence involving the third central character (Marcus), who is represented, appropriately enough, by a cat. From *Blind Husbands* on, von Stroheim demonstrated an almost mystical faith in the power of a pictorially dense or symbolically layered image to convey psychological essences, and this impulse comes to full fruition in *Greed*.

Throughout von Stroheim's body of work, the focus on narratively significant details is counterbalanced and given a very different inflection by the use of totems—black cats, half-concealed moons, and ominous crucifixes are especially prominent. This effect was strengthened, at least upon the initial release of the films, by an evocative use of selective color. In *Blind Husbands*, the flames in a candelabrum were hand-tinted in one scene using the laborious Handschiegl process, as were the flames that envelop the tower near the end of *Foolish Wives* and the gold objects in *Greed* (figure 1.3). Even von Stroheim's obsession with authentic props and locations has a mystical quality to it. Von Stroheim insisted on renting the actual mine described in *McTeague* and having his actors work within the house that had been the site of the murder that inspired Norris' novel, so that the emotions that von Stroheim believed resided in them would somehow work their way into the film.[31] Richard Koszarski points out that von Stroheim had tried similar things in *Merry-Go-Round* (1923) the year before, bringing Emperor Franz Josef's carriage over to Hollywood, "not simply because he wanted to integrate a realistic prop. He wanted it because it was part of the true cross."[32]

For von Stroheim, "realism" was not a rigidly fixed set of codes, but a way of bringing the full range of human experience within the space of the frame. As he put it, "Everything that man could dream of, I could reproduce, and

FIGURE 1.3 Foolish Wives *(Erich von Stroheim, 1922).*

I wanted to reproduce, in my films."[33] At times, this entailed finding ways to enhance the depth of field of his images (often through the ingenious use of mirrors), locating his dramas within a dense social environment and creating multiple zones of action that frequently commented upon one another. Elsewhere, space would be deliberately flattened and pictorialized by placing a veil over the camera lens, a technique, employed inside the monk's hut and whenever Karamzin (von Stroheim) looks at Ventucci's daughter in *Foolish Wives*, that von Stroheim and cinematographer Ben Reynolds called "pastelography." At other moments, von Stroheim switches suddenly from domestic scenes to allegorical inserts, such as a pair of wizened hands clutching at coins, that resemble Hieronymus Bosch's depictions of the seven deadly sins.[34] In films like *Blind Husbands*, images like these had been contained within dream sequences, but in *Greed* they act as visionary interruptions within the central narrative, eerie intimations of "the skull beneath the skin."[35] In a similar fashion, scenes like the post-wedding dinner are made to suggest gluttony more than community by repeated cuts to deliberately grotesque close-ups of faces and objects.

All of these elements are present in *Greed*'s most dramatic scene, the murder of Trina. Filmed mainly in long takes, the scene begins as a black cat runs across the screen, with a door framed through a set of partitions creating a highly compressed sense of space. As Trina and Mac struggle, they push back through several other doors; the actual murder takes place offscreen in a tunnel that appears to recede far into the distance. Several minutes later, however, the scene ends as it began, with a closed door demarcating the limits of a very shallow visual field. The result is an accordion-like sense of space expanding and collapsing within a sustained block of time whose very theatricality (reinforced through the framing) is made uniquely cinematic. The proscenium framing of the murder also acts as an ironic echo of the equally theatricalized wedding night, linking the film's only open depiction of sexual relations with death. By concentrating the formal strategies, visual symbolism, and primal drives that course through the film, the murder scene acts as the film's hinge, deepening von Stroheim's brand of realism by pushing it beyond convention and into a more irrational realm.

Von Stroheim's obsessive methods were dependent upon the resources the studios had at their disposal, but MGM saw *Greed* as flagrantly, even defiantly, uncommercial. Knowing that his contract did not give him final cut, von Stroheim attempted to preempt cuts by production manager Irving Thalberg by holding a series of preview screenings of the complete version for a number of critics and colleagues. According to Harry Carr, one of the few people to have seen the full version in 1924, the film ran for forty-five reels from 10:30 a.m. to 8:00 p.m., and von Stroheim made it clear that his ideal was either intensive viewing or screening over two consecutive evenings.[36] Despite the public support of almost everyone von Stroheim invited, MGM eventually cut the film down, allegedly destroying the negative for the remainder to extract the silver in the nitrate.[37] Whether or not this story is apocryphal, it perfectly encapsulates the mythos surrounding the film: the masterpiece of cinematic art destroyed by the forces of commerce.

Although no one has seen the original version of *Greed* since 1924, a four-hour reconstruction—mounted by Rick Schmidlin in 1998 and made up of all the extant footage reassembled according to the original script, with stills standing in for missing scenes—gives some indication of what the experience of watching the original film would have been like. Images, themes, and motifs appear and reappear throughout the film, and the doubling and repetition quietly accumulates considerable force. Carr compared von Stroheim's method to that of Victor Hugo's *Les Misérables* (1862): "Episodes come along that you think have no bearing on the story, then twelve or fourteen reels later, it hits you with a crash."[38] In the expanded version of *Greed*, the sadomasochistic relationship of Zerkow and Maria, totally excised from the ten-reel cut and "reintroduced" in the restoration, acts as a dark mirror of the Trina/Mac one, strengthening the overall moral dynamic and, through Trina's encounter with the dead Maria, giving the film a supernatural tint. These structural echoes are further enriched by the presence of the genteel couple Old Grannis and Miss Baker, whose chaste relationship contrasts markedly with that of both Mac/Trina and Zerkow/Maria. Other motifs, like the canary and the allegorical figures, are made to resonate across and even between films in a way that suggests that von Stroheim's fundamental method was one of refinement. When Mac kisses Trina early in *Greed*, for example, a shawl is wrapped around her face so that she looks like a nun, echoing earlier scenes like the seduction beneath a cross in *Blind Husbands* and anticipating later permutations like the abduction of Gloria Swanson from a convent in *Queen Kelly* (1929).

The impression of von Stroheim's silent films as an extended series of themes and variations was reinforced by *The Wedding March* (1928) and *Queen Kelly*, his last attempts to make a "great long film." This is especially true of *The Wedding March*, von Stroheim's longest film. A witty fantasia about the fin de siècle Vienna of von Stroheim's youth, the film sardonically refers to well-known images of the past (like William Hogarth's *Marriage à-la-mode* series, 1742–1743), changing the Griffith model of legitimation to one of ironic citation that would be developed further by art historically conscious modernists in subsequent decades. *The Wedding March* may have been its director's most structurally adventurous film, a prismatic study of decadence and decay among both Old World aristocrats and the lower classes in which incidents and details echo back and forth across the body of the film. During the opening sequence, a statue of the Madonna within St. Stephen's Cathedral is juxtaposed with its "so contrasting symbol, the 'Iron Man'—a remnant of the Middle Ages." Later in the film, a superimposed vision of the Iron Man taking a Danube-Maid offscreen is quickly followed by a shot of the prince (played by von Stroheim) carrying the woman he has fallen in love with in the same direction.

Although Paramount producer Pat Powers stopped shooting on *The Wedding March* before the film was completely finished, the original rough cut of "exactly fifty reels" would have run for more than nine hours, exceeding even *Greed*.[39] In a press release after the editing of the film had been taken out of his hands, von Stroheim argued, "After a certain amount of editing had been done on *The Wedding March*, I evolved the idea of dividing the production into two films—one to be called *The Wedding March*, the other to be called *The Honeymoon*."[40] The crucial phrase here is the first one, because the original script has no break whatsoever and the division was almost certainly a compromise solution.[41] Herman Weinberg argued that von Stroheim once again wanted a dedicated two-day screening of a very slightly reduced version—with each part running slightly over four hours—or, at worst, the creation of a single four- or five-hour version with a dinner break. He got neither. *The Wedding March* was cut down from an initial 25,795 feet to a version of 10,852 feet running for under two hours. The second part, *The Honeymoon*, was not released in North America, but was distributed in a version reduced from 22,424 feet to 7,000 feet in Europe and South America.[42]

Von Stroheim was even less fortunate with *Queen Kelly*, which was produced by star Gloria Swanson and financed by Joseph P. Kennedy rather than a major Hollywood studio. Less sumptuous than *The Wedding March*, *Queen Kelly* contains von Stroheim's most complex visual experiments, and many of the images have a crystalline density. In *The Wedding March*, von Stroheim had employed a series of in-camera dissolves as a way of conveying the psychological intensity of the confession scene; in *Queen Kelly*, these are combined with lap dissolves, creating a fluid, dreamlike texture in which individual objects and figures become suffused with meaning. Unfortunately, von Stroheim included a number of elements that Kennedy felt would invariably trouble the censors, and the funding was pulled well before shooting was completed.[43] Had the film been completed in the year it was shot, it may have been the great success von Stroheim always dreamed of, but by the time Swanson tried to salvage what was left of the material in 1931, the silent cinema had been totally supplanted. Only vestiges of von Stroheim's complex and intricate narrative structure, designed to engage the attentive viewer in an active process of mnemonic association, survived the process of recutting.[44]

All of von Stroheim's major films suggest incompleteness and fragmentation, but these ideas are not worked into them, as they would be in the long-form projects completed after the end of World War II. More than most filmmakers, von Stroheim believed in total, unified works. He never stopped trying to create a monumental film and at one point even met with Thomas Mann to discuss the possibility of adapting *The Magic Mountain*, but the industrial pressures of sound film production and distribution—which, in the 1930s, usually privileged brevity and the "double bill" more than the epic (even *Gone with the Wind* was less than half the length of the full *Greed*)—were totally against him.[45] His performance as Captain von Rauffenstein in Jean Renoir's *Grand Illusion* (1937) gave a second wind to his career, but he could not shake his reputation as an uncompromising tyrant and was never again able to direct a film. Even though he worked only as an actor, von Stroheim continued to develop his fictive persona, bringing motifs from his own films into those of other directors and thereby broadening the range of his "autobiographical" project. Renoir, whose *Nana* (1926) remains the most sophisticated cinematic response to *Foolish Wives*, encouraged von Stroheim to help define the character of von Rauffenstein, and he contributed not only memorable details like a neck brace but also the aristocrat's fascination with a geranium, a private symbol that establishes continuity with other films he had directed or worked on.[46] Through gestures like this, Stroheim cemented his position as a heroic figure, celebrated in Western Europe, and later New York, as the chief exemplar of the path not taken by the Hollywood studios. Appropriately, his final role was as Beethoven in Sacha Guitry's *Napoléon* (1955).

Abel Gance's Cathedrals of Light

> I see such power in the art of the moving picture that I do not hesitate
> to regard it as the nucleus of the common spectacle which every one
> demands, as being perfectly susceptible of assuming a grave, splendid,
> moving character, a religious character even, in the universal, majestic
> sense of the word.
>
> —ÉLIE FAURE, *THE ART OF CINEPLASTICS* (1921)[47]

From the very beginning, the work of Abel Gance was impassioned, excessive, and imbued with a seemingly unshakable faith in the transformative
potential of the cinema. The following comments are characteristic of his
many public and private statements in the 1920s: "[The] whole Mediterranean
dream was spread out: Dionysus. The Great Noon. And all the arts in fusion,
caught in the coils of the Eternal Return; while the organs of light in the
Church of Music played the moving stained glass of the Cathedral of Light."[48]
Gance's extravagant language was matched by the baroque style of his imagery, which was saturated with associations but still possessed a piercingly
direct intensity. Louis Delluc, who ambivalently recognized Gance as the
most powerful figure in post–World War I French cinema, elucidated this
perfectly in 1918: "This man is far from simple. In fact, he is too close to bombast, not in words, but in thinking: he wraps the most naked ideas in the
richest clothing."[49] If von Stroheim returned obsessively to certain motifs and
themes, Gance returned repeatedly to particular clusters of images. One of
his major achievements was to find a way of investing individual images with
symbolic force while simultaneously making them integral parts of symphonic film structures.

The long-form ambitions of Griffith and von Stroheim developed out of
their film work, a byproduct of their increasingly exalted conceptions of the
cinema, but Gance's desire to create a synthetic colossus preceded his adoption of the new medium. The autobiographical fragments later published as
Prisme: Carnets d'un cinéaste are replete with references to mythological figures, which Gance uses to explain his own ideas about art: "This desire to
be Titan, to be the Atlas of all the individualities, and at the same time to
take them on its shoulders, always further and higher, is what connects the
Promethean genius and the Dionysian spirit. . . . Great art is inextinguishable."[50] Gance clearly saw himself as both Prometheus and Dionysus, a singular creator possessed of a spirit of dynamic energy, and these two myths
animate much of his film work. They are also present in his early poetry and
plays, but Gance soon recognized that his style appeared more mannered
than intense in the theater, and he searched for a medium that would enable
him to reach larger audiences. Shaken by the outbreak of World War I, he

yearned for "an instrument that, better than the word, could play upon the human imagination to try to stop this drama [the war], and [he] discovered the cinema."[51]

Gance's move into the cinema was influenced by his friendship with the pioneering, Italian-born film theorist Ricciotto Canudo. In 1911, Canudo published the important essay "The Birth of a Sixth Art," which functioned as a sort of manifesto for many artistically ambitious filmmakers of Gance's generation. "The cinematograph . . . cannot today be an art," Canudo wrote, but "for several reasons, the cinematographic theater is the first abode of the new art—an art which we can just barely conceive. Could this abode become a 'temple' for aesthetics?"[52] Gance fervently believed it could, and, in his own writings, he frequently applied religious metaphors to the cinema, his "Cathedral of Light." Unsurprisingly, Gance too referred to his images as hieroglyphs: conjecturing that with the cinema, perhaps one day images "could start a new alphabet, a kind of hieroglyphic ideography, which will gradually extend, in an amazing way, the domain of our intellectual exchanges."[53] For Gance, the idea of art as the gateway to universal mysteries was informed by Friedrich Nietzsche, whom he at one point explicitly associates with Prometheus: "The thought of Nietzsche proceeds by fire. It heats or it burns. Those who do not know are frightened like the Aryans before Prometheus."[54] Like a less ironic version of Nietzsche's Zarathustra, Gance wanted to use cinema to "create new psychological values," and his repeated invocations of classical myths and the Romantic idea of creative genius point to the grandeur as well as the internal contradictions of his wildly utopian projects.[55] Whereas Zarathustra describes the cathedral in terms of perpetual struggle ("How divinely the vault and the arch bend and break each other as they wrestle"), as a parable in stone demonstrating that "struggle and inequality and war for power and supremacy are found even in beauty," Gance claimed that his projected monuments would do no less than bring about world peace.[56]

The relative modesty of those early Gance films that are extant belies the nature of his aspirations. In his first public statement on the cinema, Gance made the following declaration:

> Let the cinema be naturally grandiose and human instead of what the popular novels of the past fifty years have been to literature. Let it be innovative instead of following either a maudlin sentimentality or the mechanical comic film which seems in fashion because the true way has yet to be mapped out. Let it not be especially theatrical, but allegorical, symbolic. To plumb the depths of each civilization and construct the glorious scenario that sums it up, embracing all the cycles of all the epochs, finally to have, I repeat, the cinematographic classic that will guide us into a new era—this is one of my highest dreams.[57]

Gance made a few short films for Le Film français the year this text was published, and he began planning out versions of his great "cinematographic classic" shortly thereafter, but his career did not begin in earnest until he started work for the prestigious company Le Film d'art in 1915. The war created a production situation plagued with difficulties ranging from film stock shortages to heightened censorship restrictions, but it also provided Gance with a new outlet for his messianic impulses. As he explained in a notebook of 1916: "Until 1914, I suffered only for myself, but for the last two years, I have suffered for everyone else. . . . Oh, to walk naked between two trenches and make each side hesitate to fire, for fear of killing one of their own."[58] Gance's repeatedly professed pacifism notwithstanding, several of his early films do contain clear propaganda elements, treated in a characteristically charged manner. *Les Gaz mortels* (1916), for example, is the story of an inventor who consents under pressure to create poison gas, resulting in a metaphorically loaded conflagration, with shots of toxic fumes approaching a civilian village interspersed with images of a snake about to attack a sleeping child. The eschatological bent of Gance's fecund imagination was well suited to an era in which, as Stéphane Audoin-Rouzeau and Annette Becker have argued, many ascribed an almost supernatural power to *La Grande Guerre*.[59] Scenes like this would recur in subsequent films.

Gance's most influential response to the war was *J'accuse* (1919), which, with a running time of more than three hours, was the most ambitious film he had made up to that point.[60] Initiated by Pathé as another propaganda project, *J'accuse* was instead turned into a powerful protest against the war and the "universal stupidity" that brought it about, using Émile Zola's famous attack on the court-martial of Dreyfus as a model. Previous Gance films like *La Dixième Symphonie* (1918) had occasionally taken melodramatic situations to the point of hysteria, using extremely rapid cutting to simulate a creative epiphany.[61] In *J'accuse*, these elements are still present, but they are given a dramatically different context by the film's historical traction—most evident through the use of documentary battle footage late in the film and the use of soldier's letters as the basis for several intertitles—and its insistent use of symbolic figures, often shown inhabiting narrative space through superimposition. Gance makes frequent recourse to Renaissance paintings, but, as Jay Winter has pointed out, he also responds to folk traditions, incorporating some of the *images d'Épinal* that had been revived during the war.[62] In his acknowledgment of this popular iconography, Gance brought his treatment of the war—consciously, if schematically, structured around the different vantage points embodied by particular characters—closer to the mentality of many of his viewers. Significantly, however, the protagonist Jean Diaz is a mystical poet, who "narrates" the film's return-of-the-dead sequence and ends the film with a desperate cry against the sun, an ode to the death of

Romanticism done in a style with echoes of Novalis' *Hymns to the Night* (1800).[63]

Gance was not alone in fusing Romantic imagery with a language of allegorical classicism in the last years of the war. Many aspects of *J'accuse* have their origins in the nineteenth-century aesthetics Gance implicitly allied himself with, but the film is also related to the so-called return to order that swept through the arts in 1918 and 1919. In this way, classicism was re-envisioned as a response to the horrors of the war, a way of reasserting tradition by linking an idea of civilization with roots in the ancient world to an idealized, often feminine, beauty, and setting that up as a bulwark against the muddy chaos of the trenches and everything they represent. The key advocate for these ideas during the war was Guillaume Apollinaire, a friend of Gance's who called for a national poetry that would reinvigorate old myths with distinctly modern styles.[64] This is precisely what Gance endeavored to do in *J'accuse*, interweaving advanced techniques like the propulsive editing of the film's final battle sequence with more traditional depictions of French life and culture. In several cases, the film fuses the two strains together, most memorably in the ghostly superimposition of dead soldiers marching above the Arc de Triomphe (figure 1.4).

The war gave Gance a sense of calling and mission. In the program notes for *J'accuse*, his goals are compared to those of the great epic poets:

FIGURE 1.4 *War dead superimposed above the victory march through the Arc de Triomphe in* J'accuse *(Abel Gance, 1919).*

Since the great Red Tragedy has not had its Homer and its Rouget de Lisle [the composer of "La Marseillaise," 1792], since the tears, the blood, the widespread suffering, the gestures of the heroes and the starry eyes of the dead have not yet found their sculptors and their painters, we have tried humbly to create a lyricism of the eye and to make the images sing.[65]

Before making *J'accuse*, Gance had been preoccupied with *Ecce Homo* (1918, unfinished), which he described as a "vast prologue" to a project called *The Kingdom of the Earth*—one of the proposed "Great Gospels of Light"—that attempted to synthesize the different religious traditions of the world.[66] Realizing that he would not be able to make such a film in 1918, he abandoned *Ecce Homo* and decided to temporarily set these quixotic ideas aside by making *J'accuse*. Yet, for Gance, a great film could only be large, and after *J'accuse* became one of the most widely seen films of its era, he reconceived it as part of a massive trilogy that would include *Les Cicatrices*, focusing on postwar life, and a third film devoted to the formation of the League of Nations. Gance soon postponed these plans when he realized that the "instruments of cinema [were] too imperfect to construct [his] Cathedrals of Light."[67] He focused his energies instead on *La Roue* (1922), the full version of which lasted for six hours.[68]

With its small cast of characters and elaborate use of flashbacks, *La Roue* is the most novelistic of Gance's films, but it also intermingles different myths (here Oedipus and Sisyphus, rather than Prometheus, dominate) and models (the Passion of Christ, a notion of genetic predestination derived from Zola, the cosmic perspective of Hugo) in a way that is meant to suggest the Drama of Man. Gance described the film as a symphonic study in the contrast between the world of "locomotives, rails . . . and fumes" and the world of "snows, summits, and solitude."[69] Accompanied by an innovative score by Arthur Honegger, the full version of the film had a triumphant premiere at the Gaumont-Palace cinema in 1922.[70] In this respect, Gance was more fortunate than von Stroheim, but, like *Foolish Wives* (which was released the same year and also ran for thirty-two reels in its original form), *La Roue* was severely shortened for general release, first to five hours and finally into versions running for roughly half that length.[71] Even some of the film's many admirers questioned the decision to make a film devoted almost exclusively to four principal characters so long, but Gance saw the film's duration—with its longueurs, detail, and gradual shifts in tone—as inextricably bound to its form. As he explained to Jean Mitry in 1924, "This was the length I wanted, and I endeavored to make a work [richer] in nuances than in action. I could obviously condense it; but if dramatic intensity might be strengthened, the psychological interest and the style would be weakened."[72]

The scale of *La Roue* paled in comparison to that of its follow-up, *Napoléon* (1927), a "giant moving fresco" that Gance hoped would create a new relationship between the viewer and the image.[73] The original plan entailed the production of a series of six three-hour films—*Arcole, 18 Brumaire, Austerlitz, Retreat from Moscow, Waterloo,* and *Saint-Hélenè*—that would begin in 1782 with Napoleon as a cadet at the Royal Military Academy of Brienne and end with his death in 1821. Since the creation of the first film took three years and went heavily over budget, none of the subsequent episodes were made.[74] The finished film, *Napoléon vu par Abel Gance,* ended with the beginning of Napoleon's Italian campaign and, at least in some versions, included two "triptych" sequences in which three images were projected side by side on an enormous screen.[75] Gance held two all-day press screenings of the full version of his film (without the triptychs), which had a projection time of over nine hours and was edited down from over one million feet of footage.[76] By contrast, the biggest Hollywood production of the year—*Wings* (William Wellman, 1927), winner of the first Academy Award for Best Picture—was edited down from 360,000 feet of footage. Even von Stroheim had shot "only" 446,103 feet of film for *Greed.*[77] *Napoléon* may well have been the largest production of its kind in the silent era, a tribute both to the density of Gance's editing (a considerable portion of the footage was needed to construct the rapid montage sequences and the triptychs) and his steadfast determination to outdo his contemporaries as well as his previous films.

As with the panoramas that inspired them, the presence of the triptych sequences necessitated special exhibition conditions, and the film was officially premiered at the Opéra de Paris on April 7, 1927, with another original score by Honegger. The premiere was considered to be one of the major cultural events of the year, and in addition to such artistic luminaries as Pablo Picasso and Jean Cocteau, the audience also included the President Gaston Doumergue, Marshal Pétain, and a young Charles de Gaulle.[78] This version, which included the triptychs, was reduced to a running time of three and a quarter hours, with Gance reportedly reworking the montage until the last possible moment. After ten more screenings at the Opéra (and, later, in Berlin and Nantes), a mostly complete, but re-edited, version then played for two months at the Salle Marivaux, beginning in November 1927.[79] Distributed outside Paris and internationally in versions of various lengths, *Napoléon* was later rereleased in alternate, sound versions edited by Gance. These re-edits, *Napoléon Bonaparte* (1935) and *Bonaparte and the Revolution* (1971), combined new footage with material from the silent era and were tailored as responses to their respective historical moments, with Napoleon presented alternately as the embodiment of lost heroic virtues and as a paragon of antiestablishment revolt.

Whatever the length or completeness of the particular print, Gance's treatment of Napoleon and his era is unabashedly Romantic. Tellingly, the director's program notes for the film begin with the assertion that "Napoleon is Prometheus."[80] In a speech to his crew at the beginning of production, he explained his overall objective in even more grandiloquent terms: "This is a film that must, and let no one underestimate the profundity of what I'm saying, a film that must allow us to definitively enter the Temple of Art through the giant gate of History."[81] *Napoléon* consists of a series of historically synoptic episodes all centered on the figure of Napoleon, who is associated symbolically with the element of fire and with his talisman, an eagle. Like Griffith, Gance attempts to authenticate his narrative by citing actual historical documents as sources for key intertitles, a strategy that presumably helped to justify his claim that *Napoléon* would be "the first great French historical film that could enter schools and help children understand that this was how it was, which, in the lycées and colleges, could advantageously replace studies of the emperor by [Hippolyte] Taine, Madame de Staël, or [François-René de] Chateaubriand."[82] This emphasis on historicity is further amplified by the cinematization of paintings like Jacques-Louis David's *Death of Marat* (1793) and Antoine-Jean Gros' *Bonaparte at the Pont d'Arcole* (1796). The dramatic appearance of the names of legendary figures like Marat, Danton, and Robespierre ("The Three Gods") serves a similar function, synechdocally connecting the film to the collective memory of the history it attempts to represent. Nevertheless, the major events and figures of the period are all seen from the vantage point of Napoleon, who is portrayed as the self-designated embodiment of the principles of the Revolution, nobly saving France from its violent excesses. At one point, when asked by Marat what his projects are, "Bonaparte" responds, "The liberation of oppressed peoples, the fusion of great European interests, the suppression of frontiers ... and ... THE UNIVERSAL REPUBLIC."[83] Following the precedent of Walter Scott, Gance invents viewer surrogate figures like Tristan and Violine Fleuri, who regards Napoleon with awe and reinforces the Promethean stature of figures like Saint-Just (played by Gance) when she cries out, "They are too great for us!"

In its conflation of historical process and Romantic aesthetics, *Napoléon* owes a considerable debt to Hugo, whom Gance acknowledged as one of his models. *La Roue* opens with a title card derived from Hugo's poem "The Graveyard at Villequier" (1847)—"I know that Creation is a Great Wheel which cannot move without crushing someone!"—and *Napoléon* was influenced on a number of levels by Hugo's final novel *Ninety-Three* (1874).[84] Many of the characterizations were drawn from the novel, and passages from it inspired two crucial scenes. A scene in which Danton speaks about the ideals of the Revolution is derived from a passage linking its productive and disturbing aspects: "At the same time as it was giving off revolution, this assembly was also producing civilization. It was a furnace, but also a forge. In that vat where terror was bubbling, progress was fermenting."[85] The "Double Tempest" in which Napoleon's flight from Corsica is juxtaposed with raging debate in the Convention also comes from Hugo:

> Minds that were a prey to the wind. But that wind was a wind of prodigy. To be a member of the convention was to be a wave of the ocean. And this was true of the greatest. The impetus came from above. There was in the Convention a will that was the will of all and none. This will was an idea, an indomitable and boundless idea which blew into the shadows from the heights of the sky. We call it the Revolution. When this idea passed, it pounced upon one and lifted up another; it carried this man away in foam and broke that man on the reefs. This idea knew where it was going, and drove the whirlpool before it. To impute a revolution to men is to impute the tide to the waves. . . . Truth and justice remain above revolutions like the starry sky above storms.[86]

Gance read this passage to the members of his cast and crew before he began shooting the sequence, using a swinging camera to simulate the effect of a pendulum, which eventually became one of the two triptychs included in the version of the film shown at the Opéra de Paris.

Hugo's influence on Gance is by no means limited to a series of quotations. Paul Claudel called Gance the "Hugo of the Cinema," and, as if he were trying to validate the association, Gance announced plans to make a life-of-Hugo film shortly after the release of *Napoléon*.[87] Gance and Hugo are, of course, also linked through their Homeric sense of narrative and their sometimes disastrously excessive artistic ambition. Most importantly, both Hugo and Gance shared a Romantic desire to replace bourgeois culture with a form of artistic renewal founded on the generative potential of communal experience, as symbolized by the cathedral in the "This Will Kill That" section of *Notre-Dame de Paris* (1831). For Hugo, the replacement of the cathedral by the press represented a decisive shift in the structure of both human thought and social organization, a redirection of creativity that the influential critic-historian Élie Faure suggested was reversed by the cinema:

> If the cinema is put in the service of a unanimous social effort capable of delivering us from *individualism* by exalting and using all the spiritual resources of the *individual* to ensure this development, then we are right to see in it the most incomparable instrument of communion, at least since the [age of] great architecture. . . . "This will kill that."[88]

The idea of film viewing as a modern cultic ritual, of going to a movie theater as the secular twentieth-century equivalent to visiting a cathedral, found early expression in Canudo's "The Birth of a Sixth Art" and attained new prominence in the post–World War I period.[89] With his explicit allusion to Hugo, Faure portrays the cinema as a new form of "collective spectacle, which will take the place of the religious dance that is dead, and of the philosophic tragedy that is dead, and of the mystery-play that is dead—indeed of all the great dead things around which the multitude once assembled."[90]

As with most French critics of the period, Faure's highest praise was reserved for "Charlot" (Charles Chaplin), but his delirious enthusiasm for the cinema and his Bergsonian stress on the vital drives of perpetually shifting forms found a perfect correlate in the work of Gance. Correspondence and published statements testify to their feelings of intellectual kinship and to Faure's role as an inspiration for Gance's conception of *Napoléon*.[91] In his 1921 biography of Napoleon, Faure characterizes Napoleon as "a poet of action" and goes so far as to argue, "From the point of view of art, [Napoleon] is, with Christ, the only spirit recognized by Prometheus on earth."[92] Gance was, in effect, echoing Faure when he claimed, "My Bonaparte was in that long line of republican idealists of which Christ was the first example."[93] For his part, Faure, who collaborated on the script, called *Napoléon vu par Abel Gance* "fire snatched from the depths of History."[94]

Not surprisingly, Gance's decision to use a historiographic model valorizing the cult of the Romantic hero was controversial, particularly among leftist critics. Although only a few of the contemporary reviews accused Gance or the film of rightist tendencies—chiding him instead simply for being old-fashioned—socialist critic Léon Moussinac described the film's protagonist as a "Bonaparte for budding fascists."[95] Before Kevin Brownlow's initial restoration was completed in 1979, most film historians argued that the film was either unconcerned with politics or fundamentally progressive, but stronger criticisms were leveled against the film after its rerelease.[96] The most vociferous critique was made by Peter Pappas, who described *Napoléon vu par Abel Gance* as "fascist" because of its persistent use of superimposition, which he claims is "the art of arbitrary unification . . . the purely subjective . . . imposition of one 'reality' upon another" and therefore a foundational element of fascist aesthetics.[97] Representative of many recent critical revaluations, Pappas' argument grossly oversimplifies the formal structure of *Napoléon vu par Abel Gance* and underplays the extent to which superimposition (of both individuals and groups) was mobilized by both left- and right-leaning avant-garde movements in the 1910s and 1920s.[98] Although the effusive celebration of Gance's hero is far removed from dialectical Marxism, the film's emphasis on the sensory power of cinematic editing and the iterative use of visual motifs sometimes evokes *Battleship Potemkin* (Sergei Eisenstein, 1925).[99] These unresolved tensions are also inscribed within the film itself, which frequently hints at the darker aspects of Napoleon's personality that would have been explored more fully in later parts of the original multifilm cycle. There is, for example, a foreboding shot in which the shadow of Napoleon is projected over the "Declaration of Rights of Man and Citizen" (figure 1.5).

Gance's turn to the Prometheus myth is similarly complex. On one level, of course, this is fully in keeping with the film's historiographic sources and the

FIGURE 1.5 *The shadow of Napoleon projected over the Declaration of Rights of Man and Citizen in* Napoléon vu par Abel Gance *(Abel Gance, 1927).*

early nineteenth-century iconography it employs. Prometheus—interpreted less as the divine intercessor of Hesiod or Ovid than as a personification of the individual creative imagination—was one of the central myths of high Romanticism, linking such otherwise dissimilar figures (all beloved by Gance) as Percy Bysshe Shelley, Lord Byron, William Blake, Chateaubriand, Goethe, and Beethoven.[100] These authors used the Prometheus myth in markedly different ways, but, with varying degrees of irony or ambivalence, all of them attached it to Napoleon, who was demonized by some (Shelley) as a tyrant and lionized by others as the supreme embodiment of Romantic "genius."[101] Byron—who once claimed to have been so enamored of the Prometheus myth that he could "easily conceive its influence over all or anything that I have written"—encapsulated this attitude in his 1814 poem "Ode to Napoleon Buonaparte," in which he yearns for the exiled ruler to "share with [Prometheus], the unforgiven, his vulture and his rock! . . . [and] in his fall [preserve] his pride."[102]

Although Gance's presentation of, and public statements about, Napoleon are consistent with this tradition of Romantic valorization, the context had changed dramatically. The first few decades of the twentieth century saw a surprising revival of the Prometheus myth, by key modernists (Constantin Brancusi linked it to his sculptural abstraction in 1911) as well as esoteric figures like composer Alexander Scriabin, whose symphony *Prometheus: The Poem of Fire* (opus 60, 1910) anticipated Gance's film in its bold multimedia transmutation of Romantic iconography. Scriabin tried to combine orchestral performance with shifting patterns of light and color to represent "the active energy of the universe," but his utopian aspirations were attached more to a mystical conception of the integrated work of art than to any particular social program.[103] By the 1930s, however, the Prometheus myth had become an ideological battleground, appropriated by groups of all political persuasions. Arno Breker used it for his 1935 depiction of the idealized Nazi body, while Jacques Lipchitz, treating the myth as a metaphor for the struggle between democracy and fascism, created a series of Cubist variations culminating in a thirty-foot plaster sculpture, *Prometheus Strangling the Vulture*, designed for the 1937 International Exhibition in Paris (figures 1.6–1.7). In North America during the same period, Paul Manship made Prometheus embody the spirit of capitalism in the gilded bronze sculpture installed at Rockefeller Center

FIGURE 1.6 Prometheus *(Arno Breker, 1935, Breker-Museum, Noervenich Castle, Germany).*

FIGURE 1.7 Prometheus Strangling the Vulture *(Jacques Lipchitz, 1953 bronze casting at the Philadelphia Museum of Art of a sculpture originally made in plaster for the 1937 International Exhibition in Paris; photograph courtesy the Philadelphia Museum of Art / Art Resource, NY).*

in 1934, while José Clement Orozco transformed the myth in one of his most important leftist mural paintings (figure 1.8). Following in the tradition of Karl Marx's repeated invocations of Prometheus, the myth was also linked to the Soviet cause in books such as Cecil Day-Lewis' *The Mind in Chains: Socialism and the Cultural Revolution* (1937) and films like *Prometei* (Ivan Kavaleridze, 1935).[104]

References to Prometheus, particularly to Aeschylus' *Prometheus Bound* (fifth century BCE), also circulated in post–World War I French film culture, a more proximate source for Gance's film.[105] The most overt manifestation of this is Marcel L'Herbier's *Prométhée ... banquier* (1921), the first important film version of the legend after Louis Feuillade's now lost *Prométhée* (1908). With the dandyish wit that he had earlier demonstrated in films like *Rose-France* (1918), L'Herbier depicts an overzealous banker tied to his desk and unable to leave for fear of missing a stock update, using his parodic reworking

FIGURE 1.8 *Paul Manship's 1933* Prometheus *statue installed in the plaza of Rockefeller Center (photograph by Samuel H. Gottscho, 1934, courtesy the Museum of the City of New York / Art Resource, NY).*

of Aeschylus to wryly comment on the all-consuming nature of the market. L'Herbier's film was made for a small cine-club audience and attempts to recuperate an idea of noncommercial art-making by concealing his mythic symbols beneath several layers of mock irony. In Gance's major films, by contrast, the figure of Prometheus is treated with absolute sincerity and is frequently aligned with Christ. Gance's particular brand of late Romanticism views the artist as a suffering martyr and demiurge, fusing these two strains together as Gustave Moreau had done in his iconic 1868 painting, *Prometheus*, in which the head of Christ is grafted atop the body of the Titan (figure 1.9). Gance's representations of his own Christ-Prometheans—Jean Diaz in *J'accuse*, Napoleon, and the prophet of *La Fin du monde* (1931)—are rendered more ambiguous by the melodramatic complexities of his narratives and the occasionally heterodox nature of his symbolic associations, but the syncretic iconography used to identify them is openly, even shockingly, direct (figure 1.10).

In making *Napoléon*, Gance attempted to fulfill his dream of 1912 by creating a massive film synthesizing all the arts that would be a "Gospel of the future, a bridge of dreams leading from one era to another."[106] He frequently compared his films to symphonies and frescoes, and, like *Napoléon*, many of his earlier works refer to masterpieces from the other arts, such as the Beethoven pieces visually "performed" in *La Dixième Symphonie* and the reproduction of Sandro Botticelli's *Birth of Venus* (1485) used as the backdrop

FIGURE 1.9 Prometheus *(Gustave Moreau, 1868, Musée Gustave Moreau, Paris; photograph © RMN-Grand Palais / Art Resource, NY).*

for the "Dance of Death" sequence in *J'accuse.* For many of the most important theorists and critics of the era (Delluc, Émile Vuillermoz, and even Gance's friend Jean Epstein), these were retrograde elements in the work of a prodigious innovator whose main achievement was his control of rhythm and the concomitant liberation of cinematic plasticity from the constraints of narrative.[107] In *La Roue*, for example, Gance alternates shots of a train with increasingly brief shots of pieces of the rail and of the surrounding landscape, gradually reducing the number of frames per shot until he is finally intercutting barely perceptible images. These montage bursts had an enormous impact on Gance's contemporaries and elicited rhapsodic praise from artists and filmmakers interested in raising the cultural status of cinema. Fernand Léger (who designed the poster for the film) spoke for many of his colleagues when he wrote, "With *La Roue*, Abel Gance has elevated the art of film to the plane of the plastic arts."[108]

FIGURE 1.10 *Abel Gance as Christ in* La Fin du monde *(Abel Gance, 1931).*

Unlike those filmmakers who called for "pure" films and an alternative cinematic avant-garde, Gance insisted that cinema must be "an art of the people," and he tried to incorporate even his most extreme poetic flourishes into the generic framework of the melodrama (*Mater Dolorosa*, 1917; *J'accuse; La Roue*) and the epic (*Napoléon*).[109] For this reason, he attempted to provide a narrative rationale for his single-frame editing by including or superimposing images of the protagonists—like young Napoleon during the snowball fight—within his montage bursts, thereby locating them within a character's subjectivity. The fact that his dramatic cutting style has such a pronounced impact on audiences, and is therefore mentioned most prominently in reviews, has tended to obscure the fact that Gance also made extensive use of compositions in depth.[110] In *La Roue*, for example, the interchange between circular forms and frames within frames (demarcated by internal objects like window panes and by creative masking) set off against diagonal movement in the distance frequently suggests an adaptation into cinema of the principles of Cubist art. Like von Stroheim, Gance also uses these layered compositions to situate the tribulations of his characters within an expansive fictional world, but the difference in their treatment of similar stylistic devices is instructive. In *Queen Kelly*, von Stroheim makes use at one point of a "triple screen" effect created through superimposition, using

FIGURE 1.11 *The mental state of Kelly expressed through the splintering of the image in* Queen Kelly *(Erich von Stroheim, 1929).*

the splintering of the image not to emphasize plastic values, but to convey complex mental states (figure 1.11).

Where Griffith's editing is dynamic and integrative, linking or rhyming action across time and space, and von Stroheim's is structured around the accumulation of subtly interrelated details, Gance's fundamental mode is ecstatic. In *Napoléon*, Gance employed virtually every technique at his disposal, and he invented several others, including a 360-degree camera mechanism that could be operated remotely.[111] All of these were introduced to increase the affective participation of the viewer, to, in Gance's words, "make the spectator become an actor . . . to involve him at every level in the unfolding of the action . . . to sweep him away on the flow of pictures."[112] Gance's objective was to enhance collective involvement in the diegetic process, and he frequently used combinations of camera movement and rapid cutting to achieve this effect, thematically connecting them to representative events. One of the most striking instances is the scene in which "La Marseillaise" is first performed. Gance alternates low-angle shots of individual figures with high-angle shots of the increasingly energized crowd (Napoleon, who has not yet "entered history," is off to the side). The length of the shots is modulated like *La Roue*, with legendary characters like Danton and anonymous faces intercut at varying speeds, steadily building momentum until finally a superimposed figure representing the Revolution appears in the Convention Hall. Although the sequence includes several paroxysmic sections, the development of the montage also creates an impression of solidarity that includes the audience watching the film as well as the onscreen characters.

The triptych sequences in *Napoléon* fuse Gance's interest in maximizing the sensory impact of his imagery with his desire to engender a greater degree of spectatorial engagement. He did not, however, want his film to become overwhelmed by technological spectacle, and he chose not to use the footage shot using the "Berton" process, which, in conjunction with a stereoscopic projection technique Gance developed in 1920, gave the images both relief and color.[113] According to Gance, "The 3D effects were very good, and very pronounced," but he felt "that if the audience saw this effect they would be seduced by it and would be less interested in the content of the film. . . . The 3D effect did not encourage the same feeling for rhythm in the audience."[114] For Gance, rhythm remained the key to cinematic poetics, and he quickly adapted the triptych technique to serve these purposes, using it to create polyphonic arrangements of distinct but related images. The symphonic aspects of his approach are abundantly evident in the final few moments of the film, in which many of the motifs used earlier are interlaced across the three screens, grounded by arch-Romantic images of Napoleon looking out over the foggy landscape from the peak of a mountain, like the figure in Caspar David Friedrich's *Wanderer Above a Sea of Fog* (1817) (figures 1.12–1.13). The orchestration of these visual elements builds in intensity until, finally, both the protagonist and the film achieve a joint apotheosis signaled by the cuts from a symbolic eagle flying across all three screens to a series of images in which Napoleon's face is connected to Promethean flames, mathematical formulas, and the waves of history.

The Brownlow restorations of *Napoléon* include only this one tinted triptych reel, but the premiere version included an even more radically contrapuntal triple-screen sequence, the "Double Tempest" montage derived from Hugo's *Ninety-Three*, which has unfortunately been lost.[115] In the first film adaptation of Hugo's novel (*Quatre-vingt-treize*, Albert Capellani and André Antoine, 1914/21), the passage from which the sequence in *Napoléon* originates had been condensed to an intertitle—"In Paris, summer of '93, among the tempests." Gance instead uses Hugo's text as the basis for an extended montage that deepens the implied relationship between the disintegration of the assembly and Napoleon's absorption of its revolutionary energies.[116] The dynamic fusion of superimposition and rapid editing is most emphatic here, and it was more pronounced in the original triptych, in which Gance was able to compose "a veritable apocalyptic fresco, a mobile symphony in which, with eight superimpositions per frame, there were sometimes twenty-four interconnected visions."[117] Within this maelstrom of densely layered images, movements were able to resonate with one another across all three screens; although it would be impossible for viewers to relate all the individual fragments together, the

FIGURE 1.12 *Napoleon looking out from a mountain peak in* Napoléon vu par Abel Gance

cumulative effect must have been extraordinarily intense. This triptych would also have provided a structural echo of the final sequence, making the fundamental interdependence of physical scale (the triple screen) and explosive plasticity within *Napoléon vu par Abel Gance* much more apparent.

Astonishing as it may seem, *J'accuse, La Roue,* and even *Napoléon* were all seen by Gance as detours on the path toward the realization of his comparative religion project, which he continued to expand throughout the 1920s.[118] For Gance, the utopian promise of silent cinema, what Faure called its "social destiny," was rooted in its constructive capacity, its ability to create a sense of community based upon shared visual experience.[119] The universality of cinema, linked throughout Gance's and Faure's writings to both science and religion, would become the foundation for a newly harmonious social construction, one in which fundamental differences would be recognized and overcome.[120] As Gance explained, his comparative religion project was intended to literalize all of this:

> This series, *The Great Initiates,* concerning the life of the apostolate of the great creators of religion, will thereby bring to the cinema hundreds of millions of new spectators: Hindus, Buddhists, Muslims, Jews, etc. These millions of spectators, who will come to the cinema, as they come to their churches, only for these great, *in-depth* religious spectacles, will thus learn, after having communed with their gods, to envisage with tolerance and understanding the beauty, the poetry, and the *similarity* of different religions.[121]

In this too, Gance reveals his deep affinity with the vigorous, if rhetorically excessive, thought of Faure:

> The mosque, the pagoda, or the cathedral express, in their ensemble, the great emotional and lyrical depths that only the enthusiasm of the crowd is

(Abel Gance, 1927) (courtesy Photoplay Productions).

capable of stirring up. And the cinema should be the mosque, the pagoda, and the cathedral at the same time. A mosque, a pagoda, a cathedral widened to reach the undefined limits of living humanity, past or future, to reach telescopic or microscopic forms and movements—the unanimous orchestra, with a thousand associated instruments, of sensitivity, and intelligence, and the multitudes in action.[122]

If this project could be completed and widely seen, Gance hoped it might be possible to bring East and West together by fusing the "contemplative serenity of the Buddha" with the energy of "Julius Caesar, Napoleon, Nietzsche, Delacroix, Shakespeare, Machiavelli, Michelangelo."[123]

The overall plan for the project also entailed the supervision of a number of films made by non-Western peoples about their own religions. Each of these films would have been supported—financially, technically, and philosophically—by an organization led by Gance in Europe, and he argued that this would help bring about the cinematic self-actualization of these different religious communities, enabling them to help "build this cathedral . . . to [contribute] to a universal religious poem."[124] Citing Novalis ("Each image is an incantation"), Gance declares that cinema is "a sort of magic" that he wants to "give to all the peoples of the earth, so that they will, thanks to it, know their religious soul more profoundly and, through it, love the common God of the future."[125] It goes without saying that, within this schema, Gance himself would have been the agent of Promethean revolution, extending the universalizing democratic ideals espoused in *Napoléon* worldwide. The "identical elements" in this cycle of films—*Jesus, Moses, Mohammed, Brahma, Confucius*, and *Buddha*—were to be "synthesized in *La Fin du monde* and *L'Annonciation*, written by Mr. Abel Gance, religious epics of the future that will be the international beginnings of the new Gospel of Light that the cinema alone can give to the future."[126]

FIGURE 1.13 Wanderer Above a Sea of Fog *(Caspar David Friedrich, 1817; photograph*
© *bpk, Berlin / Hamburger Kunsthalle / Elke Walford / Art Resource, NY).*

Making such a project happen, Gance increasingly came to recognize, would require a reorientation of the distribution networks of cinema. Despite its strong national focus, *Napoléon* was an extremely international project. The film was initially financed by the Russian émigré Wladimir Wengeroff with the support of the German financier Hugo Stinnes and groups from Sweden, Spain, Czechoslovakia, and England, as well as France, with Gance retaining total creative control.[127] This was only a temporary solution for Gance, a first step toward the establishment of a European production and distribution consortium that would have acted as an umbrella organization guaranteeing artistic freedom (and an alternative to American cinematic hegemony) for strong directors from throughout the continent. He also made a proposal to the League of Nations for the creation of a special film division, the "Section cinématographique de la SDN," which would have provided financial support to certain filmmakers and could also have contributed to international arbitration. Gance hoped that disputes between different countries could be addressed by the use of images representing their respective points of view, a conceptual shot/countershot exchange that would be resolved in Geneva.[128]

Neither project came to fruition, but while they perfectly reflect Gance's dream of the cinema, they are also representative of their historical moment, the most quixotic manifestations of an internationalist impulse shared by many filmmakers for a few short years in the mid-1920s.[129] It was, after all, in this same period that Dziga Vertov attempted to demonstrate the unity through diversity of the early Soviet state through his Whitmanian *One Sixth of the World* (1926) and Walter Ruttmann created his amalgamation of world cultures, *Melody of the World* (1929).[130] Although it was never made, Griffith also announced plans for a "pictorial history of the world" to be created with funding from both the United States and Europe, claiming that since cinema "uses a universal language [it] is, therefore, a suitable medium for the exposition of a universal history. In this film history, it is hoped to give a thorough general idea of the whole history of the world."[131] Speaking in Paris in 1926, Fritz Lang even argued that through the "silent speech of its moving images, in a language that is equally understood in all hemispheres, film can make an honest contribution to repairing the chaos that has prevented nations from seeing each other as they really are ever since the tower of Babel."[132] This idealism did not last long. Late in 1929, the First International Film Congress of the Independent Film was held at La Sarraz, and directors from the fourteen participating countries proudly proclaimed the formation of an "Internationale of the Avant-Garde."[133] Concerned about an increasingly tense political situation, the global economic crisis, and the rising costs of sound film production, it was publicly dissolved one year later at the Second Congress in Brussels.

Shortly thereafter, the tatters of Gance's *La Fin du monde*, an apocalyptic disaster movie that was also a paean to universal brotherhood, were released. Gance had hoped to expand the techniques used to unify space and time in *Napoléon*, utilizing the triple screen for the entirety of the film.[134] However, the financial caution of the film's backers, aware of Gance's reputation for overspending and the logistical difficulties imposed by sound equipment, made it impossible for him to realize these plans or to make a film on the scale he wanted, setting a pattern that would haunt Gance for the remainder of his career. Rather than reducing the number of themes, he simplified his figures into the barest archetypes, linking unrelated mythic threads together in a frequently disorienting way. To some extent, this mirrors the muddled origins of the project, which began as the third part of the war trilogy that started with *J'accuse* but is also descended from one of Gance's earliest undertakings, a 1911 "tragicomic ballet" in four acts.[135] The earlier *La Fin du monde* was developed at a time when Gance's long-term goal was the creation of a cinematic cycle in which all of Western mythology would be brought together.[136] The film Gance finally began working on in the late 1920s still bears traces of this mad ambition, and of other aborted projects like *The Passion of Jesus*, but the presence of sound makes the lofty, poetic language he adopts appear hysterically strident and renders the montage of his "dynamite images" hyperbolic.[137] Gance performed a number of audio experiments before production began, and he argued a few years later that sound "comes to us through the eyes," suggesting that "sound perspective" will allow one to realize "a synthesis, a symphony."[138] Nevertheless, the sound in the extant versions of *La Fin du monde* is, with a few notable exceptions, extremely banal, and most of the dialogue is recorded in extremely static scenes that, because of the drastic shortening of the film by the producers, are often cut together in surprisingly awkward ways.[139]

The stylistic heterogeneity and intellectual mishmash of *La Fin du monde* is perfectly complemented by its ideological confusion. The prophetic, half-crazed poet Jean Novalic (Gance) is portrayed as a Christ figure, while his brother, the astronomer Martial Novalic, uses radio broadcasts and vaguely demagogic speeches to unite all governments together. Perhaps as a result of the failure of his film division proposal, Gance views the existing League of Nations—shown to be inept in the face of pending catastrophe—with great suspicion, and although he does bring different religions together in a moment of prayer (this section of *La Fin du monde* is as close as Gance ever came to realizing the comparative religion project), this occurs only under the threat of global annihilation.[140] Despite the film's didactic expressions of faith in mankind, the overall tone is dourly pessimistic; the Christ-Promethean seer ends up in an asylum while the world parties itself to destruction. The only hope for humanity lies with the charismatic Martial Novalic, who is able to electrify the enormous audience of the "One World Congress" by announcing (like Napoleon) the formation of a Universal Republic.

Until his death in the early 1980s, Gance's language remained closely tied to that he employed in the silent era. Repositioning his triple-screen "Polyvision" as the precursor to CinemaScope in the 1950s, Gance argued that "[it] will suddenly open wide the eyes of modern man, who no longer believes in miracles. You only need to reread Nietzsche's *The Birth of Tragedy* [1872] to understand that the way ahead is the one I am indicating."[141] Gance never abandoned his belief in the power of the awe-inspiring image, reworking similar themes and sometimes even remaking the same films in the hopes of reaching his audience in more intense ways. In the decades following the failure of *La Fin du monde*, *Napoléon* remained Gance's great obsession, but he also returned to his other silent triumphs, incorporating a new version of the rising of the dead in his 1937 sound remake of *J'accuse* and later using that reworked sequence in a special Polyvision presentation in the 1950s.[142] Gance's emphatic style remained present in these later iterations, but it appeared increasingly disconnected from the complexities of the era, more ingenuous than incisive. Gance demonstrated the political naïveté that had been highlighted by *La Fin du monde* repeatedly in the years that followed. In 1939, he went to Franco-dominated Spain to begin work on a "Spanish Trilogy" that would examine the figures of Christopher Columbus, El Cid, and St. Ignatius of Loyola because "the cinema is above all a machine for resurrecting heroes."[143] A few years later, he made politically "neutral" films in occupied France, one of which (*Blind Venus*, 1941) originally included an opening dedication to Marshal Pétain. In each of these cases, Gance, who later argued that "the two words Left and Right are for me . . . antiquated," followed the same independent course he had always pursued, without fully understanding the degree to which these different historical and geopolitical contexts would inevitably shape the meaning of his work.[144]

Napoléon vu par Abel Gance was the last film of its length Gance would ever complete, but he continued to dream up ever larger projects for several decades, notwithstanding the cuts made even to his completed films. *Un grand amour de Beethoven* (1936), which originally ran for four hours, was reduced to roughly half that length by the distributor so that it could be included in double bills.[145] Within months, Gance had outlined a new project tracing the history of France, embodied by "a young and beautiful woman," from the Stone Age to the twentieth century in 122 "poetic and symbolic acts," culminating in the "Great Exposition of 1937."[146] Gance regarded each individual failure or commercial assignment as nothing more than a temporary setback, and while he was more amenable to temporary compromise than von Stroheim, he never relinquished the dream of the long, culturally weighty epic. He presented a proposal for a multipart film called *The Divine Tragedy* to Pope Pius XII in the late 1940s, worked to raise funding for a Polyvision version of *The Kingdom of the Earth* in the 1950s, and later met with Mao Zedong and Zhou Enlai to discuss the coproduction of a Polyvision epic about the Long March.[147] Without Gance realizing it, however, the unfettered idealism of the silent era had given way to the more constrained, largely studio-bound realities of sound cinema. By the time *La Fin du monde* was released, it was already an anachronism; Gance's "Era of the Image" was over, and it would be decades before anyone would attempt to revive it.

Utopia and Its Discontents

Then, sure of their own rights
And of the heavenly fire
Defiant rebels mocked, not till then
Despising mortal ways,
Chose foolhardy arrogance
And strove to become the equals of gods.

—FRIEDRICH HÖLDERLIN, "THE RHINE" (1801–1802)[148]

Beginning in 1934, the Nuremberg Rallies concluded with a "cathedral of light" designed by Albert Speer, in which 130 antiaircraft searchlights projecting to a height of more than 20,000 feet were combined to simulate the appearance of an enormous building (figure 1.14).[149] There could be no clearer manifestation of the collapse of the silent era rhetoric of figures like Gance. By 1934, the image of a Napoleonic unifier of Europe and the idea of a "Universal Republic," presented with such enthusiasm in the 1920s, had taken on much darker implications. As Leni Riefenstahl's *Triumph of the Will* (1935) demonstrates, the rituals and pageantry of the Nuremberg Rallies were predicated upon a highly orchestrated combination of speech and imagery, an ersatz cinematic hybrid that was explicitly derived from the Wagnerian *Gesamtkunstwerk*. To attempt to recuperate these ideas in the post-Nazi period, to retrieve the Romantic cathedral from its misappropriation, required a realignment of the elements that constituted that fusion. In his introduction to the epic theater piece *Mahogany* (1930), Bertolt Brecht famously argued that "witchcraft . . . intended to produce hypnosis, is likely to induce sordid intoxication," and that this form of *Gesamtkunstwerk* must be resisted by making "words, music, and setting . . . more independent of one another."[150] For Brecht, a more dialectical synthesis could be achieved only through the heightened self-consciousness made possible by the meaningful

FIGURE 1.14 *Albert Speer's cathedral of light at the 1937 Nuremberg Rally (photograph ©
bpk, Berlin / Foto Marburg / Heinrich Hoffmann / Art Resource, NY).*

juxtaposition of elements that retain their own identity. This is precisely what Manoel de Oliveira in his seven-hour *The Satin Slipper* (1985) and especially Hans-Jürgen Syberberg in films such as the seven-and-a-half-hour *Hitler, a Film from Germany* (1977) tried to do, using a surfeit of talk to establish a new relationship with the image-oriented aesthetics of the silent cinema and its operatic models.

The major long-form films of Oliveira and Syberberg are the most extreme of the many important works released during a fifteen-year period running from the early 1970s to the mid-1980s in which cinematic opera was pursued with greater seriousness than at any point since the advent of sound. Other representative films from this era include *Ludwig* (Luchino Visconti, 1972), *The Death of Maria Malibran* (Werner Schroeter, 1972), *Moses and Aaron* (Jean-Marie Straub and Danièle Huillet, 1975), *The Magic Flute* (Ingmar Bergman, 1975), *La Luna* (Bernardo Bertolucci, 1979), *Don Giovanni* (Joseph Losey, 1979), *Palermo or Wolfsburg* (Werner Schroeter, 1980), *Fitzcarraldo* (Werner Herzog, 1982), *And the Ship Sails On* (Federico Fellini, 1983), *The Power of Emotions* (Alexander Kluge, 1983), and *Carmen* (Francesco Rosi, 1984). That many of these films are influenced by Brecht's ideas reflects both the renewed interest in his work in these years and the degree to which the peculiar illusionism of opera, with its audiovisual integration of the other arts, could be used reflexively to interrogate the cinema's "hypnotic" form of spectatorship (a central issue in period debates). Syberberg, who began his career by filming performances of Brecht's Berliner Ensemble with an 8mm camera, develops this further in both *Hitler, a Film from Germany* and *Parsifal* (1982) by using a conceptually rich system of front projection to highlight the psychological processes involved in film viewing.[151] This strategy, in which an on-set projector is synchronized with the movement of the camera, effectively (and inexpensively) monumentalizes techniques more commonly used for slide shows. Static reproductions of paintings and documentary footage of rallies are able to coexist in the performance space while remaining detached, as if they were the psychic ground out of which the figures and speech emerge, or the phantasmatic echoes of the cultural models co-opted, as the narrator caustically explains, during the Nazi era (figure 1.15).

Many of the images projected in *Hitler, a Film from Germany* are canonical examples of Romantic art (such as Blake's *The Ancient of Days*, 1794; Runge's *The Great Morning*, 1809–1810; and Friedrich's *The Sea of Ice*, 1823–1824). Their prominence ironically underpins Syberberg's central argument that Nazism presented itself as the fulfillment of Romanticism and, in so doing, permanently tainted its legacy. The circus barker at the beginning declares that the film will work through sentiments that have now become "taboo," and it is no coincidence that the first part is replete with plastic dolls, phalluses, and verbal references to Sigmund Freud. Syberberg's early documentary work reveals a keen fascination with the expressive possibilities of cinematic portraiture,

FIGURE 1.15 Hitler, a Film from Germany *(Hans-Jürgen Syberberg, 1977).*

the use of the recording properties of the camera to capture gestures and faces in flux. In *Hitler, a Film from Germany*, the techniques used to explore the construction of a cinematic star image (*Romy, Portrait of a Face*, 1966) or mythologizing narratives (*Winifred Wagner and the House of Wahnfried*, 1975) are applied to a figure who had demagogically mastered both. The narrator's language and the overall organization of the film suggest that Hitler's popular success derived from his manipulation of an essentially cinematic mode of self-presentation. Syberberg's examination of the mechanics of projection are, in this way, extended to both the Nazi aestheticization of politics, epitomized by the central gambit of Hitler as filmmaker, and the collective fantasies projected onto "our Hitler, the Hitler within us." The discordance between the scale of those projected aspirations and conventional biography makes it impossible to represent a singular "Hitler," and Syberberg instead attempts to force a confrontation with the repressed through dispersal and repetition. The extravagant aesthetic constructions of Speer and Joseph Goebbels' "Romanticism of steel" are replaced by kitsch objects and wildly expressionist physical performances, a bric-a-brac burlesque of history intended to provoke a therapeutic engagement with the irrational forces that made this form of "reactionary modernism" possible.[152]

Syberberg's choice and treatment of images is informed by his art historical studies at the University of Munich in the mid-1950s, especially by the method of Hans Sedlmayr, as important an influence on Syberberg as Faure was on Gance.[153] A central figure in the New Vienna School of art history in the 1920s and 1930s and an avatar of cultural pessimism in the 1940s and 1950s, Sedlmayr advocated a form of seeing that would enable a work to be "penetrated through contemplation or conceptualization."[154] Since "a work of art only exists through a particular attitude in which virtually the entire historical situation is concentrated," close analysis of salient details, however apparently minor, could facilitate insight into the entire "structure" of a particular epoch.[155] In one of his most important books, Sedlmayr applied this method to the Gothic cathedral, which he repeatedly compared to a *Gesamtkunstwerk*.[156] Like Sedlmayr's mentor Alois Riegl, Syberberg sees *Kunstwollen* in both high and low culture, in the Bayreuth presentations of Wagner as well as the culinary customs of Obsersalzberg. He also finds it in films ranging from *Siegfried* (Fritz Lang, 1924) to *Kolberg* (Veit Harlan, 1945), almost literalizing the thesis of Siegfried Kracauer's study *From Caligari to Hitler: A Psychological History of the German Film* (1947). Syberberg, however, resists both Kracauer's political engagement and Riegl's refusal of aesthetic judgment, ardently sympathizing with artists crushed by the forces of bureaucracy. Special sections of "Hell" are reserved for those who persecuted the creators of ambitious projects that parallel his own: von Stroheim, Thomas Mann, and the Eisenstein of censored or unfinished works like *Bezhin Meadow* (1936) and *Ivan the Terrible* (1944–1946). Syberberg's juxtapositions can be seen as elaborations of Eisenstein's intrashot montage (by way of Surrealist collage), and Mann's *Doctor Faustus* (1947), with its mourning for the German culture destroyed by the Nazis, offers an apposite reference point for the darkly ironic melancholy of *Hitler, a Film from Germany*. The strongest identifications of all are with von Stroheim's utopian desire to make a gargantuan film and with the sense of martyrdom that accompanied his failure. A cardboard cutout of the Iron Man from *The Wedding March*—interpreted by Syberberg as "the laughing emblem of black, strong evil, according to an old tradition"—appears at the end of the first and the final parts of *Hitler, a Film from Germany*.[157]

Openly aligning himself with the German Romantics, Syberberg has described the "Promethean gift of fire" as the "wellspring of life out of which art itself is fashioned," arguing that "film's play of dead light represents the destruction of the world, the director as demiurge."[158] Near the beginning of part four of *Hitler, a Film from Germany*, the narrator suggests that the searchlights at Nuremberg, the same lights used to construct Speer's "cathedral," were all symbolically focused on "the same point, the stairs where Hitler made his appearance." For Syberberg, Hitler functioned as the false Prometheus, whose perverse desire to act as the protagonist of his own cataclysmic *Gesamtkunstwerk* drained Western tradition—the "spiritual and intellectual legacies of Aeschylus and Sophocles, of the mystery play and

Shakespeare, of the German Romantic theater, *Sturm und Drang*, the revolutions of German classicism before Brecht"—of its authority.[159] The original screenplay includes an unfilmed scene, originally near the end of part one, that upends the Gancian paradigm by depicting two soldiers striding "as though toward eternity, in commemoration of their adored Führer," accompanied by Heinrich Heine's ballad about two grenadiers loyal "to the memory of Napoleon . . . waiting for the resurrection of their leader from the grave" and culminating in a version of "La Marseillaise" composed by Wagner.[160] Similar ideas are visualized in part two ("A German Dream"), with Hitler shown emerging from Wagner's grave in a restaging of one of Gustave Doré's illustrations for *The Divine Comedy* (1857–1868).

Syberberg's film traces a Dantean pilgrimage confined almost entirely to the Inferno, as repeated allusions to circles of Hell and the title of the final part ("We Children of Hell") confirms. The four-part structure is equally indebted to the tetralogy of Wagner's *Der Ring des Nibelungen* (and, further back, to the trilogy plus commentary mode of ancient Greek theater). Wagner's series of "music dramas" begins with the construction of Valhalla in *Das Rheingold* and ends with its destruction in *Götterdämmerung*. *Hitler, a Film from Germany* instead begins, like Syberberg's five-hour documentary on Winifred Wagner and his subsequent *Parsifal*, in postapocalyptic ruins. The concluding music of *Götterdämmerung* recapitulates the dominant threads of the earlier operas, and Syberberg's film remains metaphorically caught within these motivic loops, which are first used during the credits of part one and recur frequently thereafter. The book Syberberg published just before making *Hitler, a Film from Germany* includes a section called "My *Trauerarbeit* for Bayreuth," and this idea of mourning work may help explain the film's manic tone and the ubiquitous references to Albrecht Dürer's *Melancholia I* (1514) (figure 1.16).[161] Freud argued that melancholia entails "opposed feelings of love and hate," which "reinforce an already existing ambivalence" and manifest themselves through complex systems of projection.[162] The repetitive, oscillating form of Syberberg's film seems designed to evoke (and work through) this condition. Only by plunging into the "Black Hole" of memory could the unassailable guilt of the Nazi era be metamorphosed into what the narrator calls "the cathedral for our music."

Significantly, *Hitler, a Film from Germany* ends not with Wagner, but with Beethoven. The "Ode to Joy" from Beethoven's Ninth Symphony (opus 125, 1824) provides what little evidence there is of Paradise at the end of the film. Yet the music ends in a suspension, with the dramatic final chorus replaced by faint passages of the freedom music from Beethoven's opera *Fidelio* (opus 72, 1805) heard, according to Syberberg, "as if . . . by the inner ear."[163] Both pieces bring with them contradictory associations: the Ninth Symphony was, as musicologist Esteban Buch has pointed out, "the most frequently played work in the entire symphonic repertoire" in 1941–1942, and while *Fidelio* had been

FIGURE 1.16 Hitler, a Film from Germany *(Hans-Jürgen Syberberg, 1977).*

used to reopen the destroyed Vienna State Opera house in 1955, it had also been treated as a "prophetic" work after the Anschluss.[164] The imagery in the final section is similarly ambivalent. As the "Ode to Joy" begins, Syberberg's daughter appears with film strips draped around her head; her journey into the mists is framed by an image derived from Claude-Nicolas Ledoux's drawing *The Eye: Interior of a Theater* (1800), with a miniature reproduction of Thomas Edison's Black Maria studio trapped inside a snow globe substituting for the vision of the Theatre de Besançon in the pupil (figure 1.17). The all-seeing eye created by an artist working for the ancien régime in eighteenth-century France is thereby linked to the late nineteenth-century origins of Syberberg's own medium as filtered through the iconography of Hollywood's greatest memory film, *Citizen Kane* (Orson Welles, 1941). Both Ledoux's architecture and Welles' film had greater success in subsequent decades than they did at the time they were made, and Syberberg may have anticipated a similar response to his own work. More importantly, the juxtaposition suggests a tension between megalomaniacal manipulators of mass media (such as William Randolph Hearst surrogate Charles Foster Kane) and the state (sponsor of Ledoux's plans to redesign Paris) as well as the impossibility of art evading politics. The last gasp of the silent-era dream of complete creative control within a studio system, *Citizen Kane* was also an anti-isolationist work released a mere three months before Pearl Harbor. Syberberg's film thus

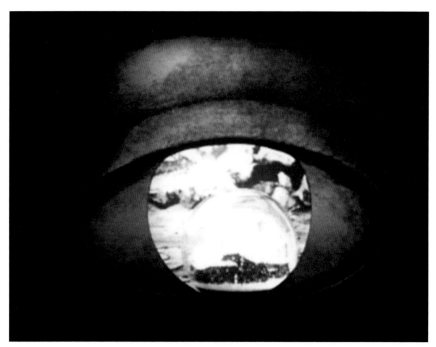

FIGURE 1.17 Hitler, a Film from Germany *(Hans-Jürgen Syberberg, 1977).*

ends on a note of profound ambiguity, poised between a modernist recognition of its material structure, an acknowledgment of its historical position,
and a yearning for a world beyond the limits of representation, for the "Grail"
that appears after the end credits.

The slow zooms and dissolves used at the beginning of *Hitler, a Film from
Germany* recall the opening of *Citizen Kane*, but where the Welles film ends
by directly reversing these movements, bringing the film full circle behind
the gates of Xanadu, the Syberberg film ends with forward movement into the
space outside the earth.[165] The implications of this shift are made clearer by
comparison to the mirrored movements that open and close *The Satin Slipper*,
Manoel de Oliveira's adaptation of Paul Claudel's theatrical behemoth. Started
in Paris in 1919 and completed in Tokyo five years later, *The Satin Slipper* was
an attempt to bridge the intellectual traditions of Old World Europe with
the nō and kabuki forms of Japanese theater.[166] In 1946, Claudel called for a
type of spectacle that would "utilize radio, dance, music, and the cinema,"
all of which were incorporated into this theological *Gesamtkunstwerk*, the
culmination of a series of almost unperformably long plays.[167] By convert-
ing *The Satin Slipper* into cinema, Oliveira was able to bring Claudel's synthetic ideal to full fruition, using overtly theatrical staging to emphasize the
fact that the most "cinematic" elements are those related to "the body and to
speech."[168] Syberberg's film combines montages of archival radio broadcasts

with exhausting and seemingly meandering verbal excursus from the actors, setting both in relation to the projected reproductions in the background to establish a Brechtian dialogue between different levels of understanding. Oliveira creates dialectical tension by complementary means, connecting Claudel's highly literary dialogues to long passages of direct address and using subtle camera movements to dynamize his own form of "primitivist" sound filmmaking.

Like Syberberg, Oliveira had a pronounced interest in the processes of cinematic construction and in the boundary between theatrical and cinematic modes of representation. Oliveira referred to cinema as a "ritual for filming rituals," and the most celebrated of his "early" works, *The Rite of Spring* (1963), uses a Portuguese passion play to consider the relationship between cinema's documentary and fictional aspects.[169] Several key films (*Doomed Love*, 1978; *Francisca*, 1981; *The Satin Slipper*) treat the unfulfilled romantic longings of the protagonists with a combination of intense passion and reflective distance, while ironically drawing attention to the structures inside and outside the narrative that determine their fate. Painted backdrops, baroque compositions, and shifts in the tonality of light are all combined to create an elaborate meditation on various forms of confinement that contains and defuses the affect of the Romantic melodrama characteristic of Oliveira's sources, without disavowing the underling emotions. Inverting the poesis of the unbridled image, Oliveira instead emphasizes sound and voice, frequently pushing his imagery toward the presentational stasis of the tableau vivant. In *The Satin Slipper*, he reduces film to its most basic elements, using simple cuts to connect otherwise disconnected locations in the manner of Georges Méliès (also a reference point for the moon imagery in *Hitler, a Film from Germany*).

Claudel's experiments with extreme duration were exactly contemporaneous with those of Gance.[170] Their explorations of temporal scale were mutually reinforcing, and they both collaborated with Honegger to develop new forms of audiovisual montage (the script for *The Satin Slipper* includes several references to cinematic techniques).[171] As with Gance and Wagner, Claudel's work combined progressive and reactionary elements, and the universalist vision of *The Satin Slipper* is inextricably wed to attitudes and assumptions that would now be regarded as chauvinist imperialism. Although a severely abridged version was presented in occupied France in 1943, the full text (lasting approximately eleven hours) was not performed theatrically until 1987, two years after the release of Oliveira's film.[172] Adapting the play more than a half-century after its creation presented a group of interconnected challenges—logistical and ideological—that Oliveira addressed by including maps of the world onscreen and by using the paired movements at the beginning and end to enclose the main body of the work within the space of both the theater and the cinema.

FIGURE 1.18 The Satin Slipper *(Manoel de Oliveira, 1985)*.

FIGURE 1.19 The Satin Slipper *(Manoel de Oliveira, 1985)*.

Although Oliveira's *The Satin Slipper* is generally faithful to the original play, he modified the opening in which the narrator describes Claudel's four-part (or "four-day") structure and summons up musical instruments one by one, with the camera slowly moving backward to follow the movement of the audience members streaming in. This introductory sequence, a Brechtian "baring of the device," ends with a zoom into the space of the movie screen (figure 1.18). After a title card announcing the beginning of the first "day," a brief montage of historical paintings is accompanied by a voiceover situating the film's narrative amid the sixteenth-century transition of power away from Portugal to Spain with the death of crusading King Sebastian, the mythic embodiment of the spiritual-temporal "Fifth Empire" explored by Oliveira in several other films.[173] Nearly seven hours later, the film concludes with a crane movement that resolves into a bird's-eye view, clearly showing the edge of the stage on which the action has been performed, the cameras used to "record" it, and a chorus repeating the word "listen" and calling for the "deliverance of all trapped souls." Extended to both the audience and the onscreen characters, this benediction is applied most directly to protagonist Rodrigo, who appears here and at the end of the prologue strapped to a mast, merging the iconography of Christ and Odysseus (figure 1.19).[174] "Delivered" from the film's diegetic boundaries but still figuratively caught between multiple levels of artistic representation, Rodrigo remains adrift, wandering toward an uncertain future, as the film ends.

Much like the Syberberg of *Hitler, a Film from Germany*, the Oliveira of *The Satin Slipper* eschews definitive resolution and foregrounds the mechanism of his own spectacle. In this respect, these inordinately long films are emblematic of post-1945 attempts to revitalize the seemingly compromised project of cathedral-building Romantic modernism. Acknowledging the historical fissure separating the 1970s and 1980s from the silent era, both directors end their most ambitious films with an original sound/image synthesis suggesting a perpetual search, a Grail quest linked to the structure of cinema itself.

Toward the Temenos

GREGORY MARKOPOULOS' *ENIAIOS*

The power of fire, or Flame . . . we designate by some trivial chemical
name, thereby hiding from ourselves the essential character of wonder
that dwells in it as in all things.

—THOMAS CARLYLE, *ON HEROES AND HERO WORSHIP,
AND THE HEROIC IN HISTORY* (1840)[1]

You scare me, forests, as cathedrals do!
You howl like organs; and in your damned hearts,
Those mourning-chambers where old death-rales ring,
Your De Profundis echoes in response.

—CHARLES BAUDELAIRE, "OBSESSION" (1861)[2]

Eniaios *at the Temenos, June 2004 (courtesy Noah Stout).*

In June 2004, June 2008, and June 2012, spectators from over a dozen coun-tries convened in an open field in Greece to attend the premiere of the first eight cycles of Gregory Markopoulos' *Eniaios*.[3] The most demanding and intransigent of all twentieth-century avant-garde film projects, the wholly silent *Eniaios* is a monumental re-editing of the nearly one hundred films that Markopoulos had made over the course of five decades (1947–1992). Completed but not printed just before Markopoulos' death in 1992, the film was divided into twenty-two cycles running for three to five hours each, with a total esti-mated projection time of nearly eighty hours. Even more remarkable than its length was its dependence on the particular characteristics of its screening environment, the Temenos. Named after the ancient Greek word for a sacred precinct, Markopoulos' Temenos was located in Lyssarea, a small hilly area located approximately three thousand feet above sea level on the western side of the Peloponnese that also houses the village where Markopoulos' father was born. Lyssarea is part of Arcadia, the mythic birthplace of lyric poetry and the home to hundreds of ancient houses of healing. By choosing it as the site for his Temenos, Markopoulos acknowledged that one of its func-tions was to isolate the viewer from the vagaries of ordinary time, purging him of media pollution and allowing him to reconnect with the rhythms of the natural world. In both scale and form, *Eniaios* is the most ambitious film ever made. Yet in its harmonization of viewing space and image and its emphasis on the mythic resonance of particular locations, it also constitutes a radical reformulation of the issues that preoccupied Markopoulos through-out his career, one that gives new meaning to the aspirations of the postwar avant-garde.

Eniaios and the Avant-Garde Long Form

From the late 1940s through the early 1960s, one measure of ambition in the avant-garde cinema was the creation of works of approximately feature length, such as Hans Richter's *Dreams that Money Can Buy* (1946), Jean-Isadore Isou's *Venom and Eternity* (1952), and Markopoulos' own *Serenity* (1961, now lost). There were, of course, exceptions, most famously Andy Warhol's *Sleep* (1963, 321 minutes) and *Empire* (1964, 485 minutes), an eight-hour silent study of the Empire State Building from a static camera position. Although these works functioned as monuments to cinematic duration, they were both conceived and regarded more as conceptual experiments than as attempts to establish an epic avant-garde form that would develop over, rather than simply unfold within, time. There has always been considerable debate over whether or not *Empire* was even meant to be viewed in its entirety as a unified work; as Warhol scholar Stephen Koch put it, "The disjunction between the pris-tine idea and the eight-hour reality is literal and incommensurable."[4] In form, tone, and sensibility, Warhol's longest films could not be more different from the mythopoeic epics of the early 1960s, although their very notoriety helped to catalyze a critical discussion about extreme duration that set the stage for the long-form projects that began to develop toward the end of the decade.

Here, as in so many aspects of the 1960s avant-garde, Stan Brakhage played a decisive role. Even including the *Prelude*, his *Dog Star Man* (1961–1964) ran for a highly compressed seventy-five minutes, but he subsequently isolated all the different superimposed layers and expanded the work into the four-hour landmark *The Art of Vision* (1965). Brakhage had not originally intended to "unpack" *Dog Star Man* and did so in an effort to help explicate and give an overtly musical inflection to its structure, to present the "visual symphony that *Dog Star Man can be seen as* and also all the suites of which it is composed."[5] As the Bach-inspired title indicates, the film, for all its richness, possesses an overt pedagogical element that is unusual for Brakhage, but it is precisely the explicitness of its attempt to redefine the parameters of epic cinema that enabled it to act as a model and a benchmark for other filmmakers.[6] Even the 250 minutes of *The Art of Vision*, however, paled in relation to the twenty-four-hour *Book of the Film* that Brakhage first announced in 1968 while working on *Scenes from Under Childhood* (1967–1970), the beginning of an extended autobiography. The project remained in flux for most of the next two decades, and, as P. Adams Sitney has pointed out, Brakhage "tended to speak of *The Book of the Film* as an aesthetic entity he was slowly coming to understand," with a variety of films included in different configurations and sometimes with alternate titles.[7] Although Brakhage outlined the preferred sequencing, which also underwent changes, in catalogs of his work, *The Book of the Film* does not appear to have had any public presentations as a complete entity, and the entire project came to an unexpected end with the dissolution of his marriage to Jane Collum in 1986.

The repeated changes and intuitive shifts within Brakhage's projected film stand in marked contrast to Hollis Frampton's *Magellan*, a preplanned 369-day project that would trace a "metahistory" of cinema. In an interview with Bill Simon, Frampton identifies the start of his work on *Magellan* as 1971, the year he published an essay entitled "For a Metahistory of Film: Commonplace Notes and Hypotheses," in which he proposes "to extricate cinema from [its] circular maze by superimposing on it a second labyrinth (containing an exit)—by positing something that has by now begun to come to concrete actuality: we might agree to call it an infinite cinema."[8] *Magellan* was designed to "pass from *The Flicker* [Tony Conrad, 1966] through *Unsere Afrikareise* [Peter Kubelka, 1966], or *Tom, Tom, the Piper's Son* [Ken Jacobs, 1969], or *La Région centrale* [Michael Snow, 1971] and beyond, in finite steps (each step a film), by exercising only one perfectly rational option in each move," with approximately two to five minutes of film screened each day of the year and longer films of up to an hour shown on days of particular significance, like the winter and summer solstice.[9] Frampton saw *Magellan* as a project, like James Joyce's *Finnegans Wake* (1939), that would "produce its own spectators, so to speak," and the utopianism of its conception resides in both the belief that the project could sustain interest over such a long period and the related idea that, by tracing a nonlinear "metahistory" of cinematic development, a history of human consciousness could also be mapped out.[10]

Sitney has suggested that, among other things, this schema was informed by Frampton's then friendly, but agonistic, relationship with Brakhage and his serial projects. The fact that other prominent artists Frampton was in regular contact with at the time were then engaging in their most ambitious projects may also have played a role in his thinking. It was, after all, in the years around 1971 that Michael Snow released his *La Région centrale* (180 minutes) and initiated his most exhaustively encyclopedic work *Rameau's Nephew by Diderot* (1974, 270 minutes), and it was in 1972 that the Tate Gallery purchased the massive installation *Equivalent VIII*, which Frampton's close friend Carl Andre had constructed several years before. *Magellan* was expected, in its final form, to run for thirty-six hours, which would have made it the longest serial film ever made up to that point, but Frampton was able to complete only approximately ten hours before his death in 1984. Crucially, Frampton insisted that he did not intend for his work to be viewed in a single sustained sitting, describing a hypothetical "marathon screening" as a nightmare. At the same time, he also maintained that "the last thing [he] would think about imposing on anyone is some ecclesiastical duty, as it were, of marching off to somewhere every day for a year to see what is typically two minutes of film."[11] Frampton remained uncertain what venue would be most appropriate for his film cycle, realizing that the costs would be prohibitive even for a dedicated avant-garde screening space like Anthology Film Archives, and he considered finishing it in video rather than leaving it incomplete.

More deliberately unfinished, but also begun in the late 1960s, was the ongoing diary project of Jonas Mekas: *Diaries, Notes, and Sketches.* Markopoulos and Mekas are rarely discussed together, but Mekas' frequently in-camera editing certainly reveals at least an affinity with, if not a debt to, the Markopoulos films he wrote about so effusively in the *Village Voice*.[12] Brakhage and Frampton were unable to complete their long-form epics because of personal circumstances, but Mekas' autobiographical project was conceived as a work in progress, continually expanding through a series of films with lengths running from a few minutes to five hours up until the present day. Often misunderstood as the work of a quixotic nostalgist, Mekas' best films are characterized by a complex tension between the perpetual present-tenseness of the onscreen images and the frequent reminders on the soundtrack that they are fragments of memory. This tension is developed furthest in Mekas' longest and richest film, the twelve-part *As I Was*

Moving Ahead Occasionally I Saw Brief Glimpses of Beauty (2000, 320 minutes), in which the director uses the voiceover to periodically highlight the gap between the time when the images, primarily from the years 1972–1985, were filmed and the moment of editing, around the turn of the millennium. On several occasions, Mekas draws attention to the passing of time, describing his late-night editing sessions or asking the viewer to measure the duration of a minute with him. The film itself proceeds nonsequentially, jumping backward and forward between events both major and minor in a highly subjective manner.

Mekas acknowledges the constraints of his own perspective repeatedly over the course of the film, announcing in one part that the footage being shown of his children is a record only of the way he sees them and may not correspond to their own experiences. At several points, this recognition turns into doubt about the relationship between a filmed "record" and a lived memory, and this begins to affect the cutting, with title cards such as "Why Am I Filming All of This?" acting as both structural and mnemonic interruptions. The entire film seems to be an elaborate attempt to map out the process the creative mind goes through in sifting through the fleeting events passing before it, and these formal disruptions are correlates for moments of psychic crisis. The ebullient affirmations of the film's final reel ostensibly act as testaments to a mental triumph over the quicksand of memory, but their ecstatic excess—and the frequent invocations of "my friends"—also points to a sort of overcompensation and serves as a reminder of a fundamental loneliness that will not and cannot be assuaged. In this context, Mekas' repeated use of the overture from Richard Wagner's *Parsifal* (1882) is telling. It appears in most reels of the film and, in almost every case, it is used to link images of traveling with footage of friends. Friedrich Nietzsche excluded the prelude from his virulent attack on Wagner's last and most difficult opera, writing that there was a perfect clarity in "the music as descriptive art, bringing to mind a shield with a design in relief on it . . . and finally, a sublime and extraordinary feeling, experience, happening of the soul, at the basis of the music."[13] This description vividly encapsulates the resonance of the *Parsifal* overture for Mekas, for whom it seems to connote memories of the Old Europe he was forced to leave in the 1940s and to suggest an insatiable desire for a past that cannot be recovered.[14]

In *As I Was Moving Ahead Occasionally I Saw Brief Glimpses of Beauty*, Mekas declares, "I am a Romantic, I believe in Romanticism" (figure 2.1). This also holds true for Brakhage—though not for Frampton, whose *Magellan* was partially intended as a critique of Romantic idealism—but it was Markopoulos who most systematically employed Romantic iconography, motifs, and ideas to underpin his extraordinary ambitions. Markopoulos saw very little of the long-form serial projects of Brakhage, Frampton, and Mekas, but his own plans for a dedicated screening space, and for what would eventually become

FIGURE 2.1 As I Was Moving Ahead Occasionally I Saw Brief Glimpses of Beauty *(Jonas Mekas, 2000)*.

Eniaios, were first developed during the same period, in the years between 1967 and 1971 when he rapidly extricated himself from the New York avant-garde community. These four filmmakers were all born within a few years of one another, and while the methods, forms, and ultimate implications of their projects differed radically, they all shared a utopian belief that the full potential of cinema could be realized only in works whose temporal scale bucked the normal patterns of film exhibition and inspired new forms of concentrated attention on the part of the spectator. Although it is only now being printed, Markopoulos' project stands alone most conspicuously in having been brought to completion in an integral form before the filmmaker's death.

If for Mekas, Wagner's *Parsifal* represents an abiding yearning, for Markopoulos it represented a dream realized. Wagner's final, five-hour opera was first performed in 1882 at the Bayreuth Festspielhaus built for him in the 1870s because he wanted to dissociate performances of his work from what he saw as the empty commercial spectacle of nineteenth-century Grand Opera. *Parsifal* was initially reserved for exhibition only in that space, where performances could take on the character of a sacred ritual that would unite pagan and Christian traditions. By 1970, Markopoulos had become similarly disenchanted with the commercialization of avant-garde exhibition spaces, which he felt had "compromised before compromise was necessary," and his sojourn in Europe quickly became a self-imposed exile.[15] He removed all of his films from circulation and issued directives to archives instructing them not to screen the films in their possession, envisioning instead the creation of a dedicated viewing space, the Temenos, in which the "specters" of printing, distribution, and projection would be "vanquished" (figure 2.2).[16] The conscious model for the Temenos was the special performance house in Bayreuth, and Markopoulos at one point considered Graubünden as the site.[17] Appropriately, one of the final films that Markopoulos publicly exhibited was *Sorrows* (1969), a dense, rapturous study of the house King Ludwig II secured for Wagner in Triebschen, Switzerland. Unlike Wagner, Markopoulos was unable to find a patron willing and able to sponsor the creation of a building devoted exclusively to the screening of his work. He nevertheless decided that the "Justified Province" would be Greece, and began work on *Eniaios*, "a cycle far removed from the politics of *filmmuseums, cinémathèques,* and *film festivals,*" which was designed for presentation in an open air amphitheater within the as-yet-unbuilt Temenos complex.[18]

Markopoulos' long-standing identification with Wagner deepened in 1967, the year he attended a performance of *Siegfried* (1876) in West Berlin and began discussing plans for what would become the Temenos.[19] Speaking of his exile in a 1968 letter, Markopoulos writes, "I feel like Wagner when he left his homeland" and mentions that he has agreed to direct two operas—one for film and one for the stage.[20] Later that year, he annotated a volume of Wagner's

FIGURE 2.2 *The screen at the Temenos, June 27, 2008 (copyright Richard I. Suchenski).*

writings, paying special attention to the "Artwork of the Future" essay in which his ideas about the *Gesamtkunstwerk* are elucidated. Markopoulos' many references to the cycles of *Eniaios* in his published and unpublished writings are a testament to the influence of Wagner, who saw *Der Ring des Nibelungen* (1848–1876) as the inauguration of a new form, a cycle of "music dramas" rather than a series of operas. Markopoulos shared Wagner's belief that everything possible—such as concealing the source of the image— should be done to encourage an immersive, cathartic artistic experience, but he did not share Wagner's investment in multimedia spectacle.[21] Where Wagner incorporated painting, music, trompe l'oeil set design, and theater into a comprehensive presentation, Markopoulos proposed an alternative *Gesamtkunstwerk* that could subsume and contain all of the other arts within the space of the projected image. Markopoulos ultimately concluded that the architectural splendors of the Festspielhaus or the Doge's Palazzo in Venice (both sites he visited in the early stages of Temenos planning) would be a distraction from the work, finding inspiration instead from much more modest sources:

> Often here in these mountains, where I came seeking the site . . . I noticed from my excursions on foot or on the train the tiny specks of churches appearing out of nowhere. Some of them I entered. I noticed their beautiful shapes. It is, perhaps, these shapes which will mould the future Temenos of the Twenty-First Century. For I reflect that if I produce my films so simply, then that principle must also be applied to what my Temenos shall be; a sanctuary where one may approach Understanding.[22]

Markopoulos' attachment to the values Victor Hugo associates with the cathedral is evident, but, like these small churches, the Temenos was meant to harmonize with its environment, to create a ritual space that exists both inside and outside the surrounding landscape. In this, Markopoulos is following the model of Goethe, who merged the imagery of the forest and the cathedral in "On German Architecture" (1773), depicting the facade of the Strasbourg Cathedral as a "far-spreading tree of God . . . with a thousand branches, millions of twigs, and leaves like the sand of the sea."[23]

"Towards a New Narrative Film Form"

Markopoulos' Temenos was intended to bring about a total fusion of interior and exterior space, and, in this respect, it brought to fruition a concern with landscape and environment that was a major, generally unremarked-upon element of the earlier films that he eventually reconfigured into *Eniaios*. In this regard, it is worth considering Sergei Eisenstein's essay "Nonindifferent Nature," by far the most sustained treatment of the topic of landscape by a major film theorist. Written between 1945 and 1947, just as Eisenstein was completing his work on the unfinished *Ivan the Terrible* "triptych" (1944–1946)—the most substantial attempt to construct a long-form modernist film between the 1920s and the 1960s—the essay connects examples from the histories of painting, literature, and music to detailed formal analysis of his own films, arguing that cinema dialectically synthesizes all of the other arts, absorbing their best properties and serving as their highest stage. Consequently, in cinema, "Landscape can serve as a concrete image of the embodiment of whole cosmic conceptions, whole philosophic systems," acting as "a complex bearer of the possibilities of a plastic interpretation of emotion."[24] This is possible because "landscape is the freest element of film, the least burdened with servile, narrative tasks and the most flexible in conveying moods, emotional states, and spiritual experiences," and is thus capable of facilitating contrapuntal rhythmic constructions by acting as the "inner plastic music" of a film.[25] Eisenstein's "nonindifferent nature" is little more than the temporalization of the pathetic fallacy, but his conception of landscape as a malleable frame through which cinematic rhythm can be modulated provides a model that can be usefully applied to a wide variety of adventurous films, including those of Markopoulos.

Markopoulos disavowed the influence of Eisenstein, but it was a similar concern with the "inner plastic music" of the film image that animated the use of landscape in his early psychodramas (*Psyche*, 1947; *Lysis*, 1948; *Charmides*, 1949; and *Swain*, 1950).[26] Produced on a shoestring budget and edited by hand without the use of a splicer, these early films demonstrate a rhythmic cohesion and a precisely modulated control of color that was extremely unusual for an "avant-garde" filmmaker of his generation. The professionalism and technical control of these films may reflect Markopoulos' unfinished training as a film student at the University of Southern California, where he acted as student observer on the films of Hollywood directors like Fritz Lang, Alfred Hitchcock, and Jules Dassin and took classes with Josef von Sternberg, whom he deeply admired. From von Sternberg, Markopoulos adopted a posture as an unrepentant "aesthete," and an attentiveness to the composition of all aspects of the film image.[27] This concern for the artistic properties of the individual image led Markopoulos to employ a production method in which he did not give his actors their dialogue or allow them to know what scene was going to be played until the moment of shooting, making it possible for him to compose the performances within the setting as an element of the entire film image. The settings themselves, both natural and architectural, were frequently used to convey particular symbolic meanings, usually in connection with the dominant colors of a scene. As a result of Markopoulos' highly elliptical narrative strategies, they also functioned as receptacles for the scene's emotions, imbued with the longings of the characters. There is a crucial section in *Psyche*, for example, where a young man places his hand on the shoulder of the titular protagonist and she throws her head back; the harmonization of her bold red lipstick, pale green dress, and golden hair with the green grass and the orange twilight sun in the background gives her carefully calibrated pose an erotic intensity that, through the repeated cuts away from the lovers, is displaced onto the hilly landscape they inhabit (figures 2.3–2.4). Markopoulos includes brief flashes of this landscape throughout the film, using it as both a structuring element and a metonymic conduit for remembered emotions.

The intertwining of landscape and the processes of memory is made even more explicit in the rapid narrative recapitulations that Markopoulos used to create fluid transitions between scenes and to end his films. In these recapitulations, representative images from earlier parts of the film flash by in rapid succession, remaining onscreen for a fraction of a second.[28] By intercutting shots of character interaction with the empty spaces where those interactions took place, Markopoulos' montage clusters create dense networks of associations in which landscapes assume a central role. Since the images in these clusters are scrambled out of sequence, they also suggest the interrelated simultaneity of spatiotemporal events and create an intensified viewing experience by encouraging the spectator to actively participate in the (re) construction of the narrative. In the 1960s, these patterns provoked frequent comparisons to Alain Resnais, but Markopoulos' memory structures, which prefigure the formal strategies of *Eniaios*, anticipate Resnais' parallel innovations by at least a decade.[29]

FIGURE 2.3 Psyche *(Gregory Markopoulos, 1947) (courtesy Temenos Archive).*

FIGURE 2.4 Psyche *(Gregory Markopoulos, 1947) (courtesy Temenos Archive)*.

Like Resnais, Markopoulos was invested in a highly abstracted form of narrative filmmaking. *Psyche*, for example, is derived from an unfinished novel by Pierre Louÿs, which Markopoulos successfully distilled into the barest fragments of a narrative without abolishing the overall sense of fictive coherence. Markopoulos continued to make oblique literary adaptations throughout the 1950s and 1960s, using works by such authors as Nathaniel Hawthorne, Aeschylus, and Honoré de Balzac as springboards for increasingly elaborate feature-length narrative films. In the four major features of his artistic maturity (*Serenity*, 1958; *Twice a Man*, 1963; *Himself as Herself*, 1967; *The Illiac Passion*, 1967), Markopoulos developed a highly sophisticated film form that allowed him to hold multiple levels of visual and temporal awareness in a state of dynamic tension with one another. The polyphonies of these films were created and sustained by Markopoulos' use of single-frame editing, which he theorized in his most important essay, "Towards a New Narrative Film Form":

> In the beginning of the motion picture, the film frame had great potential. But with the introduction of sound, a part of the frame was relegated to the service of the sound track. Aesthetically opposed but artistically united, sound and image failed to achieve that poetic unity in cinema that everyone had envisioned. . . . The film frame which creates each shot or composition has been neglected; it has been understood only as a photographic

necessity. I propose a new narrative form through the fusion of the classic montage technique with a more abstract system. This system involves the use of short film phrases which evoke thought-images.[30]

In his early films, Markopoulos sustained the methods of earlier montage-oriented directors like Eisenstein, Abel Gance, and D. W. Griffith by cutting lengths of continuous film into fragments, but by the time he made *Gammelion* in 1968, he was shooting only "short phrases" that could be edited together in a modular fashion.[31] Consequently, Markopoulos' system differs from Eisensteinian montage insofar as it replaces references to the continuing shot with the repetition of clusters of differing frames integrated through similarities of composition, orientation, or shot scale. In this way, individual images are able to reverberate throughout a film, with each appearance marked by a profusion of contrapuntal frame-to-frame collisions that create additional layers of resonance.

From *Gammelion* on, the autonomy and constitutional integrity of the individual film frame was reinforced through the near-exclusive use of stationary shots taken from a camera held at a fixed position. By fusing these static shots with openly reflexive gestures, Markopoulos shattered the illusion of cinematic movement, drawing attention instead to cinema's identity as a series of still images stitched together on a strip and then projected sequentially. On one level, Markopoulos' decision to work with the single frame seems to represent, like Stéphane Mallarmé's use of the letter and Paul Cézanne's use of the brushstroke, a modernist reduction of his medium to its most fundamental, constitutive unit. The resulting atomization of the film image is, however, counterbalanced by the harmonization of the "short film phrases." One index of Markopoulos' deep-seated Romanticism is his enthusiastic embrace of the film director's ability to imaginatively assemble these discontinuous image clusters into unified visionary edifices. By treating film footage as raw material for editing rather than "as images in movement," it was possible, he believed, to give it "a far greater and extraordinary Movement."[32]

Markopoulos' modulation of all aspects of film structure included the use of the measure of film frames as an organizing motif and a bearer of meaning. In *Twice a Man*, Markopoulos turns the number of frames used when a character is introduced into a sort of leitmotif for that figure. Thus, when the "Artist Physician" is referred to via three frame shots toward the end of the film, he is linked to the protagonist Paul, who was introduced at the beginning of the film using shots of exactly the same length.[33] Since the conventional spatiotemporal coordinates of representational filmmaking are transformed beyond recognition by Markopoulos' frame-by-frame editing, this somewhat esoteric numerological coding helps to give structural shape to, and facilitate the subliminal apprehension of, the narrative. Even more significant in this respect is the interweaving of figures into their environments through the elegant combination of cuts and dissolves. Nowhere is this more apparent than in the opening scene of *Twice a Man*, in which a shot of the "Artist-Physician" looking off into the distance from a ferry is intercut six times with brief images of the New York skyline. With each iteration, the images of New York become longer until finally the skyline becomes dominant, transforming the returns to the human figure into mere echoes of the original shot.[34] This highly flexible technique allowed Markopoulos to temporally distend the force of traditional shot/countershot exchanges, deepening the threnodic implications of the film's complex flashback structure. By repeatedly using these montage clusters to connect empty landscapes to particular characters, Markopoulos turned the former into relays for the symbolic and emotional meanings transmitted across both time and space, providing necessary connective tissue to a disjunctive narrative.

Twice a Man begins with two minutes of black leader projected to the sound of falling rain. Markopoulos claimed that the darkness allowed the spectator to "rest his eyes, so that the initial visual and psychological impact of single frames and clusters of frames would be more readily apprehended."[35] It also establishes the key sound motif of the film, creating a psychological distance between sound and image that is made even more acute by the use of superimposition. In *The Illiac Passion*, by far Markopoulos' most complex feature, these sound/image contrasts are developed even further, with the director's incantatory reading of Henry David Thoreau's 1843 translation of *Prometheus Bound* and excerpts from Béla Bartok's *Cantata Profana* (Sz. 94, 1934) acting in counterpoint to the densely layered images. The structure of Bartok's piece, consisting of a chorus of voices bracketed by a single tenor, mirrors that of the film, which begins with a lone male figure (Prometheus) crossing the Brooklyn Bridge and ends with that same figure near a lighthouse (figure 2.5). In between, Prometheus interacts with twenty-four other characters associated with figures in the Greek Pantheon, with each, according to Markopoulos, representative of one of his "selves."[36]

More than in any of the films before or after it, Markopoulos mythologized all aspects of *The Illiac Passion*, using costumes, objects, and gestures to set up symbolic links between particular deities. By using fades throughout the film, Markopoulos was able to isolate groups of characters into myth-specific subnarratives. The combination of these fades and of repeated montage phrases made it possible to subsume a seemingly limitless variety of interactions into the larger story of Prometheus. In lieu of the flashback bursts he had used in his earlier films, Markopoulos inserted shots featuring Prometheus throughout the film and included scenes in which characters are seen to relate through superimposition, montage editing, or sounds even though they occupy different subnarratives. Unadorned landscapes (mostly shot in Central Park and the New York Botanical Gardens) act as pivot points where the disconnected

FIGURE 2.5 *Prometheus in* The Illiac Passion *(Gregory Markopoulos, 1967) (courtesy Temenos Archive).*

space and time elements of the film briefly come together before splintering into new permutations.

The first images of *The Illiac Passion* are similarly oriented around locations: a fence at dawn, light reflecting off a large body of water, and finally the "adamantine bridge" that the protagonist will shortly ascend and which, for Markopoulos, suggests the binding of Prometheus.[37] Although the primary inspiration for the film was Aeschylus, the depiction of Prometheus moving gradually toward a unity within polyphony and a concomitant sense of freedom from the constraints of both space and time mirrors the overall arc of Percy Bysshe Shelley's *Prometheus Unbound* (1820). An earlier, more utopian plan for the film would have made this implicit connection even deeper by "showing each country's ruins and then ... [summing] up all the types of architecture," thereby providing a correlate to Shelley's "unclassed, tribeless, and nationless" humanity.[38] Having united all the different situations of the film within what Markopoulos called the "very Being" of the protagonist, *The Illiac Passion* ends with a repetition of the same set of landscapes that opened the film, a circular return that further interiorizes the interlocked narratives at the center of the film. Taken together with the use of Thoreau's translation on the soundtrack and the reflexive shots of Markopoulos working at an editing table in the middle of the film, these consonances with Shelley's radical reworking of classical antiquity point to a move away from heroic binaries, a dispersal of the fire of Promethean inspiration across the body of the film, that will have profound implications for *Eniaios*.

Although it wasn't possible to print the film until 1967, Markopoulos finished *The Illiac Passion* in 1965; by the time it was released, he had moved away from multicharacter narratives, devoting much of his time to short films edited entirely in-camera. By exposing film for a set length measured by the frame counter on his Bolex camera and inserting fades—either through an in-camera mechanism or by blocking the lens with his hand, rewinding, and then filming again—Markopoulos was able to create a variety of nuanced effects within the camera itself. One obvious advantage of this method is that it reduced the cost of making films, eliminating postproduction expenses and minimizing laboratory fees, an important factor for a filmmaker living as impecuniously as Markopoulos.[39] Markopoulos also believed that this method had aesthetic value, for, as he put it, "by editing in the camera one must be more exact; the idea and the image more concentrated; the result a more brilliant appeal to the mind and dormant senses."[40] In other words, by disallowing the possibility of "covering" a scene with backup or replacement footage, in-camera editing gives increased urgency to every cut, forcing a more concentrated approach to shooting and an intensified focus on the potential resonances of each shot.

Markopoulos' switch in production method was accompanied by the separation of figure and ground in his work, with most of his later films operating in one of two mutually exclusive modes: compilations of individual or group portraiture and "films of place."[41] The portrait films, shot mostly in close-up, were studies of the physiognomy of the sitters that were given texture through the use of a wide variety of angles and the inclusion of relevant objects, often via superimposition. In *Galaxie* (a 1966 compilation of twenty-four individual portraits, each shot in an interior space that is in some way emblematic of the subject's professional life), for example, Jasper Johns is shown staring at the camera with one of his paintings; Jonas Mekas is shown reading an issue of *Film Culture*; and shots of Maurice Sendak's face are intercut with drafts of the cover of *Where the Wild Things Are* (1963).[42] The "films of place," by contrast, were studies of particular locations, shot using only natural light with forms tailored to the personal, historical, and religious associations of their subjects. In these films, Markopoulos divested landscapes and interior spaces of their narrative functions, allowing them to articulate meaning on their own terms.

Frustrated by what he saw as the degeneration of film culture, in 1967 Markopoulos left the United States for Europe, where he would spend the rest of his life. The first film that he made there was *Bliss* (1967), an in-camera-edited study of the eighteenth-century Church of St. John on the Greek island of Hydra. The film contains no musical excerpts, instead making use of the muted sounds of braying sheep to evoke the symbolism of the church and remind the viewer of its countryside location. *Bliss* was shot using two reels of Ektachrome film, which intensified the natural sunlight streaming into the church through doorways and windows (Markopoulos enhanced this effect by shooting at twelve frames per second in the dimmer parts of the church).[43] The rhythmic structure of the film is based entirely on the interaction of these streams of light, sometimes superimposed in patterns suggesting the icons on the wall. These icons, and the frescoes that accompany them, gradually progress from images of Jonah in the mouth of the whale and the Virgin Mary embracing St. Anne to scenes from the life of St. Demetrius before finally settling on a depiction of the patron saint of the church in a pose of benediction (figure 2.6).[44] The film builds slowly, connecting flashes of light from different entry points in the vestibule first through gradual montage and then through a multiple superimposition, simultaneously grounding the viewer within the church and simulating the internal movement of a religious ritual. All of the shots in the second half of *Bliss* last for less than a second, but the careful framing situates each in its sacerdotal context. The editing-driven movement between these still images mirrors the devotional path a supplicant would take through the nave to the altar, a connection further reinforced by the shift in the final moments of the film to low-angle shots of the light streaming through the windows in the dome. The implied movements of the camera suggest spiritual ascent, while the triple superimposition of light shimmering through a circular array of windows provides the film with an ending

FIGURE 2.6 Bliss *(Gregory Markopoulos, 1967) (courtesy Temenos Archive).*

that is both euphoric and structurally meaningful. Where the oneiric tone of films like *Ming Green* (1966) suggested the almost-hermetic spaces of personal memory, the luminous images of *Bliss* subtly depict the unique conjoining of the local and the numinous characteristic of religious architecture and sacred space.[45]

After making *Bliss*, Markopoulos fulfilled a long-standing dream by shooting *Gammelion* at the Roccasinibalda Castle in the south of Italy (figure 2.7). Like Markopoulos' earlier films, *Bliss* combines short film phrases and continuous shots, but *Gammelion* consists entirely of brief, consistently spaced flashes of totally static imagery separated by black leader. Even here, in a film totally devoid of characters and plot, Markopoulos tries to retain vestiges of narrative by reading passages from Rainer Maria Rilke on the soundtrack ("To be loved means to be consumed. To love is to give light with inexhaustible oil. To be loved is to pass away, to love is to endure"), including shots of paintings depicting mythological courtship, and flashing images of a rose.[46] Within this schema, landscapes take on an even more prominent role than usual, and Markopoulos' editing emphasizes the sensuous vitality and metaphoric resonance of his locations. *Gammelion* opens with a number of one- or two-frame flashes of rocks, and the film gradually traces a circuitous path through a forest and up to the castle in the distance, suggesting a journey charged with psychological meaning, without implying that the camera stands in for the

FIGURE 2.7 Gammelion *(Gregory Markopoulos, 1968) (courtesy Temenos Archive).*

subjectivity of an unseen protagonist in the manner of early Brakhage. During the second half of the film, the camera passes through the various rooms of the castle complex, and Markopoulos opens up deep space through the careful selection of light sources while also stressing its enclosure through repeated cuts to walls, grills, and bars. Despite the improvised mode of shooting, *Gammelion* possesses a remarkable structural rigor, and it ends by showing the landscapes visible at the beginning from an opposite angle, reorienting the overall development of the film within the exterior environment.

More than any film before it, *Gammelion* anticipates both the form and the mode of *Eniaios*, in which journeys through landscapes and architectural sites are given complex associations related to both their status as sacred spaces and the pilgrimage aspect of the Temenos. Markopoulos first envisioned this new form while editing *Bliss* in May 1967, including a diagram in his diary for a film composed in sections of variable lengths with many superimpositions, separated by "single frames and white leader, like a mosaic."[47] However, the existence of *The Mysteries* (1968) indicates that the overall development of Markopoulos' work in this period was by no means linear. Made shortly after *Gammelion*, *The Mysteries* is a feature-length psychodrama, shot with professional actors in Munich, that is edited like *Twice a Man*, suggesting that Markopoulos was still considering different stylistic options depending on the subject of the film.[48] By contrast, the silent portrait films of major European figures, usually artists or writers, that Markopoulos began shooting in 1968 and 1969 utilize a structure that is remarkably similar to that of *Eniaios*. Indeed, *The Olympian* (1969), Markopoulos' portrait of Alberto Moravia, is included in the fourth cycle of *Eniaios* with only minor changes. As in Markopoulos' earlier portrait films, the subjects of these late portraits are depicted with objects symbolizing their work—such as hands, drawings, books, or film strips—often in superimposition. However, Markopoulos edits them in a more complex way, combining very brief shots from multiple perspectives to create, over time, a cubistic layering of space. In *The Olympian*, Markopoulos alternates single frame shots of Moravia facing the camera and then in profile to create an afterimage effect that is amplified by the juxtaposition or superimposition of brief flashes of movement frequently lasting for four to eight frames. The interrelation of these glimpses of movement with sections of black leader creates an impression of interpolated motion that manages to convey the essential mood of the sitter through fragments of gestures and facial expressions.

With the form that would become characteristic of *Eniaios* in mind, Markopoulos shot more than sixty additional films in the 1970s and 1980s, although most of them were never printed. The twenty-two cycles of *Eniaios* incorporate footage cut from the camera originals of all of these films, as well as from the films released before Markopoulos left for Europe. Reel-length segments from earlier films like *Twice a Man* were worked into different cycles at particular points.[49] The structure of *Eniaios*—brief flashes of imagery, often single frames, separated by long sections of black leader—transforms these images so thoroughly, however, that even when still images from the same film appear sequentially, they touch, but do not cross over, the threshold of narrative development. Markopoulos claimed that the "basic clue of Revelation in film" was the space between frames, and he had emphasized separations between images as early as *Swain*.[50] In *Eniaios*, he takes his modernist reduction of cinema into its most fundamental elements to a limit point in which the earlier relationship is inverted. Tantalizing glimpses of imagery seem to emanate out of an enveloping field of darkness, endowed with the hieratic power of hieroglyphs.[51]

Markopoulos' references to hieroglyphs revive a set of ideas generated during the Romantic period and first applied to cinema in the 1910s. Indeed, in developing the strategies used in *Eniaios*, Markopoulos was extending the aesthetics of the most ambitious directors of the silent era, including their belief in the power of the long form. He frequently identified Erich von Stroheim as his favorite filmmaker, and his use of symbolic images reverberating between films was an extension of von Stroheim's method (as was his treatment of the in-camera dissolves von Stroheim had used in *The Wedding March*, 1928, and *Queen Kelly*, 1929). Markopoulos also wrote a fascinating "letter" to "Wark" (Griffith) telling him how much he admired the purity of his images and describing the ways in which his mode of expression had been usurped by commercial forces.[52] The in-camera editing strategies Markopoulos developed were an elaboration of techniques that had been employed in earlier films like *Intolerance* (1916), and both directors created visual scrapbooks full of images they wanted to restage or allude to. Yet, although he could barely have known his major works (which lay in tatters until the 1970s), the filmmaker Markopoulos most resembles is Gance.[53] Like Gance, Markopoulos hoped to use dense montage and cinematic plasticity to expand the perception of the spectator. Markopoulos was more sober than his predecessor, less willing to embrace the ecstasies of art without introducing a counterelement and much less interested in fusing radical form to popular spectacle, but he was similarly open to using every conceivable means to enhance the impact of his images. While he was developing *Eniaios*, Markopoulos made detailed plans for a triple-screen version, in which different sections of the same film would be reconfigured contrapuntally across an enveloping space much as they would have been with Gance's Polyvision.[54] Markopoulos also considered reversing films and even projecting certain sections both forward and in reverse, an experiment he had previously attempted in *Twice a Man Twice*, a double projection from 1967.

For many years, Markopoulos remained attached to the idea of incorporating sound into *Eniaios*. With the exception of a few portrait films, all of the films Markopoulos made after 1969 were shot and released without sound, and he was already discussing the removal of sound from his films during their presentation at the Temenos in 1973. As he explained in a letter to Robert Freeman, "Certainly the Temenos idea denotes a peace, silence/ Meditation. I think it must be done a step at a time: if the sounds go, then I must then wait to see about removing the titles, and decide how the films would then be presented."[55] Markopoulos removed the original soundtracks of his sound films shortly thereafter. During the course of re-editing his films into *Eniaios*, however, Markopoulos considered including voiceover reading from the source texts of particular films, much as he had earlier done in *The Illiac Passion*. Partially inspired by his close study of Jean Sibelius' song cycles, Markopoulos hoped to add thematically relevant sounds at the end of a reel or cycle, treating natural effects like thunderclaps and bird songs as sonic equivalents to his landscape shots.[56] By the mid-1980s, Markopoulos had changed his mind, deciding that sound would detract from, rather than add to, his images, and he began speaking instead of the imagined (synesthetic) sounds the images would summon, what he called "the sounding image."[57] Late in 1990, as Markopoulos was nearing completion of his massive project, he writes even more enthusiastically of "the return of the image in its entirety; the sound removed, the space of the image regained."[58]

"A Supreme Art in a Dark Age"

> It is each individual New Cinema Film Spectator who breathes life
> to the images with and without thought; images which must come
> to life at the touch of each individual spectator's eyes. The elements
> are primitive fire, and the measures of holy light which make films
> possible.
>
> —GREGORY MARKOPOULOS (1968)[59]

Markopoulos believed that cinema was "without a doubt a supreme art in a dark age," one capable of having a healing function.[60] In a crucial essay that anticipates the Temenos project, he writes that the "filmmaker as physician of the future will some day realize and utilize sound and image as a mere accessory to the greater keys of a future editing form. . . . In referring to Form I mean specifically a multi-dimensional Cinema."[61] The Temenos screenings bring this ideal to fruition, with the positioning of the screen under the night sky and the persistent presence of projected black leader on it affirming its status as an object and drawing the viewer's attention to the natural sources of light (the moon, the stars, etc.) around it, thereby allowing the images of *Eniaios* to resonate with the unique characteristics of the screening environment. The mountain path that the prospective viewer has to take in order to

get to the Temenos site provides ample opportunities to scan the surrounding countryside, making it clear that the screen on which the images will
be projected exists *within* the landscape below. As a result, the filmed landscapes that appear on the screen create echo effects that deepen the relationship with the viewing environment and invest the Temenos space with some
of the mythic associations of the locations that are represented. Tellingly,
many of the films that Markopoulos shot with *Eniaios* in mind depict sacred
spaces such as the Theater of Dionysus, Epidaurus, Chartres Cathedral, and
the Asclepium of Kos (figure 2.8). The last of these is particularly significant
because Markopoulos saw the Temenos screenings, and the journeys required
to attend them, as functionally equivalent to the Asclepian pilgrimages of
ancient Greece, in which patients traveled to therapeutic sites in remote locations to undergo "sleep healing." In similar fashion, Markopoulos wanted
to use the extended measures between the images projected at the Temenos
to create an "intuition space" in the midst of the unsullied natural beauty
of Arcadia that would unite "film as film" to the mythic landscapes of the
ancient world and allow for spiritual renewal.[62]

Markopoulos' conception of the Temenos as a space outside of history with
the power to smooth over the shocks of modernity is, of course, profoundly
Romantic. It is therefore unsurprising that the central myth of *Eniaios* is that
of Prometheus, with twenty-seven reels of imagery from *The Illiac Passion*
interwoven throughout the twenty-two cycles at points of maximal intensity

FIGURE 2.8 Eniaios *(Gregory Markopoulos, 1947–1992) (courtesy Temenos Archive).*

(figure 2.9). The elision of the original narratives of the individual films included in each cycle transforms the human figures into mythic symbols, and the prominence of *The Illiac Passion* causes many of these figures to seem like echoes, or perhaps alternate manifestations, of Prometheus. In the third cycle, for example, a brief moving shot of Prometheus walking toward the camera from *The Illiac Passion* is followed nearly an hour later by an image of the protagonist of *The Mysteries* walking toward the camera in almost exactly the same position. The original contexts for both of these shots were very different, but the synchronicity of gesture and screen position within the same cycle of *Eniaios* creates a new relationship that further reinforces the centrality of Prometheanism to the project and suggests a concordance with Karl Kerenyi's reading of Prometheus as the "archetypal image of human existence."[63] Prometheus had long fascinated Markopoulos, who included book illustrations of his torment in *Lysis* (1948) and scripted a utopian project about the myth the following year. The *Prometheus* project, which underwent many changes, was intended to be a "truly 'universal' film" shot in multiple countries and multiple languages with Prometheus depicted as uniting the major religious traditions of the world, much like the mythic figures in contemporaneous works like Robert Graves' *The White Goddess* (1948) and Joseph Campbell's *The Hero with a Thousand Faces* (1949).[64] In diminished form, this

FIGURE 2.9 *Promethean fire in* Eniaios *(Gregory Markopoulos, 1947–1992) (courtesy Temenos Archive).*

project eventually became *The Illiac Passion*, and one of the key questions raised by *Eniaios* is whether it shares or reconfigures the Prometheanism of Markopoulos' earlier work.

The Romantic poets of the nineteenth century, with whom Markopoulos strongly identified, all agreed on the centrality of the Prometheus myth, but they disagreed on its ultimate meaning. One stream of Promethean Romanticism, epitomized by Lord Byron, celebrates the untrammeled greatness of the artist who breaks free from the tyrannical constraints of society and towers over ordinary mortals, setting him up as a figure fit for worship. The other stream, epitomized by Shelley and Ralph Waldo Emerson, recognizes that such a system results only in yet another form of mastery and calls instead for an "unbinding" of the creative imagination, in which it could be used to help each individual attain the highest perfection of his or her intellectual and moral nature.[65] The messianic tone of many of Markopoulos' writings, particularly his insistence that the film spectator should "accept the fact that he must serve . . . [lifting] the veil of his discontent and [looking] upon the form that is the Being of Light, his God," recognizing "the miracle which these works are," suggests the all-consuming Promethean narcissism of a figure like Wagner.[66] By contrast, the Temenos booklet distributed to the spectators in 2004 includes an essay, "Eikones Auton," in which Markopoulos writes that "the creative man seeks to give the Spectator those parts of himself which allow him, the creative man, to be creative." Seen in conjunction with his repeated use of the phrase "beloved spectator," his vision of the filmmaker as physician, and the ideal of sleep healing, this essay supports an alternate interpretation of *Eniaios* as a work designed to enrich, and open up possibilities for, each viewer.

Crucial to this interpretation is Markopoulos' proposed rereading of the myth of Narcissus. Even when not identified as such, Narcissus figures had featured prominently in Markopoulos' work since *Swain*, where the myth was linked aesthetically to absolute (male) beauty in much the same way as it is in the work of Symbolist poets like Mallarmé and Paul Valéry.[67] In "Entheos," an essay dedicated to Giorgione that was included in the 2004 Temenos booklets, however, Markopoulos claims that Narcissus has been misunderstood, that there are "those who are afraid to seek their own reflection; and, those who brood about Narcissus within their own time, misunderstanding the legend of Narcissus within his own time." By shifting the focus of the myth toward self-reflection, Markopoulos is following the lead of the early German Romantics, particularly the Schlegels, and possibly distancing himself from the homoerotic rereadings of Narcissus by postwar poet-critics like Parker Tyler and filmmaker Willard Maas.[68] In Friedrich Schlegel's *Lucinde* (1799) and August Wilhelm Schlegel's sonnet "Narcissus" (1800), a new mythology of artistic creation is proposed in which Narcissus experiences the confrontation with his reflection consciously and is reimagined as a symbol of the mystical dignity and unique position of poetry. Thus, August Wilhelm Schlegel can link the observation of one's own reflection to the search for truth, famously writing, "Every poet is really Narcissus" without the pejorative connotations attached to the myth since the early Renaissance.[69] Given the breadth of his reading and his deep interest in German poetry, Markopoulos may well have known these works; he certainly knew Rilke's "Narcissus" of 1913, in which, as in the *Duino Elegies* (1922), self-reflection becomes a yearning for true being.

In his own essay, Markopoulos develops this further:

> There is the reflection of one's self; and, there is the reflection of that Reflection apart from one's self; that is the point beyond which there is Understanding. Between the reflection of one's self, and, the reflection of that Reflection, or, the part beyond one's self, there has been the surface of the Visible Image. But this surface of the Visible Image has escaped the knowledge of the audience. The reflection of the Visible Image from its surface, depending on its size, has always lessened the understanding of the audience, for to captivate and allure is not to understand what is before one.

Markopoulos suggests not simply that the Temenos projections would establish a relation with the projected image that would enable reflection rather than solicit consumption, but also that the use of brief images of concentrated force would make possible a triangular configuration of self, screen, and eye. The spacing of the images would encourage the viewer to complete the circuit by investing part of himself in the film while simultaneously reflecting upon his own reading of the images onscreen (Markopoulos is here fusing the participatory optics of ancient authors like Plotinus with an idiosyncratic reading of Martin Heidegger).[70] In this way, the Romantic conception of Narcissus as signifying the elevated status of the poet is extended to the viewer, transferring the locus of creativity to the community engaged in watching and deciphering the film.

Toward the end of the same essay, Markopoulos makes an important reference whose meaning is not immediately obvious. After observing that "the Temenos will seek for a surface respecting the Image in the Classic sense," he provides the following example: "There is a rock which drips with water which (they say) comes from Okeanos." The passage is from Euripides' *Hippolytus* (428 BCE), and the rock in question is linked elsewhere in the play to the "rock of Asclepius."[71] The occasionally esoteric concealment of meaning in Markopoulos' writings is matched by the source play, which makes no other mention of Asclepius despite the fact that, according to legend, it is he who helps to cure the illness affecting Phaedra.[72] Robin Mitchell-Boyask has argued that the writing of Euripides' play was motivated by the epidemic that struck Athens in 430 BCE.[73] The cult of Asclepius and the eventual development of the Eleusinian mysteries were then linked to a fundamental shift in worldview brought about by the combination of the plague and the Peloponnesian War (431–404 BCE), leading to a widespread sense of a civilization collapsing from within.[74] Markopoulos' idea of the Temenos is similarly linked to an apocalyptic sense of culture, especially film culture, having collapsed, and this gives an added layer of meaning to his invocation of Asclepius. According to Epidauran tradition, Asclepius is an aspect of Apollo who embodied a form of healing light shined from within darkness, hence the "sleep healing" associated with his cult and the symbolic rebirth connected to the Eleusinian mysteries.[75]

The *temenoi* of ancient Greece were all dedicated to a specific divinity, and, appropriately, *Eniaios* begins with an hour-long "dedication" in which shots of the landscape surrounding the funeral pyre of Hercules are interspersed with blinding white flashes of light, spelling out the message "The Soul of the Eyes" in Greek letters using a system of alphanumeric coding.[76] Like Asclepius, a human physician who was eventually made into a demigod, the figure of Hercules symbolically epitomizes the idea of movement between the divine and human realms. During the mythic pyre, the human elements of Hercules were burned away, leaving only those parts of himself that could be raised to the status of godhood.[77] By shooting the monument to this mythic event in such a spare, almost punishingly difficult way, Markopoulos is forcing the Temenos pilgrims to undergo a sort of liminal initiation in which they too are cleansed of the media imagery imbibed on a daily basis and prepared for the unusual form of what lies ahead. Although the dominant image of the dedication reel is the stark white light that is repeatedly flashed onto the screen, the orientation of the single frame images of the site suggests, as in *Gammelion*, an overall sense of motion. Having become acclimated over the course of nearly forty minutes to the simulated movement in concentric circles around the site, the intermittent appearance of moving images in what follows comes as a visual shock, with the pyre of Hercules linked, both metaphorically and structurally, to the Promethean fire that will appear at regular intervals over the course of the film, connecting the dedication to the main body of *Eniaios*.

Mythic Themes, Portraiture, and Films of Place: The Structure of *Eniaios*

The relationship between the form-language of a mathematic and
that of the cognate major arts, is in this way beyond doubt. The
temperament of the thinker and that of the artist differ widely
indeed, but the expressionist methods of the waking consciousness
are inwardly the same for each. The sense of form of the sculptor, the
painter, the composer is essentially mathematical in nature.

—OSWALD SPENGLER, *THE DECLINE OF THE WEST* (1918)[78]

Markopoulos devised three categories for his work when he edited *Eniaios*—mythic themes, portraiture, and films of place—and he appears to have excised everything that does not relate directly to one of these themes. Thus, the version of *Psyche* shown as part of the first cycle of *Eniaios* is composed entirely of faces, buildings, and landscapes that have been decontextualized and stripped of the illusions of movement. The brevity and intermittence of the images disperses the energy accumulated by the montages of the original film, with the *Eniaios* "version" of the hand-on-the-shoulder scene lasting more than forty minutes and becoming almost monodic. The gradual form of imagistic development employed in *Eniaios* does, however, generate its own form of intensity, encouraging a diffuse attentiveness that makes it possible to take notice of otherwise elusive structural elements. There is, for example, a remarkable consistency in the gaps between images within each cycle. In the first cycle, the gaps were generally in five-, eight-, eleven-, or fifteen-second increments, and the images themselves were further subdivided into groups of three, four, or five similar images, with each cluster using a gap length that was consistent with the relative proximity of both the characters to each other and the camera to the characters and spaces onscreen. The shortest gaps, of approximately five seconds, were used when the man and the woman were together in frame in medium close-up, while the fifteen-second intervals were used when the man was seen by himself in long shot or when there were cuts from the man to his environment. Like more architectonic versions of the coded frame measures used in *Twice a Man*, these are the temporal equivalent of Wagnerian leitmotifs, and in addition to creating a heightened awareness of the complex relationships developed in *Eniaios* between characters and landscapes, they create links between cycles that grow in resonance with each iteration.[79]

Each of the twenty-two cycles of *Eniaios* is connected through a series of visual relationships, symbolic correspondences (between sites and myths), and rhythmic patterns, setting up a complex web of remembered and implied associations within which slight variations can take on profound significance. In this way, the idea of cumulative development is built into a work that was meant to be screened at regular intervals and viewed as a total unit either through an intensive three-week pilgrimage or over the course of a number of successive visits.[80] Here too the annual Bayreuth performances of the *Ring* cycle loom in the background, but the sheer temporal scale of *Eniaios* exceeds Wagner's ambitions by a large margin. There is no cinematic equivalent to this sort of presentation. Frampton's metahistory was intended to be an encyclopedic compendium of individual films connected conceptually, while the long-form autobiographical projects of Brakhage and Mekas grew in direct accord with the personal situations of their makers so that sequencing is related more to changes brought about by age and experience than to an overall structural progression.[81] It is not yet possible to view *Eniaios* in its entirety, but the consecutive screening of the third, fourth, and fifth cycles over three nights in June 2008 amply demonstrated how each successive cycle gives a new inflection to those that preceded it.

After a humorous portrait of artistic duo Gilbert and George that stresses their exhibitionism through repeated shots of hands and shoes, the main part of the third cycle begins with an eighty-minute reworking of Markopoulos' earlier *Genius* (1970). The longest film in the cycle, *Genius* is a variation on Faust that features three prominent art world figures: famous patron Daniel-Henry Kahnweiler, David Hockney, and the Argentinean Surrealist Leonor Fini. The film establishes connections between the orientation of glances, the positioning of bodies, and the arrangement of color harmonies, much as Eisenstein does in parts of *Ivan the Terrible*. The overall rhythm, however, develops in a fugue-like fashion, setting up and disrupting expectations serially so that, for example, an alternation of two characters in a predictable A-B-A-B pattern is suddenly interrupted by the insertion of an image of a third character, which becomes the first link in a new, more complex chain.

Genius incorporates many of the strategies of the individual portrait films, including representative artworks where appropriate and compressing spatial perspectives together through the rapid alternation of shots from different angles. The cubistic presentation of space in the film is complemented by the presence of Kahnweiler, suggesting that one of the main goals of the third cycle is to highlight the roots of *Eniaios*' form in the major art movements of the early twentieth century, a theme explored after *Genius* in portraits of Édouard Roditi and Barbara Hepworth.[82] Although he was deeply invested in the tactics of modernism, Markopoulos remained uncomfortable with its rhetoric, complaining about "the civilized chasms today called culture—Pop and otherwise the Modern" and preferring to see his own work as an extension, rather than an abnegation, of tradition.[83] In *Swain*, Markopoulos included one of his own paintings, done in the style of Abstract Expressionism, on a bridge. When the female protagonist sees it, she reacts in horror and Markopoulos cuts to a close-up of the surface, emphasizing its dissonant textures and associating them with the confused emotions of the character. Abstract Expressionism is depicted both as the exteriorization of subjective states—and hence as a late manifestation of Romanticism—and as a source of disruptive anxiety. In this context, the presence of living embodiments of early modernism within Markopoulos' only version of the Faust legend suggests a reading of *Genius* as a film about the sort of double bind addressed by Thomas Mann in his *Doctor Faustus* (1947), in which modernism itself is ambiguously depicted as a Faustian pact.

This ambivalence about the project of modernism was certainly shared by Giorgio de Chirico, and his portrait opens the fourth cycle, which is thematically focused on artists and ideas of Greek or Italian origin. An Italian-born artist raised in Greece, de Chirico's career epitomizes the issues explored in this cycle; the "metaphysical paintings" he made before and during World War I were hailed by virtually the entire French avant-garde and made him a Surrealist hero, but he spent the half-century after 1918 publicly disavowing the "degeneracy" of modernism and repositioning himself as an academic classicist perpetuating a tradition going back to Titian. Among de Chirico's most important works are a series of paintings he made on the myth of the awakening Ariadne, who was abandoned on the island of Naxos after providing the thread that Theseus used to escape from the labyrinth.[84] Because of her associations with weaving, some scholars, including John Ruskin, have seen the figure of Ariadne as connected to that of Arachne, the impeccably skilled artist who was turned into a spider by Athena as punishment for her pride.[85] This may help to explain why Markopoulos structured the fourth cycle so that the portrait of de Chirico is followed by the *Eniaios* version of *Bliss*, which includes a number of shots of a spider dangling from a thread near the entrance to the church.

The application of the *Eniaios* form to *Bliss* serves two mutually reinforcing ends: it takes the formal design of the original film to its logical endpoint and, in so doing, helps to clarify the role and function of iconicity within the project as a whole. In accordance with Orthodox tradition, neither version of *Bliss* actually shows the altar directly, but, according to Jeffrey Stout, they do depict the *menalia*, the candelabra placed in front of the iconostasis, which serves "as the 'membrane' connecting [the sanctuary] to the nave."[86] The title of the fourth cycle, "Nefeli Photos," can be translated as "Clouds of Light," a reference, among other things, to the "cloud of witnesses" mentioned in Hebrews 12:1, who, in Orthodox tradition, manifest themselves through and within the iconostasis. Pavel Florensky explains that the material iconostasis "does not, in itself, take the place of the living witnesses, existing *instead of* them; rather, it *points toward* them, concentrating the attention of those who pray upon them—a concentration of attention that is essential to the developing of spiritual sight."[87] Although they lack an explicit liturgical function, Markopoulos uses the literal icons and the iconic form of the *Bliss* reel to clarify what he is doing in *Eniaios*, suggesting that the entire film can be seen in relation to the idea of sacred vision made possible through the iconostasis. During the 2008 Temenos projections, these implications were strengthened by the repeated appearance of an extremely pale blue light between some of the images within the church; in context, this suggested the direct emanations of pneumatic inspiration, giving additional resonance to the linkage in the *Bliss* reel and elsewhere of candlelight, fire, and the underlying Promethean/Asclepian myth structure of *Eniaios*. In this way, the *Bliss* reel also helped to clarify the film's relationship to modernism. Markopoulos adopted the iconic, fragmented, and temporally distended form of *Eniaios* not simply to create a sense of shock or estrangement from the structures of contemporary existence, but also to make possible a new form of vision capable of reconstituting isolated images into a unified totality.[88]

One partial explanation for the cycle's title is provided by *Cimabue! Cimabue!*, which depicts the restoration of Cimabue's *Crucifixion of Santa Croce* (1288), the major work of art damaged during the 1966 Florentine flood, largely through shots of hands working in various capacities, implicitly valorizing the act of creative labor. By situating *Cimabue! Cimabue!* immediately after *Bliss* in the cycle, Markopoulos also imbues these acts with sacred value. The most densely edited section of *Eniaios* screened in 2008, *Cimabue! Cimabue!* contains at least four thousand splices over the course of its hour-long running time, and its active alternation of images across short gaps lasting at most two or three seconds made the rhythmic patterns operating throughout *Eniaios* more evident. When the film was first completed in 1972, Markopoulos publicly acknowledged its importance:

> With CIMABUE! CIMABUE! I have wandered through the dangerous regions of the inferno and purgatorio and arrived with the final shot of Silvio Loffredo, hands folded in the Gallery Pananti, Firenze, where his footage was shot, before my philosophy of Cinema. What I had suggested once, the filmmaker as physician of the future, has transpired.[89]

The last claim is particularly important because it links *Cimabue! Cimabue!* and its thematic exploration of art restoration to the Asclepian ideals fundamental to *Eniaios*. In addition to the meticulous craftsmen involved in preparing and presenting works of art to the public, *Cimabue! Cimabue!* lovingly portrays a number of the people—poets, patrons, and friends—who support them. Given the film's central position within the cycle, this suggests that the "witnesses" in the "clouds of light" include all of those involved in making, preserving, and understanding works of art, an ideal of elective community that could be extended to include the pilgrims to the Temenos as well as the local Greeks of Loutra who make visits possible.

Cimabue! Cimabue! is followed in the fourth cycle first by *The Olympian* and sections from *The Illiac Passion* and *Eros, O Basileus* (1967), and then by two films that once again emphasize landscapes. The first of these is *Chronion*, an extraordinarily beautiful depiction of the cypress grove outside the Asclepium of Kos at dawn. The high horizon line and red-tinged sky evoke the conventions of Romantic landscape painting, and especially of the dawn shown in Caspar David Friedrich's epochal altarpiece, *The Cross in the Mountains* (1807–1808). Even as it evokes the iconography of German Romanticism, however, *Chronion* also resonates with the site at which it was shot; the cypress grove on Kos was planted to celebrate the ending of a ravaging plague, and the rising of the sun over it is regarded, according to some scholars, as a natural symbol for the mysterious powers of Asclepian healing.[90] Appropriately, the fourth cycle ends with the first reel of images taken from *Twice a Man*, Markopoulos' earlier retelling of the myths of Hippolytus and Asclepius. Seen after *Chronion*, the repeated shots of Hudson Bay at dusk seem less like memory triggers or montage pivots or even as records of actual New York locations than as reverse images of the mythic landscapes shown in the preceding films.

Whereas the third cycle explored the roots of *Eniaios'* unusual form in twentieth-century modernist practice and the fourth cycle reflected on the ultimate meaning of that form, the fifth cycle redirects the focus toward the pilgrimage aspects of the Temenos. The first five reels (nearly three hours) of the fifth cycle, whose title translates roughly as "The Great Chasm," are taken up by a single film, *Hagiographia*, a study of the ruins of Mistra that begins, like the dedication reel, with a long series of white flashes and then proceeds in the style of *Gammelion* (figure 2.10).[91] An ancient Byzantine site that also functioned intermittently as a mosque, Mistra is charged with layers of associations that Markopoulos alludes to over the course of the film, gradually shifting from exteriors to images of bas-reliefs and icons. Sacred space is given another inflection in the one-reel study of *Epidaurus* that appears later in the same cycle, after another reel of images from *The Illiac Passion*. Where most of the shots of *Hagiographia* are frontal, *Epidaurus* begins with high-angle shots of the stones on the ground, using them to trace a path toward the temple steps, an uncharacteristic gesture that foregrounds the pilgrimage thematic of the cycle by suggesting devotional movement. The film of Epidaurus is also

FIGURE 2.10 Eniaios *(Gregory Markopoulos, 1947–1992) (courtesy Temenos Archive)*.

FIGURE 2.11 Eniaios *(Gregory Markopoulos, 1947–1992) (courtesy Temenos Archive).*

made to resonate, through similarities of subject and environment, with the study of Kos at dawn in the fourth cycle, a striking example of the way in which each cycle builds off the one that precedes it.

Sequencing can also create unexpected implications. At the end of the third cycle, for example, the close proximity of *The Illiac Passion* and *The Mysteries* caused the protagonist of the latter film to seem like another figuration of Prometheus. By contrast, in the reel of *The Mysteries* that appears in the fifth cycle, the same man is compared to a reclining statue in a rare example of simulated shot/countershot within *Eniaios*. Epidaurus is the central site of the Asclepian cult, and the statues there are traditionally seen as marking the emergence of pathos and suffering within Greek art. The precise identity of the Munich statue is unclear, but, positioned at the very end of the fifth cycle, its appearance takes on another level of potential meaning, suggesting that, within *Eniaios*, the title of *The Mysteries* may no longer allude to individual romantic longing but to the ceremonies at Eleusis.[92]

Since only the first few cycles have been printed, it is not yet possible to determine how successfully the grand ambitions of *Eniaios* were realized. It is apparent from the small amount that has been screened so far, however, that the intensity of the film is inextricably bound to the unusual nature of the Temenos viewing experience. The mountain air and the late screening times

(typically running from 10:00 p.m. to 4:00 or 5:00 a.m.) magnified the hypnotic effects of the imagery. This sensation was especially pronounced during the screening of *Hagiographia*, where the combination of extreme length,
a heavily distended rhythm, and the similarity of the trees in Mistra and
Lyssarea encouraged a consideration of the relationship between the onscreen
landscape and the one the viewer inhabits (figure 2.11). The sustained gaps,
sometimes as long as thirty seconds, between single-frame flashes created
afterimages that dissipated gradually and seemed to echo off the sky above
and the fields around the screen. Consequently, when, after nearly two hours
on the third day of screenings, the filmed light bursting through one of the
windows in a dark section of the Mistra site perfectly matched the angle of the
light streaming onto the screen from the projector, the result was genuinely
ecstatic. This harmonization could not have been planned during shooting or
editing, but it is a vivid example of the type of effect made possible by and at
the Temenos, a momentary fusion of the sacred space depicted onscreen and
the ritual space of viewing—a perfect synchronicity of imagined, filmed, and
projected light. Moments like this made it clear that, whatever else they may
or may not represent, the Temenos screenings of *Eniaios* have the capacity to
give viewers a renewed sense of the revelatory potential of cinema.

"We Are No Longer Innocent"

THE LONG-FORM AESTHETIC OF JACQUES RIVETTE

A film must be, if not an ordeal, at least an experience, something which makes the film transform the viewer, who has undergone something through the film, who is no longer the same after having seen the film. In the same way that the people who made the film really offered up troubling personal things, the viewer must be upset by seeing the film; the film must make his habits of thought go off their beaten tracks: so that it can't be seen with impunity.

—JACQUES RIVETTE (1968)[1]

It takes more courage to pull down the old gods than to adopt new ones.

—ÉLIE FAURE, EPIGRAPH TO MARCH 1964 ISSUE OF *CAHIERS DU CINÉMA*[2]

La Belle Noiseuse *(Jacques Rivette, 1991)*.

Unscreened at traditional venues and isolated from the metropolitan centers of film culture, the films Gregory Markopoulos made after he left the United States stood to the side of the main artistic currents of the era. Nevertheless, the tone of Markopoulos' published statements, the profoundly idealistic nature of his project, and his abiding faith in the power of symbolic imagery can be seen as strongly related to—even emblematic of—the strain of post–World War II film culture that consciously attempted to revive the euphoric optimism of the 1920s and came to full fruition in the late 1960s. The dialectical opposite can be found in the films Jacques Rivette made during roughly the same period, long-form epics concerned less with the idea of spiritual transformation than with the ethics of artistic production and a form of quietly pervasive paranoia rooted in the disintegration of utopian models. As Rivette put it, with bracing directness, in the extended 1968 *Cahiers du cinéma* interview "Time Overflowing": "I believe more and more that the role of the cinema is to destroy myths, to demobilize, to be pessimistic. Its role is to take people out of their cocoons and to plunge them into horror."[3]

For most writers, the defining characteristics of Rivette's filmmaking are his use of improvisational acting and protracted pacing, both of which are frequently presented as challenges to conventional notions of film authorship and viewing.[4] Almost all of Rivette's films are over two hours long, and several run for more than four hours, notwithstanding the fact that only one of them (*Joan the Maid*, 1994) contains the sort of dramatic events crucial to Hollywood-style epics. This unusual approach to duration created considerable impediments to the distribution of Rivette's films, but his refusal to accommodate his work to the conventions that dictate that a three- or four-hour film must have a commensurately expansive narrative scope has been celebrated internationally by critics inclined to ascribe political importance to deviations from dominant practice. Robin Wood even claimed that the "'unjustified' length of [Rivette's] films . . . represents an act of cultural transgression."[5] Rivette, however, has repeatedly insisted that he has no intention of deliberately provoking audiences and makes such long films because he believes their rhythms foster a unique form of intensity that encourages deeper cinematic immersion. In his most formally adventurous works—*L'Amour fou* (1968), *Out 1* (1971), *Out 1: Spectre* (1972), *Céline and Julie Go Boating* (1974), *Duelle* (1976), *Noroît* (1976), and *Le Pont du nord* (1981)—Rivette reflexively opens up diegetic space in complex ways, setting multiple levels of meaning and viewing against one another without abandoning the hypnotic powers of narrative illusionism.

Partially because of the emphasis on *jouissance* and *jeu* in the contemporaneous critical writings of Roland Barthes and Jacques Derrida, Rivette's most radical experiments are often understood to pivot around the different narrative mechanisms, imagined and actualized, that are dispersed throughout his films.[6] Certainly, "play" is an integral element of Rivette's style, manifested in the thematic interest in chess-like games and the nature of performance as well as the vertiginous interchange between different layers of intertextual reference. What is underrecognized in critical discussions of Rivette's work is the importance of mythology and ritual. In a 1973 interview, Rivette expresses his admiration for then recent films by Miklós Jancsó, Ingmar Bergman, and Werner Schroeter, claiming that what interested him is the fact that they "tend towards the ritual, towards the ceremonial, the oratorio, the theatrical, the magical, not in the mystical so much as the more devotional sense of the word, as in the celebration of Mass."[7] The drumbeats and incantatory chanting used in the opening credits of *L'Amour fou*, the theatrical performance that opens *Out 1*, and even the three knocks on the door at the beginning of *The Nun* (1966) all point toward the sorts of ceremonial effects that Rivette evidently saw as constitutive of one form of cinematic modernism. Hence the repeated analogizing, in the films of the 1960s and 1970s, of theaters and arenas, the ritualistic rehearsals of classical or classicizing plays with mythic themes (Shakespeare's *Pericles*, 1607–1608; Racine's *Andromaque*, 1667; Aeschylus' *Prometheus Bound*, fifth century BCE, and *Seven Against Thebes*, 467 BCE), and the portrayal of collective performance as a utopian enterprise.[8]

The fact that these films are equally preoccupied with failure and negation—with the fact that the plays are not performed, the mysteries are not explained, the relationships do not hold—gives a very different inflection to Rivette's much-vaunted playfulness. Play, in this context, is a defense mechanism, a way of staving off the fear that encroaches when the projects or quests the characters embrace collapse in on themselves. When Claire and Sébastien, the central couple in *L'Amour fou*, reach a crisis point in both their marital and professional lives, the response is to degenerate into infantile antics and role-playing, which seems harmless until they begin blithely smashing through the walls of their apartment with a sledgehammer. Like more unreconciled versions of the repressed behavior that is chaotically unleashed in the post–World War II Howard Hawks comedies that Rivette wrote about with such wild enthusiasm, the wanton self-destruction of Claire and Sébastien suggests a retreat into a private domain that promises temporary security through hermetic enclosure.[9] In Rivette's films, liberation from social constraints is often inseparable from madness; like the bacchanals of Claire and Sébastien, the convulsive laughter of Céline and Julie in *Céline and Julie Go Boating* frequently suggests imbalance as much as freedom. The most potent example of this in Rivette's work is the laugh Joan of Arc lets out toward the end of her trial, a jarring eruption of childish energy that chillingly suggests the anguish brought about by total isolation.

Although they are never the dominant emotions, terror and anxiety are almost invariably lurking in the background of Rivette's films, suddenly

FIGURE 3.1 The Nun *(Jacques Rivette, 1966).*

coming into full view on the face of an actor or (more often) an actress, gen-erally shown in medium close-up (figure 3.1). In some instances, these act as physiognomic expressions of a claustrophobic entrapment also expressed architectonically through the carefully calibrated alternation of shots in which characters walk deep into the background through corridors or

FIGURE 3.2 La Belle Noiseuse *(Jacques Rivette, 1991).*

doorways—expanding the viewer's sense of spatial boundaries—with space-compressing shots in which objects or architectural features dwarf the human figures. In other cases, these fugitive glimmers of inquietude seem to emerge not from spatial entrapment but from the uncertainty brought about by movement into unknown territory. Late in *La Belle Noiseuse* (1991), for example, there is a moment when the artist Frenhofer sets Marianne up in a pose and then leaves her standing there alone; genuine panic briefly flashes across her face, a reaction that seems to come as much from the actress as from the character she is playing, a characteristically Rivettian blurring of representational levels that is rendered even more startling by its position just after one of the film's few jump cuts (figure 3.2). Whether or not moments like this were in any way planned before shooting, they function as spontaneous interruptions, points of rupture where the smooth veneer—of the narrative space and of the human face—begins to crack, and something usually withheld is unexpectedly exposed.

"Every Shot Is an Event"

My cinema is not a cinema of montage; it is a cinema of continuity,
of events during shooting.

—JACQUES RIVETTE[10]

Like most directors associated with the French New Wave, Jacques Rivette began his career as a film critic. Yet while some of his most lucid pieces—especially his "Letter on Rossellini" and his review of Gillo Pontecorvo's *Kapò* (1959)—have exerted a lasting influence on international film culture, Rivette seems to have viewed his writing primarily as a prelude to his filmmaking. When he characterizes *Beyond a Reasonable Doubt* (Fritz Lang, 1956) as being about clandestine forms, expresses an interest in "movement from the Interior," and describes the mental processes the viewer goes through in transforming narrative puzzles into conceptual patterns, he is speaking more about his own work than the late films of Fritz Lang.[11] Nowhere is this double consciousness more explicit than in an aside in the "Letter on Rossellini," where, after observing that "with the appearance of *Voyage to Italy* [Roberto Rossellini, 1954], all films have suddenly aged ten years," he writes, "Here is our cinema, those of us who in our turn are preparing to make films (did I tell you, it may be soon)."[12] In other *Cahiers du cinéma* texts, he implies that the essence of cinema lies in its capacity for revelation, claiming that Alfred Hitchcock's films make it possible to see the "space between something exterior and something very secret" and arguing elsewhere that "the goal of every work of art" is the disclosure of a "secret figure."[13]

Rivette's emphasis on a veiled, secretive world lying just beyond the material surface of things accords very strongly with the Catholic tenor of much of his early criticism and also provides an important context for his repeated allusions to a "breach" opening up in the most vigorous cinema of the 1950s.[14] In the "Letter on Rossellini," he writes that *Voyage to Italy*, whose form conveys subjectivity through shots focusing on inquisitive looking rather than dramatic development, "opens a breach . . . that all cinema, on pain of death, must pass through."[15] The term is used again, several months later, to describe the dynamic styles of American "auteurs" like Nicholas Ray and Anthony Mann, who incorporated discontinuous cutting into the bodies of their films and thereby presented an alternative to the "conventions of classical editing"; in Rivette's words, "Those punches, weapons, dynamite explosions have no purpose other than to blast away the accumulated debris of habit, to create a breach."[16] Intriguingly, he suggests that the function of this breach is to allow filmmakers to "pass beyond the long period of submission to the manufactured product and openly renew links with the tradition of 1915, [D. W.] Griffith and Triangle [Studios]," to reconnect with the more lyrical aesthetics of silent cinema and rediscover "naïveté."[17]

This idea of reviving an approach to filmmaking associated with the early silent cinema was expressed more directly in Rivette's first, most manifesto-like essay, "We Are No Longer Innocent," in which he calls for a return to the principles of "simple writing," of a documentary-like attentiveness to the "universe of life; the camera reduced to the role of witness, an eye."[18] Implicitly recapitulating the language of German Romanticism, Rivette argues that this sort of filmmaking would be "always a tentative adventure, a continual improvisation, a perpetual creation."[19] While these would remain fundamental values for the rest of Rivette's career, his relationship to the mythical purity of silent cinema would change in the late 1950s and early 1960s as he became more attached to contemporary developments in the other arts and to the historical predicament of the postwar generation. Asked in a 1963 *Sight and Sound* interview whether the cinema had once reached "a sort of state of grace, which it has lost today," Rivette tellingly responded, "Yes . . . but since it is lost, it isn't worth talking about."[20]

Paris Belongs to Us (1961), Rivette's first feature film and one of the earliest works of the French New Wave, epitomizes his attitude and approach at that time.[21] The film includes a number of shots of characters standing atop buildings looking down at the city of Paris, along with an overall sense of menace and potential danger that suggests the World War I–era work of Louis Feuillade (figures 3.3–3.4). The film also includes a resonant insert shot of the Tower of Babel from Lang's *Metropolis* (1927), cropped to emphasize the director's metonymic use of hands. Yet while Rivette adopts visual strategies from the silent era, he does so in a way that is fully conscious of the historical events that have intervened, transforming the forms so radically that

FIGURE 3.3 Les Vampires *(Louis Feuillade, 1915–1916).*

FIGURE 3.4 Paris Belongs to Us *(Jacques Rivette, 1961).*

they seem strikingly contemporary. Entrenched in its late-1950s milieu, *Paris Belongs to Us*—which, unlike most of Rivette's later work, is a totally scripted film—includes charged references to Francoist Spain, Joseph McCarthy, atomic bombs, and even then potential presidential candidate Richard Nixon. All of these are methodically interwoven into an ever-expanding conspiratorial web by a young woman (Anne) who gets involved with a theater troupe attempting to put on Shakespeare's *Pericles* and begins finding hidden meanings in every situation. Like the protagonist, the viewer is gradually inculcated into this obsessively suspicious mode of viewing. Although Rivette does make room for a number of the exploratory shots (either traveling along the street or taking in the surroundings from the perspective of cars or trains) that are characteristic of the New Wave in this period, the spaces they depict are rendered progressively more threatening until even the Arc de Triomphe begins to appear ominous. Late in the film, one character portentously says, "In 1945, one person [Hitler] died, but the greatest conspiracy still continues" and makes vague allusions to "their" attempts to regain power, but it has already become clear to both Anne and the viewer that this is hysterical bombast, a pointless and dangerous misappropriation of Resistance rhetoric that testifies to the self-defeating Cold War paranoia that leaves the characters paralyzed.

The melancholic, disillusioned mood of *Paris Belongs to Us* stands in stark contrast to the youthful ebullience of the iconic films fellow New Wave directors—and *Cahiers du cinéma* colleagues—Jean-Luc Godard (*Breathless*, 1960, and *A Woman Is a Woman*, 1961) and François Truffaut (*The Four Hundred Blows*, 1959, and *Shoot the Piano Player*, 1961) were making at the same moment. In its intellectualized treatment of characters with a debilitating obsession with historical traumas, *Paris Belongs to Us* is much closer to a film like *Hiroshima mon amour* (Alain Resnais, 1959), an impression reinforced by its modernist score. Philippe Arthuys' Bartok-inspired music perfectly matches the constantly shifting, unstable sense of space in *Paris Belongs to Us*, which, like the nebulous "conspiracy," manages to seem simultaneously sprawling and foreclosed.[22] It also points to Rivette's abiding extracinematic interest in modernism among and between the arts. For Rivette, following André Bazin, cinema was "impure, complex, between the novel, theater, painting, music, dance, etc.," a nexus of different influences given new meaning by their position within a film.[23] Throughout the 1950s, Rivette's touchstones were early twentieth-century figures like Igor Stravinsky and Henri Matisse, both of whom are treated as paradigms in a number of critical articles. He describes the cinematic problems addressed by Resnais as "parallel to those that Stravinsky sets himself in music—an alternating succession of exaltation and repose . . . the search for an equilibrium superior to all of the individual elements of creativity."[24]

A quote by Stravinsky was used as the epigraph for *Cahiers du cinéma* shortly after Rivette became editor-in-chief, and during his tenure, the journal opened up to such avowed cinematic modernists as Michelangelo Antonioni and to major figures in culture and the arts more generally. "Modernity" became one of the most frequently used words in the journal, and, as contributor André S. Labarthe has explained, Rivette conceived of the word "in terms of the opposition to classical culture and of integration in new artistic forms."[25] In this sense, the sudden prominence of the term signaled a movement away from the inveterate "classicism" of previous editor Éric Rohmer, as well as a shift in Rivette's own critical concerns. It was with this expanded notion of artistic modernity in mind that he conducted a lengthy interview with Pierre Boulez and reread *Monsieur Verdoux* (Charles Chaplin, 1947) from the perspective of the present, comparing the attitude of Chaplin toward his fictive persona "to [Bertolt] Brecht before his [1939 play] *Mother Courage*, to [Jean] Fautrier before his [1943–1945 painting and sculpture series] *Otages*, to Boulez before his *Structures* [serialist works composed between 1951 and 1961]."[26]

Rivette tried to achieve a similar synthesis in his own filmmaking, describing his second feature, *The Nun*, as a "film in the spirit of Mizoguchi [Kenji]," but also as a film originating with "the ideas of Boulez . . . the idea that each shot had its own duration, its tempo, its 'colour' (that is, its tone), its intensity and its level of play."[27] For the first time in *The Nun*, Rivette made striking use of extended cuts to black leader, which become more frequent as the film goes on. Where filmmakers like Markopoulos incorporated passages of empty leader to redefine the viewer's relationship to (and perception of) onscreen imagery, Rivette used it to emphasize the temporal elisions in the narrative while also making individual sequences feel like cells of isolated space-time, a formal correlate to the fractured isolation experienced by the young protagonist. Adapted from Rivette's own 1963 stage production of Denis Diderot's text, *The Nun* created a scandal in France, but in its dependence on a tightly formulated script and the supple performance of a well-known star (Anna Karina), it was as close as Rivette would come in this period to making a traditional "art film."[28]

With his three-part 1966 documentary on Jean Renoir, Rivette's aesthetic took a decisive turn in a new direction. Rivette had long been one of Renoir's most fervent admirers (when *The Golden Coach* opened in 1952, he was apparently so enraptured by the film that he watched it continuously from 2:00 p.m. to midnight), but the detailed study, on an editing table, of the director's entire corpus "made [him] see things differently."[29] Titled *Jean Renoir le patron*, after Jean Paulhan's 1952 text on Georges Braque, the resulting film was part of the *Cinéma de notre temps* series supervised by Labarthe and Janine Bazin for French television, and it was made with the lightweight 16mm equipment that Rivette felt enabled one "to do things which were possible in the silent days but were practically impossible . . . during the first thirty years of the sound film."[30] By virtue of its size, low cost, and mobility, this equipment facilitated not only location filming, but also a higher shooting ratio, encouraging a more exploratory approach to cinematic form, with the overall shape of a film developing in relation to the events being recorded rather than a set of preplanned ideas.

By the time *Jean Renoir le patron* was made, 16mm synchronized sound cameras were associated primarily with cinéma vérité, the subject of a contentious debate that would affect many filmmakers in this period. The phrase was coined by sociologist Edgar Morin in a 1960 article for *France observateur* as a direct translation of Dziga Vertov's *Kino-Pravda*, but it very quickly became an umbrella term encompassing a number of documentary approaches with different methods and assumptions.[31] One strand, centered in North America around the National Film Board of Canada and Robert Drew's Drew Associates, advocated a minimum of authorial intervention, transforming the camera into a sort of objective witness, which would purportedly allow more immediate access to reality and "cinematic truth." For Richard Leacock, one of the chief theorists of "Direct Cinema," the filmmaker should function "as an observer and, perhaps, as a participant capturing the essence of what takes place around him, selecting, arranging, but never controlling the event. [By doing so], it would be possible for the significance of what is taking place to transcend the conceptions of the filmmaker, because, essentially, he is observing the ultimate mystery, the reality."[32] This can give Direct Cinema films like *Primary* (Robert Drew, 1960) the impression of what Vertov called "life caught unawares," but they are often founded on an epistemological contradiction in which the mediating presence of the filmmaker at all levels of production (shooting and "selection" as well as editing) is problematically ignored. In the work of filmmakers like Jean Rouch, cinéma vérité instead refers to a complex, reflexive effort to provoke situations out of which "truth" might emerge rather than an attempt to use the camera to unselfconsciously document external events. Rouch, who abandoned the term cinéma vérité after it became clear that it was being interpreted in radically different ways outside France, developed an unusual rapport with his subjects (who often participated in a number of unrelated films), and he used these relationships to provocatively blend fictional and documentary modes in a way that deeply influenced Rivette.[33]

Chronicle of a Summer (Edgar Morin and Jean Rouch, 1961), widely regarded as a virtual manifesto for cinéma vérité, includes a scene near the end in which the individuals interviewed elsewhere in the film attend a screening of the compiled footage and comment upon their own self-presentations. Codirector Morin helps lead the discussion from the front and expresses his concerns about certain people who he thought exhibited too much of themselves, pushing the project in the direction of melodrama. At least one of the scenes is revealed to be a constructed performance, and several of the interviewees express frustration at the images they see of themselves onscreen, but in a postscreening coda, Rouch and Morin, walking through the halls of the Musée de l'Homme, agree that their way of involving their subjects in the cinematic process has great potential. Within the projects shot and directed by Rouch alone, before and after *Chronicle of a Summer*, the intrusion of fictional elements into an ostensibly documentary framework is taken much further. This is especially true of *The Human Pyramid* (1961), an experimental study of a group of students at a lycée on the Ivory Coast, in which the participants were invited to incorporate their own narratives and desires into the film.

Unlike *Chronicle of a Summer, The Human Pyramid* makes no pretense to objectivity, opening with two precredit sequences that both complicate and clarify the unusual approach of the film: a brief shot of two of the central characters walking the streets of Paris "after" the events depicted in the main body of the film is followed by a scene of Rouch explaining his method to the students and soliciting their active collaboration. In subsequent scenes, present-tense events are intermingled with flashbacks and fantasies, while the soundtrack becomes a fluid amalgam of directly recorded sound, post-synchronized dialogue, reflections from some of the participants, and third-person narration by Rouch. These representational registers flow into one another without clear differentiation, giving the film a disarmingly dream-like atmosphere that is disrupted by a final sequence that metaphorically and literally depicts the takeover of fiction, as Rouch stages the death of "Alain," the one entirely constructed character in the film. Although it is not immediately evident to the lycée students, the "suicide" of Alain is a moment of pure artifice, a simulation of the fictional deaths that bring closure to many narrative features. By concluding his open-ended experiment with this surprising intrusion, Rouch forces the viewers to re-evaluate what they have just seen, drawing attention both to the inevitable presence of fictional tendencies within even the most uncontrolled filmmaking situation and to the director's role as the intellectual agent shaping the complex matrix of perspectives presented in the film.

It is this conception of cinéma vérité that Rivette's documentary on Renoir is responding to. Although it appears to be more naturalistic than *The Human Pyramid*, the *Portrait de Michel Simon par Jean Renoir ou Portrait de Jean Renoir par Michel Simon ou La Direction d'acteurs: Dialogue* episode of *Jean Renoir le patron* makes similarly sophisticated use of audiovisual montage to activate the different resonances of the footage, creating a portrait whose deceptively complex form mirrors that of its subject. Large portions of the film depict director Jean Renoir and his former actor Michel

Simon talking about various matters in real time on a particular day. The roving camera generally stays close to them, but it also moves around the table at various points, capturing interviewer-director Rivette, some of the camera equipment, and other people present in the same space. While the earthy conversation of Renoir and Simon is engrossing, the viewer is never allowed to forget that this seemingly casual encounter between friends is mediated by the director and crew, and the final film includes shots of clapboards, of someone putting a hand over the camera lens, and even of a blank screen as the camera battery is reloaded. Even more pronounced intervention occurs as sequences from films Renoir and Simon made together are inserted at unexpected moments. There are no clear transitions separating these excerpts from the main body of the film, and the sound from the conversation continues over (or at least bleeds into) the clips, creating a dialogue between remembered, lived, and represented experiences, which become increasingly intertwined as the film progresses.

Unlike many of its partisans, Rivette was fully conscious of the fundamental artificiality of cinéma vérité techniques, and he felt that its interest as a style comes "from the moment you realize it's a creator of artifice (and not, I repeat, of lies). But one which, by comparison with the traditional method, is more directly in touch with that particular artifice which constitutes the act of *mise en scène*, of filming."[34] In *L'Amour fou*, Rivette sets both methods against one another by positioning 16mm footage in a vérité style within the larger frame of a 35mm narrative fiction. The 16mm material was shot by Labarthe as a faux documentary of a troupe, led by theater director Jean-Pierre Kalfon, preparing to perform Jean Racine's *Andromaque*. Using a Coutant 16mm camera capable of synchronized sound, Labarthe and his crew inquisitively get in close to their subjects, creating a sort of confrontational intimacy by filming human faces in extreme, slightly hazy close-up from a low angle. By contrast, the 35mm sections, which show the Labarthe documentary being filmed and also depict the romantic dramas of Sébastien (Kalfon) and his wife Claire, are shot with a large, and largely impassive, Mitchell camera and are lit much more clearly.

The distinction between the two film formats is mirrored in the demarcation of the two narrative streams of *L'Amour fou*—the scenes focusing on the married life of Claire and Sébastien are generally shot in enclosed domestic spaces, while the rehearsals take place inside a theater with audience members frequently present and the equipment used for the documentary clearly visible. Both sections have their own rhythms and sonic environments; the scenes inside the apartment use natural light, include a number of shot/countershot exchanges, and feature very few nondiegetic sounds, all in accordance with the conventional codes of cinematic realism. These scenes contrast markedly with the rehearsals, which generate intensity through the switches back and forth between the two different cameras, with their attendant differences in framing, visual texture, and sound quality. The tension between the highly localized sound associated with the 16mm equipment and the much more atmospheric sound present in the 35mm shots, for example, helps keep the two levels of filming distinct even as it paradoxically makes the (16mm) "documentary" footage look more stylized.

The narrative motor for both plots is Claire's decision, very early in the film, to leave the play her husband is directing, because she is concerned about the recording of the rehearsals by Labarthe's unit. When she is replaced by Sébastien's ex-girlfriend Marta, a wedge is driven between their personal and professional lives, and Rivette uses the extended duration of the film to depict the slow disintegration of both the couple and the troupe. The choice of Racine's *Andromaque* as the play being rehearsed reinforces this, because its portrayal of unrequited passion leading to despair and eventual madness has a number of concordances with the entangled web of interpersonal relationships in the film. Rivette claims that he tried to downplay easy comparisons during shooting, but he was certainly aware of the structural echoes, and they are underscored at several points.[35] Feeling increasingly isolated and desperate to communicate her feelings to her husband, Claire begins compulsively reading into a tape recorder the lines of the role she was supposed to perform, at one point reciting a long passage from a key speech:

> Where am I? What have I done? What must I do?
> What clouds my heart? What cleaves my brain in two?
> All through the palace, aimlessly I move.
> Alas, I know not whether I hate or love.
> Oh, with what cruel eyes he took his leave!
> No pity in them, no pretense to grieve.
> Was there a moment's pain or mercy shown?
> Could I extract from him a single groan?
> Dumb to my sighs, unmoved by my dismay,
> Did he seem touched by me in any way?
> And still I pity him! Worse yet, my heart
> Is cowardly enough to take his part![36]

This language is from act five, scene one, when Hermione deliberates, in soliloquy, about her request to have Orestes arrange to kill Pyrrhus, who has spurned her for Andromaque. In *L'Amour fou*, Sébastien himself plays Pyrrhus, and the triangulation of roles and perceptions is made apparent by cutting from the private monologue of Claire, who uses this moment of concentrated subjectivity within Racine's play as an indirect expression of her own dilemma, to Marta performing the same lines onstage. Sequences like this make the relationships between the different characters ambiguous and blur the boundaries between public and private space. When Labarthe suddenly interviews Marta in her room rather than the theater, the effect is of a breach of trust, even a sort of violation, which ironically makes the ethical importance of these distinctions clear.

The echoing symmetry of *L'Amour fou* also extends to the relationship between Sébastien and film director Jacques Rivette. After several months of conversation, Rivette left Kalfon free to direct the production of *Andromaque* as he wished, giving putative justification to Labarthe's film-within-a-film and setting in motion a set of dynamic mechanisms out of which the main conflicts would emerge.[37] Much as the fictional psychodrama filmed in 35mm outside the theater begins to contaminate the rehearsals, however, Kalfon's approach as theater director increasingly parallels the method Rivette laid out before shooting. For Rivette, "The guiding principle was to let things happen by themselves without ever forcing them, to be there as a witness."[38] In the 16mm interviews with Labarthe, Sébastien explains that "seeing the rushes [for Labarthe's documentary] really helped me because it seemed that it was too . . . directed, too manipulated," and he expresses an interest in breaking down rigid hierarchies of control, allowing the actors to discover the essence of their characters on their own and achieving a unity of parts and actions. The result is a labyrinthine mise en abyme in which real-life theater director Kalfon, playing the fictional role of theater director Sébastien staging a production of *Andromaque* that is being documented by a 16mm unit, espouses the same ideas about mise en scène as Rivette, the person directing the 35mm feature that subsumes all of these other elements within it.

A number of critical commentators over the past four decades have taken these statements at face value, claiming that "in *L'Amour fou*, the director has almost vanished, as far as possible."[39] Yet this is undermined even within the film-within-a-film, with Labarthe telling a frustrated Sébastien that "playing [the lead role of] Pyrrhus while acting as director is more than simply adding a role to the director's duties, it's also a way of directing." Even as he tries to relinquish some of his authority, his controlling influence (like Rivette's) reasserts itself indirectly.[40] Like the theater director within the film, Rivette let the performers and collaborators develop their own roles as much as possible, simply observing the *Andromaque* rehearsals for several days as he tried to find a way of fluidly guiding this process without draining it of vitality. The dynamic nature of this approach is manifested in the finished film, but the authoring presence of Rivette and his colleagues is continually apparent on the level of editing, through the overt manipulation of the soundtrack as well as the cutting of the unplanned elements that emerged serendipitously from the filmmaking situation—the repetition of lines, the shifting tones of the interviews, and the rhyming of actions and events in different sections of the film. Even the impression of lassitude, the rhythmic slackening encouraged by the long takes, is worked into a larger temporal structure whose presence is reaffirmed through the periodic return of title cards announcing the amount of time that has passed.

Collaborative improvisation is only one aspect of Rivette's method. The true experiment in *L'Amour fou* was to construct a form that would develop out of the dialectical interchange between predetermined and contingent elements in such a way that it would appear self-generated. In this, the film is connected to contemporaneous developments in the arts more generally, and Rivette has acknowledged that "formally the great ambition of the film was to seek an equivalent in the cinema for [Karlheinz] Stockhausen's recent research: this mixture of what is constructed and what is by chance, which also necessarily implies duration."[41] Stockhausen's signature achievement, developing out of musique concrète and its integration of both concrete and synthetic sounds, was to reorient composition around a "directionless time-field" in which a wide range of tones, structured around a basic temporal interval or "fundamental," could interact.[42] Other composers (John Cage, Pierre Boulez, Luigi Nono) were exploring the aleatoric component of composition at the same moment, but embedded within these many variations is a notion of artistic liberation that is inextricable from questions of authorship. Paradoxically, the intense efforts to free music, cinema, or painting from the supposed authoritarianism of direct personal expression recapitulated the absolutist rhetoric of modernism, drawing attention back to the heroic efforts of the creator through what Krzysztof Penderecki has called "the utopian quality of its Promethean tone."[43]

Rivette remains presciently aware of this paradox, thematizing it through the Kalfon character at the same time as it is reproduced formally and ultimately circumscribing all the unplanned elements of the film. Like *Ugetsu* (Mizoguchi Kenji, 1953), a film Rivette has expressed his admiration for repeatedly (Claire listens to a record of the soundtrack music in one scene), *L'Amour fou* begins with a circular pan up and ends with a circular pan down on an almost identical image.[44] In Mizoguchi's case, this conveys historical cyclicity, a cosmic idea of the relative insignificance of the events portrayed in the film that is fully in accord with the precepts of the Nichiren Buddhism he had recently embraced.[45] In *L'Amour fou*, by contrast, the same arrangement makes it seem as though the film were closing in on itself, constrained within the limits of the frame. Even this contains ambiguity, however, because the first and last sounds in the film are of a child crying, which metaphorically suggests the childlessness of the central couple, and symbolically stands in for Andromaque's child Astyanax, while also serving as a perfect example of the unpredictable elements fortuitously captured during shooting.[46] This simple sound encapsulates the double bind of *L'Amour fou*, insistently pointing to the uncontrolled world outside the closed circle that it is, through its rigorous repetition, firmly enclosed within.

Noli me tangere

It is useful to study the rules that Aeschylus obeyed; however, it is better still to discover the values that led Aeschylus to take these rules into consideration.

—JEAN PAULHAN, EPIGRAPH TO FEBRUARY 1965 ISSUE
OF *CAHIERS DU CINÉMA*[47]

Whatever is fitted in any sort to excite the ideas of pain, and danger, that is to say, whatever is in any sort terrible, or is conversant about terrible objects, or operates in a manner analogous to terror, is a source of the sublime; that is, it is productive of the strongest emotion the mind is capable of feeling.

—EDMUND BURKE, *A PHILOSOPHICAL ENQUIRY INTO THE ORIGIN OF OUR IDEAS OF THE SUBLIME AND BEAUTIFUL* (1757)[48]

Like *The Nun*, *L'Amour fou* was a source of controversy upon its initial release, and this time it found Rivette fighting against the same producer, Georges de Beauregard, who had supported Rivette throughout the lengthy censorship battle over *The Nun*. De Beauregard understood that the aura of notoriety attached to *The Nun* would increase its commercial prospects, but he evidently felt that the four-and-a-quarter-hour length of *L'Amour fou* was an unjustifiable obstacle to its release, and he insisted on a drastic reduction. When Rivette refused, "on the grounds that his experiment is pointless without this freedom from conventional time-limits and traditional boundaries," a two-hour abridgement, which he subsequently disowned, was prepared.[49] A single screening of the original cut was held at the Cinémathèque française in May 1968, and it played at one Parisian art house later that year, with the abridgement put into general release by Cocinor Films in January 1969.[50] The complete version was better attended than the two-hour cut, proving Rivette's point that "to make a film appear shorter, it is necessary to elongate it," and setting the stage for *Out 1*, his most radical exploration of cinematic duration.[51]

After successfully utilizing a number of uncontrolled variables to create an austerely rigorous work, Rivette wanted to take his experiments with the boundaries of cinema further by making a film whose overall length would be established only at the end of production. He secured an "Advance on Receipts" from the Centre national de la cinématographie (CNC) on the basis

of a four-page outline and was able to make the film—eventually dubbed
Out 1 to signify its opposition to the mainstream—thanks to the support of
Stéphane Tchalgadjieff, an innovative producer with whom he would remain
affiliated for the remainder of the decade. Rivette's project was conceived as
a modern equivalent to the serial format developed in the United States and
France during World War I, a film made in multiple parts without a definite
ending in mind, and Tchalgadjieff agreed to begin the project "without knowing if the film would last six hours, twelve hours, eighteen hours, or twenty-
four hours!"[52] At this stage, Rivette apparently hoped that French television
(ORTF) might help distribute it, but ORTF refused. Since the film's thirteen-
hour length also made theatrical distribution completely impractical, *Out
1* received only a single public screening (as a work print) at the Maison de
la Culture in Le Havre, over two days on October 9 and 10, 1971. A description of the film was published on the cover of the arts section of *Le Monde*,
along with a Rivette interview and a short piece, tellingly titled "*Out 1*: Voyage
beyond the Cinema."[53] This cut of the film was called "*Noli me tangere*," the
Latin translation of the phrase ("Touch me not") that the risen Christ said to

FIGURE 3.5 Noli me tangere *(Titian, circa 1514; photograph © National Gallery,
London / Art Resource, NY).*

Mary Magdalene when she recognized him, an allusion that mocks the film's pretentions while also positioning it within a rich iconographic lineage (figure 3.5).[54] *Out 1* was not exhibited again anywhere until the 1989 Rotterdam Film Festival.

Eventually, more than twenty years after its production, *Out 1* was broadcast and released on videotape, possibilities that Rivette dismissed in 1971 as "utopian."[55] Since it is broken up into sections generally running for ninety to one hundred minutes, the film could conceivably be watched episodically, but its true impact comes only from sustained viewing. Rivette later admitted that showing it in parts on television would have been "a disaster," and suggested that the "ideal thing was to see it in two days, which allowed one to get into it enough to follow it, with the possibility of stopping four or five times."[56] He similarly insisted that the film was intended for cinematic exhibition: "It is 16mm [the standard format for television production in the 1970s], but it was made with the big screen in mind: it has a meaning on the big screen which it wouldn't have on the small screen. Even visually it is composed of elements implying a massive image—a monumentality is putting it too grandly but that's it nevertheless."[57] For Rivette, the scale of the projected image and the concentrated viewing made possible by a theatrical screening is tied to the transformative potential of the experience, which would have been further heightened by the awareness that this was the only possible way to see the film.[58] Far from incidental, the length was an essential part of the film's meaning:

> The relationship to the thirteen-hour film is a relationship totally falsified at the outset by the fact of the performance. Even in *L'Amour fou* this came into play for the spectator to a certain extent—the idea of going into an auditorium and getting out four and a quarter hours later—but at least it kept within reasonable limits, it was still feasible, only a little longer than *Gone with the Wind* [Victor Fleming, 1939], though without the bonus of the Civil War. Whereas twelve hours forty minutes . . . it may not be the first time a film has run for so long, but at any rate the only equivalent in my opinion—and even then it isn't so long—is when [Henri] Langlois shows a [Louis] Feuillade serial at the Cinémathèque, starting at six in the evening and going on till one a.m. with three little breaks.[59]

Serials like Feuillade's *Fantômas* (1913–1914) or *Les Vampires* (1915–1916) would originally have been screened in small, regularly spaced intervals over a period of several weeks, and Langlois' decision to screen them intensively had little historical justification. Yet Feuillade's films exerted an influence in the post-1945 period (above all on Rivette) precisely because these marathon screenings made them simultaneously absorbing and disorienting, impressions strengthened by Langlois' practice of removing all intertitles from the prints.[60]

Feuillade was by no means the only major director of serials, but he was the most prominent and, thanks to the support of studio head Léon Gaumont, he was also the most fully in control of his films. Embraced by the Surrealists, who nevertheless could not even remember the name of the person who directed their beloved *Les Vampires*, Feuilade's major works were held in contempt by critics concerned with lending an air of artistic respectability to the cinema. Louis Delluc, for example, regarded Feuillade as the embodiment of everything against which the emerging French avant-garde was struggling, claiming that *"Judex* [1916–1917] and *The New Mission of Judex* [1917] . . . are more serious crimes than those condemned by court-martial."[61] The individual films were largely forgotten by the time Feuillade died in 1925, but they were revived by Langlois when the Occupation ended, and in them critics like Francis Lacassin felt they had discovered a "third possibility," a hybrid alternative to the then famous opposition of the cinema's fantastic and realistic impulses (incarnated, respectively, by Georges Méliès and the Lumières).[62]

A political conservative attached to the idea of mass cinema, Feuillade made films that were fully in the feuilleton tradition of popular fiction, with clearly defined heroes chasing remarkably clever villains across a Paris envisioned in terms of middle-class culture. Yet by situating dangerous events within the well-lit avenues of an urban environment captured with documentary accuracy (although they were not intended as such, films like *Fantômas* are among the best visual records of pre–World War I Paris), Feuillade turned realism on its head, defamiliarizing a city whose Gothic buildings and crisscrossing streets could appear comforting or threatening depending on the context. Over the course of each of Feuillade's serials, spaces are connected in unexpected ways, through invisible tunnels and secret passages as well as windows, doorways, and ceiling lights. By the end of the war, space in Feuillade's films had become porous, opening up in all directions, often through startling juxtapositions: the interior of a bourgeois house is suddenly connected to a group of red-tinted ruins framed like liminal portals, while an innocuous set of stairs leads the characters into a subterranean cavern that appears to recede infinitely. It is this kind of unconscious surrealism—in which a sharply articulated space is deformed and rendered eerily abstract through simple shifts in perspective or the appearance of incongruous details—that made these films seem so poetically dreamlike to directors like Rivette, who playfully acknowledges his debt to Feuillade with the rooftop gun battle in the final episode of *Out 1*.

As Rivette's comments about the unorthodox way he viewed these serials indicate, *Out 1* was also a tribute of sorts to the idea of cinema exemplified by the Cinémathèque française under Henri Langlois. Langlois viewed programming as a form of montage, arranging screenings so that very different types of films would be screened back to back, revealing previously unseen connections. A Douglas Fairbanks comedy would be followed almost immediately by a film of Luis Buñuel or Andy Warhol, and this model of cinematic integration informed Rivette's thinking about both film criticism and filmmaking.[63] Rivette kept up to date on developments in both commercial and avant-garde cinema, describing Alfred Hitchcock's *Marnie* (1964) as a partial inspiration for *L'Amour fou* while also expressing admiration for "structural" films like Michael Snow's *La Région centrale* (1971) and Ken Jacobs' *Tom, Tom, the Piper's Son* (1969).[64] The deliberate pacing and formal precision of these films could potentially be related to *Out 1*, but its distended form reflects the strong influence of Jean Rouch's *Petit à petit* (1969–1971), a comic inversion of his earlier "ethno-fictions." *Petit à petit* includes a group of satirical scenes in which two men from the Ivory Coast travel to Paris and explore it anthropologically with the help of a map and guidebook; these scenes are both visually and conceptually echoed in the exploratory wanderings of Colin in *Out 1*, but it was the way in which Rouch's film was presented at the Cinémathèque that had the greatest impact on Rivette. Rouch's approach entailed the accumulation of masses of material designed to capture the sensation of a long journey between different cities (*Jaguar*, 1957–1967) or different countries (*Petit à petit*), which could result in films of indeterminate length, posing the question, later pursued by Rivette, of when and how to make cuts. Although it was eventually released commercially in a tight, ninety-seven minute form, *Jaguar* was presented in a three-hour version at a single Cinémathèque screening in 1957.[65] Rouch continued this practice for subsequent films, holding special screenings of an eight-hour rough cut of *Petit à petit*, before reducing it to a four-hour television version and a ninety-minute theatrical print (at one point, he expressed a desire to make a film running for twenty-four hours).[66] Rivette "was so impressed by the original that [he] refused to see the shorter versions," and this idea of a "first assembly" animates the thirteen-hour version of *Out 1*, which strategically incorporates a few awkward dialogues, stammers, and hesitations in an attempt to draw attention to the risks associated with a production method reliant on chance.[67]

It is in its treatment of cinematic time that *Out 1* appears most original. The serial form mastered by Feuillade relied upon a series of surprising plot twists that produced sufficient narrative tension to make audience members want to see the next episode. Rouch's films generate a more malleable form of temporality by surrounding images suggestive of present-tense subjectivity with postsynchronized sound, making it seem as though time is unfolding in relation to the personal rhythms of the individuals portrayed. In *Out 1*, both tendencies are dialectically interconnected, so that the overarching plot (whose true nature always remains obscure) and the interactions of the various characters appear to be on two separate temporal tracks that intersect only occasionally. This impression is heightened by Rivette's predilection for long takes, which sometimes run as long as the 16mm camera battery can handle.[68] The unusual latitude offered by the thirteen-hour length of the film and the spectatorial commitment it demands enabled Rivette to adopt a form of extremely diffuse development, beginning the film in the midst of a long rehearsal sequence and delaying any elaboration of the motivating plot until the end of the second episode (more than three hours in). Rivette has characterized this section as an "exposition in the manner of [Honoré de] Balzac," the pseudodocumentary delineation of different social spheres, which are gradually transformed as the fictional elements proliferate. In this way, Rivette reworks the basic parameters of the Rouch paradigm, giving it a new inflection by shifting the focus away from the interdependence of fiction and documentary and toward the unstable relationship between different levels of performance.

There was no script for *Out 1*, but Rivette and his "cowriter" Suzanne Schiffman worked out a schematic diagram listing all of the characters and the places in which their paths would cross.[69] Each of the actors was encouraged to spontaneously create his or her own dialogue within each of these cells, without knowledge of scenes other than the ones in which they were participating or awareness of the overall arc of the project. Even those familiar with experimental improvisation in theater—like Bulle Ogier, who had worked closely with Lettrist Marc'O, or actor-director Michael Lonsdale—claimed that, for the actors, the method "was anguish: when one performed, everything seemed completely abstract. You did not know what to do, nor what to say, nor why. Rivette knew, Suzanne [Schiffman] also; we [the actors] floundered completely."[70] This restless struggling for clarity on the part of the actors was used constructively in the film, keeping the boundary between performer and role perpetually ambiguous in a way that thematically resonates with the characters' search for deeper understanding of a conspiracy that remains forever out of reach. In a similar fashion, the idiosyncrasies of the various performers became crucial elements of the film. For example, when it became clear that the most famous actor in the cast, Jean-Pierre Léaud (Colin), had difficulty improvising, Rivette and Schiffman redirected his manic energy by giving him, in the form of letters, recondite fragments of texts by Balzac and Lewis Carroll, which he then tried to decipher onscreen.[71] In every case, the uncertainties experienced by each of the actors eventually meshes with the confusion of the characters they play, resulting in hysteria or madness driven by exhaustion (Thomas, Michael Lonsdale), alienation (Pauline/Émilie, Bulle Ogier), or interpretive delirium (Colin).

A superficial reading of the method employed in *Out 1* would suggest that Rivette has taken the "de-authoring" of *L'Amour fou* to its limit, setting the performers loose in a world where the godlike director is both unseen and silent, thereby enabling a participatory form of collective creativity. As *L'Amour fou* demonstrated, however, Rivette is acutely aware of the inevitable tendency for this type of utopian system to self-destruct, for structures of domination to reassert themselves through other means.[72] In *Out 1*, directorial control is decentralized and displaced, but it is abundantly evident—through the unseen grid of meetings that is functionally equivalent to the conspiratorial fiction some of the characters are trying to comprehend, the letters around which the plot is structured, and surrogate figures like Lonsdale, who, like Kalfon in *L'Amour fou*, plays a patriarchal theater director. Above all, the authorial "hand" of Rivette is present in the choice and editing of the images, which continually feature identifiable hallmarks of his style. In *Out 1*, Rivette assumes the position of a demiurge, creating a situation in which, like pieces on a moving chessboard, both the performers and the characters are hemmed in by unseen forces, even while they maintain the illusion of total agency.

Similar issues are addressed by the two theater groups, each trying to present a modern adaptation of a play by Aeschylus. One troupe, organized by a woman named Lili, attempts to reinterpret *Seven Against Thebes* by stressing words and gestures, trying to locate the meaning behind the words by repeating or chanting particular syllables in various configurations. The rival troupe, led by Thomas, works instead with *Prometheus Bound*, using theurgic group activities to restage the struggles of the Titan. Improvisation and experimentation are central to both projects, but the Prometheus group is much freer in its physical actions, and the actors are also much more cohesively aligned around their "leader." After an exercise involving a totemic mannequin standing in for Prometheus, Thomas leads the first of several discussions about the meaning of Aeschylus' play, a mixture of therapy and textual analysis that the various characters, including Thomas, humorously stumble through. In one such sequence, at the beginning of the second episode, the characters assemble a variety of different texts and objects that they feel provide ways into the play—including poems about Prometheus by Goethe ("Prometheus," 1774) and Percy Bysshe Shelley (*Prometheus Unbound*, 1820), a short text by Samuel Beckett, and a Japanese theatrical mask—and Thomas instructs troupe members to "speak in the name of Prometheus," to try to communicate his thoughts in a contemporary idiom. Thomas claims that he wants to divide Prometheus' creative energies among the group, but he is invariably the one adopting the lead role in the theater exercises, subtly manipulating the other performers in a way that keeps them subservient, re-enacting the system of mastery that Shelley endeavors to "unbind."

Unlike Abel Gance or Markopoulos, Rivette does not openly endorse the rhetoric of Romanticism, and his treatment of the Prometheus myth reflects this.[73] Yet the parodic manner, poised between wry irony and sardonic wit, in which the different attempts to summon or represent the gods are portrayed in *Out 1* only partially conceals the underlying seriousness of the enterprise. Here, as in his other films, Rivette remains committed to the project of reconnecting mythic and quotidian realms, setting up analogies between the daily lives of ordinary characters who frequently have symbolic names (like

"Achille" in *Out 1* or "Virgil" in *L'Amour par terre*, 1984) and the performances of plays that once had profound ritual functions. *Prometheus Bound*, one of Aeschylus' final plays, was the first part of a tragic trilogy that differed from earlier versions of the creation myth by ascribing political significance to Prometheus' resistance to the gods and metaphorically relating his seizure of fire to the creative energies of mankind. "All arts that are mortal come from Prometheus," the Titan proudly declares.[74] *Seven Against Thebes*, on the other hand, was the third part of a much earlier, Oedipus-oriented trilogy consisting primarily of a series of incantatory dialogues in which Theban citizens express their thoughts about the hostile army outside their gates. Original, fifth century BCE performances would have been part of a larger Dionysiac festival and would have helped to establish a communal space outside the bounds of normal social life. Both troupes in *Out 1* seek an equivalent for this in a world in which ancient languages are virtually incomprehensible and ancient myths have no place.

Unable to rely on audience familiarity with a shared repertoire of archetypes, the two troupes attempt to make ancient theater relevant by searching for preverbal modes of expression, allowing them to circumvent the formulaic patterns of habitual speech. For Johann Gottfried von Herder, it was "Prometheus' divine spark" that "ignites in the human soul . . . the first characteristic marks to serve as elements of language."[75] It is unlikely that anyone involved with *Out 1* was thinking of Herder while making the film, but the objective of both troupes is to reconnect the "divine spark" of Prometheus with the primal roots of human communication. Before making *Out 1,* Rivette had worked with Jean Gruault on an unproduced film about Herder's more celebrated contemporary, Jean-Jacques Rousseau, and both the Thebes troupe's focus on inarticulate sounds and the Prometheus troupe's focus on symbolic movements could be seen as instantiations of the ideas outlined in Rousseau's 1781 "Essay on the Origins of Languages."[76] Rousseau identified "sacred fire" as the origins of human community and argued that spoken language was preceded by a language of gesture and nonverbal sounds, elegizing the melodic cadences that "the Greek tongue had and ours lacks."[77] By reversing this arc, the two troupes attempt to reclaim the lost origins of poetry and music, substituting the rhythmic communication appropriate to the time of Aeschylus for the more codified, wholly word-oriented forms of modern speech.

In their primitivist attitude toward the distant past, the projects of the Thebes and Prometheus troupes strongly resemble the 1960s theater work of Peter Brook and Jerzy Grotowski.[78] Both Brook and Grotowski wanted to purify theater, reviving ancient ritual by means of images or strategies derived from Greek mythology, a "rediscovery of the terror and awesomeness of the original semi-religious theater" that is fully in keeping with Rivette's emphasis on the cinematic sublime ("For me, the most powerful pleasure in cinema—and this is something that interests me more and more . . . is connected with terror and anguish").[79] Brook taught his actors to express internal states "by pure thought transfer, adding vocal sound and physical rhythms 'to discover what was the very least he needed before understanding could be reached' and developing a body language 'beyond psychological implication and beyond monkey-see-monkey-do facsimiles of social behaviorism.'"[80] The ultimate manifestation of this was *Orghast* (first presented at the ancient theater of Persepolis in 1971), a synthetic fusion of myths symbolically enacted within the being of Prometheus that utilized a series of dead, ceremonial languages to bypass intellectual understanding.[81] Grotowski's writings and public statements place an even greater emphasis on religious metaphors than Brook's, and he tried to restructure the forms of drama around the figure of the performer, arguing that "the actor must not *illustrate* but *accomplish* an 'act of the soul' by means of his own organism," turning the human body into a transmitter of hieroglyphic images.[82] Within *Out 1*, the Thebes troupe is aligned more closely with the practices of Brook, while the therapeutic emphasis on process of the Prometheus troupe brings them closer to the ideas of Grotowski, although there is just as much shared ground between them as there would have been in the Paris theatrical scene at the time the film was made.

Much like the assimilation of the ideas of Stockhausen and Boulez in *L'Amour fou*, the incorporation of avant-garde theatrical models into *Out 1* is a sign of the film's larger ambitions. Unlike *L'Amour fou*, however, *Out 1* masks its modernism within a realist framework that is only occasionally challenged. Rivette includes the same sorts of "visual silences" used, like the gaps in Anton Webern's compositions, as rhythmic punctuation in the previous two films, but these are marked in *Out 1* not only by stark cuts to black leader, but also by shots of public squares. *Out 1* is also much more clearly rooted in a particular moment, April and May 1970, the time of shooting indicated during the opening credits. The chronological specificity of the film is fully in keeping with its pseudodocumentary realism, and it also provides a key to understanding the larger political agendas at work within the film. The repeated references by members of "The Thirteen" (a cabal named after Balzac's *History of the Thirteen*, 1834–1835) to events two years before make it clear that this loose organization was formed in the mid-1960s and dissolved after the events of May 1968.[83] This was precisely the moment when Brook came to Paris (where he would cofound the International Centre for Theatre Research, CIRT, in 1970) and when Grotowski's major book, *Towards a Poor Theatre* (1968), first appeared, providing an additional context for the strategies of the two theater troupes in *Out 1*.

It eventually becomes clear that both Lili and Thomas were members of "the Thirteen" and that their attempts to adapt classical plays are introversions of collective enthusiasm in the aftermath of May 1968, a point that Thomas makes explicit in a monologue late in the film. When Colin confronts him with questions about the relationship between Balzac's Thirteen and *Prometheus Bound*, he jokingly responds by demonstrating a card game called "Thirteen," but this leads him to see affinities that he had been oblivious to before. As he explains to former coconspirator Étienne:

> You know I started Prometheus . . . I realized that I can't find Prometheus . . . and I wonder if I haven't made some kind of link . . . between *The History of the Thirteen* and Prometheus . . . the real Thirteen. For me, it's Prometheus in a way, he's a symbol of the Thirteen. He's a symbol because . . . it's a way for us to commit without knowing the ultimate end or goal. But what matters in my work, is first of all to do something. And then, through that work, you find out what the goal is. I'm discovering it through talking about it. . . . I have the feeling that we, to put it bluntly, we can change something that's nailed down, that's Prometheus, that makes a link and we can open things up and show people. . . . Things grow out of a decision made by some group, that's how things start to move. To me, Prometheus symbolizes what is prevented, and with the group, we can find enough energy to change things.

Rambling as they are, Thomas' comments perfectly articulate the vague utopianism motivating both the elusive "Thirteen" and his theatrical troupe—the desire to lead a collective (inevitably run by a superelite that wants to "hold a whole society in their hands") toward an undefined goal, to take some sort of decisive action, regardless of its practical consequences, in the hopes of liberating the revolutionary energies embedded within an ancient legend.

In *Out 1*, this sort of imprecise, conspiratorial idealism serves only to defer the disillusionment brought about by the realization that there are, in fact, forces totally outside the control of the individual members. Over the course of the film, Rivette makes the ultimate vanity and vacuousness of their desire for domination clear through comically deflating imagery, the cinematic equivalent of Balzac's mock-heroic prose.[84] Like Balzac's Thirteen, the secret society in Rivette's film has "broken up, or at least dispersed," and the members have assumed places in civil society.[85] The clandestine organization in *Out 1* is a ruse, an empty shell that, by insisting on the contemporaneity of the film—on its status as a collective portrait of a certain strata of Paris in 1970—Rivette is able to use as a double-edged mechanism, a device that both draws out the quixotic aspirations of the different characters and propels the self-generating narrative. Over the course of thirteen hours, the viewer, like Colin, undergoes a series of perceptual shifts, slowly becoming inculcated into an alternative history of Paris, only to discover that the quest for the true meaning of the city leads nowhere. Colin refuses to relinquish this search, responding to someone suggesting that his pursuit may be empty, "But that would mean that the magical, mysterious world I've been living in is nothing but illusion. And that is impossible!" In the final episode, the camera quietly observes as Colin, unable to rein in his speculations, appears to lose his sanity and Thomas, having failed to complete his reworking of Aeschylus, ends up sobbing alone on a beach, ironically in the position of the fallen Prometheus.

More than any other Rivette film, *Out 1* depicts the dissolution of utopian fantasies, with the extended duration making it possible for the viewer to share the enthusiasm of the participants in the idea of a secret world and then to watch helplessly as their illusions of control are shattered and despair overtakes them. The use of unrestrained improvisation is the formal analogue to this thematic process, and it creates a vertiginous sense of space and time expanding outward, accumulating layers of mythic or metaphoric references, only to collapse into banality (before ever so slightly opening up again in the final moments). In this way, Rivette's longest films develop the Romantic irony described by Friedrich Schlegel in the *Athenaeum Fragments* (1798). Like Schlegel, Rivette subscribes to a chaotic model of the universe, and he remains profoundly invested in volatile artistic structures that generate intense sensations even as they unravel. It is that double movement that separates Rivette's work from the demystifying principles of modern deconstruction, which skeptically insist on the illusoriness of all attempts to find patterns in human experience without a concomitant affirmation of the power of the creative imagination to transform these fictions into new forms. Although he is not an inveterate Romantic like Novalis or Lord Byron (or Gance), Rivette is a consummate Romantic ironist insofar as his films are predicated on the never-ending pursuit of a point where dialectical opposites would be momentarily conjoined, a fragile equilibrium that simultaneously leads outside and within itself. As he explained in an article on Mizoguchi:

> Everything finally comes together in that search for the central place, where appearances, and what we call "nature" (or shame, or death), are reconciled with man, a quest like that of German high Romanticism, and that of a [Rainer Maria] Rilke, [a T. S.] Eliot; one which is also that of the camera— placed always at the exact point so that the slightest shift inflects all the lines of space, and upturns the secret face of the world and of its gods.[86]

The ever-changing relationship between these different elements is encapsulated in a pair of images from the final hour of *Out 1* (figures 3.6–3.7). The first shows Pauline/Émilie staring off blankly into a series of reinforcing mirrors, a vortex that replicates, in microcosm, the push-pull formal structure of the film, suggesting both infinite expansion and total enclosure. It is also, as the most overtly stylized image in the film and an example of one of the director's quintessential obsessions, the clearest expression of Rivette's visual signature, an inescapable reminder of the presence and authority of the filmmaker. The second

FIGURE 3.6 Out 1 *(Jacques Rivette, 1971).*

FIGURE 3.7 *Final shot of* Out 1 *(Jacques Rivette, 1971).*

is the final shot of the film, a five-second coda that shifts the meaning of every-thing that has preceded it by showing Marie, an actress from the Thebes troupe, standing at the Porte Dorée by Léon-Ernest Drivier's 1931 statue of Athena, the goddess of cities, knowledge, and heroic enterprises. Marie had gone to look for stolen money earlier in the film, and by cutting to show her still standing there—after both troupes have dispersed—this final image renews the plot, opening up alternate interpretations of the conspiracy and adding yet another unexplained mystery to the film.[87] With this final winking image, Rivette visualizes the "to be continued" that he claimed, in an interview with Marguerite Duras, should appear at the end of all films, slyly demonstrating how fiction, like conspiratorial thinking, rises like a phoenix from its own ashes.[88]

Cinematic Phantoms

Every perfect thing of its kind leads beyond its kind.

—GOETHE, EPIGRAPH TO OCTOBER 1964 ISSUE OF *CAHIERS DU CINÉMA*[89]

When you called my work epic a moment ago, you reminded me of [Raymond] Queneau's theory that there are two categories of the novel: those that derive from *The Iliad*, and those that descend from *The Odyssey*. The former have to do with battles and strife; the latter concern themselves with strange voyages, with discovery and return, and with the way these things are reported. My films are obviously epic in the Odyssean manner.

—JACQUES RIVETTE (1975)[90]

Unlike his silent predecessors, who were more interested in realizing the total-ity of the long-form works they imagined than with theorizing the experience of the viewers, Rivette gave considerable thought to what the experience of watching his thirteen-hour film would be like. In interviews, he insisted that the fact that, in narrative terms, "almost nothing happens for the first three or four hours," causes receptive viewers to experience "purely the *durée*."[91] Martin Even, in the *Le Monde* review of the 1971 screening, describes the audience as discussing "duration, the distortion of time, at the beginning fictional time, then real time," and ends his piece by writing, "It is a quarter after midnight (already Monday), and time has truly lost all significance."[92] Rivette's lack of concern for traditional narrative flow and his use of deliberate longueurs have led critics like Jean Durançon to argue that he is "the least rhythmic of cineas-tes."[93] *Out 1* does indeed include several extremely long sequences, notably the theater rehearsals, that go on much longer than is apparently "necessary," but even though it may not be apparent until much later, the film possesses a clear rhythmic structure. As in *L'Amour fou*, sustained vérité-like segments are regularly interrupted by insert shots and broken up through cross-cutting. The unobtrusiveness of the editing in most of Rivette's films has tended to obscure the fact that it is meticulously layered, creating subtle links that allow sequences to resonate with each other in both space and time.

Throughout *Out 1*, Rivette sets up a series of perceptual expectations and then plays with them, editing carefully around speech so as to maximize the interpretive possibilities of particular sequences, and encouraging the acclimated viewer to make assumptions that are shown to be mistaken minutes or hours later. A similar sort of distortion occurs on the level of mise en scène, through slight shifts in the arrangement of space or the appearance of an object in multiple unrelated locations. The fact that the fictional apparatus that appears to structure the film is ultimately revealed to be a trap, and that certain key plot questions (like the identity of Igor) remain unresolved, further reinforces the impression that *Out 1* is concerned with the sheer presence of time, with duration for its own sake. Yet by cutting in such a way that even the longest, most inert theater exercises or discussions are made to interact with other sequences that suggest possible redirections of the plot, Rivette imbues every minute of the film with potential narrative importance, creating an unusual form of suspense. It is here that *Out 1* differs most significantly from the conceptual gambits of Warhol, which Rivette was certainly aware of, as well as the "sculpted" time of contemporaries like Andrei Tarkovsky. In films like *Andrei Rublev* (1966/1969) and *Solaris* (1972), Tarkovsky refined the temporal strategies associated with filmmakers like Antonioni—whose films had made narrative *temps morts* pivotal to the critical debates of the 1960s— by using glacially hypnotic pacing and hypersensitive long takes, energized by fleeting shifts in rhythm, as the basis of a new film form. Tarkovsky draws out his sequence shots until they appear drained of conventional meaning, paving the way for epiphanic moments of spiritual plenitude. Rivette does just the opposite, flooding his sequences with possible meaning only to empty them out minutes or hours later.

It is through editing that Rivette "really starts to see the film," and in a 1974 interview, he claimed that he wanted "to return, though with quite different methods, aims, and end products, to the old Dziga Vertov idea: that the montage should be conceived with the project and not merely with the exposed film."[94] The thirteen-hour version of *Out 1*, which was edited over the course of six months by Rivette and his frequent collaborator Nicole Lubtchansky, bears this out. Having experimented with various means of connecting the different micronarratives in the film—at one point they even considered treating *Out 1* as a series of interlinked short films—Rivette and Lubtchansky finally decided to stack the narrative sequences next to each other in rough chronological order, using sporadic cross-cutting to generate an expanding network of possible connections while also leaving long sequences shot with handheld cameras largely intact. These are often continued for seconds or even minutes past the point at which the narrative interest has receded, making the camera appear almost aggressive by holding steadily on the actors after their improvised performance has run its course. This is Rivette's way of finding the cracks he praised so effusively in films by directors like Hitchcock and Otto Preminger, of capturing the moment where the fissures and seams of the performances become visible and self-display gives way to self-exposure.

In the shorter, commercially distributed version of *Out 1*, almost all of these moments are gone. Although the four-and-a-half-hour cut, whose title, *Out 1: Spectre* (1972), draws attention to its filial relationship to the long-unseen source, is made up almost entirely of footage used in the full thirteen-hour *Out 1*, its jagged, brittle form makes it into a radically different work, oriented around structural rhymes and contrasts rather than narrative immersion. To maximize these differences, Rivette hired an editor, Denise de Casabianca, who was not already familiar with the material, and the two of them spent close to a year reconstituting the film.[95] In place of extended sequences and gradual development, different plots are continually juxtaposed next to or intercut with one another, generally without establishing transitions, forcing the viewer to actively process overlapping threads as soon as they appear. Sometimes scenes from totally unrelated sections of the film are linked through deceptive matching, with cuts that connect one character looking offscreen to the right with another looking in the opposite direction, even though they are in totally different spaces. At other points, material from the earlier film is dramatically reconfigured by being repositioned in a new context. This is especially true of the ending, a shot of Colin playing with a small reproduction of the Eiffel Tower while he counts up to thirteen over and over again. This scene passes by unremarkably in the thirteen-hour version, but by placing it at the end, immediately after an enigmatic series of shots that includes images of "empty" crossroads as well as several characters who are now isolated from the theatrical troupes, it functions not as a comic interlude, but as a distillation of the obsessive-compulsive anxiety that permeates *Out 1: Spectre*.

One model for the editing of the shorter cut is Jean-Daniel Pollet's *Méditerranée* (1963), a forty-five minute film that circles ritualistically around the same cluster of imagery, creating different, and ever more mysterious, meanings with each iteration. Far more than an elaborate Kuleshov experiment, Pollet's film possesses a mythic narrative shell, within which each of its images—an Egyptian statue, an apple, the steps of an ancient theater, and so on—operates like an ideogram (figure 3.8).[96] As Pollet explained decades later, the sequencing of the images was not predetermined but was developed, by trial and error, over the course of six months of arduous assembly, much like Rivette's film.[97] *Méditerranée* was one of a handful of titles screened as part of

FIGURE 3.8 Méditerranée *(Jean-Daniel Pollet, 1963).*

an international conference on montage in 1969 that Rivette participated in, writing afterwards that

> one might, very schematically, distinguish four [film historical] moments: the *invention* of montage ([D. W.] Griffith, [Sergei] Eisenstein), its deviation ([Vsevolod] Pudovkin-Hollywood: elaboration of the techniques of propaganda cinema), the rejection of propaganda (a rejection loosely or closely allied to long takes, direct sound, amateur or auxiliary actors, non-linear narrative, heterogeneity of genres, elements or techniques, etc), and finally, what we have been observing over the last ten years, in other words the attempt to "salvage," to re-inject into contemporary methods the spirit and the *theory* of the first period, though without rejecting the contribution made by the third, but rather trying to cultivate one through the other, to dialectise them and, in a sense, to *edit* them.[98]

Where a filmmaker like Markopoulos saw himself as reviving the lost first tradition of pure montage, Rivette was committed to an expanded notion of synthetic montage, in which each stage of the film would be dialectically related to the next, a process for which the open form of *Méditerranée* provides one key point of reference. Yet while *Out 1: Spectre* and *Méditerranée* are equally reliant on structural elisions, they proceed by inverse methods. Pollet's film spirals outward, using color clashes along with disjunctures between Philippe Sollers' allusive voiceover narration and the internal logic of the editing to drive the individual shots away from one another, blocking any association that would allow full apprehension of the events being depicted, even as the repetitions in the montage intractably pull each image back into the orbit of the shots that surround it. By contrast, *Out 1: Spectre* creates the impression of two parallel circles that, both fully enclosed, touch at only one point—the moment (placed just before the intermission) where the representatives of the different narrative strands briefly intersect in the aptly named L'Angle du hasard boutique.

The most important addition to *Out 1: Spectre* is the insertion of a large number of evocative, black-and-white still shots. In true serial fashion, each episode of the final version of the thirteen-hour cut of *Out 1* opens with short excerpts from the preceding episode, along with several carefully selected stills. In *Out 1: Spectre*, still images are spread across the film, acting as constant intimations of the material that has been excised, shards of the subjacent form that would remain (for almost two decades) unseen. Rivette claims that he "spent most of the editing time of *Spectre* selecting them" and that they "should be seen as a kind of machine, an electronic computer that interrupts the general dream of the characters in *Spectre*."[99] Accompanied by an electronic hum, the stills initially appear to open up new interpretations of the sequences they buttress, but they eventually become completely inscrutable; like the frequent appearances of black leader, they continually disrupt the flow of the film, refusing to allow it to fully cohere. By standing in for missing scenes and reflexively pointing to the full work for which this is the "spectral" shadow, the stills make *Out 1: Spectre* appear totally constructed and artificial, dialectically inverting the basic parameters of the earlier film. The self-generating fictional mechanism of *Out 1*, with its illusions of performative autonomy, here devours itself, rigidly foreclosing all possible openings by insistently drawing attention to the film's status as a composite of preexisting footage and to the invisible authorship that shapes it. In this way, the idea of fictional incompleteness is incorporated, in high modernist fashion, into the body of the film, which is organized around a series of deliberate subtractions. To paraphrase Picasso's famous maxim, in the case of *Out 1: Spectre*, filmmaking is a sum of destructions.[100]

Having reached the ne plus ultra of the trajectory that began with *L'Amour fou*, Rivette decided to continue his experiments on a parallel track, replacing an investigation of cinema's documentary affinities with an exploration of its oneiric aspects. This move reflects, in part, "the total refusal of France in the seventies. It was something I suddenly didn't want to see any more."[101] The first project Rivette initiated after *Out 1* was called *Phénix*, a film (intended for Jeanne Moreau and Michael Lonsdale) in which the biographies of Sarah Bernhardt and Eleanora Duse would have been fused with Gaston Leroux's *Phantom of the Opera* (1910). The original scenario coyly alludes to the mythic origins of cinema, beginning, "The action of this film takes place over six days and six nights, inside a grand *théâtre parisien*, at the end of the last century (very exactly December 1895)," a reference to the public premiere of the Lumière brothers' Cinématographe at the Salon Indien of the Grand Café on December 28, 1895.[102] Because of scheduling conflicts, *Phénix* was never made, but the same concerns are evident in *Céline and Julie Go Boating*, the first feature Rivette completed after five years working with (and through) the *Out 1* material. One of Rivette's most quickly made films, *Céline and Julie Go Boating* is also one of his most entertaining, a comically reflexive demonstration of the cinema's dual status as both a distorting reflection of the world and a shared hallucination.[103] The two titular protagonists create a space of enchantment within their otherwise ordinary lives by using magical sweets to "enter" fictional projections, which they eventually infiltrate and take over. Unsurprisingly, the boundaries separating the highly stylized film-within-a-film, ensconced within a Victorian mansion, and the naturalistically shot scenes in the contemporary world become extremely tenuous, especially after a scene in which Céline and Julie don Feuilladesque costumes, sneak into a library, and steal an enormous book. Passage between the two domains is initially marked by the bright red imprint of a hand, but the different layers are also interposed through direct cuts. For all its playfulness, *Céline and Julie Go Boating* is among Rivette's most rigorous films, held together by a prismatic montage in which brief fragments from the different zones of the film are interspersed with cuts to black leader and even, on a few significant occasions, the sort of photographic stills used in *Out 1: Spectre*.

One result of the distribution problems created by both versions of *Out 1* is that Rivette was required by contract to turn *Céline and Julie Go Boating* into a film of "normal length" (the resulting film ran for 192 minutes).[104] Not content to simply accept the standard formula for film production and exhibition, Rivette initiated a new project in 1974, fulfilling the dream of perpetual cinema by planning a series of four loosely interrelated films, all shot back to back, with editing to commence only after shooting on the final film was finished.[105] Totally unlike *Out 1*, each of these films would be shot with preplanned scripts, in 35mm and the wider aspect ratio then dominant in commercial cinemas. Having taken his journey through the "house of fiction" as far as it could go, Rivette worked instead to make films in which plastic values assumed a more essential role than narrative.[106] Each of the four films in the series would be a modernist reworking of a particular genre: a love story, a film noir, a musical comedy, and a Jacobean tragedy/adventure film. Having secured funding for the entire series, Rivette finished two of the films (*Duelle* and *Noroît*, both from 1976), but collapsed after two days of shooting on the third, *Marie et Julien*, bringing the entire project to a halt. Rivette eventually made a very different musical comedy in 1995 (*Haut bas fragile*), and he finally succeeded in filming *The Story of Marie and Julien* in 2003—with different actors and a revised script—but, of the four films originally planned, only *Duelle* was completed and released in the 1970s.[107]

Rivette's series was entitled *Les Filles du feu*, an allusion to Gérard de Nerval's 1854 book of the same name, and it was conceived as an alternative cinematic mythology founded on the idea of cinephilia. This is reflected in his choice of genres, cinematic references—Jacques Tourneur's *Anne of the Indies* (1951) and Lang's *Moonfleet* (1955) for *Noroît*; Orson Welles' *The Lady from Shanghai* (1947) and the films of Val Lewton for *Duelle*; *Vertigo* (Alfred Hitchcock, 1958), the cinema's supreme siren song, for *Marie et Julien*—and especially in the lavish attention paid to pure surface textures. Rivette's mastery of image and sound has never been more apparent than in these films. In contrast to the grainy, 16mm appearance of *Out 1* and *Céline and Julie Go Boating*, both *Duelle* and *Noroît* make use of tonally rich colors, shifting pools of light that sculpt figures in space, and an emphatically expressive sound design. By positioning characters at the very edges of cavernous or mirror-filled spaces and slowly turning the camera, Rivette also makes space seem elastic, continually expanding into areas beyond the limits of the frame. Live musicians are frequently visible improvising the soundtrack onscreen, but because of the flagrant artificiality of the rest of the films, this unusual tactic, like the occasional shifts to blue- or red-tinted stock, intensifies the overall sensory experience of the film. It also adds yet another layer of cinephilic allusion, evoking the aesthetics of silent film presentations more than Brecht's "Chinese theater" techniques, a point reinforced by the presence in *Duelle* of Jean Wiener, a veteran of the silent era who had been composing scores for important French films since 1922.

The debt to Nerval, a mid-nineteenth-century conduit for the transmission of German Romantic ideas to France, is most evident through the cryptic symbolism of the films, each of which was "divided into three main sections, three acts, corresponding to the three lunar phases."[108] These were phantasmatic works, films in which sun and moon goddesses descend to the earth, magical invocations are uttered, and burning substances are discovered under the earth. They were also exercises in purely elemental cinema; *Noroît*, for example, begins with a shot of the sea at dawn, uses images of the sun and the earth as structural markers, and ends with a shot of corpses on the ground in deepest night. In these films, Rivette attempted to construct a pure choreography of filmic space centered on the physical actions and corporeality of the performers, "the movement of bodies, their counterpoint, their inscription within the screen space," rather than the psychological states they project, a move away from conventional signifiers of emotions that heightened the abstract energy of the films.[109] Contemporary dance is as important to these films as music had been to *L'Amour fou* or *Out 1*, leading Rivette to cast Jean Babilée in *Duelle* and employ a number of dancers from Carolyn Carlson's company in *Noroît*, a film that ends with a dance of death, complete with burning torches and group chants. *Duelle* also ends with an enigmatic ritual accompanied by flames, but it provides an opening into a "mirror world," an enchanted space lurking just behind the real Paris (in yet another link to

Nerval). The alternate title for the series of films, shown in the opening credits of both *Duelle* and *Noroît* is *Scènes de la vie parallèle*, and transfer between the two "parallel" realms is accomplished by means of spells and magical objects. Throughout *Duelle*, movement across this frontier happens mainly by means of a necklace and a summoning phrase, often marked by shifts in light or the presence of a large glass surface. In the final shot, the protagonist turns toward the camera and begins her incantation. As she finishes, there is a cut to a black screen and the sound of a train passing, suggesting passage beyond the diegetic world of the film, movement across an invisible axis separated, appropriately enough, by the movie screen.

"The True Tradition Lives in Contradiction"

When [George] Balanchine did a choreography to my *Danses concertantes* [1942], he approached the problem architecturally and not descriptively. And his success was extraordinary for one great reason: he went to the roots of the musical form, of the *jeu musical*, and recreated it in forms of movements. Only if the film should ever adopt an attitude of this kind is it possible that a satisfying and interesting art form would result.

—IGOR STRAVINSKY (1946)[110]

After recovering, Rivette completed his "contract" for the four-film series with the hastily shot *Merry-Go-Round* (1979), a film that is only intermittently related to the principles laid out in the original proposal. It was followed in 1981 by *Le Pont du nord*, a full-fledged return to contemporary France after a full decade in the realm of the fantastic. Where *Duelle* takes place inside a largely defamiliarized Paris, *Le Pont du nord* responds directly to the malaise that set in during the last years of the Valéry Giscard d'Estaing presidency, including a plethora of references to the major scandals of the era. With characters reading newspaper stories about the suicide or murder of ministers and the Goldman affair, *Le Pont du nord* is Rivette's most politically trenchant film, and while its targeted criticism was partially mooted by the surprise election of François Mitterrand several months before the film's release, it treats all of these contemporary events as part of a secret history of the French capital.[111] In the film, Rivette systematically alternates between images of buildings under construction and shots of iconic statues, like the bronze replica of *The Lion of Belfort* (Frédéric Bartholdi, 1880) in the Place Denfert-Rochereau—a symbol of French Resistance and an important site of May 1968 protests that also marks the entrance to the Catacombs—highlighting them in a way that invites comparison with the work of the filmmakers Jean-Marie Straub and

FIGURE 3.9 Le Pont du Nord *(Jacques Rivette, 1981).*

Danièle Huillet (figure 3.9). Straub and Huillet frequently combine formal concentration with a focus on the particular histories and structures of major cities, using extremely long shots that roam through a location as a way of interrogating the compression of historical forces that it embodies or represents, as in the circular movement at the Place de Bastille in *Too Early, Too Late* (1981) or the twenty-minute drive through the streets of Rome in *History Lessons* (1972). In both of these films, the deliberate solidity of statuary, as artistic manifestations of cultural moments, is framed statically and set off against the constant motion of cars and other vehicles. In *Le Pont du nord*, by contrast, the camera moves in circles around the statues, which function less as historical palimpsests than as mythic guardians, symbols of the clandestine interactions that influence modern life from behind the scenes.

For all the attention it pays to concrete spaces and historically specific situations, *Le Pont du nord* is every bit as concerned with games and magic as *Céline and Julie Go Boating*. Rivette's treatment of Paris is informed by the nineteenth-century literary tradition, fusing the meandering narratives of Eugène Sue's *Mysteries of Paris* (1842–1843) with the panoramic mapping of Victor Hugo, but it also contains elements of childlike play. This is also true of *Le Pont du nord*'s partner film, *Paris s'en va* (1981), a twenty-five-minute short made as part of a series sponsored by the European House of Photography that attempted to recast the omnibus film *Paris vu par . . .* (1965) for the year 1980. *Paris s'en va* uses the same locations as *Le Pont du nord*, and it is edited

FIGURE 3.10 Le Pont du Nord *(Jacques Rivette, 1981).*

around a children's rhyme narration derived from "The Game of the Goose." In both films, two women, Marie and Baptiste, wander through the city like Don Quixote and Sancho Panza, an implied reference given added resonance when Baptiste claims that a statue of a dragon at an amusement park is actually alive, like the windmill in Cervantes' novel. As in earlier Rivette films, however, these fantasy projections carry with them an undercurrent of genuine danger, capped off by the death of Marie in *Le Pont du nord. Paris s'en va* opens with a dedication to "amateurs," and that applies equally to the inquisitive characters and to the films, Rivette's final forays into 16mm filmmaking. The limitations of the medium are apparent throughout, with booms occasionally visible in parts of the screen and sound that becomes tinny or difficult to process when the actors move away from the microphone, anticipating a final scene in which, as Baptiste does battle with a mysterious man, the narrative system breaks down and the lines of the camera's viewfinder become visible (they are accompanied by the sound of the rolling camera). With this gesture, Rivette totally disrupts the illusionistic space of the film, giving the characters freedom of action while simultaneously visualizing their ineluctable containment within a grid structure (figure 3.10).

From *Le Pont du nord* on, almost all of Rivette's films take on a retrospective quality that finds thematic expression in narratives of loss and renewal. Rivette continued to argue that filmmaking should always entail a process of discovery and adventure, but the idea that each film challenges the assumptions of the ones that preceded it is replaced by a sense of temporal passage, with a new focus on the lives of characters trying to put their lives together again after a long hiatus. It is revealed very early in *Le Pont du nord*, for example, that Marie was released from prison with a previous history of radicalism (for this and other reasons, it is possible to see the character as an extension of the terrorist played by the same actress, Bulle Ogier, in Rainer Werner Fassbinder's 1979 film *The Third Generation*). In *Haut bas fragile*, the character played by Anna Karina—whose very presence evokes an earlier era of filmmaking as well as the unfilmed musical intended to be the third part of *Les Filles du feu/ Scènes de la vie parallèle*—longingly recalls the time when she tried to be a painter "long ago." This changed notion of time also manifests itself through an amplified intertextuality, an internal networking of otherwise unrelated films that is often linked to the idea of an abandoned quest. Coded images recur in a number of different configurations, and the names of characters (like Henri de Marsay in *Gang of Four*, 1988) and even entire films (*The Duchess of Langeais*, 2007) covertly allude to phantom works like *Out 1*. The most powerful metaphor for the spiritual journeys of Rivette's characters is of a battle with dragons, a trope that recurs frequently in the late films: through the fire-breathing amusement park ride of *Le Pont du nord*, the small reproduction of a Raphael painting of St. George and the Dragon in *Gang of Four*, repeated visual references to the Rue du Dragon, and especially the verbal quotation of Rilke's *Letters to a Young Poet* (1929) in Rivette's final film, *Around a Small Mountain* (2009): "Perhaps all the dragons of our lives are princesses who are only waiting to see us once beautiful and brave."[112]

The idea of personal quests as sacred missions is central to both of the long-form films Rivette made in the early 1990s, *La Belle Noiseuse* and *Joan the Maid*. The latter, at almost six hours in length, is the only Rivette film that qualifies as a historical epic, a modernist rendition of the Joan of Arc story that is fully conscious of its two most artistically commanding precursors, *The Passion of Joan of Arc* (Carl Theodor Dreyer, 1928) and *The Trial of Joan of Arc* (Robert Bresson, 1962). Much of Rivette's film is made up of fluidly choreographed long takes in which the actors are able to calibrate their performances organically, creating an absorptive rhythm that is rendered strangely unreal by the highly saturated, almost Fauvist color (whose full impact can be registered only through 35mm projection). This impression is heightened by the highly mobile camera, which continually tracks and pans through space, keeping spatial configurations in flux even as it fixes the characters within a materially specific environment. Unlike Bresson or Dreyer, Rivette frequently stages lengthy scenes in extreme depth, and his focus on unstable triangular compositions in the various interiors continually draws the eye toward light-filled passageways like corridors and hallways, pushing spatial geometry to the border of abstraction.

The narrative form of *Joan the Maid* is similarly complex. Although the wealth of period detail and the overall sense of accumulation developed over the course of the film's running time help convey the lived experience of history, this history is always mediated by its representation, most obviously through the sudden appearance of intertitles and cuts to black leader. Evocative of the section breaks in medieval epics as well as the conventions of silent cinema, the intertitles are used to bridge highly elliptical sequences, keeping the synoptic progression of events clear, while the often startling switches to black leader mark gaps whose duration can be determined only retrospectively. This has the simultaneous effect of keeping the viewer involved in the unfolding of the narrative and preventing this meticulously researched historical reconstruction from descending into cliché. Rivette uses these narrative leaps both to downplay the ideologically charged pageantry typically associated with his subject and to reinterpret the forms adopted by his predecessors, skipping past most of the period covered by *The Passion of Joan of Arc* with a single intertitle, "After 4 Months of Trial." When the film resumes, Joan is shown in the center of a courtyard being condemned, and the camera slowly completes a semicircular pan in which every figure is positioned on the periphery. Where Dreyer had used circular camera movements to isolate Joan from her inquisitors, Rivette instead uses a mobile establishing shot to visualize her entrapment within an open-air space. Allusions build upon one another in highly resonant ways; as a visibly terrified Joan is escorted to the stake, Rivette switches for the first time to close-ups of her feet—in an open quotation of the Bresson film—and birds can be heard faintly chirping in the background. Within moments, however, the birds are drowned out by the rising crackle of flames and Joan's six, progressively more intense repetitions of "Jesus." Questions of the world beyond this one are left completely outside the bounds of this profoundly materialist film, which ends with Joan's final, desperate cry and a hard cut to black.

If *Joan the Maid* can be seen as a final summation of Rivette's pessimism, its affirmative counterpart is *La Belle Noiseuse*, a four-hour study of the relationship between a painter and his model that is also the director's *ars poetica*. Even though the full version of the film, which ran almost exactly as long as *L'Amour fou*, won a major prize at the 1991 Cannes Film Festival, Rivette was forced by contract to produce a shorter, two-hour version, *Divertimento* (1992). Since the best shots had already been incorporated into *La Belle Noiseuse*, *Divertimento* consists almost entirely of outtakes, and Rivette acknowledges its status as a commercial compromise by restructuring the final scenes so that the film ends with the painter Frenhofer—who has just exhibited the painting he has spent most of the film working on—asking his agent Porbus if they can "talk about figures." Reducing *La Belle Noiseuse* involved not only

FIGURE 3.11 La Belle Noiseuse *(Jacques Rivette, 1991).*

the removal of the voiceover narration of Marianne, the model for the epon-
ymous painting, but also the elimination of the sequence shots used during
most of the painting sessions, blocks of unbroken time injected in the midst
of a tightly constructed narrative. Duration—along with the intermittent
boredom and distraction that occasionally goes with it—is used to accord the
creative process with a sense of immensity, to imbue the fastidious, concentrated work of a portrait painter with an appropriate level of temporal magnitude. By subtly altering the soundtrack so that the natural sounds of birds
and planes audible in the more plot-oriented sections of the film are largely
silenced and replaced by the reverberations of footsteps and the rustle of bris-
tles on canvas, these sequences seem to exist outside the flow of narrative
time, acquiring a temporal density that allows the weight of the human body
to be first registered and then transformed. Rivette reinforces this by framing for the anachronistic 1.37:1 "Academy" ratio of width to height, using the
added vertical space to visually complement the horizontal canvases shown
onscreen, drawing the viewer's eye deep into the image (figure 3.11).

     Although it is certainly not unique in this respect, *La Belle Noiseuse* is one of
Rivette's more complicated literary adaptations, wedding elements and motifs
from Henry James' "The Figure in the Carpet" (1896) and Edgar Allen Poe's
"The Oval Portrait" (1842) to Balzac's influential 1831 novella, *The Unknown*

FIGURE 3.12 *Pablo Picasso (1881–1873),* Painter Before His Easel, With a Long-Haired Model, *from Honoré de Balzac's* Le Chef-d'oeuvre inconnu, *1927, published 1931. © 2015 Estate of Pablo Picasso / Artists Rights Society (ARS), New York. Etching from The Louis E. Stern Collection of The Museum of Modern Art, New York. Digital Image © The Museum of Modern Art / Licensed by SCALA / Art Resource, NY.*

Masterpiece, which art historian Dore Ashton has argued should be read as a "fable of modern art."[113] The ambiguous story of a painting so advanced—with merely a single foot representing an entire figure—that it cannot even be adequately seen in the present was embraced by a number of key modernists including Paul Cézanne, Arnold Schoenberg, Rilke, and especially Picasso, who created a series of illustrations for a 1931 reprinting of the Balzac text (and whose *Ma Jolie,* 1911, similarly contains a single stray foot) (figure 3.12).[114] The young painter of the original Balzac story is Nicolas Poussin, but while the story is moved back to the seventeenth century, the key references are to artistic Romanticism, and in particular to Eugène Delacroix.[115] Balzac describes the young model, lover of Poussin, as appearing before Frenhofer "in the innocent posture of a terrified Circassian girl carried off by brigands to some slave dealer," and the painter explains that anyone who saw his unseen masterpiece would suppose that "he saw a woman lying on a velvet coverlet, her bed surrounded by draperies, and, at her side, a golden tripod exhaling incense," both characteristic of many Delacroix canvases.[116] Tellingly, creative genius is compared to the "divine fire" of "Prometheus' torch," analogizing painting and male virility.[117] This connection is drawn out in Picasso's drawings, which are, in turn, playfully referred to in the first cinematic treatment of

The Unknown Masterpiece, Sidney Peterson's *Mr. Frenhofer and the Minotaur* (1948). Peterson employs anamorphosis to critique the inherent voyeurism of the camera, and he displaces his concerns with the nature of representation by taking the latent sexual metaphors of Balzac to a reductio ad absurdum in which Joycean puns ("Belle wrought-up") are intermingled with tongue-in-cheek Freudianisms ("mini-mini-mini-tour") and reflexive jokes about both the source text and the privileged space of the artist's studio ("Oh, it comes from 'respectable literature.'" "My mistake, of course").

Rivette approaches this constellation of issues from a very different angle, addressing questions of modernist form and Romantic genius from within a stable, almost "classical," spatiotemporal environment in which neither the basic structuring system of shot/countershot editing nor the recording properties of the camera are overtly disrupted. Rather than parodying the erotic sublimation involved in the creation of nude portraits (and painting more generally), he turns it into a challenge for both spectator and filmmaker, treating the subject with the chaste modesty one would expect of the critic who once argued that "the filmmaker judges that which he shows, and is judged by the way in which he shows it."[118] In a 1991 interview, he specifically insisted that he "shot many close ups of the face of Emmanuelle Béart, but not of her body. It was something that had been totally forbidden. There are traveling shots where the camera approaches the body, certainly, but never

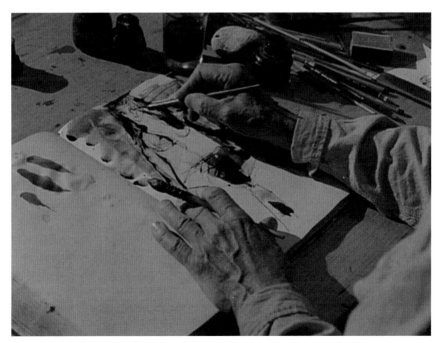

FIGURE 3.13 *Bernard Dufour's hands in* La Belle Noiseuse *(Jacques Rivette, 1991).*

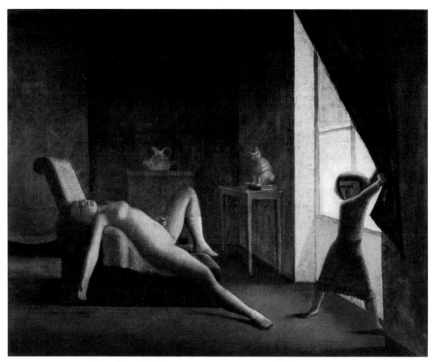

FIGURE 3.14 La Chambre *(Balthus, 1952–1954, private collection. © 2015 Artists Rights Society [ARS], New York / ADAGP, Paris).*

close-ups. Never."[119] Within the film itself, this distinction is reversed. Like the viewer, Marianne becomes acclimated to the display of her naked body, but she is warned by the painter's wife (and former model) Liz to refuse if Frenhofer asks to paint her face. What Frenhofer is after is "the whole body. I don't care about your lips, legs, breasts, I want more. I want everything. I'll take everything. I'll get it out of you and put it in this frame." It is this desire to contain life within a work of art that Liz argues is shameless. As in Poe's "Oval Portrait," the outer limit of portraiture is the painting of the human face, because a true rendering entails the vampiric transfer of personality onto canvas.

Rivette had long wanted to make a version of what became *La Belle Noiseuse,* "the image of a possible relationship between a director and an actress," and he had been considering projects of this kind since the early 1960s, when he tried to make a film with Jean Fautrier.[120] He eventually decided to work with Bernard Dufour, whose nudes, like Fautrier's, evoke figuration largely through abstract outlines and whose hand is shown working throughout *La Belle Noiseuse* (figure 3.13). Yet the constrained poses Frenhofer asks Marianne to adopt and his insistence that she stand "as if you were stretched up to the ceiling," pushed to the point just before the body begins to crack, suggest a more surprising source, the enigmatic Balthus. Balthus was almost certainly an influence on Rivette's earlier film of *Wuthering Heights* (1985), which is transposed to the early 1930s, the moment when this fellow traveler of the Surrealists completed his series of illustrations on the same themes, several of which are openly cited in the film.[121] Steeped—through his friendship with Rilke and his philosopher brother (translator of Friedrich Hölderlin and Friedrich Nietzsche)—in German Romanticism, Balthus made a number of works in which Dionysian energy rests uneasily beneath a placid, severe surface, treating symbolic rites of passage with forms that look back to the Old Masters while retaining the psychosexual concerns of his own era.[122] Although Rivette's use of the nude female form in *La Belle Noiseuse* is much less confrontational than that of Balthus, both the filmmaker and the painter share an interest in an eccentric, sometimes mannered, realism in which the torquing of bodies is used to endow space with metaphysical possibilities (figures 3.14–3.15).

With the exception of a few surprise jump cuts, the sittings in *La Belle Noiseuse* are presented as directly as possible, through simple camera setups, carefully orchestrated mobile long takes, and smooth transitions. The switches in film stock, discordant music, or cuts to black that had been so prominent in films like *L'Amour fou* or *Noroît* are nowhere to be found, and Rivette instead gives the accretion of time during the sittings profound implications. While

FIGURE 3.15 La Belle Noiseuse *(Jacques Rivette, 1991).*

FIGURE 3.16 La Belle Noiseuse *(Jacques Rivette, 1991).*

the young Nicolas, who paints from photographs, clings to a materialist conception of the artwork ("For me, painting is the stroke"), Frenhofer uses ever more grandiose language to describe his ambitions: "Can't you hear the forest? The forest murmuring all the time. The forest and the sea mixed together, that's what painting is." For Frenhofer, painting is a leap into the unknown, a search for the absolute and "the invisible," whose stakes could not be higher; by visualizing the true form of a human being, he believes that his painting could express "whirlwinds! Galaxies, the ebb and flow" of the cosmos.

As in the Balzac story, Rivette makes it possible to see Frenhofer's rhetoric as either self-delusion or a direct emanation of the Romantic imagination, but it also becomes clear that the process of searching, like the experience of actively watching the film, is as important as the final result. Marianne is speaking for the viewer as much as her character when she claims that, after adjusting to Frenhofer's method, she "lost the sense of time. I could be one hundred years old or a baby. I feel I'm in a tunnel with no light, no rain, no wind, no sun, no cold, no warmth. . . . There's just a very small light, right at the end, flickering." The sense that the painting sessions exist in a space outside normal time is deepened by the numerous sacramental or Christological metaphors in the film, the culmination of a tradition going back to Rivette's early criticism and continuing through *Joan the Maid* (where Rivette plays the role of Joan's parish priest). When she first walks into the studio, Marianne

FIGURE 3.17   La Belle Noiseuse *(Jacques Rivette, 1991).*

says that it is "like a church," and when Liz finally sees the completed painting, she draws a small cross on the back of it (figure 3.16). There is, in fact, a
Passion narrative carefully woven throughout the film, but one that is partially concealed through the "sacred indirections" Tony Pipolo has identified in Bresson's late work, with the major landmarks moved "back" by
two days.[123] An opening title announces that it is "a Monday at the beginning of July, between three and four," but this is the film's version of "Spy
Wednesday" ("you sold my ass," Marianne says to Nicolas in the evening),
and the session in Frenhofer's studio the next day culminates in Gethsemane-
like doubt ("Maundy Thursday"). Twelve bells can be heard on the film's third
day ("Good Friday") as Liz and Magali jokingly refer to a friend who died at
the biblical age of thirty-three but "was nothing like Jesus"; inside the studio,
Marianne adopts a crucifixion pose and listens as Frenhofer talks about "getting her out of her body" and mentions a friend who died after completing a
sculpture of the Resurrection.

Rivette's most significant departure from Balzac's novella is the addition
of a sequence showing Frenhofer burying the true painting in a wall the night
before the public presentation of his fake portrait (figure 3.17). Like Balzac,
Rivette depicts the making of the masterpiece as a revitalization of the energies of an artist who is well past his prime, but he makes the experience
equally transformative for the model (who, as if inverting James Joyce's 1922

novel *Ulysses*, ends the film with the word "no"), and he adjusts the references to the past so that they resonate autobiographically with his own artistic itinerary. Early in the film, Porbus mentions that the last book about Frenhofer was published in 1974, the crest line for Rivette's most creatively fertile period. Liz later asserts that ten years ago Frenhofer "quit searching, just when you should have gone all the way," much as Rivette largely abandoned his radical formal experiments after completing *Le Pont du nord* in 1981, a decade before *La Belle Noiseuse*. In this respect, *La Belle Noiseuse*, which includes several visual references to previous films, can be seen as the supreme manifestation of Rivette's retrospective turn, and also as an explanation for the shift in his approach.

Frenhofer helps explain his decision to retreat from his innovative path when he says that if he "goes the whole way, there's blood on the canvas." In May 1990—shortly before he began shooting *La Belle Noiseuse*—Rivette reviewed and completed postproduction on the thirteen-hour cut of *Out 1*, removing a sequence in which Jean-Pierre Léaud has an unstaged nervous breakdown onscreen in the process.[124] Editor Nicole Lubtchansky mentioned in an interview that Rivette's directorial method in *Out 1* was designed to push improvisation to precisely this point: "In *Out*, one saw the terrified look of Bulle [Ogier] toward the camera—one knew that she was panicked, that she did not know what to do, but Jacques did not say 'Cut.' He always waited until something else happened, even if the scene was scripted."[125] Two adults other than Frenhofer see the finished canvas in *La Belle Noiseuse*, and their reactions make it clear that the painter had succeeded in his objective, that he had used his medium to visualize the true essence of his subject. Within the quasi-religious ethics of art-making expressed in the film, and adopted by Rivette at the same moment, that sort of revelation is the unique achievement of an intense artistic exchange; because it exposes deeply private truths, it needs to remain a secret. By cutting around the canvas and refusing to provide the countershots to the images of Liz and Marianne looking, Rivette tantalizes the viewer, who, after four hours, surely expects to be shown the completed canvas. All that is revealed is a brief glimpse of legs against a red background, the equivalent of Balzac's vestigial foot and just enough to make it clear that this painting differs from the blue-covered one shown at the end. "Blood" may indeed be on this canvas, but the "resurrection" it represents remains invisible to those not prepared for it, as the indifferent response of the young Magali (who helps bury the painting in the wall) demonstrates. Frenhofer declares that it "is Titian [he has] done," and his *Belle Noiseuse* functions as a modernist *Noli me tangere*, emphasizing questions of belief and process rather than visual evidence.

Balzac's Frenhofer is a slightly mad idealist who has taken his artistic vocabulary so far that it appears incomprehensible to everyone else. Whether or not this makes him a visionary, Frenhofer does embody, in his total dedication, the Romantic conception of artistic genius, an idea that in *La Belle Noiseuse* is viewed through the coolly abstracted lens of twentieth-century modernism. For Rivette, the great paragon of this dynamic is Stravinsky, whom he includes on the soundtrack in *La Belle Noiseuse*, for the first and only time.[126] In one scene midway through, Magali is shown dancing to a passage from *Pétrouchka* (1911), but it is *Agon* (1957), which is used in the opening and closing credits, that is most important to the film. Originally a collaboration with George Balanchine, the plotless *Agon* abstractly depicts the relationship between artist and model, with erotic tension manifesting itself in the shift from strenuous tension to fluid movement. In *Agon*, the third in a series of ballets thematically focused on Greek mythology, Stravinsky stands on the cusp of atonality, fusing the seething, full-bodied musical texture of his early work with aspects of twelve-tone musical composition and complementing both with elaborate physical movements derived from seventeenth-century court dances. Appropriately, *La Belle Noiseuse* includes several scenes in which characters pass through large rooms, move apart, and assemble in shifting groups, with the lateral movements of the camera balancing out the circular movements of the figures within, much like the form of a Baroque sarabande. Space is stretched and expanded by the positioning of characters at diagonal ends of the frame, and, as in the Stravinsky ballet, it becomes an arena within which an array of male-female relationships, mythological or Christological narratives, and formal issues are worked out. The title of *Agon* refers at one and the same time to a contest, a conflict, or the Holy Agony, and by including it Rivette puts his film in dialogue with the paradigms of musical modernism.[127] Like *Agon, La Belle Noiseuse* is a work that goes backward in order to go forward, opening into radical newness by integrating artistic tradition and depicting art-making as a struggle in which both everything and nothing happens.

{ 4 }

The Sense of an Ending

JEAN-LUC GODARD'S *HISTOIRE(S) DU CINÉMA*

The Gods have not returned. "They have never left us."
They have not returned.

—EZRA POUND, CANTO CXIII (1969)[1]

And yet it might prove worth while to take up the theme of the
Aetna-song again in order that now, having more knowledge, more
earnestness, more perception than formerly, one could spy on the
limping smith in the demon-infested, iron depths of his smithy, blind
from the glare of the underworld, nevertheless able, by virtue of this
blindness—oh, the blindness of the singer—to see the splendor of the
ultimate heights: Prometheus embodied in Vulcan—redemption in the
form of calamity.

—HERMANN BROCH, *THE DEATH OF VIRGIL* (1945)[2]

A catastrophe is the first strophe of a love poem.

—JEAN-LUC GODARD[3]

Nouvelle vague *(Jean-Luc Godard, 1990).*

Approximately one minute before the end of the final section (*Les Signes parmi nous*, 4B) of *Histoire(s) du cinéma* (1988–1998), Jean-Luc Godard's meditation on the mutual imbrications of history and cinema in the twentieth century, the inimitable voice of Ezra Pound appears on the soundtrack, reading a section from the first of his *Cantos* (1915–1972):

> But first Elpenor came, our friend Elpenor,
> Unburied, cast on the wide earth,
> Limbs that we left in the house of Circe
> Unwept, unwrapped in sepulchre, since toils urged other.
> Pitiful spirit.[4]

This is the first time either Pound or Elpenor had been referred to, and no immediate explanation is given for the inclusion of this excerpt, which is accompanied by a clip from Orson Welles' *Othello* (1952) and preceded by four images linked together by cuts and superimpositions. Taken as discrete units, none of these seemingly unrelated (and unlabeled) images—a close-up of a man's eye from *Mr. Arkadin* (Orson Welles, 1955), a still photograph of a human eye about to be sliced from *Un chien andalou* (Luis Buñuel and Salvador Dali, 1929), a shot of an editor cutting a strip of film, and a shot of Godard in profile (both taken from *JLG/JLG—Self-Portrait in December*, 1994)—helps to elucidate the enigmatic text. Viewed as elements of an elaborate audiovisual montage chain, however, they suggest that Pound's carefully enunciated words could be indirectly linked to the structure of filmmaking and to Godard's project. Like Godard, Pound is invested in stitching together different ideas and periods, using the spectral encounter between Odysseus and his dead friend Elpenor to reflect upon the ways in which the ghosts of the past endure into the present, as manifested through a language that is informed by historical experience. After all, as Pound makes clear at the end of the canto, his words are a translation of a translation of *The Odyssey* (Homer, eighth century BCE), rendered according to the conventions of Old English verse.[5] Godard's mode of quotation throughout *Histoire(s) du cinéma* is similarly aggregate, intermixing images, sounds, and texts stripped from their original contexts and reintegrated into a new matrix. Often this entails the collage-like layering of disparate materials, but sometimes this occurs through transposition, as in the moment in the preceding section (*Le Contrôle de l'univers*, 4A) when Alain Cuny recites a long text on Rembrandt by Élie Faure that Godard has refashioned as a reflection on cinema.[6] Godard's repositioning of the Pound extract makes it, too, resonate with larger ideas of cinema, connecting Elpenor—the forgotten friend of Odysseus who died "unwept, unburied" and begs to be remembered—to his elegiac lament for his medium not through simplistic metaphor, but through a dense weave of implied associations that steadily accumulate gravity even as they resist fixed, unitary meaning.

The Pound reading is only one of hundreds of extracts packed within the thirty-eight minutes of *Les Signes parmi nous* (4B), which is only a small section of an eight-part magnum opus. Lasting for nearly four and a half hours in its entirety, *Histoire(s) du cinéma* has the following structure (dates listed are based on the first public exhibition of individual sections; Godard continued to make modifications after these initial screenings and the formal completion date for the entire work is 1998):

1. *Toutes les histoires* (1A, *All the Histories*, 1988, 51 minutes)
2. *Une histoire seule* (1B, *A Single History*, 1988, 42 minutes)
3. *Seul le cinéma* (2A, *Only Cinema*, 1994, 26 minutes)
4. *Fatale beauté* (2B, *Deadly Beauty*, 1994, 28 minutes)
5. *La Monnaie de l'absolu* (3A, *The Currency of the Absolute*, 1995, 27 minutes)
6. *Une vague nouvelle* (3B, *A New Wave*, 1995, 27 minutes)
7. *Le Contrôle de l'univers* (4A, *The Control of the Universe*, 1997, 27 minutes)
8. *Les Signes parmi nous* (4B, *The Signs Among Us*, 1997, 38 minutes)

Although Pound is rarely mentioned as an influence on the overall conception of *Histoire(s) du cinéma*, there are striking and highly revealing affinities between it and the *Cantos*. Other critics, notably Colin MacCabe and Jonathan Rosenbaum, have pointed instead to another modernist landmark—James Joyce's *Finnegans Wake* (1939)—as a model, but despite Godard's obvious and professed interest in Joyce's work (made especially evident when the Jean-Paul Belmondo character in *Pierrot le fou*, 1965, talks of succeeding where Joyce failed and writing a novel that would be about "what goes on between people"), their longest works offer very different experiences.[7] Joyce's final novel is a torrential overflow of description that seems to move in ever-expanding and never-ending circles whose shape is only clear at the end. The constant superimposition in *Histoire(s) du cinéma* sometimes gives the impression of seamless flow, but this is invariably interrupted by the startling juxtapositions in the montage (like the pairing of the magnified eye from *Mr. Arkadin* with the sliced eye of *Un chien andalou*), preventing the viewer from ever becoming fully acclimated to the jarring rhythms of the work.

Like the *Cantos*, and unlike *Finnegans Wake*, there are also a number of relatively clear, discursive passages in *Histoire(s) du cinéma*, which provide points around which the whirlwind of associations can momentarily coalesce. Where Pound fixates on details of political economy, Godard focuses on twentieth-century history and especially the cataclysm of World War II, but they both work through thinly veiled autobiography, making frequent references to friends who are fellow artists, and adopting a retrospective approach in which earlier moments of personal history are recalled and held up against the chaotic uncertainty of the present.[8] Pound's emphasis on the precise meaning and "thingness" of words is paralleled by Godard's stress on "*juste*" images, and the momentum of both the *Cantos* and *Histoire(s) du cinéma* is driven by the accretion of fragments grouped into fluid arrangements, "vortices," that echo back and forth across the body of the work.[9] In a 1913 essay, Pound compared the poetic "epic to a temple, the *Commedia* [Dante's *Divine Comedy*, 1308–1322] to a cathedral," and later defined his goal as the creation of a "poem containing history."[10] Godard had a similarly exalted conception of his cinematic epic and a comparable obsession with shattered ideals, with Pound's invocations of lost civilizations (Ithaca, Renaissance Venice, Byzantium) occupying a position in the *Cantos* that is roughly equivalent to Godard's explicit portrayal of cinema as the lost "utopia" of the twentieth century.[11]

Godard's project also resembles Pound's insofar as they are both long-form works made over an extended period of time without an end in sight, continually expanding works-in-progress publicly released in provisional forms before reaching their final, never entirely stable, states. Pound began the *Cantos* during World War I, and they ended only with his death more than fifty years later (the "definitive" version was compiled posthumously).[12] Godard worked intensively on the *Histoire(s) du cinéma* project for approximately ten years between 1988 and 1998, but it had been gestating for more than a decade before that and continues to inform his subsequent work, with films and videos like *Les Enfants jouent à la Russie* (1993), *The Origins of the 21st Century* (2000), *Liberté et patrie* (2002), and even the montages at the beginning of *Notre musique* (2004) and the end of *Film socialisme* (2010) acting as more specialized addenda or "annexes."[13] Although Godard had been considering a film historical work since the early 1970s (and had developed early versions of some of his later montage strategies in films like *La Chinoise*, 1967, and *Le Gai Savoir*, 1968), the immediate impetus for what became *Histoire(s) du cinéma* was a proposed collaboration with Henri Langlois that ended with his abrupt death in 1977.[14] Langlois had invested most of his energy in the 1970s on the creation of a Museum of Cinema. As part of that initiative, he arranged an exhibition at the Palais des congrès in March 1974 entitled "Paris à travers le cinéma, de Louis Lumière à Jean-Luc Godard," which included a twelve-hour compilation film made up of excerpts from nearly two hundred representative works.[15] Godard was impressed by Langlois' compilation, and it helped generate ideas for a film-based history of cinema, which he initially wanted to call, after André Malraux, *The Metamorphosis of the Gods*.[16]

"Cogito ergo video"

> There is a kind of poetry . . . which begins as satire in the absolute
> difference of ideal and real, hovers in between as elegy, and ends as
> idyll with the absolute identity of the two . . . this sort of poetry should

unite the transcendental raw materials and preliminaries of a theory of
poetic creativity—often met with in modern poets—with the artistic
reflection and beautiful self-mirroring that is present in . . . the lyric
fragments of the Greeks, in the classical elegy, and, among the mod-
erns, in Goethe. In all its descriptions, this poetry should describe
itself, and always be simultaneously poetry and the poetry of poetry.

— FRIEDRICH SCHLEGEL, ATHENAEUM FRAGMENT 238 (1798)[17]

The short-lived project Godard and Langlois committed to in 1976 was supported by producer Jean-Pierre Rassam and would have been released as
both a film and a series of videocassettes.[18] Langlois had been giving lectures
on film history at Concordia University in Montreal, and when he died in
1977, Godard agreed to take his place.[19] In the preface to the published version of these lectures, *Introduction à une véritable histoire du cinéma*, Godard
speaks as if this was a failed effort, but he has subsequently identified the
1978 Montreal lectures and the resulting book as a key step in the development of what would eventually become *Histoire(s) du cinéma*.[20] Godard
met with representatives from the International Federation of Film Archives
(FIAF), trying to persuade them to make their collections available for his
use, and he announced in 1980 that he would make "in the form of a film,
the *Introduction à une véritable histoire du cinéma*, showing the unknown
aspects of this history: first aspect, to see the cinema more than to read it.
It is the only history that one can see."[21] As Michael Witt has documented,
Godard persuaded the Rotterdam Arts Foundation to invest in his developing film history project, and he conducted several associated seminars there
in 1980 and 1981.[22] Reports in journals like *Variety* indicated that Godard was
now working on a "history of the cinema in images being done for a Dutch
foundation"; at the 1983 Venice Film Festival, Godard instead declared that
he was pursuing his history of cinema project in collaboration with Canal
Plus in France.[23] Contracts were signed with the emerging television network in 1984.[24]

The fact that a monument to, and eulogy for, the history of cinema was
made on video and supported by financing from a television network is not
the least of *Histoire(s) du cinéma*'s ironies. Although Godard has been one
of the most trenchant critics of television for decades, he has made a number of films—including the militant "Groupe Dziga Vertov" films of the late
1960s and early 1970s—at least partially with funding from television networks or with the promise of television exhibition in mind. In the late 1970s,
he even embarked on a pair of multipart analyses of French society made, in
collaboration with his partner Anne-Marie Miéville, for the newly formed
Institut national de l'audiovisuel (INA): first, *Six fois deux (Sur et sous la communication)* (1976, twelve programs totaling approximately ten hours) and

then *France/tour/détour/deux/enfants* (1979, twelve "movements" totaling approximately five hours).[25] The former interrogates the nature and function of mass media, while the latter, organized around a series of interview-based dialogues with children, directly addresses the structure of television by parodying many of its conventions. Hoping to subvert the medium from within, Godard continued to make self-critical meditations intended for public broadcast throughout the 1980s—primarily short video works, but also *Grandeur et décadence d'un petit commerce de cinéma* (1986), a metafictional feature about the creation of a TV movie in the vein of *Contempt* (1963).

Since the mid-1970s, the period in which he moved his studio from Grenoble to Rolle, Switzerland, Godard's depictions of television, and his descriptions of it in interviews, have become increasingly caustic and despairing.[26] *Comment ça va?* (codirected with Miéville, 1978) includes a scene in which television is compared to a cancerous infestation, an idea elaborated further in a 1982 interview in which Godard calls television "a mutation" and "the great defeat."[27] Godard later describes his 1985 feature *Détective* as "a film shot . . . under the Occupation of the cinema by television and all kinds of magazines," a point he makes onscreen near the beginning of *Soft and Hard: A Soft Conversation on Hard Subjects* (codirected with Miéville, 1986), a work "made in the epoch of television."[28]

What most differentiates the cinema and television, in Godard's view, is the fact of projection, which he consistently differentiates from televisual diffusion.[29] As he explains in *Soft and Hard*, with cinema "one projects oneself" on the screen, while television projects itself upon the spectator.[30] The Godard of the 1980s, in other words, inverts the presumptions of the "apparatus theory" that had emerged simultaneously with the Maoist-Althusserian rhetoric of the Groupe Dziga Vertov films: television, which is "all powerful, like royalty, like the Church during the Middle Ages," exerts an almost fascistic control over the viewer's imagination, whereas the distance between viewer and screen in the cinema creates the possibility of an authentic and liberating engagement with the projected image.[31] What is lost under television's influence is "the proper part of the film, that is to say the image, [which] has diminished greatly."[32] The pre–*Histoire(s) du cinéma* work that is most explicit about this is the underrated *King Lear* (1987), a film made, as William Shakespeare the Fifth explains in the film, "in a time now where movies and more generally art have been lost and must somehow be reinvented." To help make this possible, Professor Pluggy—played by Godard in the self-deprecating, director-as-mad-jester style he adopted throughout the 1980s—tries repeatedly to demonstrate the true nature of cinema and the cinematic image, at one point using small models and a mock theater to simulate the effect of projection. Godard has repeatedly argued that cinema is the last art with direct ties to a representational approach originating in ancient Greece, and the movie theater is presented here as a reconstructed version of Plato's cave, a unique type of space where the light "must come from the back," with its reflection off the screen enabling alert viewers to see glimpses of otherwise hidden realities.[33]

With projection and the spectatorial receptivity that goes with it, this idea of cinema can survive even if "films" are produced and exhibited only on video.[34] Although more than half of his work since 1970 has been done using one video format or another, Godard has long remained ambivalent about video, which was depicted as having a Cain-and-Abel-like relationship with film in *Every Man for Himself* (1980).[35] He has nevertheless tried to constructively utilize each new technical development, mixing 16mm and video material in *Ici et ailleurs* (codirected with Jean-Pierre Gorin, 1970–1976) and *Comment ça va?*, filming live video monitors with a 35mm camera in *Numéro deux* (1975) and *Passion* (1982), and producing a series of video "scenarios" to accompany many of the features made during the 1980s. *In Praise of Love* (2001) dialectically relates both poles of this dynamic by setting the luminous, 35mm black-and-white footage of Paris in the first half against the heavily oversaturated video palette of the second half, and ending with a jerky and pixelated digital homage to the Lumières that points, with characteristic ambiguity, toward cinema's capacity for perpetual renewal.

Video dilutes the projected image, drastically reducing its tonal range, but it also makes it much easier to interrelate different sorts of imagery, the primary reason Godard employed it for *Histoire(s) du cinéma*. Film prints were screened before each of Godard's Montreal lectures, but the process was too cumbersome to facilitate a direct dialogue with particular scenes or aspects of the films in question, which is one reason he regarded the enterprise as a partial failure.[36] Shortly thereafter, Godard began collecting videocassettes; he could barely stand to watch them, but they would make it possible for him to extract small segments of different films.[37] He later hired two assistants to help with the acquisition and cataloging of the nearly three thousand tapes he consulted, and to teach him the video-editing techniques he would need to complete all the necessary work manually. As Godard explained, "In 35mm, this project would have been impossible to realize. With video, one can erase the canvas and begin again. By hand, by *instinct*."[38]

What would have made 35mm work impossible was the expensive and time-consuming lab work required for the reprinting of all the individual excerpts from celluloid back to celluloid. Video editing made the selection and juxtaposition of disparate footage much simpler, but, despite the density of many of his superimpositions, Godard restricted himself to a limited number of (largely) analog-based editing options and was not being disingenuous when he claimed that he worked primarily with techniques that have been around since the time of [Georges] Méliès.[39] Indeed, the project is intended to resist the amnesiac teleology of "the digital," in which, as Godard explained, "modern democracies turn technical thought into a separate domain" and thereby "incline towards totalitarianism."[40] He has insisted that, unlike video, new media forms derive from information technology. By contrast, "*Histoire(s)* was cinema" precisely because of the possibility of, and connection to, projection.[41]

While Godard was making *Histoire(s) du cinéma*, individual sections were transferred to 35mm and screened in that format at festivals and cinematheques as they became available.[42] Regardless of whether they are viewed in 35mm or on video, however, the second-degree nature of the imagery is readily apparent, amplified by the extreme fragmentation and overlapping of the source material. This is counterbalanced by the use of techniques, such as the flicker-like alternation of images and black screen or the insertion of the clattering sounds of a film projector, that evoke the memory of an older, more intense form of cinematic experience by simulating some of its peripheral effects. The periodic recurrence of these and other devices helps give *Histoire(s) du cinéma* a sense of overall structural cohesion that separates it from his earlier, more explicitly televisual, series-based video works.[43] Although the eight sections of *Histoire(s) du cinéma* could be watched individually—and indeed, as draft elements, that is how they were initially presented—it was designed as an integral work, the only genuinely long-form project by a director whose features typically run for eighty to one hundred minutes.[44] This long-form structure gives Godard room to integrate a narrative of death and rebirth both within the work as a whole and within the dialectically paired sections. The atrocities detailed in *Toutes les histoires* (1A) pave the way for the theological arguments of *Une histoire seule* (1B), much as the discussion of nineteenth-century modernist painting in *La Monnaie de l'absolu* (3A) anticipates the comments about the French New Wave in *Une vague nouvelle* (3B), while the analysis of its precursors in *Le Contrôle de l'univers* (4A) sets the stage for the retrospective melancholy of *Les Signes parmi nous* (4B).

Getting *Histoire(s) du cinéma* into this finished form was, however, evidently a problem for the man who famously said that films should have "a beginning, a middle, and an end, but not necessarily in that order."[45] After the entire work was completed, Godard referred to the final, eight-part structure as if it had been predetermined, but the plan changed repeatedly over time.[46] Both *Toutes les histoires* (1A) and *Une histoire seule* (1B) run for approximately fifty minutes, as per the original agreement with Canal Plus. They were premiered at the Cannes Film Festival and then exhibited on the network in May 1989, with additional support from rival network FR3.[47] There was then a gap of several years before additional sections, all running for less than thirty minutes except for *Les Signes parmi nous* (4B), were completed. La Sept (now Arte) was briefly involved, but eventually almost the entire project fell under the auspices of Gaumont, thanks to the ardent support of production head Nicolas Seydoux, who felt that a studio with the longevity of his should fund at least one noncommercial project like Godard's.[48] Seydoux agreed not only to finance the remaining parts of the project, but also to coproduce the accompanying book (released by the prestigious Gallimard) and to make the company's catalog accessible, which is undoubtedly one of the reasons why a large percentage of the French film excerpts are from Gaumont titles.

The original schema appears to have remained in place for several years because an outline published when the Museum of Modern Art mounted the 1992 exhibition *Jean-Luc Godard: Son + Image, 1974–1991* lists ten sections.[49] These ten titles also appear sequentially in the background of later sections in the final version of *Histoire(s) du cinéma*. Godard claimed that he could have continued to expand the series for two more decades, and ending it clearly took an act of will (along with pressure from Gaumont).[50] *Histoire(s) du cinéma* was screened as a unit in September 1997 at the Ciné Lumière in London, and the "final" version officially debuted in November 1998. Godard made modifications throughout this period, and he created handmade copies of several paintings to circumvent rights complications.[51] He continued to edit the project even after its completion, allegedly making minor adjustments of various kinds before its release (by Gaumont) on DVD in 2007. In 2004, certain sections were also condensed and reworked into a 35mm feature film, *Moments choisis des Histoire(s) du cinéma*.

In a fundamental way, this sense of *Histoire(s) du cinéma* remaining open and in process is profoundly connected to Godard's overall artistic framework. Many of Godard's earliest films have titles (such as *Une femme mariée: Fragments d'un film tourné en 1964 en noir et blanc*, 1964) that suggest a predilection for unfinished movements and unresolved gestures, an active dynamism that privileges exploratory initiations over definitive conclusions. Godard makes an uncredited cameo appearance in Éric Rohmer's first feature, *The Sign of Leo* (1959), as a man who listens repeatedly to the opening movement of a Beethoven piece, compulsively restarting the record every few seconds, and he does much the same thing in many of these early films. Whether or not the source of the music is shown onscreen, Godard regularly interspersed brief fragments of classical music throughout his 1960s films, often from the beginning of a movement.[52] Although he sometimes used Mozart, Godard usually relied upon one of the middle- or late-period Beethoven string quartets, with their sophisticated call-and-response structures, sometimes working this into the fabric of the films by restarting a piece from the moment it had been left off fifteen or twenty minutes before. This created a form of continuing dialogue that Godard extended further by reusing some of the same pieces in subsequent films, connecting them not simply with their own histories as artworks, but also with their use in previous Godard films. When sustained passages of the same quartet (Beethoven's String Quartet Number 16, opus 135, 1826) heard in pieces throughout *Two or Three Things I Know About Her* (1967) are performed live onscreen in *First*

Name: Carmen (1983), for example, the impression is of a musical dialogue played out across the entire corpus of the filmmaker.[53]

This same dialectic is also worked out in films such as *One + One* (*Sympathy for the Devil*, 1968), one of the many Godard works that deconstructs artistic production while also endowing the creative process itself with vital force. Sinuous tracking shots of the Rolling Stones rehearsing the titular song in a large studio space are continually interrupted by sequences representing political events happening outside (often filmed in lateral, rather than circular, pans), as if Godard was trying to momentarily grab hold of a contemporaneity, an artistic and political present, that is always slipping away. Here too, Godard insisted on leaving the film open, cutting to black without ever allowing the complete song to play through and pulling his name off the film after the producer added it to most release prints.[54] As the first full feature completed after Godard announced the first of his many retreats from filmmaking (1967's *Weekend* having ended with a title card reading "*Fin de cinema*"), *One + One* was a sort of new beginning and—like *Numéro deux* in the 1970s, *Every Man for Himself* in the 1980s, *In Praise of Love* in the 2000s, and *Film socialisme* in the 2010s—it speaks to a yearning for reinvention that complements the structural trajectory of the individual films.

Godard's insistence on an unending oscillation between destruction and reconstruction both within and between his films puts him fully in line with the Romantic poetics espoused by Friedrich Schlegel in the *Athenaeum Fragments*.[55] These influences have been underrecognized in the critical literature, but they are evident even in Godard's earliest work; the first script he completed and pitched to producer Pierre Braunberger was an adaptation of Goethe's *Elective Affinities* (1809), which Braunberger estimated would have run for at least five hours.[56] Godard's criticism in this same period frequently includes incongruous statements like the assertion that cinema is "a perpetual aesthetic inauguration" (in a 1958 review of a Frank Tashlin comedy), and the films themselves are replete with narratively gratuitous shots of natural landscapes, some of which include observers positioned in accordance with the iconographic tradition of the *Rückenfigur* (figures 4.1–4.2).[57] There is even a scene a few minutes into *Breathless* (1960) where the protagonist turns to the camera and speaks in praise of mountains and the sea. By the time he repudiated and "remade" *Breathless* for the first time with *Pierrot le fou*, Godard expressed a desire to film "the presence of nature, which is neither romantic nor tragic."[58] Although this is in keeping with the growing turn toward epistemological questions in his work, it is undermined by the many shots that seem to luxuriate in natural idylls and even by the director's own description of the film as the story of "the last romantic couple" done in the tradition of *La Nouvelle Heloïse* (Jean-Jacques Rousseau, 1761) or *The Sorrows of Young Werther* (Goethe, 1774).[59] In a fascinating 1966 interview with Robert Bresson, Godard argued that "to be an actor is to be romantic, and not to be an actor,

FIGURE 4.1 Contempt *(Jean-Luc Godard, 1963)*.

classical," explaining that the former mode involved the "sublime" and could represent "a certain kind of poetry" that could be creatively mixed with other cinematic elements.[60]

Seeming contradictions are precisely that. Nothing in Godard's work is ever straightforward or unidirectional, and each film always includes or strives for its opposite, dialectically interrelating different stylistic devices (long takes broken up by jump cuts, extended tracks intercut with handheld camera work), intellectual impulses, and points of view. A portrait of Novalis is pierced with an arrow by the student radical played by Jean-Pierre Léaud in *La Chinoise*, but the third section of the film includes onscreen text spelling out the French titles for Goethe's two *Wilhelm Meister* novels, ironically linking the character to the paradigmatic Romantic Bildungsroman (a work whose publication Schlegel saw as comparable in importance to the French Revolution).[61] In the same year, Godard released *Two or Three Things I Know About Her*, the most essayistic of his works up to that point and a film focused almost entirely on the urban landscape of Paris, as well as *Weekend*, most of which takes place in pastoral settings. The scene in *Weekend* where Léaud appears as Saint-Just reading speeches from the late eighteenth century in the middle of a landscape sets the tone for many of the films that follow. This late-1960s return to origins is framed by the ideas of Rousseau, whose *Émile, or On Education* (1762) was the basis for *Le Gai Savoir*, a film made in "Year Zero." Although this was probably intended as a reference to Roberto Rossellini's film about postwar Germany (*Germany Year Zero*, 1948), it also suggests the postrevolutionary France of the late eighteenth century and its attempts to recalibrate the Gregorian calendar.[62]

This holds equally true for the didactic Groupe Dziga Vertov films that began that year and lasted until 1972. In the late 1960s and the 1970s, these films were held up by some critics and theorists as the paragon of collaborative, progressive filmmaking, ideologically minded projects in which the Romantic artist had been displaced by a collective.[63] Yet if these films were

FIGURE 4.2   Chalk Cliffs on Rügen *(Caspar David Friedrich, 1818–1819; photograph © bpk, Berlin / Museum Oskar Reinhart am Stadtgarten, Winterthur, Switzerland / Hermann Buresch / Art Resource, NY).*

so genuinely "authorless," why is it that Godard appears before the camera so frequently in *Vladimir and Rosa* (1970), that his voice can be heard so distinctly during the Marxist-Leninist debate of *Wind from the East* (1970)?[64] Moreover, if these films represent such a radical break with the past, why do they, like *Weekend* and for that matter *Pierrot le fou*, repeatedly depict characters wandering through beautiful landscapes, discussing contemporary political issues such as women's rights by referencing the French Revolution?[65] This is Marxism read through the lens of early Romanticism, and Godard belatedly recognized it as such, telling a journalist for the *New York Times* in 1992 that this period was, for him, "political romanticism. I loved Mao as I loved Goethe."[66] In both *Détective* and *Hélas pour moi* (1993), Romanticism is defined through a passage from the end of Joseph Conrad's *Lord Jim* (1900) in which the expression of moral conviction engenders belief.[67] Godard's notion of Romanticism is, in this sense, very close to that of influential poet and essayist Charles Péguy, who argued that an idealizing *mystique* united Catholicism and revolutionary republicanism (Péguy is mentioned by name in both *In Praise of Love* and *Histoire(s) du cinéma*).[68]

Romanticism, connected to his own youth and adolescence, would take on a fresh meaning for Godard during the years of historical and personal reflection that culminated in *Histoire(s) du cinéma*. The creation of *Germany Year 90 Nine Zero* (1991)—an exploration of post-unification Germany that functions as both a sequel to *Alphaville* (1965) and a pendant to the then ongoing *Histoire(s) du cinéma* project—seems to have brought these allegiances to the fore (figures 4.3–4.4). In a 2001 interview with Alexander Kluge, Godard described the biographical significance of the film:

> With [*Germany Year 90 Nine Zero*], I came to terms with my youth, which was molded by my father. I later discovered that my father loved Germany very much and had lived there, but I didn't know that at the time. As a young man, I discovered the German Romantics. I even read books that people don't read anymore—Novalis, Jean Paul, [Jakob Michael Reinhold] Lenz, [Clemens] Brentano, [Gerhard] Kurz, all of them. The German Romantics moved something in me, more than the French did. In a way, I think I paid a debt I owed to Germany by making that film.[69]

The twentieth-century French intellectual traditions with which Godard, the son of a Swiss father and a French Protestant mother, has aligned himself are inextricably bound with his experience of early German Romanticism. In 1994, he explained that he was "very influenced by German Romanticism" as a

FIGURE 4.3 Germany Year 90 Nine Zero *(Jean-Luc Godard, 1991).*

FIGURE 4.4 Riverbed in the Fog *(Caspar David Friedrich, 1820, Wallraf-Richartz-Museum, Cologne; photograph © Rheinisches Bildarchiv Köln).*

child: "It was Novalis or the young Goethe that made me know Sartre."[70] The proposal for the cinematic "self-portrait" he made that year, *JLG/JLG—Self-Portrait in December*, is even more explicit: "Remember the author of *Nausea* [Jean-Paul Sartre, 1938], but also of *Cahiers pour une morale* [Jean-Paul Sartre, 1983], Jean-Paul, like he of the *Confessions* [Jean-Jacques Rousseau, 1782], and like the German Romantic [Jean Paul], all having nourished me: a man, nothing but a man, who is worth one and who is worth all."[71]

Sartre aside, the central mediating figure for Godard throughout this period was Malraux. Godard has been quoting Malraux since the 1950s and the art historical method developed and practiced in his three-volume book *The Psychology of Art* (1947–1949)—in which forms from widely different cultures and periods are compared with one another in an "imaginary museum" made possible by photographic reproductions—is the most overt model for the historical juxtapositions in *Histoire(s) du cinéma*.[72] In a few cases, Godard even selects the same images used by Malraux, although his own comparisons place less emphasis on morphological similarities than on the historical transformation of particular approaches to image-making. Malraux was equally central as the avatar of a certain type of politically engaged, twentieth-century Romantic humanism; from him, Godard also adopted an idea of art born, like fire, from what it consumes, which resonates very strongly with the writings of Schlegel.[73] Variations of this appear in many of the films made during the period Godard was developing *Histoire(s) du cinéma*, and with it came a new poetics of fire that, like the idea of projection, finds its clearest cinematic expression in *King Lear*. In a scene that includes at least one visual reference to the final sequence of Andrei Tarkovsky's *Nostalghia* (1983), Professor Pluggy explains that art "is born and it is burnt. It begins from the thing it ends. At the same time. Birth and death, linked, like mouth and breath. . . . It is born from what it destroys."[74] At several other moments in the film, the flame of a candle is held up against darkened reproductions of paintings by Francisco de Goya and Rembrandt, a form of citation that would become central to *Histoire(s) du cinéma*.[75] As in *Nostalghia*, where the simple act of carrying a continuously burning candle across a drained pool in a single unbroken take is treated as a redemptive act, Godard suggests that in a world where the conviction in art has been lost, the cinema alone retains the power to cast light.[76]

"Montage, My Fine Care"

My films are of the present and of myths.
—JEAN-LUC GODARD (1995)[77]

Underpinning Godard's late work generally, and *Histoire(s) du cinéma* in particular, is an idiosyncratic and expanded notion of montage. For Godard, "montage" refers not simply to the connections between, or even within, shots, but to a mode of vision and experience that lies dormant in raw footage and needs to be discovered through the process of selection and sequencing that is the foundation of the filmmaker's art. In a 1989 lecture to the film school La Fémis, Godard explained this in Malrucian terms, "In montage, one encounters destiny."[78] Godard had used similar language in the most well-known of his early essays, "Montage, My Fine Care" (1956), where he writes that editing "can restore to actuality that ephemeral grace neglected by both snob and film-lover, or can transform chance into destiny."[79] In both cases, montage is described using organic metaphors ("a heart-beat," "something soft, having time to breathe") and is specifically connected to existential notions of choice, the decisive acts through which the freedom of shooting is converted into the fixed structure of a projectable film, but the contrasts are equally revealing.[80]

In 1956, montage is presented as an aspect of temporal construction that is inseparable from mise en scène: "Knowing just how long one can make a scene last is already montage, just as thinking about transitions is part of the problem of shooting."[81] Godard also isolates one particular use of the brief shot that he sees as fundamental to cinema, the use of glances:

Cutting on a look is almost the definition of montage, its supreme ambition as well as its submission to mise en scène. It is, in effect, to bring out the soul under the spirit, the passion behind the intrigue, to make the heart prevail over the intelligence by destroying the notion of space in favour of that of time.[82]

The example Godard provides is the sequence at the Royal Albert Music Hall in Alfred Hitchcock's remake of *The Man Who Knew Too Much* (1956). In his review of Hitchcock's *The Wrong Man* (1956) several months later, Godard once again underscores the interdependence of mise en scène and montage, but he places special emphasis on the use of long close-ups in which Henry Fonda stares "abstractedly, pondering, thinking, being."[83] What Godard finds extraordinary in them is their ability to "convey the basic data of consciousness," something they can do precisely because they happen within the normal shot/countershot syntax of classical narrative cinema, a system in which montage is a constitutive but unprivileged element.[84]

Pensive close-ups play an equally important role in *Breathless*, and Godard would soon prove to be one of the cinema's great portraitists, especially of women. In film after film, Godard includes strikingly framed shots of faces held long past the point at which they serve any explicit narrative or dramatic function. These lingering images may have the quality of loving affection (as in many of the portrait shots of Anna Karina in the films of the early 1960s), ethnographic probing, or both, but they almost always depict people in the act of thinking (figure 4.5). The shots act as meditative pauses, contributing to the shifting rhythms of Godard's features, and the montage generally

FIGURE 4.5 *Nathalie Baye in* Détective *(Jean-Luc Godard, 1985).*

supplies a clear logic for their inclusion by grounding the characters in a particular space. In *Histoire(s) du cinéma*, Godard uses similar images, culled
from throughout the history of the arts, to demonstrate cinema's status as
the heir to a pictorial tradition that he (once again following Malraux) sees
as centered on the enigmatic figures of Édouard Manet (figure 4.6).[85] Excised
from their original contexts and divorced from their narrative motivation,
however, the close-ups of women looking in the *Histoire(s) du cinéma* function as an endless series of incomplete shot/countershots, malleable parts of
a continuing dialogue that testifies to the cinema's power to embalm beauty
and to be "a form that thinks," soliciting questions without ready answers.[86]

Indeed, by the 1980s, Godard's conception of montage had become altogether more ambitious and mysterious, a way of using intershot relationships
to create "something like [utopia]."[87] This notion of montage exceeds even
that of Sergei Eisenstein, who developed an increasingly inclusive notion of
montage that eventually encompassed the core of both European and East
Asian modes of representation and that he saw as the highest stage of artistic
development. For Godard, by contrast, montage is completely and even defi-
nitionally the property of the cinema: "The cinema is the invention of montage. And montage did not exist in the other arts."[88] Although Godard shares

FIGURE 4.6 *Detail of* Nana *(Édouard Manet, 1876–1877, Kunsthalle Hamburg) superimposed with text reading "I know what you are thinking" in* La Monnaie de l'absolu *(3A) of*
Histoire(s) du cinéma *(Jean-Luc Godard, 1988–1998).*

Eisenstein's investment in dialectical thinking, he breaks with his predecessor's conception of artistic progress, positing instead—in both *Histoire(s) du cinéma* and many of his interview comments—the idea of art engaged in a series of complex negotiations with a multilinear history. More than a synthesis, montage provides access to a new artistic space, a unique moment in which past, present, and future are able to cross-penetrate.[89] Embedded within this notion of montage is the possibility of organic creation, even of a sort of life-giving magic: "In montage, the object is living, while in shooting it is dead. It is necessary to resuscitate it. It is sorcery."[90]

As Godard's sense of montage becomes more vast, it also becomes more restrictive. In *Seul le cinéma* (2A), he tells Serge Daney that neither Eisenstein nor Welles had achieved a true montage; their discovery was the power of angles. He elaborated on this further in the lecture he gave in 1995 upon receipt of the Theodor Adorno Prize:

> Eisenstein himself found the angle, preceded by El Greco and [Edgar] Degas. When one looks at his famous images of three lions in *October* [1928; the lions are in Eisenstein's earlier *Battleship Potemkin*, 1925], if the three lions make an effect of montage, it is because there were three shot angles, not because there was a montage.[91]

In Godard's formulation, Eisenstein had mastered the mechanism of montage, but not its ultimate goal: the use of separate images to generate a synthetic Image, the one thing that montage alone can do. By the middle of the 1980s, this had become a mainstay of Godard's commentaries both within and outside the films and, as with his ideas of projection, it was expressed most directly in *King Lear*:

> The Image is a pure creation of the soul. It cannot be born of a comparison, but of a reconciliation of two realities that are more or less far apart. The more the connections between these two realities are distanced and true, the stronger they get to be, the more it will have emotive power. Two realities that have no connection cannot be drawn together usefully. There is no creation of an image. Two contrary realities will not come together. They oppose each other. One rarely obtains forces and power from these oppositions. . . . An image is not strong because it is brilliant or fantastic, but because the association of ideas is decent and true. The result that is obtained immediately controls the truth of the association. Analogy is a medium of creation; it is a resemblance of connections. The power or virtue of the creative image depends on the nature of these connections. What is great is not the image, but the emotion that it provokes. If the latter is great, one esteems the image at its measure. The emotion thus provoked is true because it is born outside of all imitation, all evocation, and all resemblance.

Versions of these ideas are included in *Passion, Keep Your Right Up* (1987), *JLG/JLG—Self-Portrait in December, Notre musique*, and *Les Signes parmi nous* (4B). The underlying principles are central to the aesthetics of his post-1980 work, suggesting a way to use implicit affinities or concordances to create new relationships out of diverse and even contradictory materials.

The central source for Godard's comments about the Image— unsurprisingly, never cited in any of the films or videos where it has appeared—is Pierre Reverdy. A poet with a penchant for mysticism, Reverdy was a friend of Pablo Picasso and Georges Braque who was championed by André Breton in the first "Manifesto of Surrealism."[92] Reverdy started and ran the journal *Nord-Sud*, which published a number of important Dadaist and Surrealist texts during its brief existence (from 1917 to 1918), including "L'Image," the poem that Godard borrows from in his discussions of montage.[93] That Godard's often repeated theory of the authentic Image has its roots in Surrealism reinforces its crucial place in his artistic genealogy. Godard shares with the Surrealists not only an interest in psychic disorientation and a puckish desire to upend the staid proprieties of middle-class culture, but also a commitment to transforming photographic realism from within, using it to facilitate the intuitive perception of a lyrical realm more unitary than the one we ordinarily inhabit.[94] In this sense, Godard's "Image" could be seen as a contemporary equivalent of the Surrealist "marvelous," which, in the words of Louis Aragon, is an "eruption of contradiction" that reveals the artificial character of rationalized reality.[95]

Reconciling these twin montage impulses—for Surrealist rupture and historical dialectics—within *Histoire(s) du cinéma*, and the related films and videos initiated in its wake, necessitated a radical reformulation of the space of the projected image. Godard's pre-1968 films provoked active engagement through the use of shock cuts, sudden alterations of arrangement or even structure that work only if the spatiotemporal coordinates of illusionistic representation are otherwise respected. A collage-like impression of overlapping layers was created by interspersing different materials, but they were invariably linked to the main body of the narrative through hard cuts (figure 4.7). The detritus of the outside world could thus be brought into the larger audiovisual frame of the film, but, despite all the intellectual pirouettes they evoked and the narrative friction they created, the basic documentary recording tendencies of the camera remained unchallenged by these juxtapositions. During his Groupe Dziga Vertov phase (1968–1972), Godard used a number of different techniques to represent the misperceptions of the viewer (splashing paint on the camera in *Wind from the East*, for example), but even the most strident and astringently confrontational of those films were still constructed primarily through the collision of discrete images and sounds. When different media were reflexively inserted within the same space as the "characters"—as in the use of advertising in films like *Made in USA* (1966) or

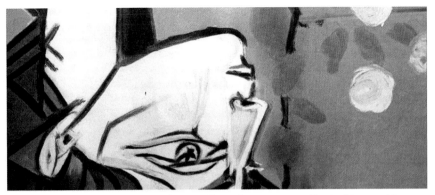

FIGURE 4.7 *Pablo Picasso's* Jacqueline aux fleurs *(1958, private collection) inverted in* Pierrot le fou *(Jean-Luc Godard, 1965).*

the use of video cameras in *Numéro deux*—the individual elements retained their relative autonomy (figure 4.8). It was only with the turn toward superimposition in *Histoire(s) du cinéma* that Godard could truly place "two realities that are more or less far apart" within the same contiguous space. Since this "space" is always shifting, with no single image allowed to attain complete self-sufficiency, the basic operating conditions of collage, which presupposes a stasis that enables the tenuous boundaries among the various elements to be apprehended, are supplanted, creating the grounds for a genuinely polyvalent montage.

Godard's knowledge of world cinema is expansive, and he has acknowledged the "distance montage" theories of Armenian filmmaker Artavazd Pelechian, with the repetition of imagery across the body of a film generating a "spherical" momentum, as a useful point of comparison.[96] Given his formal obsessions, however, the most conspicuous lacuna in *Histoire(s) du cinéma* is the near-total omission of the North American avant-garde, the main arena

FIGURE 4.8 Made in USA *(Jean-Luc Godard, 1966).*

in which a non-Soviet conception of montage was worked out. The presence of shots from Maya Deren's *Meshes of the Afternoon* (1943) in the 2002 short *Liberté et patrie* accentuates the absence of such films from the four and a half hours of *Histoire(s) du cinéma*. *Les Signes parmi nous* (4B) includes the reading of a long, modified excerpt from the 1971 text in which Hollis Frampton maps out his *Magellan* project, and his name is cited onscreen, but no mention is made of Stan Brakhage, the filmmaker whose work *Histoire(s) du cinéma* most resembles visually.[97]

For far too long, film history has maintained a false opposition between Brakhage's exteriorization of subjectivity and the "Brechtian" artifice of Godard, generalizations derived entirely from their most famous early works (their later works remaining largely unseen and comparatively underdiscussed). Yet with the benefit of hindsight, it becomes increasingly clear that Godard and Brakhage—notwithstanding their many important ideological, formal, and contextual differences—are two poles of a larger mid-century modernist project that challenged the naive assumptions that the film screen is a direct window onto the world, focusing instead on the structure of perception. The questions of the gardener in *Nouvelle vague* (1990)—who asks, "What is grass before it has been given a name?" and ponders whether it lies inside or outside himself—unconsciously echo the opening passage of Brakhage's "Metaphors on Vision":

> Imagine an eye unruled by man-made laws of perspective, an eye unprejudiced by compositional logic, an eye which does not respond to the name of everything but which must know each object encountered in life through an adventure of perception. How many colors are there in a field of grass to the crawling baby unaware of "Green"? How many rainbows can light create for the untutored eye? How aware of variations in heat waves can that eye be? Imagine a world alive with incomprehensible objects and shimmering with an endless variety of movement and innumerable gradations of color. Imagine a world before the "beginning was the word."[98]

Godard too is interested in making each moment of his films "an adventure of perception," part of a continually evolving form of visual thinking that would attack the presumptions of Western logocentrism, and since 1980, he has devoted himself to an exploration of prelinguistic imagery.[99] The attitudes of Godard and Brakhage toward narrative differ considerably, but the respective strategies they have employed to articulate the self's relationship with the world have increasingly converged in the decades since the expressive possibilities of handheld camerawork were redefined by *Anticipation of the Night* (1958) and *Breathless*.[100] Godard's use of multiple superimposition in video work like *Histoire(s) du cinéma* has striking correlates with Brakhage's use of it in both partially and fully hand-painted work, as do his abrupt cuts away from images at the end of an overlapping dissolve—leaving a particular image onscreen just long enough for it to be registered as a composition before the visual field is once again transformed—and his use of the back-and-forth fluttering of images lasting a mere fraction of a second.[101] For his part, Brakhage's incorporation of text and preexisting footage as subjacent material within densely layered montages—in films like *23rd Psalm Branch* (1967), *The Dante Quartet* (1987), *Agnus Dei Kinder Synapse* (1991), *Untitled: For Marilyn* (1992), and *Night Mulch* (2001)—parallels techniques used more ironically by Godard.[102]

Brakhage and Godard met and respected one another, but what matters more than any direct personal contact is the existence of a shared desire to reconfigure the basic parameters of Eisensteinian montage so that the transitions between superimposed images could suggest the dynamism of vision as well as thought.[103] The most likely reason filmmakers like Brakhage were excluded from *Histoire(s) du cinéma* is relative inaccessibility; as Godard has mentioned, work like this could be seen only at the Cinémathèque française and, crucially, videotapes of Brakhage films were not readily available in Europe until *Histoire(s) du cinéma* was nearly complete.[104] Although he apparently knew Gregory Markopoulos well during the 1950s, it would have been even harder for Godard to see any of *Eniaios* (1947–1992).[105] Nevertheless, in its long-form restructuring of classical myths and its radical reformulation of montage, *Eniaios* may present a useful counterpoint to *Histoire(s) du cinéma*. Like Markopoulos, Godard makes frequent use of a black screen throughout his film, a technique he had early experimented with in *Pravda* (Groupe Dziga Vertov, 1969) and *Struggle in Italy* (Groupe Dziga Vertov, 1971).[106] Godard's idiosyncratic conception of cinematic projection harmonizes surprisingly well with the triangulation of viewer, screen, and eye that Markopoulos postulates in his essay "Entheos," and both filmmakers used similar sorts of medical metaphors. The son of a doctor, Godard frequently characterized himself as a physician during the period he was making *Histoire(s) du cinéma*, suggesting, like Markopoulos, that he was going to use cinema to cure media pollution.[107]

In its foregrounding of historical patterns, however, Godard's project diverges radically from the profoundly ahistorical *Eniaios*. Where *Eniaios* bestows sacralized images "purified" of their nonmythic contexts to the viewer across extended gaps, *Histoire(s) du cinéma* offers instead an excess or overflow of images with a conflux of potential and embedded meanings. The image clusters in *Histoire(s) du cinéma* have such historical traction that the rapid interweaving of one or two frame shots, and even the use of passages of black, seems to suggest film catching in the projector gate, unable to smoothly proceed forward, an idea visualized at several points by the appearance (and sound) of a strip running forward and backward in fits and spurts on an editing table.

It is thus no surprise that the central myth of *Histoire(s) du cinéma* is not that of Prometheus but that of Orpheus. Romantic Prometheanism manifests itself throughout Godard's late work in the association of flames with artistic creativity and the depiction of the artist as demiurge, but the Titan's struggles are rarely thematized as overtly as they are in the work of Markopoulos, Abel Gance, or Jacques Rivette. The deepest affinities are with the "anxious reflection eating away at us like Prometheus' vulture" that Germaine de Staël—another Swiss-born figure with ties to France and a commitment to dialectical thought—described in *On Germany* (1813), her celebrated treatise on the emergence of the Romantic sensibility (alluded to in both *Germany Year 90 Nine Zero* and *Histoire(s) du cinéma*).[108] The Orphic myth, on the other hand, is central to Godard's work, and it is featured prominently in *Alphaville* and *Nouvelle vague* as well as *Histoire(s) du cinéma*, where it is represented by the recurring image of a boatman from Carl Theodor Dreyer's *The Bride of Glomdal* (1926).[109] Son of Calliope, the Muse of epic poetry, and (at least in some versions) the sun god Apollo, who taught him his art, the figure of Orpheus symbolically fuses cinema's facility for storytelling with its dependence on light. Godard's emphasis is on Orpheus' attempt to recover his lost beloved Eurydice, which resonates with the underworld quest theme in *Histoire(s) du cinéma* and points to the challenges of retrospection. An onscreen text in *Seul le cinéma* (2A) declares that "the cinema authorizes Orpheus to return without killing Eurydice," and Godard uses almost exactly the same terminology to define art in a contemporaneous interview: "Art is that which permits you to go back, and to see Sodom and Gomorrah without dying. Art permits us to do that because it is seen from a distance."[110] If the cinema enables Orpheus to look back, it also enables Lot's wife to witness History in the midst of its unfolding, changed not into a pillar of salt, but into the "silver salts which fix the light."[111]

The Museum of the Real

Beauty is nothing but the beginning of terror, which we are still just
able to endure.

—RAINER MARIA RILKE, *DUINO ELEGIES* (1922)[112]

To call Godard a Romantic modernist is not to disregard history and politics, but rather to highlight the means by which he engages with them. His Victor Hugo—referred to repeatedly in the late work—is the Hugo of the poor, the *misérables* described in *In Praise of Love*, but also the Hugo who decried the atrocities of the 1876 Serbian-Ottoman War, in a text that is read out by Godard himself and cited at the beginning of *La Monnaie de l'absolu* (3A).[113] As with the use of photographs depicting Richmond, Virginia, during the American Civil War in his lecture to students in *Notre musique*, Godard provides the context only at the end, thereby emphasizing the cyclical returns of history and the barbarism of modern warfare without ignoring the specificity of events. When Godard reads the part of Hugo's text referring to Europe's refusal to intervene to prevent the "annihilation of a people," the viewer inevitably thinks of the Holocaust; when the source, "Pour le Serbie" (1876), is (uncharacteristically) acknowledged onscreen, it carries with it intimations of the twentieth-century history of conflicts in the region, from the Balkan Wars of the 1910s to the 1990s Yugoslav wars that were ongoing at the time *Histoire(s) du cinéma* was in production. Godard's montages operate in a similar manner, bringing together forms and ideas not according to diachronic patterns but through provocative collisions, creating a constant tension in which the history of cinema, "this affair of the nineteenth century that resolved itself in the twentieth," is inseparable from a History that is always in motion.[114] This slippage is contained even within the title of the series, as Godard explains in *Toutes les histoires* (1A), "actuality of history, history of actualities, histories of cinema, with an s, with an SS." Godard's words are immediately followed by the voice and an image of Adolf Hitler, the figure referred to more frequently than any other in *Histoire(s) du cinéma* and the personification of the events with which the present can never be comfortably reconciled.[115]

Among other things, Godard wanted *Histoire(s) du cinéma* to function as a serious work of historiography. He has mentioned Jules Michelet's multivolume *Histoire de France* (1833–1867) in interviews, and he alludes to both Walter Benjamin and Michel Foucault within *Histoire(s) du cinéma*, but the overarching model is Fernand Braudel, the dominant figure in the postwar Annales school.[116] Braudel's emphasis on social history is perfectly suited to Godard's project, with its fixation on the lived texture of history as manifested through images and sounds, aspects of experience that, Godard argues, cinema alone is capable of directly rendering:

> When Joyce wrote *Finnegans Wake*, which is the sum of all that can be written, he said, "I": it is literature, but not the history of literature. In the same manner, sculpture or painting cannot make its own history, whereas the cinema can truly tell a story, as we have always said. I wanted to tell the story of History, through the cinema.[117]

Underlying these arguments is the conviction that the cinema's unique bond to history stems from its direct rapport with reality. Godard is perhaps the most ardent and proselytizing follower of André Bazin, but, fully aware of the myriad ways in which images can be manipulated and of the multiple levels of mediation involved in the creation of a film, he places little value on the much-vaunted concept of "indexicality." For Godard, realism consists not of a one-to-one relationship between film strip and world, but of a fact-based orientation operating at every level of cinematic construction, a historicity that adheres to filmed material and endures even when images and sounds are recontextualized. This is what enables him to invoke complex histories through small details, like the recitation of part of a German cavalry poem

("*Morgenrot, Morgenrot*"), documentary footage of refugees, or a speech by Marshal Pétain, even when those images and sounds are interlaced with very different material.[118]

Although the soundtrack is just as essential as the imagery to the form of *Histoire(s) du cinéma* (and was, in fact, released independently as a CD set), Godard's comments invariably privilege cinema's capacity to encapsulate historical processes visually. "My idea," he explained, "is to say: There, that's what cinema was. The fact that we see it, that we can still project it, it's like when [Heinrich] Schliemann discovered some ruins and said: 'Well, Troy must have happened there.' That's the way it is."[119] For Godard, this was the true mission of the cinema, a moral imperative that, he suggests, it relinquished in the midst of World War II. In its inability to document the Holocaust as it occurred, "The cinema totally failed its duty. There were six million people shot or gassed, principally the Jews, and the cinema was not there. . . . In not filming the concentration camps, the cinema totally resigned."[120] Godard's insistence that the concentration camps needed to be shown in cinemas has embroiled him in a decades-long debate with Claude Lanzmann that has led to some misguided accusations of anti-Semitism.[121] Lanzmann, whose nine-and-a-half-hour *Shoah* (1985) famously makes use of no archival imagery, has publicly called for a total prohibition of Holocaust footage, at one point saying that if any visual record of the camps in operation existed, it should be destroyed. "I made *Shoah* against all archives," Lanzmann declared, arguing on another occasion that "there is indeed an absolute obscenity in the project of understanding."[122] For Godard, by contrast, showing is an ethical act, not only because it may help to prevent the very historical repetitions emphasized throughout *Histoire(s) du cinéma*, but also because it authenticates the self's relationship to the external world. It is, in other words, a gesture of faith in reality.

The Godard/Lanzmann dispute has its roots in much older debates over the biblical proscription of graven images, whose stake is the status of vision itself. Yet, perhaps surprisingly, Godard's iconophilic arguments are fully in accord with those of Frankfurt School theorist Siegfried Kracauer, who addresses the question of Holocaust imagery just before the end of his *Theory of Film* (1960):

> In experiencing the rows of calves' heads or the litter of tortured human bodies in the films made of the Nazi concentration camps, we redeem horror from its invisibility behind the veils of panic and imagination. And this experience is liberating in as much as it removes a most powerful taboo.[123]

"Even scratched to death, a simple 35-millimeter rectangle saves the honor of reality," Godard says in *Toutes les histoires* (1A), accompanied by a shot from a fictional reconstruction of the last days of Hitler and Eva Braun, as well as a documentary shot of corpses. For Godard, who has remained one of the most vocal critics of *Schindler's List* (Steven Spielberg, 1993) and the contemporary

FIGURE 4.9 *Superimposition of a cropped and rotated image taken from* Noli me tangere *(Giotto, 1305–1306, Arena Chapel, Padua) and a shot from* A Place in the Sun *(George Stevens, 1951) in* Toutes les histoires *(1A) of* Histoire(s) du cinéma *(Jean-Luc Godard, 1988–1998).*

"Holocaust industry," what was needed was for the cinema to properly show the camps as they were, to make the fact of what took place evident to everyone without sentimentality or artifice. Yet as the example above makes clear, making things visible is a question of relationships and point of view as much as it is a question of direct recording. When Godard talks about the "failure" of the cinema to show the Holocaust, he is referring not only to the inability of newsreel cameramen to film the gas chambers in operation, but more generally to an unwillingness to develop a cinematic form that would make clear what happened and what was lost between 1939 and 1945.

This is exactly what Godard tries to do in the most-discussed section of *Histoire(s) du cinéma*, the moment in *Toutes les histoires* (1A) where Godard says, "If George Stevens had not used the first 16mm color footage at Auschwitz and Ravensbrück, Elizabeth Taylor would never have had her place in the sun."[124] Accompanying this sentence is a chain of images that proceeds as follows (figure 4.9):

(1) An image of corpses in an extermination camp that was taken from *D-Day to Berlin*, a 1985 compilation of color footage shot by the wartime unit run by George Stevens

(2) A shot of Elizabeth Taylor cradling an obscured object from *A Place in the Sun* (George Stevens, 1951) superimposed with the first image
(3) A return to (1)
(4) A shot of Elizabeth Taylor in close-up from *A Place in the Sun*
(5) (2) without the superimposition, so that it becomes clear that Taylor is holding onto Montgomery Clift
(6) An image of a corpse from *D-Day to Berlin*
(7) A shot from *A Place in the Sun* showing Taylor slowly lowering her body
(8) A rotated section of Giotto's *Noli me tangere* (1305–1306), framed so that the hands of Mary Magdalene (reaching out to touch Jesus in the original composition) are pointed down
(9) A superimposition of (7) and (8) so that Mary Magdalene's hands appear to be reaching out to Taylor as she rises up

Jacques Rancière has criticized this sequence, questioning Godard's decision to rotate the Giotto image and decrying his "neospiritualism."[125] What Rancière, and other similar commentators, appear to be missing is the complex irony of the juxtaposition. Iconographically, the *Noli me tangere* depicts the first sighting of the risen Christ, who tells Mary Magdalene not to touch him (in one of the most enigmatic passages of the New Testament) since he is about to depart the earth and has "not yet ascended to the Father."[126] In forbidding touch, the *Noli me tangere*, virtually alone among the traditional Christological scenes, affirms the power of sight to register that which is about to vanish. By connecting Giotto's painting with the scene from *A Place in the Sun*, Godard is not endowing the Stevens film with sacred value or suggesting that it represents the rebirth of the true cinematic image, because what he is lamenting is that the image of the Holocaust comes through, if it does at all, only *indirectly*, by means of a narrative that does not address it as such. "How marvelous to be able to look at what we cannot see," Godard says immediately after the Giotto/Stevens superimposition, "what a miracle for our blind eyes."[127]

For Godard, following Rossellini, what matters is not so much what is recorded by the camera as the attitude the filmmaker takes to it in the work.[128] "What there is in newsreels of the war says nothing. It does not judge," Godard declares in *Toutes les histoires* (1A), followed by a shot from Fritz Lang's *M* (1931) and the onscreen text, "Only the hand that erases can write." The text is an epigram attributed to fourteenth-century German theologian Meister Eckhart and, as so often in Godard's work, the quotation is only partial (Godard elides the final words from the sentence, "Only the hand that erases can write the truth").[129] Several minutes later, he continues, "We've forgotten that small village, its white walls and olive trees, but we remember Picasso, that is, Guernica." By repositioning material like the Giotto image, Godard implies, cinema can create new relationships that, because of their remove from mimetic transcription, can facilitate a more profound connection with history.

In both his films and writings, Godard has always treated the boundary between fiction and documentary as porous. As a result, the transformation or reinvigoration of preexisting material is seen to deepen rather than threaten the integrity of an artwork. Godard's predisposition toward oblique adaptations is a corollary to this and it may also be the reason why the one European director celebrated in *Histoire(s) du cinéma* for salvaging some modest dignity for the cinema during the war is Bresson.[130] Very shortly after the claim that a 35mm rectangle can save the honor of reality, Godard inserts a shot from *Les Anges du péché* (Robert Bresson, 1943), in which a young novice in a convent bows down before Mother Superior, with a shot of the tracks leading to Auschwitz from *Shoah* superimposed in the middle (figure 4.10).[131] Like the Giotto/Stevens juxtaposition that follows several minutes later, the Bresson/*Shoah* pairing crystallizes the loss of the cinema's documentary inclinations—the image from *Shoah* standing in for what cannot be shown—while at the same time suggesting one of the ways in which even narrative cinema can engage with the larger cultural matrix from which it emerged. Once the novice

FIGURE 4.10 *Superimposition of shots from* Les Anges du péché *(Robert Bresson, 1943) and* Shoah *(Claude Lanzmann, 1985) in* Toutes les histoires *(1A) of* Histoire(s) du cinéma *(Jean-Luc Godard, 1988–1998).*

completes her prostration, a title card reading "failure at the Gestapo" appears and Godard switches to an image from Bresson's follow-up film, *Les Dames du Bois de Boulogne* (1945), a contemporary drama derived from Denis Diderot with a production severely affected by the conditions in wartime Paris.[132] Through the friction generated by the back-to-back juxtaposition of these seemingly discordant elements, Godard is able to suggest the contradictions and dilemmas of a historical moment—the period of the Occupation and the Resistance—that is epitomized by Bresson's wartime films.[133]

For Godard, television "makes forgetting, while the cinema made memories," an idea that is succinctly embodied in *Histoire(s) du cinéma* by a short sequence from the 1912 Gaumont film *Le Mystère des roches de Kador* (Léonce Perret), which depicts an amnesiac woman who suddenly recalls the traumatic past she has suppressed when confronted by a movie screen.[134] By recording, editing, and then reprojecting the world, cinema "shows" things, making ideas and histories manifest and allowing viewers to come to terms with events that cannot be contained by language. Yet the cinema can sometimes neglect its duty, merely "doing pretty things to pretty girls" (*Fatale beauté*, 2B). In *La Monnaie de l'absolu* (3A), Godard reads a memo from David O. Selznick: "I want [Dolores] Del Rio and Tyrone Power in a romance with a South Seas setting. The story doesn't matter, so long as it is called *Bird of Paradise* [King Vidor, 1932] and at the end Del Rio jumps into a volcano."[135] Within the studio system, great auteurs can be forced by contract to direct films with insipid scripts, and even at their most incisive and powerful, as in the shots of Ethan Edwards lifting up Debbie from *The Searchers* (John Ford, 1956) that appear frequently in *Histoire(s) du cinéma*, these films can be an instrument of cultural imperialism.[136] Hollywood, with which Godard has always had a love/hate relationship, is the power of Babylon, represented by an image from *Intolerance* (D. W. Griffith, 1916) with overlay text reading "The World for a Nickel" and followed by a phrase that is frequently repeated in the works of this period, "Trade follows films."[137] The spirit of Resistance that Godard attributes to Bresson in *Histoire(s) du cinéma* is at one and the same time a question of historical circumstance and of formal originality, the struggle to resist "a certain uniform way of making movies" and the dominance of the American corporate model.

Bresson is an isolated figure, a powerful exception in the midst of a French film culture that "was never liberated from the Germans or the Americans." The real revolution, in Godard's view, comes with Italian Neorealism and specifically with *Rome, Open City* (Roberto Rossellini, 1945), a film that allowed Italy "to reclaim the right to look itself in the face." Like Bresson, Welles, and Hitchcock, Rossellini is referred to in one form or another in every section of *Histoire(s) du cinéma*, often through brief, iconic fragments: an excerpt of Pina falling to the ground in *Rome, Open City*; or Karen climbing the volcano in *Stromboli* (1949); a still from *Joan of Arc at the Stake* (1954); or the sound of the murdered partisans falling into the water from the end of *Paisà* (1946). In these and other instances, Godard plays off the intrinsic power of the sequences, while also treating them as symbols of their period.

On two significant occasions, however, Italian Neorealism is dealt with in more detail, the only movement other than the French New Wave to receive dedicated attention. *Toutes les histoires* (1A) ends with a long excerpt from *Germany Year Zero*, showing a young boy, Edmund, wandering through the ruins of a Berlin building before falling to his death. The entire sequence is a long excursus in the midst of a discussion of American cinema exerting its economic power over Europe both before and then after World War II ("if World War I allowed American cinema to ruin French cinema . . . with the advent of television, World War II allowed it to finance, that is to ruin, European cinema"), and it is bracketed on both ends by a superimposed still from *La Strada* (Federico Fellini, 1954) that shows actress Giulietta Masina holding her hands over her face.[138] The moving images from *Germany Year Zero* are frequently interspersed with passages of black and the moments both before and just after Edmund falls are amplified through the use of slow motion. The audio from Rossellini's film is gone, replaced by a sonic montage incorporating Paul Hindemith's symphony *Mathis der Maler* (1934), silence, garbled passages of sound from the original film, and Godard, in voiceover, reading an uncited passage from Ludwig Wittgenstein's posthumously published book, *On Certainty* (1951). Wittgenstein's text focuses on hands— "Looking won't reassure me. Why trust my eyes, if I have doubts? Why check my eyes to see whether I see my hands?"—and Godard accordingly uses the fusion of the images from the Rossellini and Fellini films to create a montage cluster pointing to both the epistemic crisis of the postwar world and the shifting nature of the image within Neorealism.[139] With its historical boundaries implicitly marked by the two films, Neorealism is depicted as offering a genuine European alternative to the aesthetics of Hollywood filmmaking for a few short years, with Fellini's work functioning, according to André Bazin's famous phrase, as the "voyage to the end" of the movement that began with Rossellini's war trilogy.[140]

Godard's manipulation of both the sound and image tracks from *Germany Year Zero* is consistent with the strategies employed throughout *Histoire(s) du cinéma*—if only the "hand that erases can write," then distortion is a virtual prerequisite for montage—and it also sets the stage for the return to Neorealism nearly three hours later at the end of *La Monnaie de l'absolu* (3A). There Godard observes that "it was a strange thing, however, how the Italian cinema became so great, when from Rossellini to [Luchino] Visconti, from [Michelangelo] Antonioni to Fellini, sound was never recorded with images." In separating the images of *Germany Year Zero* from the attached soundtrack at the end of *Toutes les histoires* (1A), Godard draws attention to the new alliance of production method (location shooting using both nonactors and nonsynchronous sound) and aesthetic framework inaugurated by the films of Rossellini, using the fissure between image and sound to demonstrate the capacity of footage shot independently of a script to capture a concrete historical situation in all its ambiguity.[141] At the end of *La Monnaie de l'absolu* (3A), Godard again accentuates the autonomy of images and sounds by including an extended montage from key Neorealist films accompanied, somewhat comically, by a 1983 Italian pop song, *La nostra lingua italiana* (Riccardo Cociante and Gaio Chiocchio). The true "sound," however, comes from elsewhere; in the major Italian films of the post-Resistance period, "the language of Ovid and Virgil, Dante and [Giacomo] Leopardi passed through the images," Godard declares, superimposing passages from Lucretius, Dante, and Ovid as text throughout the sequence.

As if to emphasize that this process largely eludes conscious recognition, the texts are in the original languages (Latin or Italian), but each excerpt—from Book IV of Lucretius' *On the Nature of Things* (first century BCE); Book XV of Ovid's *Metamorphoses* (8 CE); Ovid's *Cures for Love* (ca. 1 CE); Canto XXIV of Dante's *Inferno* (1314); and Canto XX of the *Purgatorio* (1318–1319)—has an implied relationship with the images it is linked to.[142] These associations range from the autobiographical ("The man who protests to the world 'I'm not in love,' is," attached to images of Godard's ex-wife Anne Wiazemsky from Pier Paolo Pasolini's *Teorema*, 1968) to the metaphorical ("As soon as his voice ceased, the god disappeared. With him, sleep departed too, and kindly daylight followed hard on the heels of sleep," tied to images from Visconti's *The Leopard*, 1963) to the philosophical ("When the first [image] perishes and a new one is born and takes its place, the former seems to have changed its attitude," a passage from Lucretius accompanied by a blank screen).[143] In every instance, however, the cuts are structured around the visual patterns onscreen. By relegating both sound and text to supporting roles, this montage suggests that the faint remnants of the premodern literary world are able to "inhabit" these Neorealist films because the system of audiovisual synchronization foundational to cinema since the early 1930s had been fractured, allowing images to once again speak for themselves.

"A Truth That Says, Believe"

Religion is only the frame and the pretext for the creative energy
of man as it reaches its summit and as it lends to him the enthusiasm which it draws up from the consciousness of itself. There is
no "religious art." Any art is religious in its essence; and, with love
doubtless—of which it is the spiritual flower—it is the sole creator and

also the sole reliable evidence of that grand intoxication which moves mountains and which is called religion.

—ÉLIE FAURE, *THE SPIRIT OF THE FORMS* (1927)[144]

In interviews about *Histoire(s) du cinéma*, Godard has offered up extraordinarily grand claims for the significance of Rossellini's work. The Italian literary tradition can come into the Neorealist image because "there is a space of miracles," he declared at one point, expounding further in a subsequent discussion:

> *Rome, Open City* is a film of resistance because it is a film of resurrection. It is not by chance that this work comes from Italy, the nation the most absent from the war and at the same time a guardian of Christianity. Only Christianity has held images. St. Paul said almost this: "The Image will come at the time of the Resurrection."[145]

Godard has made similar statements on several occasions, including in *Une histoire seule* (1B), arguing that the Pauline conception of sacred images is something that he "as a director . . . can begin to understand."[146] Godard has never explained where in St. Paul's writings he found the words "The Image will come at the time of the Resurrection," which, even accounting for variations in translation, appear nowhere in the Epistles. It is likely that Godard is condensing and paraphrasing a number of passages, especially 1 Corinthians 13:12 ("For now we see through a glass, darkly, but then face to face") and 1 Corinthians 15:49 ("And we have born the image of the earthly, so shall we bear the image of the heavenly"). St. Paul's comments refer eschatologically to the resurrection of all souls at the end of time. Godard, however, takes this to refer more generally to the power of the cinematic Image to act as both imprint of reality and emanation of the sacred. As he put it in a 1983 interview (and as he reiterated in *Toutes les histoires*, 1A), the cinema is "a very evangelical matter, and it's not by chance that the white screen is like a canvas . . . [like] the linen of Veronique, the shroud that keeps the trace, the love, of the lived, of the world."[147] In the formulation developed in *Fatale beauté* (2B), the cinema is "neither an art, nor a technique, but a mystery."

Godard uses similarly religious language to describe his experience of the screenings on the avenue de Messine at the first version of the Cinémathèque française, which Jean Renoir once described as "the church for movies."[148] Godard has also compared public film screening to a Mass, and this is related throughout his late work to a new poesis of light.[149] Caroline Champetier, the cinematographer for several Godard films in the 1980s including *Keep Your Right Up*, has argued that this motivated his decision to shoot his later films using the full frame even though virtually every cinema would have projected the films cropped to a widescreen ratio like 1.66:1: "The idea, for

him, [was that] the shot was not [a question] of space, or of environment, or
of framing, but of a force, an impulse—very often a pulsation of light."[150] The
phrase "what Goethe said before he died" is repeated so often in *Keep Your
Right Up* that it becomes a running joke, predicated on the assumption that
the viewer knows Goethe's (possibly apocryphal) final words, "More light!"[151]
Godard develops the references further in *Germany Year 90 Nine Zero* and
puns on light incessantly in *Histoire(s) du cinéma*.[152] "One evening we went
to Henri Langlois' and then there was light," Godard declares in *Une vague
nouvelle* (3B), later observing, "The true cinema was that which could not be
seen, because it was still prohibited, always invisible. Such was our cinema,
and it has stayed with me, and Langlois confirmed it for us. Yes, that is the
right word *exactly*."[153]

What Langlois, called "L'Ange" in *Une vague nouvelle* (3B), confirmed for
his young acolytes above everything else was the universalizing power of the
silent cinema. "With silence, people opened their eyes, together," Godard
announced in an interview. "Everyone was equal before the image."[154] For
Godard, more perhaps than for any of his colleagues, the silent era was a
period in which the deities of film, those whose creative powers were diminished immeasurably by the coming of sound, walked the earth, and he
emphasizes this throughout *Histoire(s) du cinéma*.[155] Just before announcing
that Langlois had shown the young cinephiles light, Godard pairs William
Blake's *Ancient of Days* (1794) with a shot of Napoleon adrift at sea from the
"Double Tempest" section of Abel Gance's *Napoléon* (1927), both cropped
with an overlay reading "The Museum of the Real." Accompanying these
images is a text by Braudel about the Siege of Toulon. In linking Braudel's
words to the fusion of a section of *Napoléon* with the painting of Blake,
Godard highlights Gance's attempt to renew the Romantic tradition and
the cinema's ability to reveal the fabric of historical experience through the
montage of wholly fictional imagery, connecting both to "the identity of the
New Wave."[156]

If Gance's films are used here and throughout to suggest the power as
well as the excess of a cinematic visionary, Erich von Stroheim, whose portrait recurs at key points in *Histoire(s) du cinéma*, is depicted as an Icarus-
like fallen hero, a martyr to the burgeoning power of Hollywood.[157] Fifteen
minutes into the first section of *Histoire(s) du cinéma*, a title reading "factory
of dreams" appears onscreen, followed by a partial reproduction of Gustave
Moreau's *Jupiter and Semele* (1894–1895), which is linked—first by an iris and
then via superimposition—to an image of von Stroheim, an association that
is, in its own way, just as rich as the linkage of *Napoléon* and Blake (figure
4.11). In the original myth, Semele, encouraged by Juno, asked the disguised
Jupiter to appear in all his glory, precipitating her own death (since mortals
cannot look upon the gods without perishing).[158] The parallel with the career
of von Stroheim is evident, but the use of Moreau's testament to late Romantic

FIGURE 4.11 *Cropped detail of* Jupiter and Semele *(Gustave Moreau, 1895, Musée Gustave Moreau, Paris) superimposed with a photograph of Erich von Stroheim in* Toutes les histoires *(1A) of* Histoire(s) du cinéma *(Jean-Luc Godard, 1988–1998).*

aesthetics adds additional layers of resonance. Where Picasso, in his 1930 drawing *Loves of Jupiter and Semele*, focuses on the human act of coupling, and Tintoretto, in his 1545 *cassone* panel (*Jupiter and Semele*), emphasizes the essential narrative structure of the myth by having Jupiter occupy the central third of the composition, Moreau's painting depicts the intercourse of a mortal and a god as a moment of suspension, literally poised between ultimate consummation and the disintegration of the body into ash.[159] There could be no clearer fusion of Eros and Thanatos, with the erotic force of the subject sublimated into a mélange of impenetrably arcane signs and symbols. Insofar as this symbolism can be seen to evoke what Malcolm de Chazal has called "a point-state where death and birth meet halfway," the painting embodies the poetic cycle of creation and self-destruction central to *Histoire(s) du cinéma* and Godard's late work more generally.[160] By virtue of its 1895 completion date and its implicit mythic context—the birth of Bacchus, who was taken from his mother's womb and "sewn into his father's thigh" after the events portrayed in the painting—the image could also be related to the birth of cinema, deepening the implied connection between the artistic temperament of a figure like von Stroheim and the voluptuous abandon of "Hollywood" (the focus of *Toutes les histoires*, 1A).[161]

FIGURE 4.12 *Cropped detail of* Le Chapeau de paille *(Portrait of Susanna Fourment,
Peter Paul Rubens, 1622–1625, National Gallery, London) in* Fatale beauté *(2B) of*
Histoire(s) du cinéma *(Jean-Luc Godard, 1988–1998).*

As always, there is a danger of making Godard's montages cohere too easily as texts, when the point is to create audiovisual relationships that extend
out in multiple directions at once, much like the use of recurring motifs in
the work of directors like von Stroheim. For von Stroheim, this functioned
as both a sign of his authorship and a sort of secret code, a hieroglyphic
system of correspondences that connected both individual films and his
entire corpus to larger symbolic, religious, or occult systems. In *Histoire(s)
du cinéma*, repeated images, sounds, or sequences—like the frequent return
to the Teutonic Knights of *Alexander Nevsky* (Sergei Eisenstein, 1938) or the
Liebestod of *Duel in the Sun* (King Vidor, 1946)—function as modernist meta-
communication, a way of putting Godard's films in dialogue with both one
another and with the history of the arts.[162] For example, Peter Paul Rubens'
Le Chapeau de paille (Portrait of Susanna Fourment, 1622–1625) is used
throughout Godard's late work, appearing in *Fatale beauté* (2B), *JLG/JLG—
Self-Portrait in December, The Old Place* (1999), *In Praise of Love,* and *Notre
musique* (figure 4.12). In each of the later iterations, the appearance of this
Rubens painting recalls its use in the earlier films while also functioning as
cinematic shorthand, condensing Godard's arguments about the tendency
for male artists to frame women "from the bust" into a single image. This is

FIGURE 4.13 *Frontal view of the* Isenheim Altarpiece *(Matthias Grünewald, 1512–1515, Musée d'Unterlinden, Colmar, France; photograph courtesy Album / Art Resource, NY).*

the pictorial equivalent of Godard's frequent musical quotations, and, in at least one instance—the use in *Histoire(s) du cinéma* of Hindemith's *Mathis der Maler* and Matthias Grünewald's *Isenheim Altarpiece* (1512–1515)—the two streams are powerfully interrelated.

The crucifixion on the front of Grünewald's famous polyptych, designed for a hospital chapel run by Antonine monks devoted to easing the suffering from gangrenous disease, includes an image of St. John the Baptist pointing toward the body of Christ. Next to his hand, the Latin phrase, "*Illum oportet crescere me autem minui*" ("He must increase, but I must decrease," John 3:30) is inscribed on the surface of the painting (figure 4.13). In order to reinforce the lesson contained in this text, Grünewald disregards the conventions of just proportion developed during the Renaissance, making the suffering Christ dominate in the manner of sacred images developed before the advent of linear perspective. The painting's visual structure suggests a strong reassertion of Catholic faith, but its unusual (and iconographically unnecessary) reliance on text has made it central to later Protestant arguments about visual representation; Karl Barth kept a reproduction by his desk throughout his career and excluded it from his more general condemnation of images, while

FIGURE 4.14 *Detail of St. John the Baptist and the Latin inscription of the* Isenheim Altarpiece *(Matthias Grünewald, 1512–1515, Musée d'Unterlinden, Colmar, France) superimposed with text reading* "Histoire(s) du cinéma" *in* La Monnaie de l'absolu *(3A) of* Histoire(s) du cinéma *(Jean-Luc Godard, 1988–1998).*

Paul Tillich went so far as to claim that it is the "greatest German picture ever painted."[163] In *Histoire(s) du cinéma* and several other films, Godard crops Grünewald's frontispiece to emphasize the figure of St. John the Baptist and the inscription, using it as a totem for the conflict between text and images in his films (figure 4.14).[164]

From the lengthy verbal digressions of *Breathless* and *My Life to Live* (1962) through the logorrhea of films like *Un film comme les autres* (1968) and the superimposition of texts in countless video projects, there has always been a tension between the visual and textual modalities of Godard's work that is given greater philosophical and theological significance in the years surrounding the creation of *Histoire(s) du cinéma*. The writings Godard uses matter a great deal to his work, but what he objects to is the way in which printed words can become rigid, even oppressive models of authority (this too echoes St. Paul: "For the letter killeth, but the spirit giveth life").[165] By extracting phrases from their sources—without, it should be noted, making it impossible to trace their origins—and putting them in dialogue with other audiovisual or textual materials, Godard makes them part of an active and dynamic process and keeps them from solidifying into "texts." It is the irreducible polyvalence of images that underlies Godard's strong preference for the silent cinema:

> With silence, there was no need to talk in order to be understood—it was the speech of silence. . . . Then the text, the scenario, returned to power [with the coming of sound], at the moment when Stalin became Stalin, Hitler, Hitler. The scenario, the texts, the programs, the scenarios, and the camps.[166]

Godard retains the historical friction generated by these associations, while also underscoring the dire consequences of their implications, when, in *Notre musique*, he further crops the Grünewald image to isolate the figure of St. John the Baptist and then cuts to an image of a concentration camp victim with the word *juif* in the upper left, a cut bridged through a verbal chain going from "The Tables of the Law" to "The Holy Scriptures" and finally "The People of the Book."

These same concerns informed Paul Hindemith's *Mathis der Maler*, a musical response to the *Isenheim Altarpiece* that is one of the most frequently excerpted pieces of music in *Histoire(s) du cinéma*. In addition to Protestant sympathies, Grünewald is also said to have supported the peasants in the Peasants' War (1524–1525), and Hindemith draws parallels to the contemporary political situation in Nazi Germany in both his symphonic (1934) and operatic (1935–1938) portraits.[167] Throughout *Histoire(s) du cinéma*, Godard uses extracts from the third movement of the symphony as sonic counterparts to the visual allusions to the *Isenheim Altarpiece*, reflexively emphasizing the formation of a synthetic montage image by focusing on a section at the beginning of the movement that attempts to musically represent the moment of artistic creation.[168] Most powerfully, in *La Monnaie de l'absolu* (3A), the cropped image of St. John the Baptist appears in superimposition with the words "*Histoire(s) du cinéma*," shortly before this extract from *Mathis der Maler*, dedicated to the "Temptation of St. Anthony," is used. Grünewald's depiction of one of these temptations—in which St. Anthony is beaten to death by demons in a cave, revived, and then beset once again by the same demons before a sudden flash (which St. Anthony believes came from God) causes them to flee—had appeared several minutes before. Superimposed with El Greco's *Christ Throwing Traders from the Temple* (1600), it visually encapsulates the narrative of death and rebirth developed in *Histoire(s) du cinéma* (figure 4.15). Cropped and partially veiled by superimposition, however, it is as concealed within the audiovisual fabric of *Histoire(s) du cinéma* as Grünewald's rendering of the scene, visible only when the altarpiece is fully open, is buried inside its architectural frame. Godard proves himself here to be an ardent follower of Bresson's maxim, "Hide the ideas, but so that people find them. The most important will be the most hidden."[169]

FIGURE 4.15 *Detail of* Christ Throwing Traders from the Temple *(El Greco, 1600, National Gallery, London) superimposed with a detail of "The Temptation of St. Anthony" panel from the* Isenheim Altarpiece *(Matthias Grünewald, 1512–1515, Musée d'Unterlinden, Colmar, France) in* La Monnaie de l'absolu *(3A) of* Histoire(s) du cinéma *(Jean-Luc Godard, 1988–1998).*

What Godard is suggesting is that the historical "rebirth" brought about by Neorealism is a kind of resurrection, the revitalization of an approach to cinematic image-making that was first consigned to a passive role by sound and then compromised further by World War II. This type of cinema offers something to the viewer, a secular faith that the postwar generation, steeped in Sartrean ideas of commitment, could believe in, an idea that comes out most clearly during a sequence in *Une histoire seule* (1B) that begins with Godard declaring, "The cinema, like Christianity, is not founded on historical truth." Godard's voiceover is accompanied by a complex montage that includes audio or visual references to Arthur Honegger's *Pacific 231* (1923); Giotto's *Flight into Egypt* (1304–1306); Ingmar Bergman's *Prison* (1949); Rossellini's *Joan of Arc at the Stake*; *I Confess* (Alfred Hitchcock, 1953); *Judex* (Louis Feuillade, 1916–1917); *The Princess of Clèves* (Madame de La Fayette, 1678); William Faulkner's *Absalom, Absalom!* (1936); *Genuine* (Robert Wiene, 1920); and *The Spiders* (Fritz Lang, 1919–1920). The triple repetition of the phrase "the cinema like Christianity" creates the impression that the "film" is caught in the projector, a conceptual stutter that is overcome only when Godard continues (in French):

It offers us a [historical] narrative and says: now believe! But not, believe this narrative with the belief appropriate to a historical narrative, rather: believe, through thick and thin, which you can do only as the result of a life. Here you have a narrative, don't take the same attitude to it as you take to other historical narratives![170]

The source, a 1937 note from Wittgenstein, becomes clearer when Godard repeats the last phrase in German, *"wie zu einer anderen historischen Nachricht"* ("as you take to other historical narratives"), and then reads the final sentence of the text ("Make a *quite different* place in your life for it") in both French (*"Donne-lui une place* tout autre *dans ta vie"*) and German (*"[Laß sie] eine* ganz andere *Stelle in Deinem Leben einnehmen"*).[171] After using these linguistic shifts to invoke the post-Babel confusions of speech, the screen goes black, and an excerpt from the soundtrack of Fritz Lang's *M* is intertwined with the beginning of the third movement of Hindemith's *Mathis der Maler*.[172]

In the text Godard quotes from, Wittgenstein is addressing the structural significance of faith to Christian belief, ideas that Godard—buttressed by the cinematic, musical, and literary allusions listed above—explicitly analogizes to the relationship between viewer and screen in the cinema. Even here, however, the montage remains destabilizing and paradoxical, with the audio excerpt from *M* continuing over an image of an emaciated hand from a 1947 Alberto Giacometti sculpture, strongly evoking (yet again) the irredeemable atrocities of World War II. In what follows, however, Godard makes his strongest audiovisual "argument" for the power of the cinema in the postwar world: the Giacometti hand is linked via dissolve to a still image of Joan of Arc's hand on the floor in Bresson's *The Trial of Joan of Arc* (1962). Although it is one of Bresson's least-known films, Godard returns to *The Trial of Joan of Arc* more than any other, using its spare concentration of gesture and portrayal of Joan—always shown, in the excerpts selected for *Histoire(s) du cinéma*, in chains—to stand in for the martyrdom of an art form besieged by institutions that constrain its spiritual power.[173] Godard superimposes text with the still, beginning an extended, punning dialogue in which he again alludes to the paraphrase from St. Paul: *"viendra"* appears over the *Trial of Joan of Arc* image; followed by an image of a hand preparing to take communion (*"Oh! Temps"*); an image of the couple from *The Story of the Flaming Years* (Yuliya Solntseva, 1961); an image of Johannes and Maren from the end of *Ordet* (Carl Theodor Dreyer, 1955) (*"Oh! Temps"*); a still of an empty bed with the imprint of a body from Hitchcock's *Psycho* (1960); and finally a moving shot from *Un chien andalou*, ending just before the eye is sliced (*"l'image viendra au temps de la resurrection"*).

This short excerpt is as densely packed as the rest of *Histoire(s) du cinéma*, but, coming immediately after the Wittgenstein text, at least one strong thread appears—what "the cinema alone," through the montage-driven transformation of conventional vision, can do is summon an Image of that which exceeds the boundaries of sight. Whatever iconic "purity" it may have had in an earlier period, this Image is perpetually in flux, its plenitude accessible only through the matrix of contrapuntal collisions on which its visibility depends. In *Le Contrôle de l'univers* (4A), Godard refers to *Ordet* as one of only two films in the history of cinema that successfully presented a miracle, and the shot he selects in this sequence is of the moment *before* Johannes raises his sister-in-law from the dead.[174] Unlike Dreyer, Godard leaves the definitive moment offscreen, instead using associational montage to hint at transformational potentialities that remain, within *Histoire(s) du cinéma*, unfulfilled. "For me, montage is the resurrection of life," Godard declared in an interview. "It is the sense of utopia, of possible resurrection, that I have found in montage, which means that if I am alone, it is a shame, but it is bearable."[175]

Think with Your Hands

The purely corporeal can be uncanny. Compare the way angels and
devils are portrayed. So-called "miracles" must be connected with this.
A miracle must be, as it were, a sacred gesture.
—LUDWIG WITTGENSTEIN (1946)[176]

After showing the famous shot of an eye about to be spliced in *Un chien andalou* midway through *Une histoire seule* (1B), Godard inserts a series of three seventeenth-century paintings—Rembrandt's *The Vision of Daniel* (1650), Caravaggio's *David with the Head of Goliath* (1609–1610), and finally a "close-up" of the head in Rembrandt's *The Anatomy Lesson of Dr. Deyman* (1656) (figure 4.16). All of these have conceptual links to the film sequences and stills that preceded them, focusing as they do on images shorn from the body and on the boundary between life and death.[177] There is also a fixation on cutting, on hands as an instrument of separation and division, which Godard reinforces by returning to the puncturing of the eye in Buñuel's film, connecting the image that he had held offscreen up until this point to a simple title card reading "*le cinéma.*" In the years when he was making *Histoire(s) du cinéma*, Godard sometimes implied that, like the unseen subjects of Rembrandt's *The Anatomy Lesson of Dr. Deyman*, he was working like a surgeon, using montage to open eyes rendered complacent by industrial consumer life. In the Montreal lectures, Godard instead compared his practice to that of a carpenter, an idea that resonates with both his artisanal production method and the many images of manual labor in his films.[178] On other occasions, he has described his approach to the editing of images and

FIGURE 4.16 *Detail of* David with the Head of Goliath *(Caravaggio, 1609–1610, Galleria Borghese, Rome) superimposed with text reading "The image will come at the time of the resurrection" in* Une histoire seule *(1B) of* Histoire(s) du cinéma *(Jean-Luc Godard, 1988–1998).*

sounds as like that of a sculptor.[179] Godard's desire to exert direct control over the images in his films also led him to help develop a handheld 35mm camera that would have "the technical simplicity and flexibility of Super-8 so that a nonspecialist [like Godard] could use it for spontaneous, brief shots that could be intercut with 35mm work done by professional cinematographers."[180] For Godard, hands are the most concrete manifestation of the self's interaction with the world of objects and things, the instrument for physical activity, and the vouchsafe of corporeal existence (figure 4.17).

"The true condition of man is to think with his hands," Denis de Rougemont declared in *Penser avec les mains* (1936), a personalist treatise that is read out at length in *Le Contrôle de l'univers* (4A).[181] At the same time, hands are also the conduits for creativity—that which makes possible the writing of a text, the performance of a musical composition, or the filming of a moment in time. Malraux ends *The Voices of Silence* (1951), the revised single-volume edition of *The Psychology of Art*, with an encomium about the artistic power of hands, using language that connects very strongly with *Histoire(s) du cinéma*:

> Humanism does not consist in saying: "No animal could have done what we have done," but in declaring: "We have refused to do what the beast

FIGURE 4.17 *A hand over a television screen in* First Name: Carmen *(Jean-Luc Godard, 1983).*

within us willed to do, and we wish to rediscover Man wherever we discover that which seeks to crush him to the dust." True, for a religious-minded man this long debate of metamorphosis and rediscoveries is but an echo of a divine voice, for a man becomes truly Man only when in quest of what is most exalted in him; yet there is beauty in the thought that this animal who knows that he must die can wrest from the disdainful splendor of the nebulae the music of the spheres and broadcast it across the years to come, bestowing on them messages as yet unknown. In that house of shadows where Rembrandt still plies his brush, all the illustrious Shades, from the artists of the caverns onwards, follow each movement of the trembling hand that is drafting for them a new lease of survival—or of sleep.

And that hand whose waverings in the gloom are watched by ages immemorial is vibrant with one of the loftiest of the secret yet compelling testimonies to the power and the glory of being Man.[182]

"The trembling hand" in the midst of a creative act appears frequently in Godard's late work. In films like *Une femme mariée: Fragments d'un film tourné en 1964 en noir et blanc,* Godard, inspired perhaps by the opening of *Hiroshima mon amour* (Alain Resnais, 1959) and the early 1960s work of Antonioni, had used cropped images of hands and other body parts to suggest an eroticism that had been detached or abstracted from tenderness. After

1968, hands are instead linked to acts of production—organic and sexual as well as artistic—while in films like *Numéro deux*, they are used to suggest the compulsive creativity of a filmmaker at an intellectual impasse. By the time Godard returned to feature filmmaking and began planning out *Histoire(s) du cinéma*, hands had attained both a heightened prominence and a new autonomy, linked to a conception of montage that was both abstrusely allusive and emphatically concrete. "In montage," Godard declared in one interview, "one has a moment physically, like an object, like this ashtray," and both *King Lear* and *JLG/JLG—Self-Portrait in December* include scenes in which strips of film are held and connected together by hand (figure 4.18).[183] The frequent shots of hands in *Nouvelle vague* are similarly tactile, but they resonate along a number of overlapping metaphoric axes. Like the hands at the end of Nicholas Ray's *On Dangerous Ground* (1952), they suggest the possibility of genuine connection, while also, through their linkage across a single matching cut, making tangible the largely invisible effects of editing. By adjusting focus so that the outstretched hands stand out from the blurred landscape in the background, Godard is able to fixate on their physical surfaces, the ways in which they evoke aging bodies, while also pointing in the direction of the ineffable.[184]

FIGURE 4.18 *Film being worked by hand in* JLG/JLG—Self-Portrait in December *(Jean-Luc Godard, 1994).*

In treating hands as he does in *Nouvelle vague*, Godard invokes the most iconographically charged depiction of outstretched hands in the Western canon, the divine touch in Michelangelo's *The Creation of Adam* (1508–1512). Godard never refers to the Sistine Chapel image directly, but the relationship between sacred love and physical contact informs much of the work made during the period of *Histoire(s) du cinéma*. In *Scénario du film Passion* (1982), for example, Godard assigns a privileged place to another sort of "divine" love, Tintoretto's painting *The Marriage of Bacchus and Ariadne* (1578), which he describes as embodying both the subject of his film—one man and two women—and the idea of a sacred trinity (figure 4.19).[185] *Scénario du film Passion* is the longest and most substantive of the video "sketches" that Godard completed in this period, and, like the others, it is replete with images of hands in motion—operating an editing table, gesticulating to the viewer, or raised, like those of a suppliant, before a movie screen. Like Stéphane Mallarmé's blank page (to which it is compared), the screen remains "empty" throughout the video, but images of several of the canvases re-enacted as tableaux vivants in the accompanying feature (*Passion*) are superimposed with an image of Godard himself. As in Ingmar Bergman's *Persona* (1966), the screen becomes a metaphor for the Cartesian separation of the body and the psyche, a surface

FIGURE 4.19 *Detail of* The Marriage of Bacchus and Ariadne *(Jacopo Tintoretto, 1578, Palazzo Ducale, Venice) superimposed with Jean-Luc Godard in* Scénario du film Passion *(Jean-Luc Godard, 1982).*

on which psychological yearnings and needs can be projected. Yet by layering dim reproductions of canvases on top of pixelated video imagery, Godard subsumes everything onscreen within the visual imagination of the film-maker in the center. In "matching" the central touch in the Tintoretto canvas with the outstretched arms of the director, Godard goes even further, turning those same hands into expressions of his demiurgic authority.

Godard ends *Une histoire seule* (1B) with a brief sequence that cinematically distills this dynamic. After an extended montage that focuses on the lost innocence of the cinema by linking post-1945 film icons like *La terra trema* (Luchino Visconti, 1948) with proto-cinematic materials from the late nineteenth century, Godard inserts an intertitle reading "*au paradis perdu*" and includes sound of Maria Casarès reading a passage from Martin Heidegger's 1946 essay, "What Are Poets For?"

> Poets are the mortals who, singing earnestly . . . sense the trace of the fugitive gods, stay on the gods' tracks, and so trace for their kindred mortals the way toward the turning. . . . But who has the power to sense, to trace such a track? Traces are often inconspicuous, and are always the legacy of a directive that is barely divined. To be a poet in a destitute time means: to attend, singing, to the trace of the fugitive gods.[186]

When this text had been quoted earlier in *Une histoire seule* (1B), it was accompanied by images of the "gods" themselves—the founding figures of United Artists—but here, intercut with Leonard Cohen's "If It Be Your Will" and the voice of a man discussing Christian theology, it is attached to a brief sequence from Hitchcock's *Vertigo* in which Scottie Ferguson uses his hands to rescue "Madeleine" from drowning in San Francisco Bay. In *Nouvelle vague* (which was made the following year), Godard riffs on the same *Vertigo* sequence, but gives it added weight by structurally paralleling two partial drownings, the first leading to death and the second to a sort of resurrection.[187] By virtue of its position within this montage constellation, the drowning sequence also has religious connotations in *Une histoire seule* (1B), but Godard gives it a different inflection by quoting the Acts of the Apostles in overlaid text reading "we are all here."[188] In bringing all of these elements together, Godard indirectly elucidates his own double position within *Histoire(s) du cinéma*: the Romantic elegist (a "poet in a destitute time") using fragments of a lost world to memorialize fallen deities; and the modernist reflexively interrogating the mnemonic structure of his medium.

Throughout *Histoire(s) du cinéma*, Godard uses the ashes of the past to memorialize an auteurist pantheon, with major filmmakers doubling as substitutes for the heroic figures of the ancient world. If von Stroheim is presented as a modern Icarus, Hitchcock, "the greatest creator of forms in the twentieth century," is Godard's Prometheus. The penultimate section of *Histoire(s) du cinéma*, *Le Contrôle de l'univers* (4A), contains a long tribute to

Hitchcock that interrelates images of tightly framed body parts and objects from throughout his corpus, emphasizing the director's still unmatched ability to fuse the codes of narrative "realism" with a sense of pure form that hovers on the border of pictorial abstraction. If Hitchcock is, as Godard suggests, "with Dreyer, the only one who knew how to film a miracle," it is because he links it to the motion of hands, framing his images to isolate gestures like the touching of rosary beads in *The Wrong Man*, and thereby making visible the corporeal manifestations of the sacred. Like the Dreyer of *Ordet*, who uses the conventions of pastoral romance and the "rhythm-bound restlessness" of a long-take aesthetic to conceal the spiritual agency of Johannes until very late in the film, Hitchcock deflects attention away from the religious implications of his narrative by adopting a location-driven style derived from Neorealism and exhaustively detailing the specifics surrounding the arrest of Manny Balestrero.[189] In a unique precredit sequence, a silhouette of Hitchcock declares that "everything you see in this film is absolutely true," misdirecting the first time viewer's attention toward the surface effects of the film's style while audaciously deepening the impact of the "miracle"—in which, following the prayer of Balestrero's mother, the criminal is discovered and arrested—at the end of the film. The unusual nature of

FIGURE 4.20 *Superimposition of a photograph of Alfred Hitchcock and a detail of* Madonna of the Rosary *(Caravaggio, 1607, Kunsthistorisches Museum, Vienna) with text reading "The Artist" in* Le Contrôle de l'univers *(4A) of* Histoire(s) du cinéma *(Jean-Luc Godard, 1988–1998).*

the scene is reinforced by Hitchcock's use of superimposition, a technique that was rarely employed in his sound features and constitutes a decisive rupture in the midst of a film shaped, as Godard himself noted in the 1950s, by a rigorously "classical" mise en scène.[190] Godard amplifies this quality by superimposing a photograph of Hitchcock with the sequence from the film, implying that the true agent of fate in the film is the filmmaker, envisioned here as both creator and puppeteer (figure 4.20).

For Godard, the movement of hands in *Le Contrôle de l'univers* (4A) was orchestrated "in order to show the classic gesture of the old cinema, when there were no more shots. . . . [As in] painting, the cinema is thought with the hands; all creators think with their hands."[191] In *Histoire(s) du cinéma*, Hitchcock is portrayed as the embodiment of both classical form and directorial power, "the only *poète maudit* to meet with success, failing where Alexander, Caesar, Hitler, and Napoleon had failed, in controlling the universe." At the same time, however, Godard also draws attention to the way in which Hitchcock's deceptive classicism masked his transformation of Romantic motifs, extracting only the moments of *l'amour fou* in *Vertigo* and drawing out their underlying implications at the end of *Une histoire seule* (1B) by juxtaposing the shot of Scottie Ferguson and "Madeleine" from *Vertigo* with an image of a boat at night from Albert Lewin's postwar recuperation of Wagner (by way of Giorgio de Chirico), *Pandora and the Flying Dutchman* (1951). In the same interview in which he spoke of hands as demonstrating a "classic gesture," Godard refers to the unification of contraries by asserting, "the Classics, that is us," an allusion to Hugo's *Hernani* and its famous reconciliation of Classicists and Romantics.[192] *Hernani* was first performed in February 1830, several months before the July Revolution, and it became the standard-bearer for French Romanticism in theater by absorbing the strategies of eighteenth-century Classicism.[193] *Breathless* occupies a position within film history that is analogous to *Hernani*'s within the corpus of literary Romanticism—a point Godard himself makes by situating it at the halfway point of his *The Origins of the 21st Century*. By alluding to this nineteenth-century debate, Godard is commenting upon his own hybrid position. Rather than Oedipally resisting his predecessors, he intimates that his style emerges from the absorption of theirs; as he put it in an interview for *Histoire(s) du cinéma*, "I have always been a Romantic bound by a Classical key."[194]

However much it may owe to Hitchcock, *Histoire(s) du cinéma* was made in a postclassical film culture, and it is explicitly aligned with the "other cinema" celebrated in the montage of hands that occurs near the end of *Les Signes parmi nous* (4B). This culminating cluster of gestures is accompanied by Godard's voiceover reading of the modified Frampton text and is initiated by an aged hand and a pair of photographic portraits of himself. The series of hands that follows includes stills from *Un chien andalou; The Joyless Street* (G. W. Pabst, 1925); *In a Lonely Place* (Nicholas Ray, 1950); *Beauty and the Beast* (Jean Cocteau, 1946); and *The Trial of Joan of Arc.* The choice of films suggests an array of interpretive possibilities, but the primary thread linking them together is Godard's own history as a critic and the viewer's memories of previous *Histoire(s) du cinéma* sections. By implicit contrast with the Hitchcock montage in *Le Contrôle de l'univers* (4A), the far less totalizing montage at the end of *Les Signes parmi nous* (4B) suggests the rougher, more jagged rhythms as well as the potential for aesthetic or spiritual elevation (signaled above all by the communion scene from Bresson's *The Trial of Joan of Arc*) that define the "other" cinema. In this respect, the turn to Hitchcock in *Le Contrôle de l'univers* (4A) is also an elegiac turn toward Godard's own origins, the final moment in which popular and art cinema moved roughly parallel to one another, formal experiments could comfortably be wedded to tightly constructed narratives, and "the trembling hand" of the artist did not need to assert itself by proxy, but could be hidden in plain sight.

À *la recherche du paradis perdu*

In order that we may understand one another, it is well to cast a glance at the present state of my Memoirs. What happens to every contractor working on a large scale has happened to me: I have, in the first place, built the outer wings of my edifice, and then, removing and restoring my scaffoldings in different positions, I have raised the stone and the mortar for the intermediate structures: it used to take several centuries to complete a Gothic cathedral. If Heaven grant me life, the work will be finished by stages of my various years; the architect, always the same, will have changed only in age.

—FRANÇOIS-RENÉ DE CHATEAUBRIAND, *MEMOIRS FROM BEYOND THE TOMB* (1849–1850)[195]

Yes: if, owing to the work of oblivion, the returning memory can throw no bridge, form no connecting link between itself and the present minute, if it remains in the context of its own place and date, if it keeps its distance, its isolation in the hollow of a valley or upon the highest peak of a mountain summit, for this very reason it causes us suddenly to breathe a new air, an air which is new precisely because we have breathed it in the past, that purer air which the poets have vainly tried to situate in paradise and which could induce so profound a sensation of renewal only if it had been breathed before, since the true paradises are the paradises that we have lost.

—MARCEL PROUST, *TIME REGAINED* (1927)[196]

In 1980, Godard claimed that "the domination of Gutenberg" has resulted in a sort of blindness, for which, by restoring to death its "tremendous force," films like those of Hitchcock are the cure.[197] Godard's modification of the Hugolian paradigm challenges that of Malraux, who had inverted the assumptions of Élie Faure by suggesting that the supplanting of cathedrals by "picture-palaces" represented the diminished idealism of a world devoid of supreme Truth: "The creative imagination is put to the service of amusement and, with the break-up of man's inner world, the arts of delectation—entertainment for its own sake—sweep the board."[198] Malraux first made arguments of this kind in his 1940 essay "Sketch for a Psychology of Cinema," which Godard annotated by hand while working on *Histoire(s) du cinéma*.[199] Godard's most important annotation comes after Malraux's declaration that, with its power of distraction, the cinema becomes a type of "journalism . . . constrained to have recourse to an element from which art cannot be permanently banned: the element of the Myth."[200] "And the life of the best cinema . . . consists in being crafty with the myth," Godard responds, in what could be seen as a declaration of principles for a work devoted to the cinematic mythos that "begins with *Fantômas* [Louis Feuillade, 1913–1914] and ends with Christ."[201] These two poles are central to *Histoire(s) du cinéma*, which treats cinema as both a site of dubious escapism and a ritual act, transforming the ephemerality of a medium predicated on mass reproducibility into an audiovisual monument with some of the structural weight and embedded cultural memory of a cathedral.[202]

When watched as an intensive unit, *Histoire(s) du cinéma* creates the impression of gradual ascent, with the fugal repetitions intermittently evoking the sensation of rapture, momentary glimpses of transcendent release that are inextricable from the constant reminders of the twentieth century's horrors. Godard's claim that the best way to watch *Histoire(s) du cinéma* is to "enter the image without a name or a reference in mind" suggests that the viewer will take in the layers of reference in much the same way that a cathedral visitor absorbs the pedagogical program of stained glass windows elevated far above eye level, through the diffusion of light.[203] Yet if *Histoire(s) du cinéma* can be seen as a cathedral-like work, it is also an echo chamber, a labyrinth of the mind, which language is able to penetrate only in the most halting way. The many repetitions, half-starts, and pauses reflect not only Godard's resistance to historiographic transparency, but also the deliberately unstable positioning of his own authorial interventions. Godard provides one possible explanation when, anticipated by a single onscreen definition of cinema as "time lost" and "time found" in *Seul le cinéma* (2A), he cries out "Albertine" at the beginning of *Fatale beauté* (2B).[204] This allusion to Marcel Proust's masterwork announces early in *Histoire(s) du cinéma* that it is, on at least one level, a fictionalized autobiography ("*Histoire(s) du cinémoi*"), an extended memory piece permeated with associations that are at once hermetically private and profoundly interlinked.[205]

The significance of this idiosyncratic voiceover becomes clearer by comparison to *JLG/JLG—Self-Portrait in December*, a film made while Godard was completing work on *Fatale beauté* (2B) that he said should be viewed along with *Histoire(s) du cinéma*.[206] Complementing the Proustian reconstruction of selfhood in *Histoire(s) du cinéma, JLG/JLG—Self-Portrait in December* opens with a voiceover in which Godard declares that he is performing a role ("JLG"), carefully choosing how to present himself before an audience: "Exercise 174. Cast the roles. Begin the Rehearsals. Settle problems concerning the direction. Perfect the entrances and exits. Learn your role by heart."[207] Adopting the indirect manner of some painted self-portraits, Godard attaches his narration to open windows, a pair of his shoes, and a photograph of himself as a youth that is already "in mourning," a product of both temperament and circumstance (the photograph depicts Godard, age thirteen, in the midst of World War II).[208] In this "self-portrait in December," history may well be a nightmare from which the artist is trying desperately to awaken, but it is also a privileged memory, the point against which the self being narrated is defined.[209] Godard deepens this point by including the same photograph in *La Monnaie de l'absolu* (3A) and pairing it with onscreen text reading first "1944" and then "'94," thereby linking *Histoire(s) du cinéma* to the cinematic "self-portrait" and the semicentennial of the French Liberation.

The most openly autobiographical section of *Histoire(s) du cinéma* is the last, *Les Signes parmi nous* (4B), which opens with a joint dedication "to Anne-Marie Miéville [Godard's partner since the early 1970s] and to myself." Although there is no new footage of Godard, as there had been in every section before *Le Contrôle de l'univers* (4A), *Les Signes parmi nous* (4B) includes more images of the artist—photographs from different angles and clips taken from *JLG/JLG—Self-Portrait in December*—than any other. Yet *Les Signes parmi nous* (4B) is also the section with the most explicit verbal references to the viewer, with onscreen text building off the Eliotic "*cinéma histoire(s) / cinéma toi / ne a toi / né toi / né*" ["cinema histories / cinema you / born in you / born you / born"] that ended the preceding section to assert, punningly: "*le cinéma / à qui il appartenait, lui / à toi / é moi / toi toi / toi histoire*" ("the cinema / to whom it belongs / to you / and me / you you / your history").[210] "My story crosses these stories [of the century], their silences, their passions," Godard declared in a contemporaneous interview, continuing:

> The *Histoire(s)* is a little bit like an album of memories, mine, but also those of many others, of several generations who believed in the sunrise. The cinema, in the twentieth century, was the art that permitted souls—as one says in Russian novels—to live intimately their stories in History. We will never again see such a fusion, such adequation, such a desire for fictions

and collective History. . . . Having lived fifty years of cinema, it is normal that I end by connecting it to my own life and to the men of my time. Only the cinema could bring together this "I" and this "we."[211]

This comes across most vividly not through any of the photographic or filmic images of an aged Godard, but through a portrait of the young Arthur Rimbaud that Godard links to footage of Charles de Gaulle arriving in Paris and includes shortly before the reading of the Pound extract. That this photograph is an indirect stand-in for the filmmaker is supported by the visual similarities with the image shown in *La Monnaie de l'absolu* (3A) and *JLG/JLG—Self-Portrait in December*, as well as the fact that Godard would have been approximately the same age as Rimbaud at the time of de Gaulle's return.[212] The layers of resonance do not end there, however, because the photograph of Rimbaud also recalls the famous photograph of a boy in the Warsaw ghetto that had appeared at the beginning of this section of *Histoire(s) du cinéma*, while the images of de Gaulle are matched to an extract from *The Fall of Berlin* (Mikheil Chiaureli, 1949) showing people waiting for the arrival of another triumphant leader (Stalin) in a very different capital city. It is by bringing these seemingly unrelated elements—photographic portraiture, documentary footage, and audiovisual excerpts from fictional propaganda—together that cinema is able to fuse the "*moi*" and the "*toi*," the "vertigo of history" and the "odyssey of utopia," bringing private and public memories into dialogue with one another in such a way that the perspectives of the viewer and the filmmaker meet.

Late in *JLG/JLG—Self-Portrait in December*, Godard offers up a sort of indirect *ars poetica* by having a blind seer recite a slightly modified version of the final passages of Ovid's *Metamorphoses* in Latin. Substituting "America" for "Rome," Godard (who translates and repeats certain passages in French) analogizes his work to that of a poet:

> My work is complete: a work which neither Jove's anger, nor fire nor sword shall destroy, nor yet the gnawing tooth of time. That day which has power over nothing but my body may, when it pleases, put an end to my uncertain span of years. Yet with my better part I shall soar, undying, far above the stars, and my name will be imperishable. Wherever America [Rome]'s influence extends over the lands America [Rome] has subdued, people will read my verse. If there be any truth in poets' prophecies, I shall live to all eternity, immortalized by fame.[213]

Godard's decision to invoke this heritage in his apologia testifies to its role in his thinking at this time (there are no sustained quotes in Latin in the films made before *Histoire(s) du cinéma* was initiated) and helps explain his decision to structure his long-form epic as a mythic journey led by a fictionalized self-projection of the author. After all, the very first words to appear onscreen are "*hoc opus / hic labor est*," a passage from *The Aeneid* (Virgil, 19 BCE) that refers to the difficulties of returning from hell.[214] The passage from Pound at the very end of *Les Signes parmi nous* (4B) returns to this imagery, which, like the underworld scene in *The Aeneid*, derives from the *nekuia* in Book XI of *The Odyssey*.[215] As in *Histoire(s) du cinéma*, Pound returns again and again to central figures, looping back to remind the reader of the spiraling arc of the "chryselephantine" work. Thus, in one of the last Pisan Cantos (LXXXIII), the reader encounters "Tiresias, Thebae," the same "Tiresias Theban" who had prophesied (in the passage that begins just after the one used in *Les Signes parmi nous*) that Odysseus would "come to disaster, losing all companions."[216] Equivalent recurring motifs could be found throughout both *Histoire(s) du cinéma* and the *Cantos*, but this one is especially significant because it represents a return to the beginning and because it underscores the centrality of the Odyssean quest, which, as in the story of the colporteur Godard reads out shortly before the Pound extract, ends in near-total isolation.[217]

"You in the dinghy (*piccioletta*) astern there!" Pound cries out in Canto CIX, evoking yet again the sea journey of Odysseus while also pointing back to the central model underpinning his modernist epic by alluding to the third part of Dante's *Divine Comedy*.[218] Yet creating a *Paradiso* has proven to be an insurmountable obstacle for Romantics and post-Romantics; how can one convincingly depict the perfection of the heavens within an aesthetic framework oriented around ceaseless becoming? Pound spent the last decades of his life trying to "write Paradise," but in the final completed canto, he declares:

> I have brought the great ball of crystal;
> Who can lift it?
> Can you enter the great acorn of light?
> But the beauty is not the madness
> Tho' my errors and wrecks lie about me.
> And I am not a demigod,
> I cannot make it cohere.[219]

Godard too has struggled with the problem of endings and, at least since he began *Histoire(s) du cinéma*, with the task of completing a cinematic *Commedia*. Midway through *JLG/JLG—Self-Portrait in December*, Godard provides a dialectical pair of lateral tracking shots across a bookshelf in his home. The first shot conspicuously ends by pausing before a shelf section containing only two books, *Inferno* and *Purgatorio*, a detail repeated when the inverse movement begins shortly thereafter. In both *Nouvelle vague* and *La Monnaie de l'absolu* (3A), Godard includes quotations from both books, but nothing from the *Paradiso* (parts of *Inferno* had earlier been recited and discussed in *Contempt*).[220] The one time that Godard attempts to "film paradise," in the third part of the explicitly Dantean *Notre musique*, it is circumscribed, bisected by barbed wire and blocked by American marines, ironically literalizing the lyrics of the military anthem ("If the Army and the Navy / Ever look on Heaven's scenes / They will find the streets are guarded / By United States Marines") emanating from an onscreen radio.[221]

For Godard, paradise, like utopia, is something always anticipated and endlessly deferred. "My goal . . . is like that little poem by Brecht, 'I examine my project carefully: it's unrealizable,'" Godard, like Fritz Lang in *Contempt*, declared to Serge Daney in the central interview of *Seul le cinéma* (2A), continuing,

> because it can only be done on TV, which reduces. Or which projects you, the viewer, but then you lose consciousness, you're rejected. Whereas in cinema, the viewer was attracted. But we can make a memento of this projectable history . . . it's all we can do.[222]

In 2003, Godard was commissioned by the Centre Georges Pompidou to construct a floor-wide installation piece originally entitled *Collage(s) de France, archéologie du cinema d'après JLG* that would have applied the montage principles of *Histoire(s) du cinéma* spatially.[223] After a long and public set of

FIGURE 4.21 *Shot of a white rose from* Germany Year 90 Nine Zero *(Jean-Luc Godard, 1991), with its color changed to yellow, superimposed with text reading "factory of dreams" in* Les Signes parmi nous *(4B) of* Histoire(s) du cinéma *(Jean-Luc Godard, 1988–1998).*

professional disagreements, the plan was scrapped and Godard constructed an alternative installation at the Pompidou that was made up of the fragments of the first and entitled *Voyage(s) en utopie, Jean-Luc Godard, 1946–2006: À la recherche d'un théorème perdu*.[224] The heterogeneous materials of the three long galleries were united primarily by a single sentence that continued across the floor: "Spirit borrows from matter the perceptions on which it feeds and restores them to matter in the form of movements which it has stamped with its own freedom."[225] This passage, the final line of Henri Bergson's *Matter and Memory* (1896), was frequently quoted in works made during the period of *Histoire(s) du cinéma* and, recontextualized, it succinctly articulates the defining aims of Godard's body of work, a series of carefully arranged combinations of found material that undergo continual metamorphosis in both time and space.[226]

Unlike an installation, an epic video project aspiring to contain the history of cinema needs a conclusion, and Godard wanted to find something that would have an impact after four and a half hours that it would not have otherwise.[227] His characteristically vertiginous solution is to fuse the different levels of the work—autobiographical, historical, and aesthetic—in a synthesis that

FIGURE 4.22 *The final superimposition in* Les Signes parmi nous *(4B) of* Histoire(s) du cinéma *(Jean-Luc Godard, 1988–1998): a photograph of Jean-Luc Godard and* Study for a Portrait of Van Gogh II *(Francis Bacon, 1957, private collection).*

enables new forms of regeneration. Accompanied by a reprocessed image of a yellow rose and a photograph of himself superimposed with Francis Bacon's *Study for a Portrait of Van Gogh II* (1957), Godard tells a story of a man who "passed through paradise in a dream, and received a flower as proof of his passage, and found that flower in his hand when he awoke . . . I was that man." The image of the flower is derived from a shot of a white rose in *Germany Year 90 Nine Zero*, where—accompanied by the Sanctus from Beethoven's *Missa solemnis* (opus 123, 1824)—it had functioned as an allusion to the anti-Nazi rebel group led by Sophie Scholl ("The White Rose") in 1943 (figure 4.21).[228] Resituated and with its color changed, however, the image takes on a different meaning, evoking the "yellow of the sempiternal rose" that appears at the end of the *Paradiso*, and implicitly suggesting that Anne-Marie Miéville, whose name appears for the first time in the dedication to *Les Signes parmi nous* (4B), may have functioned as the Beatrice to Godard's Dante.[229] By moving, within the space of one minute, from the beginning of one epic poem (Pound's *Cantos*) to the ending of another (the *Divine Comedy*), Godard constructs a constellation of mutually resonating associations that, pivoting on an image that echoes earlier sections of his own epic, links origins and conclusions, "birth and death," together (figure 4.22).[230] Onscreen text credits the story to Jorge Luis Borges, which is where most scholars have left it, but Borges was also a modernist scavenger, and he took the story from Samuel Taylor Coleridge, who, in turn, had found it in a volume of Jean Paul's *Geist* (1801).[231] For Jean Paul, the story was an affirmation of an absolute world he desperately wanted to believe in.[232] For Godard, by contrast, the rose is more ambivalent, the symbol of a journey through a paradise that, always lost, hovers in the interstices of History, and can only be recovered in memory.

Conclusion

We work in the dark—we do what we can—we give what we have.
Our doubt is our passion and our passion is our task. The rest is the
madness of art.

—Henry James, "the middle years" (1893)[1]

Sátántangó *(Béla Tarr, 1994)*.

After completing *Histoire(s) du cinéma* (1988–1998), Jean-Luc Godard began work on a project that could be seen as a sort of coda, a forty-seven-minute video commissioned by the Museum of Modern Art entitled *The Old Place* (1999). This "child of the museum" addresses the shifting relationship between cinema and the art world by contrasting two empty screens: a raised screen on the wall in an open-air piazza on which a scene from Robert Bresson's *Les Anges du péché* (1943) is superimposed, inhabiting the public space as if it was recalled by collective memory, and a screen in a contemporary art performance space that is made to mechanically convulse (figure C.1).[2] The footage of this writhing screen had been used earlier in *Une vague nouvelle* (3B), as an ironic commentary on the collapse of the cinematic New Wave ("What is in the museum? T-shirts"), and it was reused in *In the Darkness of Time* (2001), the short that was paired with *The Old Place* during its French premiere at the Centre Georges Pompidou.[3] Onscreen text declares that these are "the last minutes of cinema," but what Godard is meditating upon through the repetition of this footage is the proliferation of isolated (and isolating) screens in both contemporary life and artistic practice. Shortly before this moving screen appears in *The Old Place*, Godard sets Jean-Baptiste-Siméon Chardin's idea that art "was an island whose shores he had glimpsed from far off" against Andy Warhol's claim that "art is a market for buying and selling."[4] For Godard, what is lost in between is

FIGURE C.1 Les Anges du péché *(Robert Bresson, 1943) superimposed on a screen in the middle of a piazza in* The Old Place *(Jean-Luc Godard and Anne-Marie Miéville, 1999).*

a conception of art as mystery, as spiritual elevation, as something that, like a cathedral, could "protect time."[5]

A number of artists attempted to find a way to give their media some of the (lost) properties of a cathedral in the twentieth century. Auguste Rodin's late sculpture *The Cathedral* (1909) analogizes a pair of human hands to the structures celebrated in his book *Les Cathédrales de France* (1914) (figure C.2). In the mission statement for the Bauhaus that Walter Gropius wrote in April 1919, he calls for a "cathedral of the future" that would unify the energy of society like the stone edifices of the Middle Ages.[6] Similar metaphors informed the postwar affirmations of the Abstract Expressionists, who gave their works titles like *Cathedral* (Jackson Pollock made one in 1947, Hans Hofmann in 1959); *Sky Cathedral* (Louise Nevelson, 1958); *Man and Woman in Cathedral* (David Smith, 1956); and *Cathedral—The Ascension* (Richard Pousette-Dart, 1947). The major attempts to construct cinematic cathedrals, to create massive works whose radically new form would reinvigorate vanished or fading artistic traditions, also fit into these two historical periods. Those filmmakers who—like D. W. Griffith (born 1875), Erich von Stroheim (born 1885), and Abel Gance (born 1889)—grew up in the nineteenth century

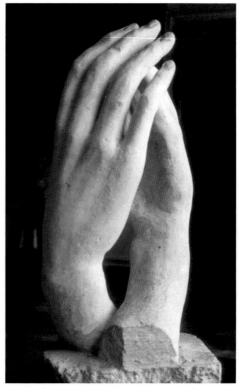

FIGURE C.2 The Cathedral *(Auguste Rodin, 1909, Musée Rodin, Paris; photograph ©* *Vanni Archive / Art Resource, NY).*

and reached their full artistic maturity during or just after World War I could, like Gropius, adopt the mantle of prophets of the future, Promethean artists whose outsized ambitions would pave the way for new conceptions of time and space. For a later generation—Gregory Markopoulos, Jacques Rivette, Jean-Luc Godard, all born between 1928 and 1930—the cinema could take on some of the properties of a cathedral only if it was in some way removed from mainstream culture, cut off from the popular energies that filmmakers like Gance and Griffith had tried to incorporate into their operatic epics.

In every case, however, these filmmakers designed works whose phenom-enological intensity was tied to their status as integral temporal experiences that could open up new affective possibilities for the spectator. Insofar as their films were predicated on ideas of continual and cumulative progres-sion, they amplified, rather than undercut, the basic viewing conditions of narrative cinema. Although screens of various kinds have often been shown reflexively in Godard's work, they are always contained within the space demarcated by the projected film image, which is equally true of the ritual, open-air projections at the Temenos. The mode of viewing required by these works contrasts starkly with the mobile spectatorship engendered by con-temporary multimedia projects like Peter Greenaway's *Ten Classic Paintings Revisited* (2006–present) and Bill Viola's *Going Forth by Day* (2002), attempts to apply the principles of the *Gesamtkunstwerk* within a multiroom gallery setting (figure C.3).[7] It also differs significantly from the type of intermittent viewing encouraged by more recent long-form works by directors like Lav

FIGURE C.3 Leonardo's Last Supper *(Peter Greenaway, 2010, installed at the Park Avenue Armory, New York; photograph courtesy James Ewing/OTTO).*

Diaz or Wang Bing, which, made entirely with inexpensive digital equipment, are no longer conceived as continuous units and are instead intended, like the longest films of Warhol, to be viewed in pieces, with the audience members coming and going as they please.[8] The idea of monumentality endures, but the concentrated, auratic power of the immersive film experience—reinforced in *Eniaios* (Gregory Markopoulos, 1947–1992), *Out 1* (Jacques Rivette, 1971), and *Histoire(s) du cinéma* by the anachronistic embrace of the full frame—has been displaced.[9]

Digital video works like the ten-hour *Evolution of a Filipino Family* (Lav Diaz, 2004) and the nine-hour *West of the Tracks* (Wang Bing, 2003) are products of a globalized, post-Communist world that is very different from the one that shaped the filmmakers discussed above. Early in *The Old Place*, Godard inserts a montage of red flags immediately after text reading "Photos of Utopia," and while he, more than any of the other moving image creators, remains acutely aware of the ease with which idealism transforms into horror, he also recognizes that the political utopianism represented by the Internationale provided a foil, a dialectical counterpoint through which or against which ambitious art could define itself.[10] "Nobody cares about Russians anymore," Godard muses in *La Monnaie de l'absolu* (3A), and part of what he is reacting to with the footage of the convulsing screen is the diminished stakes of art in a world where politics is, for many, no longer a question of life and death. Perhaps this is why almost all the films from the 1990s that are referred to in *Histoire(s) du cinéma*—like the Šarūnas Bartas and Aleksandr Sokurov films included in *Le Contrôle de l'univers* (4A) and *Les Signes parmi nous* (4B)—come from post-Soviet cinemas or reflect upon its legacies.[11]

The one long-form, modernist epic to emerge from this period, Béla Tarr's *Sátántangó* (1994), brings both of these strands together and consciously presents itself as the last work of its kind, which it almost certainly is.[12] In 2009, Tarr prepared a lecture for the Museum of Modern Art, and what he wrote about experimental filmmaker Gábor Bódy applies equally to his own seven-and-a-half-hour film:

> His obsession with "*Gesamtkunst*" helped him achieve unbelievable accomplishments. . . . He wanted to vanquish the film industry with a monumental movie epic, but at the same time to remain in the subculture of underground film, from which he expected renewal.[13]

Straddled between narrative and experimental cinema, Tarr's film announces its formal structure with an opening shot of wandering cows that, over the course of nearly eight uninterrupted minutes, pushes past any possible allegory and into the domain of pure temporal experience.[14] Tarr uses the rich tonalities of genuine black-and-white 35mm film stock to turn these blocks of time into exercises in precise observation—fixating on both the creases of faces and the form of beer bottles so obsessively that they appear almost equivalent, pitching the entire work on the tenuous border between photographic realism and graphic abstraction.[15] Both individual sections and the total twelve-part work are arranged according to the structure of a six-steps-forward, six-steps-back tango, a perfect metaphor for the cyclic torpor unifying the film's multiple, interlaced perspectives.[16] As explicitly as any of the other works discussed here, Tarr's film is oriented around the Romantic iconography of the cathedral, but here ruins are presented as a space devoid of solace and absolution.[17] Just before the end of the film's fifth section, a young girl, utterly without hope, climbs into the remnants of a cathedral-like space, and drinks poison. The image that follows—of mist slowly passing over the dilapidated exterior of this structure—recurs two hours later, when Irimiás, the man who persuades everyone in the village to leave for a better future, walks past it with his two companions. Irimiás falls to the ground like Saul on the road to Damascus, but he is not converted; his encounter with the residue of the sacred past may be as startling for him as it is for the viewer, but he remains a con man, a false messiah who, like Soviet Communism, makes utopian promises that can never be fulfilled.

Tarr's strongest stylistic influences are fellow Hungarian directors like Miklós Jancsó and Gábor Bódy (he has also listed the painter Pieter Bruegel), but the filmmaker to whom he responds most powerfully at the end of *Sátántangó* is Andrei Tarkovsky.[18] In the penultimate section of Tarkovsky's *Andrei Rublev* (1966/1969), the icon painter encounters a young boy who, like a film director, takes on the role of an impresario, encouraging everyone to contribute his part to the construction of a large bell. Tarkovsky includes several high-angle shots in this scene that recall the enigmatic, and equally elemental, prelude to the film, which showed an Icarus-like inventor attempt

FIGURE C.4 *The making of the bell in* Andrei Rublev *(Andrei Tarkovsky, 1966/1969).*

to fly in a hot air balloon only to come crashing back to the ground. The boy succeeds where the inventor failed because he first descends into the bowels of the earth, toiling assiduously in a spirit of fear and trembling before attempting to raise the bell over the horizon, a gesture that revives Rublev's faith and leads to the creation of his greatest masterpieces [figure C.4]. In the final section of *Sátántangó*, the doctor—a viewer surrogate who has voyeuristically observed and narrated the behavior of the other townspeople—hears the sounds of a distant bell and leaves his house, slowly traversing the flat plains of Hungary to find an isolated chapel sitting, like the memorial ruins of a Caspar David Friedrich painting, in a small wooded grove. He enters to find a crazed madman in the belfry, shouting about invaders who will never come, a relic of a past that has become wholly disconnected from the present and a history that has been drained of coherence.[19] Without saying a word, the doctor returns home and methodically boards up the central window in his house, blocking out all light and offering a powerfully materialist finish both to Tarr's cinematic monument and to one of the boldest traditions in twentieth-century art.

{ NOTES }

Introduction

1. Henri Focillon, *The Life of Forms in Art*, translated by Charles Beecher Hogan and George Kubler (New York: Zone Books, 1992), 31.

2. Friedrich Nietzsche, *Thus Spoke Zarathustra*, translated by Adrian Del Caro (Cambridge: Cambridge University Press, 2006), 110.

3. Stan Brakhage, "Brakhage meets Tarkovsky," *Chicago Review* 47, no. 4 (Winter 2001), and 48, no. 1 (Spring 2002), 42.

4. Victor Hugo, *Notre-Dame de Paris*, translated by John Sturrock (London: Penguin Classics, 2004), 193–196.

5. Walter Benjamin, "The Work of Art in the Age of Mechanical Reproduction," in *Illuminations*, edited by Hannah Arendt, translated by Harry Zohn (New York: Schocken Books, 1968), 217–251.

6. The original language title of a work will be used when no standard translation exists or the work was released internationally with a non-English title (e.g., *La Belle Noiseuse*). This applies especially to works with a title containing language-specific meanings that are lost or smoothed over in translation (like *Histoire(s) du cinéma*). Titles will also vary when it is important to distinguish between an overarching project (like Abel Gance's expansive *Napoléon*) and particular manifestations (like the film released as *Napoléon vu par Abel Gance*).

7. Longinus, *On the Sublime*, in *Classical Literary Criticism*, translated by Penelope Murray and T. S. Dorsch (London: Penguin Classics, 2000), 121–129; Edmund Burke, *A Philosophical Enquiry into the Sublime and Beautiful* (London: Penguin Classics, 1998), 114. *On the Sublime* was long attributed to the third-century CE scholar Cassius Longinus, but it is now thought to be the work of an unknown author from the first century CE.

8. Victor Hugo, *The Essential Victor Hugo*, edited and translated by E. H. Blackmore and A. M. Blackmore (Oxford: Oxford World's Classics, 2004), 25. *Cromwell*, written for seventy-seven characters and completed the same year (1827) that the first part of Goethe's *Faust* was translated into French by Gérard de Nerval, announced the birth of Romanticism and initiated a series of extremely long French plays that culminated in Paul Claudel's eleven-hour *The Satin Slipper* (1924). Hugo used the preface as an opportunity to outline his theory of drama, which he defined as "the perennial contrast, the perpetual conflict between two opposed principles that are always in existence, fighting for possession of man, from the cradle to the grave" (33). Like *Cromwell*, the second part of Goethe's *Faust* (published posthumously in 1832) was long considered unperformable, and it anticipates some of the projects discussed here in its gargantuan scale, encyclopedic impulses, and reworking of earlier creative models (particularly through the many references to Dante's *Divine Comedy*, 1308–1320).

9. Hugo, *The Essential Victor Hugo*, 65–68.

Notes to Pages 6–9

10. *Bride of Frankenstein* begins with a sequence in which Lord Byron, Percy Bysshe Shelley, and Mary Shelley comically discuss the origins of poetic inspiration, before moving into the main narrative (extrapolated from material in Mary Shelley's 1818 novel *Frankenstein; or, The Modern Prometheus*). Hitchcock frequently smuggled tropes or ideas derived from the British Romantic poets into his films, slyly alluding to Samuel Taylor Coleridge's "Rime of the Ancient Mariner" (1798) in *The Birds* (1963) and combining the story of Pygmalion with the myth of Demeter and Persephone (complete with corresponding shifts in color scheme) in *Vertigo* (1958), a film whose moments of most intense sensuousness are accompanied by music derived from *Tristan und Isolde* (Richard Wagner, 1865).

11. Longinus, *On the Sublime*, 120.

12. Goethe, "On German Architecture," in *Goethe's Literary Essays*, edited and translated by J. E. Springarn (New York: Frederick Ungar, 1964), 13–14.

13. Sergei Bondarchuk's *War and Peace*, the longest and most expensive film produced in the Soviet Union, was released in four parts between 1966 and 1967, totaling approximately seven hours in its entirety. The film was preceded by several socialist realist epics presented in the form of trilogies, such as the *Maxim Trilogy* (Grigori Kozintsev and Leonid Trauberg, 1935–1939) and *And Quiet Flows the Don* (Sergei Gerasimov, 1957–1958). *The Human Condition* was a series of three long films, adapted from a six-volume novel, that were released individually between 1959 and 1961. Altogether, the trilogy has a projection time of over nine and a half hours.

14. David Quint, *Epic and Empire* (Princeton, NJ: Princeton University Press, 1993), 9, 34.

15. Friedrich Schlegel, *Philosophical Fragments*, translated by Peter Firchow (Minneapolis: University of Minnesota Press, 1991), 31–32. Schlegel's comments in Athenaeum Fragment 116 apply beyond the specific genre of poetry. As Frederick C. Beiser has argued, "As early as 1797, Schlegel had already extended the concept of *romantische Poesie* to all the arts and sciences, and he began to talk about the *Poesie* within nature itself . . . he is *not* referring only to literary works or indeed to the products of any activity. Rather, he is talking about creative *activity*, the *process* by which something is produced" (Frederick C. Beiser, *The Romantic Imperative: The Concept of Early German Romanticism* [Cambridge, MA: Harvard University Press, 2003], 17).

16. Quoted in Marshall Brown, *The Shape of German Romanticism* (Ithaca, NY: Cornell University Press, 1979), 186. In Schlegel's novel *Lucinde* (1799), memory imbues external spaces with private associations, enabling them to become "the sacred home" of the protagonist's "sorrows and resolutions" (Friedrich Schlegel, *Lucinde and the Fragments*, translated by Peter Firchow [Minneapolis: University of Minnesota Press, 1971], 93).

17. Fragment 859 in Novalis, *Notes for a Romantic Encyclopedia* (*Das Allgemeine Brouillon*), edited and translated by David W. Wood (Albany: State University of New York Press, 2007), 155; "Logological Fragments I," Number 88 in Novalis, *Philosophical Writings*, edited and translated by Margaret Mahony Stoljar (Albany: State University of New York Press, 1997), 88; Novalis, *Hymns to the Night and Spiritual Songs*, translated by George MacDonald (London: Temple Lodge, 1992), 13.

18. Fragment 1023 in Novalis, *Romantic Encyclopedia*, 176. Laurie Ruth Johnson argues that the key term for Novalis is *Erinnerung*, which suggests a conception of memory as "an activity that requires the use of the imagination," rather than *Gedächtnis*, which "connotes the faculty of memory as a kind of storage space" (*The Art of Recollection in Jena*

Romanticism [Tübingen: Max Niemeyer Verlag, 2002], 104–105). Novalis explicitly connects this form of active memory to poetry in one of the *Pollen* (1798) fragments, writing, "Nothing is more poetic than memory [*Erinnerung*] . . ." (*Philosophical Writings*, 45).

19. Coleridge further distinguishes between a "primary" imagination, which is "the living Power and prime Agent of all human Perception . . . a repetition in the fine mind of the eternal act of creation in the infinite I AM," and a "secondary" imagination that is "an echo of the former, co-existing with the conscious will, yet still as identical with the primary in the *kind* of its agency, and differing only in *degree*, and in the *mode* of its operation." It is in this secondary mode that imagination becomes "essentially *vital*, even as all objects (*as* objects) are essentially fixed and dead" (Samuel Taylor Coleridge, *Biographia Literaria*, in *Coleridge's Poetry and Prose*, edited by Nicholas Halmi, Paul Magnuson, and Raimonda Modiano [New York: W.W. Norton, 2004], 488–489).

Percy Bysshe Shelley had a similarly vaunted conception of memory, imagination, and developing selfhood. In an implicit reversal of a Homeric invocation, his "To Jane: The Recollection" (1822) turns the "Tell me, Muse" that begins *The Odyssey* into the assertive "Rise, Memory, and write its praise!" and ends with the declaration, "Less oft is peace in Shelley's mind / Than calm in waters seen!" (lines 4 and 87–88). "Tell me, Muse" is Richmond Lattimore's translation of the first line of Homer's *The Odyssey* (New York: Harper and Row, 1967). In a nod to Vladimir Nabokov's autobiography, a more recent translation by Stanley Lombardo (Indianapolis: Hackett, 2000) renders this as "Speak, Memory."

Chapter 1

1. Dedication preceding the poem *Les Fenêtres* in the catalog for a Robert Delaunay exhibition in 1913 (Paris: André Marty, 1913). The title of this chapter derives from Abel Gance, "Le Temps de l'image est venu!" in Léon Pierre-Quint, Abel Gance, Lionel Landry, and Germaine Dulac, *L'Art cinématographique II* (Paris: Félix Alcan, 1927), 83–102.

2. D. W. Griffith, "Weak Spots in a Strong Business—XIV," *Motion Picture News* 11, no. 18 (May 8, 1915), 39.

3. Ibid.

4. Louis Feuillade's *Fantômas* (1913–1914) and Victorin Jasset's *Protéa* (1913–1919), the first major European serials, began in 1913. The American equivalent, *The Perils of Pauline* (Louis J. Gasnier and Donald MacKenzie, 1914), began the following year. Both were preceded by lengthy films released in episodes or sections, sometimes lasting several reels. Albert Capellani's *Les Misérables* was a twelve-reel film broken up into four "*Époques*" of three reels each, released at one-week intervals in January 1913.

5. In 1911, for example, W. Stephen Bush, the influential *Moving Picture World* critic who frequently expounded on the relationship between music and cinema, wrote, "Every man or woman in charge of [the] music of a moving picture theatre is, consciously or unconsciously, a disciple of Richard Wagner" (quoted in Matthew Wilson Smith, "American Valkyries: Richard Wagner, D. W. Griffith, and the Birth of Classical Cinema," *Modernism/Modernity* 15, no. 2 [2008], 229).

6. Griffith, "Weak Spots," 39.

7. Ibid.

8. Clune's Auditorium Souvenir Booklet for *Intolerance*, D. W. Griffith Papers, Museum of Modern Art.

9. In his 1841 essay "Art," Emerson wrote, "Art must not be a superficial talent, but must begin farther back in man." Earlier in the same essay, Emerson described the function of the artist in a way that the Griffith of *Intolerance* would surely have agreed with:

> The artist must employ the symbols in use in his day and nation, to convey his enlarged sense to his fellow-men. Thus the new in art is always formed out of the old. The Genius of the Hour sets his ineffaceable seal on the work, and gives it an inexpressible charm for the imagination. As far as the spiritual character of the period overpowers the artist, and finds expression in his work, so far it will retain a certain grandeur, and will represent to future beholders the Unknown, the Inevitable, the Divine. (Ralph Waldo Emerson, *Essays and Lectures* [New York: Library of America, 1983], 431–432)

10. D. W. Griffith, "Griffith to Film History of World in Gigantic Serial," *New York Globe*, May 2, 1922, 12.

11. In his posthumously published autobiography, Griffith admits that Whitman was at least as important as Dickens in his artistic development. According to the person compiling the autobiography (James Hart):

> [Griffith] had been led to tempo and parallel action in Whitman's *Leaves of Grass* by the roundtable of Flexner's bookstore, an anecdote he repeated several times in the presence of others. With his earthy ideas on sex and religion, however, Whitman had already succeeded in scandalizing rural America, and Griffith simply could not afford to openly espouse this avant-garde poet and then face Oldham County again. Dickens, however, was eminently respectable, and for Griffith to ascribe all his techniques to the popular Victorian English author was a natural ploy. (D. W. Griffith and James Hart, *The Man Who Invented Hollywood* [Louisville: Touchstone, 1972], 161)

12. Vachel Lindsay, "Photoplay Progress," *New Republic* 10, no. 120 (February 17, 1917), 76.

13. Quoted in Michelle Facos, *Symbolist Art in Context* (Berkeley: University of California Press, 2009), 47. Characteristically, Friedrich Schlegel described his novel *Lucinde* (1799) as an "eternal hieroglyph" of the "nature of love" (*Lucinde and the Fragments*, translated by Peter Firchow [Minneapolis: University of Minnesota Press, 1971], 261).

14. Quoted in Peter Selz, *German Expressionist Painting* (Berkeley: University of California Press, 1974), 101.

15. Leopold von Ranke, *The Secret of World History: Selected Writings on the Art and Science of History*, edited and translated by Roger Wines (New York: Fordham University Press, 1981), 241. Ranke had a considerable influence on late nineteenth- and early twentieth-century American historiography (he was appointed the first honorary member of the American Historical Association in 1884). Although there is no evidence that Griffith read his books, he certainly shared Ranke's belief that the narrativization of representative statements and ideas would allow one to capture the essence of a particular historical moment.

16. John T. Irwin, *American Hieroglyphics: The Symbol of the Egyptian Hieroglyphics in the American Renaissance* (New Haven: Yale University Press, 1980), 31. Whitman refers to grass as a "uniform hieroglyphic" in the "Song of Myself" section of *Leaves of Grass*

(Book III, section 6), and Irwin argues that, partially under the influence of Emerson's writings on Swedenborg, Whitman conceived *Leaves of Grass*, which he described as "the Great Construction of the New Bible," in relation to the hieroglyphic studies of Jean-François Champollion (Irwin, 20–32).

17. Vachel Lindsay, *The Art of the Moving Picture* (New York: Modern Library, 2000), 123–124.

18. Lillian Gish and Ann Pinchot, *The Movies, Mr. Griffith, and Me* (Englewood Cliffs, NJ: Prentice-Hall, 1969), 183. Miriam Hansen mentions a slightly different version of this quote as part of a discussion of the discourse surrounding cinema's position as a "new universal language" in *Babel and Babylon* (Cambridge, MA: Harvard University Press, 1991), 77. Hansen links the democratic rhetoric underlying arguments like Lindsay's to the emergence of a "classical" mode of address and what she sees as the film industry's attempts to "ensure American films' dominance on both domestic and world markets," claiming that, by the end of World War I, "any possible ambiguity or tension disappeared, and the progress of civilization became synonymous with the worldwide hegemony of the American film industry.... The universal language by which American products were to transume their foreign rivals corresponded, on the level of film style, to the emerging codes of classical narrative cinema" (78–79).

Although, as Hansen suggests, there may be some relationship between the universalist ideas celebrated by a number of critics in the 1910s and attempts by the American film industry to assert themselves internationally, the notion of film as a universal language is not a uniquely American phenomenon. European critics such as Ricciotto Canudo, Émile Vuillermoz, and Élie Faure made similar arguments about the leveling, community-generating power of the cinema both before and after their American counterparts. To cite one of the more prominent examples, in his 1911 essay, "The Birth of a Sixth Art," Canudo wrote, "It is desire for a new *Festival*, for a new joyous *unanimity*, realized at a show, in a place where together, all men can forget in greater or lesser measure, their isolated individuality. This forgetting, soul of any religion and spirit of any aesthetic, will one day be superbly triumphant" (Ricciotto Canudo, "The Birth of a Sixth Art," translated by Ben Gibson, Don Ranvaud, Sergio Sokota, and Deborah Young, in *French Film Theory and Criticism*, edited by Richard Abel, vol. 1 [Princeton, NJ: Princeton University Press, 1998], 65). Canudo's arguments reflect the influence of Friedrich Nietzsche, while Lindsay's are similarly informed by Emerson, but they both speak to a transcontinental interest in the power of cinema as a collective experience with enormous potential as an agent of social cohesion.

19. The print history of *Intolerance* is extremely complicated and a subject of scholarly debate. Griffith continued tinkering with the film even after the initial premiere, and it was further reduced by others after the shortened thirteen-reel (11,811 feet) version proved too cumbersome for most exhibitors. Additional reductions were made for a variety of reasons in the 1920s and the 1930s, and some of the footage appears to be irrevocably lost. The Museum of Modern Art, the central repository for the Griffith paper and print collections, mounted an extensive reconstruction effort in the 1980s, resulting in a film that is very close to the presumed length of the version screened at the film's premiere at New York's Liberty Theater on September 5, 1916. Some silent film scholars, notably William K. Everson and Russell Merritt, have criticized various aspects of the reconstruction effort, and at least one (Merritt) has claimed that the fourteen-reel original never existed.

Information on the restoration can be found in Eileen Bowser, "Some Principles of Film Restoration," *Griffithiana* 13, nos. 38–39 (October 1990), 172–173, and Gillian Anderson, "'No Music until Cue': The Reconstruction of David W. Griffith's *Intolerance*," *Griffithiana* 13, nos. 38–39 (October 1990), 154–169. Merritt's counterarguments can be found in "D. W. Griffith's *Intolerance*: Reconstructing an Unattainable Text," *Film History* 4, no. 4 (1990), 337–375.

20. Clune's Auditorium Souvenir Booklet for *Intolerance*.

21. Eisenstein would also develop the idea of hieroglyphics as an element of montage in essays like "The Cinematographic Principle and the Ideogram" (1929).

22. Gish and Pinchot, *The Movies*, 177–180. Unfortunately, there is little indication of what an eight-hour *Intolerance* might have been like, but Gish suggests that it may have been more formally daring:

> Every week overwhelming effects poured from the darkroom. Some of the scenes were shot in startling shapes: triangles; diamonds; diagonals; frieze-like panels that blocked out all but a long thin strip of the film; and semicircles that opened like fans. In the shots of the virgins in the Temple of Sacred Fire, the impression of sensual motion was reinforced by having the camera turn from left to right and back again, and also by having the screen frame close in, then move out, then in again. Small iris shots opened to reveal huge panoramas. Other shots contained double and triple exposures. There were huge close-ups of only the lower half of Miriam Cooper's face or of only Margery Wilson's eyes. (177)

Gish gives no specific dates for her arguments, and there is no reason to dispute her claims that Griffith had, at one point, planned to screen a much longer version of the film on two consecutive evenings.

23. Anita Loos, *A Girl Like I* (New York: Viking, 1966), 102.

24. Erich von Stroheim, "Rêves de Realism," in Freddy Buache, *Erich von Stroheim* (Paris: Éditions Seghers, 1972), 108–110.

25. Thomas Mann, *The Magic Mountain*, translated by John E. Woods (New York: Alfred A. Knopf, 1995), x.

26. Arthur Lennig, *Stroheim* (Louisville: University of Kentucky Press, 2000), 1–23.

27. Thomas Quinn Curtiss, *Von Stroheim* (New York: Farrar, Straus and Giroux, 1971), 343.

28. Erich von Stroheim, "The Merry Widow: Introduced by Erich von Stroheim," in *The Film Culture Reader*, edited by P. Adams Sitney (New York: Cooper Square Press, 2000), 53. Von Stroheim gave a similar account, with the same O'Neill reference, to Peter Noble, who wrote the first biography of von Stroheim in 1951 (Peter Noble, *Hollywood Scapegoat: The Biography of Erich von Stroheim* [London: Fortune Press, 1951], 51).

29. "'Foolish Wives' Re-censored after First Presentation," *Variety*, January 20, 1922, 38. In the same article, Carl Laemmle insists that the film was reduced from fourteen to ten reels because "the picture was too long, and not because of any actions by members of the Board of Censors."

30. These books can be found under the catalog heading STROHEIM3-B2 in the Bibliothèque du film attached to the Cinémathèque française (hereafter Bibliothèque du film).

31. Herman G. Weinberg, *The Complete Wedding March of Erich von Stroheim* (Boston: Little, Brown, 1974), 15.

32. Richard Koszarski, *Von: The Life and Films of Erich Von Stroheim*, rev. ed. (New York: Limelight Editions, 2001), 118.

33. Von Stroheim, "Rêves de Realism," 110.

34. In light of this medievalism, it is worth noting that the Oberammergau Passion Play is being advertised in the mountain town depicted in *Blind Husbands*.

35. T. S. Eliot, "Whispers of Immortality" (1920), line 2.

36. Harry Carr, "On the Camera Coast," *Motion Picture Magazine* 27, no. 3 (April 1924), 76. Since other witnesses of these previews (Idwal Jones and Jean Bertin) report slightly differing numbers of reels, Richard Koszarski argues that "it is ... likely that the film changed from day to day, perhaps even influenced by the reactions of the previous audience" (Koszarski, *Von*, 160).

37. According to Arthur Lennig, "By the time Stroheim finished editing [his original cut] of *Greed*, he had forty-two reels of *unrepeated* narrative (about 42,000 feet), a total of almost eight hours at sound speed and more than that at twenty or twenty-two frames per second" (*Stroheim*, 214–215). Knowing that cuts were inevitable, von Stroheim personally reduced the film to twenty-four reels, writing to Peter Noble that he "could not, to save my soul, cut another foot" (Noble, *Hollywood Scapegoat*, 52). When it became clear that the studio would not accept even this reduced version, von Stroheim asked fellow director Rex Ingram to see what he could do. Ingram cut the film down to eighteen reels and sent von Stroheim a telegram, "If you cut one more foot, I'll never speak to you again" (Lennig, *Stroheim*, 216). Unfortunately, MGM rejected even this version, finally deciding to adopt a ten-reel version supervised by "editorial director" June Mathis (Koszarski, *Von*, 159).

38. Carr, "On the Camera Coast," 76.

39. Erich von Stroheim, "Stroheim States Own Version of Tilt over 'Wedding March,'" *Exhibitors Herald and Moving Picture World*, February 11, 1928, 22. In his photographic reconstruction, Herman Weinberg lists the original rough cut as "50,000 feet" (consistent with von Stroheim's statement, assuming that he was referring to the standard 1,000-foot reels of the era) and says this would have run for "eleven hours," but the difference may be attributable to variation in projection speed (Weinberg, *Complete Wedding March*, 3). At the twenty-four-frames-per-second speed used almost universally by 1928, fifty reels would have run for approximately nine hours.

40. Von Stroheim, "Stroheim States Own Version."

41. As Richard Koszarski points out, the material that eventually became *The Honeymoon* began on page 107 of a 246-page script, suggesting that if the entire film had been completed as planned, it could well have run far longer than the nine hours of extant material available when production was brought to a halt (Koszarski, *Von*, 229).

42. Weinberg, *Complete Wedding March*, 3. The only surviving European print of this drastically reduced version of *The Honeymoon* (whose 7,000 feet included a 2,000-foot "summary" of the first part so that it could be marketed as an autonomous work) was destroyed in a fire in the courtyard of the Cinémathèque française several days after von Stroheim's death.

43. Richard Koszarski argues:

The suspension of shooting on *Queen Kelly* was the single most damaging blow to von Stroheim's career. Coming only three months after the disastrous premiere of *The Wedding March*, it convinced producers and public alike that not only was von Stroheim an intractable wastrel, but that the type of film with which he was so strongly identified was now definitely out of touch with audience fashion. (Koszarski, *Von*, 263)

Von Stroheim later adapted much of the unfilmed material from the second half of the film into a novel, which was written in English but published in French as *Poto-Poto*, translated by Renée Nitzschke (Paris: Éditions de la Fontaine, 1956).

44. The 1980s reconstruction and the published screenplay make it clear that particular details of clothing, decor, or movement are made to rhyme and contrast with one another both within the same section of the film—as when Kelly throws her white underpants away with the same gesture used when the queen throws a prostitute's stockings at the prince—and at different points in the narrative. For example, the third part of the screenplay begins with "former convent girl" Kelly, who has been married off against her will to Jan, walking "with majestic steps," having become "queen" of a brothel (Bret Wood, ed., *Queen Kelly: The Complete Screenplay of Erich von Stroheim* [Lanham, MD: Scarecrow Press, 2002], 171–172). She wears a "black charmeuse dress" and carries a "patent leather dog whip," much like Queen Regina earlier in the film (171).

45. Herman Weinberg mentions that Thomas Quinn Curtis invited Thomas Mann, von Stroheim, and producer Gilford Cochrane to the Astor Hotel in December 1940, hoping to bring about a film version of *The Magic Mountain* (Herman G. Weinberg, *A Manhattan Odyssey* [New York: Anthology Film Archives, 1982], 144–145).

46. Lennig, *Stroheim*, 370.

47. Élie Faure, *The Art of Cineplastics*, translated by Walter Pach (Boston: Four Seas, 1923), 20.

48. Abel Gance, *Prisme: Carnets d'un cinéaste* (Paris: Samuel Tastet, 1986), 195.

49. Louis Delluc, "Notes to Myself: *La Dixième Symphonie*," translated by Richard Abel in Abel, *French Film Theory*, 145.

50. Gance, *Prisme*, 32.

51. Undated autobiographical fragment by Abel Gance quoted in Christophe Gauthier, "Mensonge romantique et vérité cinématographique: Abel Gance et le 'langage du silence,'" *1895* 31 (October 2000), 6.

52. Canudo, "Sixth Art," 62.

53. Gance, *Prisme*, 109.

54. Ibid., 63.

55. Ibid., 109. In a note from 1915, Gance wrote:

Since Nietzsche became, for me, God, since his doctrines seem to me to summarize the highest and most sublime aspirations of man, I will not lose a day to make them better understood. Jesus, without his apostles, would not have had force. I should be the best apostle, the most persuasive. The struggle is difficult because of Nietzsche's nationality. Even better, the victory will be more beautiful. But before teaching Nietzsche, I will need to understood it thoroughly and to know his *Zarathustra* by heart. To be able to recite it as they recite the verses of the Bible. Man is something that must be surmounted. (Roger Icart, ed., *Abel Gance, un soleil dans chaque image* [Paris: Cinémathèque française, 2002], 25)

56. Friedrich Nietzsche, *Thus Spoke Zarathustra*, translated by Adrian Del Caro (Cambridge: Cambridge University Press, 2006), 78.

57. Abel Gance, "A Sixth Art" (1912), translated by Richard Abel in Abel, *French Film Theory*, 66.

58. Gance, *Prisme*, 107–108.

59. Stéphane Audoin-Rouzeau and Annette Becker, *14–18: Understanding the Great War* (New York: Hill and Wang, 2000), 94–173.

60. The original cut of *J'accuse* was in four episodes totaling 5,250 meters, but for what biographer Roger Icart has called "mysterious reasons," the film was reduced to three episodes totaling 4,350 meters before entering general release, in episodes that were sometimes run together and sometimes separated by days or even weeks (Roger Icart, *Abel Gance ou Le Prométhée foudroyé* [Lausanne: Éditions L'Age d'Homme, 1983], 106–111). The film was re-edited further in 1922 into a 3,200-meter version intended for a single, intensive screening of three to three and a half hours (depending on projection speed). This version is the most explicitly pacifist and incorporates some new footage, such as the shot of the dead walking above the victory parade on the Champs-Élysées (which took place on July 14, 1919, more than three months after Gance finished editing the first version of the film to be released publicly).

61. In *La Dixième Symphonie*, Gance attempts to create a visual synesthesia, using a series of lap dissolves combined with allegorical inserts to convey the essence and sensation of music without sound. Over the course of performing his piece before an audience, the protagonist is so inspired that he literally becomes his "master," Beethoven, much to the amazement of the audience, whose response precisely mirrors the one Gance tries to evoke in the viewer.

62. Jay Winter describes these images of conventional warfare—which began in the sixteenth century as woodcuts and became extremely popular in the nineteenth century—and Gance's adoption of them in Winter, *Sites of Memory, Sites of Mourning: The Great War in European Cultural History* (Cambridge: Cambridge University Press, 1995), 122–133. Gance's interest in these images was reaffirmed sixteen years later when he inserted a scene of a craftsman producing *images d'Épinal* celebrating Napoleonic battles early in the first sound reworking of the *Napoléon* material (*Napoléon Bonaparte*, 1935).

63. In his notebooks of the 1920s, Gance dedicates his work to Novalis and puts him at the top of a list of favorite authors (Gance, *Prisme*, 207). He also explicitly connects the cinema to Novalis' poetics in the following exchange:

Sound seems to be nothing but a broken movement, in the sense where color is broken light.—Novalis ("Last Fragments," Number 7 in *Philosophical Writings*, translated and edited by Margaret Mahony Stoljar [Albany: State University of New York Press, 1997], 154)

[Gance's reply]: And in the sense where light is broken fire, the cinema is the music and the lamentation of this light. (Gance, *Prisme*, 215)

64. The central text is the 1917 essay "The New Spirit and the Poets," in which Apollinaire writes:

The new spirit, which has the ambition of manifesting a universal spirit and which does not intend to limit its activity, is nonetheless, and claims to respect the fact, a particular and lyric expression of the French nation, just as the classic spirit is, *par excellence*, a sublime expression of the same nation. It must not be forgotten that it is perhaps more dangerous for a nation to allow itself to be conquered intellectually than by arms. That is why the new spirit asserts above all an order and a duty which are the great classic qualities manifested by French genius, and to them it adds liberty. This liberty and this order, which combine in the new spirit, are its characteristic and its strength. (*Selected Writings of Guillaume Apollinaire*, edited and translated by Roger Shattuck [New York: New Directions, 1971], 230)

65. This statement was included in the original *J'accuse* program and is quoted in Jean Mitry, *Histoire du cinéma: Art et industrie*, vol. 2 (Paris: Éditions universitaires, 1967), 257–258.

66. In 1917/1918, Gance described his ambitions as follows: "[To] develop my projects of the centralization of film theaters to control production in the years to come and make it possible to create the Great Gospels of Light with the cinema." He claims to have abandoned *Ecce Homo* after shooting one-third of it when he realized that his "subject is too elevated for everything that surrounds [him], for [his] actors even, who do not release sufficient radioactivity," and committed himself instead to films "touching the war and its lessons, because [they are] closer to the immediate mentality of spectators" (Gance, *Prisme*, 114–116).

67. Ibid., 118.

68. Upon its initial release, the film was screened over three consecutive Thursday afternoons in December 1922. Gance continued working on this version up until the last possible moment, but, for reasons that remain unclear, the film was reduced from the premiere version (containing a prologue and six 1,800-meter episodes) to a slightly shorter version consisting of four 2,300-meter episodes before it went into general release on February 17, 1923 (for more details, see Roger Icart, "Étude sur une longue copie teintée de *La Roue*," *1895* 31 [October 2000], 275–290).

69. Gance, *Prisme*, 119.

70. The original score is now lost, but Honegger's seven-minute study of a train journey, *Pacific 231* (1923), suggests that it would have contributed to the momentum of the film while also accentuating its many rhythmic fluctuations.

71. Like Griffith with *Intolerance*, Gance re-edited his own film in subsequent years for various reasons, and the shortest commercially distributed version consisted of only seven reels (at the end of the silent era in 1928). In 1929, Gance began planning an elaborate sound version, but it was never completed (Gance's plans can be found in the Bibliothèque du film, GANCE236-B71).

72. Quoted in Icart, "Étude," 276.

73. A 1923 letter by Gance in Icart, *Abel Gance, un soleil dans chaque image*, 69.

74. With Gance's blessing, director Lupu Pick made a German-language film version of the *Sainte-Hélène* script in 1929. Gance eventually succeeded in making a version of the film he had intended to be the third part of the *Napoléon* series, *Austerlitz* (1960), but the final result was very different from the original conception.

75. Gance told Kevin Brownlow in the 1960s that the premiere version included four sequences in "Polyvision": "Les Deux Tempêtes, the Return to Corsica, Le Bal des victimes, and the Entry into Italy" (Kevin Brownlow, *The Parade's Gone By . . .* [Berkeley: University

of California Press, 1968], 547). However, no known version of the film ever included four triptych sequences, and Gance did not begin regularly using the word "Polyvision" to describe his process until after World War II. As Gance explained in a 1956 radio interview, "I did not see Polyvision, as I make it now, in [the 1920s]. . . . The first idea of Polyvision [came with the triptychs for *Napoléon*], but it was actually elementary in my spirit" ("Le Bureau des rêves perdus d'Abel Gance, émission radiophonique de Louis Moillon réalisée par Albert Riera le 13 Novembre 1956," *L'Écran* 3 [April–May 1958], 17–22). The "Return to Corsica" and "Le Bal des victimes" sequences were presented as triptychs in a special presentation at Studio 28 in 1928 (under the names *Galops* and *Danses*), while both "Les Deux Tempêtes" and the "Entry into Italy" triptychs were included in the version of *Napoléon* shown at the Opéra de Paris.

76. The two screenings were held on May 9 and 10, 1927, at the Apollo Theater in Paris and were presented to great acclaim. This "Apollo" version was missing the triptychs.

A contract signed on July 30, 1926, for the international exhibition of *Napoléon* (distributed by MGM) specified that 400,000 meters of negative had been shot (Roger Icart, "Les Divers Visages du 'Napoléon' d'Abel Gance," in *Napoléon et le cinema: Un siècle d'images*, edited by Jean-Pierre Mattei [Ajaccio: Éditions Alain Piazzola and Cinémathèque de Corse, 1998], 87).

77. Koszarski, *Von*, 69.

78. Kevin Brownlow, *Napoleon: Abel Gance's Classic Film* (New York: Alfred A. Knopf, 1983), 152.

79. Icart, "Les Divers Visages," 88–89.

80. Abel Gance, "My Napoleon," translated by Kevin Brownlow in Abel, *French Film Theory*, 400.

81. Icart, *Abel Gance, un soleil dans chaque image*, 73.

82. The model for Gance's use of documents, as well as much of his Napoleonic historiography, is Jules Michelet (who wrote, "Man is his own Prometheus," in the preface to the 1869 edition of his *Histoire de France*), but his treatment is also clearly indebted to the authenticating strategies Griffith employed in *The Birth of a Nation*. The statement is from a 1923 letter by Gance reprinted in Icart, *Abel Gance, un soleil dans chaque image*, 69.

83. This exchange occurs at the conclusion of a fictionalized episode in which Napoleon communes with the dead spirits of his colleagues and proclaims his commitment to the principles of the Revolution before he sets off for Italy. Napoleon also declares, "Europe will become a single people, and anyone, wherever he travels, will always find himself in a common fatherland," thereby making him into the progenitor of the "United Europe" Gance would himself champion throughout the 1920s in various writings and projects (most notably, in the proposals he made for a film division of the League of Nations). Gance adapted this language from Leo Tolstoy's 1869 novel *War and Peace*.

84. A more recent translation renders this passage as "Your whole creation is a great wheel which to turn at all must crush someone" ("The Graveyard at Villequier," in Victor Hugo, *Selected Poems*, translated by Brooks Haxton [London: Penguin Classics, 2002], 43). Hugo's poem was written on the part of the Seine where his daughter had drowned four years before, and Gance almost certainly cited it with this history in mind, as a tribute to his wife Ida Danis, who (like lead actor Séverin-Mars) fell ill with the flu and died before *La Roue* was finished.

85. Victor Hugo, *Ninety-Three*, translated by Lowell Bair (Cresskill, NJ: Paper Tiger, 2002), 137. Gance's characterization of Danton, Marat, and Robespierre as "The Three Gods" also derives from Hugo's novel. At one point, Marat declares, "We represent the Revolution. We're the three heads of Cerberus" (106).

86. Ibid., 140–141.

87. Gance quotes Claudel—"For we must bear the Cross before the Cross bears us"— late in *La Roue* and, although it is unclear when exactly Claudel made his frequently quoted statement about Gance, it was used in advertisements for many of the director's films (for example, in *Paris Match* 406 [January 19, 1957], 57).

On November 14, 1928, Gance declared that he intended to make a life of Hugo in time to celebrate the centenary of 1830, and he had prepared the scenario by early the following year. In subsequent correspondence with Raymond Escholier, the conservator of the Musée Victor Hugo, he explains that he has postponed *La Vie de Victor Hugo* but planned to resume it once *La Fin du monde* was completed (Bibliothèque du film, GANCE424-B93).

88. Élie Faure, *Function du cinéma: De la cinéplastique à son destin social (1921–1937)* (Paris: Librairie Plon, 1953), 65–66. Quotation marks around the final sentence were added to emphasize what is clearly a reference to Hugo's novel.

89. Canudo wrote:

The cinematographic theater *is the first new theater*, the first authentic and fundamental theater of our time. When it becomes truly aesthetic, complemented with a worthy musical score played by a good orchestra, even if only representing life, real life, momentarily fixed by the photographic lens, we shall be able to feel then our first *sacred* emotion, we shall have a glimpse of the spirits, moving towards a vision of the temple, where Theater and Museum will once more be restored for a new religious communion of the spectacle and Aesthetics. (Canudo, "Sixth Art," 64–65)

The widespread adoption of these ideas later in the decade is attested to by Émile Vuillermoz, who refers to "this new religion" of the cinema in "Before the Screen: Hermes and Silence," translated by Richard Abel in Abel, *French Film Theory*, 156.

90. Faure, *The Art of Cineplastics*, 43.

91. Faure wrote the introduction to the Opéra de Paris program for the April 1927 premiere and subsequently wrote a preface to Gance's *Prisme* in 1931, in which he claims that the director is fulfilling some of his dreams for the cinema: "The man capable of writing such a book has heroically chosen the first stammerings of the visual symphony in order to flood, from its rising tide, the still floating river of our new universe" (Gance, *Prisme*, 14). Toward the end of the book, Gance in turn argued that Faure was one of the great writer-thinkers in the line of Montaigne, Cervantes, and Shakespeare (228).

92. Élie Faure, *Napoleon*, translated by Jeffrey E. Jeffrey (London: Constable, 1924), 2. Faure later writes that people are beginning to realize that "Napoleon was a poet, that art is imagined action and that action is art which is actually lived" (240). The book is dedicated to "the man, whoever he may be, among the leaders of the Universal Revolution, whatever form it may take, who will possess the divine virtue of being able to impose upon it the order which it will establish in his heart."

93. Nelly Kaplan, *Napoléon* (London: British Film Institute, 1994), 42.

94. Ibid., 44. The Bibliothèque du film contains a number of annotated volumes Gance referred to in preparing *Napoléon* (GANCE184-B64). In one book, Louis Madelin's

Napoléon (Paris: Librairie Plon, 1926), Gance marks the following passage with great enthusiasm: "Men of genius are meteors destined to burn in order to light their century" (331).

95. Léon Moussinac, "A French Film: *Napoléon*," in Norman King, *Abel Gance: A Politics of Spectacle* (London: British Film Institute, 1984), 35.

96. The influential French film historian Jean Mitry made the apolitical argument in his *Histoire du cinéma: Art et industrie*, vol. 3 (Paris: Éditions universitaires, 1967), 354. Bernard Eisenschitz makes similar claims in his article on Gance in *Cinema: A Critical Dictionary*, edited by Richard Roud, vol. 1 (New York: Viking, 1980), 404–415. On the other hand, Roger Icart, author of a meticulously researched French biography of Gance, has studied the different versions of *Napoléon* extensively and has argued that, in all versions, Gance's vision is fundamentally progressive.

97. Peter Pappas, "The Superimposition of Vision: *Napoleon* and the Meaning of Fascist Art," *Cineaste* 11, no. 2 (1981), 8–12.

98. More than a decade before it was employed by Mussolini and Hitler, for example, Dada artists like Hannah Hoch made use of superimposition in photomontages. In works such as *Lenin* (1931), Soviet artists like El Lissitzky used techniques and formal devices that are virtually identical to those used to create the famous composite images depicting Mussolini as the literal embodiment of large crowds. Jeffrey Schnapp discusses these "oceanic" images in "The Mass Panorama," *Modernism/Modernity* 9, no. 2 (2002), 243–281.

99. In 1931, Gance created a syndicate for the distribution of Soviet films in France, at least partially in the hopes that it would facilitate his plans to make *1812, La Campagne de Russie*, a Soviet coproduced follow-up to *Napoléon vu par Abel Gance*.

100. One of Goethe's most important poems, written in the same period as "On German Architecture," is entitled "Prometheus" (1774). Goethe's poem ends by depicting Prometheus as the source of human creativity:

> Here I sit, forming men
> In my image,
> A race to resemble me:
> To suffer, to weep,
> To enjoy, to be glad—
> And never to heed you,
> Like me! (Goethe, "Prometheus," translated by Michael Hamburger in
> J. W. von Goethe, *Selected Works* [New York: Alfred A. Knopf, 1999], 1071)

In a similar fashion, the third stanza of Lord Byron's "Prometheus" (1816) treats its subject as the embodiment of Romantic ideals, "[strengthening] Man with his own mind" (line 38). Beethoven wrote a ballet entitled *The Creatures of Prometheus* (opus 43, 1800–1801) and later used its theme for the finale of the 1804 Third Symphony ("*Eroica*," opus 55), often cited as the first work of musical Romanticism. Goethe's Prometheus poem was also set to music by Franz Schubert in 1819 ("Prometheus," D.674).

101. In his memoirs, Chateaubriand tellingly refers to Napoleon as "Prometheus, with the vulture at his breast, who stole the fire from heaven [and] thought himself superior to all things" (*The Memoirs of François René, Vicomte de Chateaubriand*, translated by Alexander Teixera de Mattos [New York: G.P. Putnam's Sons, 1902], 2:285). He claims that the feelings were mutual, with Napoleon telling Monsieur de Montholon that "Chateaubriand has been gifted by nature with the Promethean fire" (Chateaubriand, *Memoirs*, 3:223).

102. Byron, "Ode to Napoleon Buonaparte," lines 138–144. Byron described the pervasive influence of Prometheus in an 1817 letter to John Murray (*So Late into the Night: Byron's Letters and Journals*, edited by Leslie A. Marchand, vol. 5 [London: John Murray Publishers, 1976], 268).

103. Faubion Bowers, *Scriabin: A Biography* (Mineola, NY: Dover, 1996), 206–207. The piece was never performed with proper color accompaniment during Scriabin's lifetime. Theosophical ideas and color-music experiments also inspired Claude Bragdon's 1916 attempt to create an audiovisual "cathedral without walls" in New York's Central Park (R. Bruce Elder, *Harmony and Dissent: Film and Avant-Garde Art Movements in the Early Twentieth Century* [Waterloo, Ontario: Wilfrid Laurier University Press, 2008], 57). Shortly thereafter, Bragdon founded an organization called The Prometheans with Thomas Wilfred, whose Clavilux color organ "compositions" would sometimes last for days or even years (John Gage, *Color and Culture: Practice and Meaning from Antiquity to Abstraction* [Berkeley: University of California Press, 1999], 245–246).

104. Marx mentions Prometheus repeatedly, characteristically writing that the accumulation of wealth "rivets the labourer to capital more firmly than the wedges of Vulcan did Prometheus to the rock" (*Capital: An Abridged Edition*, edited by David McLellan [Oxford: Oxford World's Classics, 1999], 362). The most important left-leaning independent production/distribution company in late Weimar Germany—active from 1926 to 1931—was called Prometheus Films.

105. In 1921, for example, Louis Delluc wrote: "The irresistible pressure of creative minds is turning over the silent art to blood that is difficult to poison. Believe me, it will allow great figures to emerge out of creators yet to come, just as Aeschylus created *Prometheus*, as Shakespeare created *Macbeth* and *Hamlet*, as Wagner created *Parsifal*" (Louis Delluc, "From Orestes to Rio Jim," translated by Richard Abel in Abel, *French Film Theory*, 258).

106. Gance, "Le Temps de l'image est venu!," 102. Earlier in the same essay, he argued that "the cinema silently observes the other arts and, [like a] formidable Sphinx, asks itself which vital parts it will devour" (99).

107. In this respect, the review by Louis Delluc of *La Dixième Symphonie* is paradigmatic. Delluc lavishes praise on Gance's formal innovations and calls him a genius, but then chides him for the obviousness of the film's dramaturgy and, especially, for its citation of other artworks in a "vision sequence." He writes of this sequence:

> Perhaps this will please spectators. Indeed it's quite pretty to look at. But it is no good; it overlays something fine with something pretty but unnecessary. It's simply a mistake. Don't tell me, Gance, that the execution hasn't measured up to the intention. No, you were thinking of the Victory at Samothrace. I wasn't. The Victory at Samothrace suffices unto itself. Leave it where it is, unless you are devoting an essay, a poem, or a play to it. In a film, visibly present like that, it is extraneous. For three-quarters of an hour, you alone kept us interested. Would you have us believe that you aren't sufficient unto yourself? It's too late. We have only come for *La Dixième Symphonie*. (Delluc, "Notes to Myself," 145–146)

108. Fernand Léger, "*La Roue*: Its Plastic Quality," translated by Alexandra Anderson in Abel, *French Film Theory*, 272. Jean Cocteau famously said of the same film, "There

is cinema before and after *La Roue*, just as there is painting before and after Picasso" (Jean Cocteau, *The Art of Cinema*, edited by André Bernard and Claude Gauteur, translated by Robin Buss [New York: Marion Boyars, 1994], 132). Gance's friend Jean Epstein was equally enthusiastic: "The conviction that pours from *La Roue* is overwhelming. From this film was born the first cinematographic symbol. . . . The cross which turns very quickly takes the form of a wheel. That is why, at the summit of your Calvary, Gance, there is *La Roue*" (Jean Epstein, "Les cinéastes—Abel Gance," *Photo-Ciné* 8 [September–October 1927], 153).

109. In a 1929 lecture, Gance lays out three fundamental principles that guide his own work: (1) cinema is an art of the people; (2) cinema is the art of light; (3) cinema is an art for the whole of humanity (Abel Gance, "Autour de moi et du monde—Le Cinéma de demain," in Icart, *Abel Gance, un soleil dans chaque image*, 124–125).

110. Norman King argues that these sorts of carefully staged images are preparations for the more spectacular creative outbursts, but it does not seem to me that Gance's formal strategies are as monolithically oriented around the "look" as King suggests (King, *Abel Gance*, 179–206). Although the overarching presence of the director is clearly felt throughout all of Gance's major works, the films do open up aspects of perception that go beyond narrative exigency or spectatorial manipulation. In many of the pictorially deep compositions of *La Roue*, for example, there is an obsessive fixation on constantly shifting light patterns, which shimmer over faces and glint off objects to such a degree that it sometimes feels as though the film has momentarily broken free of its narrative and entered the domain of abstract sensation.

111. Kaplan, *Napoléon*, 28.

112. Gance, "My Napoleon," 400.

113. Kaplan, *Napoléon*, 38.

114. Brownlow, *Napoleon*, 143.

115. Kaplan claims that the director inexplicably destroyed it himself during one of his re-edits of the film in the 1940s (Kaplan, *Napoléon*, 9). Jean Dréville, who was present at the 1927 premiere, reconstructed this triptych using the existing footage for the Cinémathèque française restoration (Bambi Ballard, ed., *Napoléon as seen by Abel Gance* [London: Faber and Faber, 1990], 58).

116. This impression is strengthened by the two most dramatic intertitles: "Thus all the giants of the Revolution were swept, one after the other, into the raging whirlpool of the Reign of Terror," followed (after a superimposition of the Convention and a guillotine) by "And a man, the defiant sport of the Ocean, his Tricolor sail opening to the wind of the Revolution, was being triumphantly carried to the Heights of History."

117. Icart, *Abel Gance, un soleil dans chaque image*, 120.

118. In a letter to Charles Pathé, Gance went so far as to write:

I think that *Napoléon* will be for me a great projection of light into the cinematographic future, that it will show what a historical film can and should be, a living lesson for the future, but I do not believe like you that it will be my last work. For a long time, I have been plotting the series of *Great Initiates*—Moses, Buddha, Orpheus, Krishna, Jesus, Pythagoras, Mohammed . . . [leading to] the great cinematic Gospel of *La Fin du monde* that I have been preparing these years and that will be the definitive future of the new silent language between peoples. (Quoted in Icart, *Abel Gance ou Le Prométhée foudroyé*, 167)

Gance's diary from the mid-1920s includes the related admission that he would make *Napoléon* as a side project during the preparation of his beloved *The Kingdom of the Earth* and *La Fin du monde*:

January 1922—Plan for the next two years:
Dedicate soul and blood on:

1. *La Fin du monde.* Make *Napoléon* during the preparation of this.
2. *La Mort d'Orphée*, in order to slightly appease my infinite pain and in order to revive my dead beloved in *Eurydice*. [This project was soon abandoned.]
3. The Kingdom of the Earth

   (a) Actions,
   (b) Codes,
   (c) Studies

Devote my seconds to these three goals and think of nothing outside of them. (Gance, *Prisme*, 166)

119. In his writings of the 1920s, Gance increasingly placed stress on the psychological power of the cinema, observing that the "naïveté of the crowd needs the cinema" and including a proposal for a "Section d'observation et d'utilisation pratique des forces psychologiques universelles" as part of his larger League of Nations (SDN) initiative (Gance, *Prisme*, 112). He describes audiences responding to a hypothetical three-dimensional cinema (a true "Universal Psychological Force") in similar terms:

The crowd will respond as one man; the chorus of antiquity will be resurrected. The soul of the spectators will merge with that of characters and objects; all will participate in the drama through the magic of this hallucination, and they will have to restrain themselves from crying out and replying to the voices which gush out from these beings, from this prodigious nature as real as they are. (Gance, "Autour de moi," 124)

120. In an essay entitled "Vocation du cinéma," for example, Élie Faure writes:

The cinema, product of scientific culture and its technical evolution, naturally offers itself to us in order to assume this task [of expressing the collective spirit of the age], as dance and music had offered themselves to primitive people as explanations of mythic culture, as architecture had offered itself to the great synthetic religions—Hinduism, Buddhism, Christianity, Islam—in order to explain the social culture whose sublimation they manifested. Indeed, the cinema presents all the social characteristics that the Christian architecture of the Middle Ages—to take the most recent example and the one closest to a mode of expression that I would call symphonic—offered unanimously to the multitudes. (Faure, *Function du cinéma*, 88)

Similar comments can be found in an earlier essay entitled "Introduction à la mystique du cinéma":

The cinema, if we *want* to understand it, should revive and carry to its highest pitch a religious feeling whose dying flame it feeds. The infinite diversity of the world offers to man for the first time the *material* means to demonstrate its unity. A pretext of universal communion, whose deepening requires of us only a little goodwill, is offered to us, with tireless kindness. (*Function du cinéma*, 84–85)

121. Gance, *Prisme*, 247. Gance's decision to title this project *Les Grands Initiés* is an explicit reference to the 1889 work of the same name by French philosopher-poet Édouard Schuré, who argued that Jesus, Moses, Mohammed, Rama, Krishna, Hermes, Orpheus, Pythagoras, and Plato were all "initiates" of a single esoteric tradition that took on different surface manifestations. For Schuré, a friend of Nietzsche and a great admirer of Wagner whose work took a more occult turn after he met the German-Russian mystic Helena Petrovna Blavatsky, organized religion was an institutional distortion of the prophetic truths espoused by those he labeled initiates. Gance's comparative religion project was heavily influenced by Schuré's ideas, and in his own writings he implies that understanding the "similarity" of different religions will help make the universal truths that lie behind them clear.

122. Faure, *Function du cinéma*, 114–115.

123. Gance's internationalism precedes World War I. In his first published essay (1912), he had written of "a sixth art which, with one and the same sadness, will simultaneously bring tears to the eyes of the Arabs and the Eskimo and which, at the same time, will offer them the same lesson in courage and health" (Gance, "A Sixth Art," 66).

124. "PROJECT de M. Abel GANCE sur une SOCIETE MONDIALE de FILMS," archival document included in Abel Gance: Documents (1912–1929), Yale University Library, Fiche S21 11, p. 12.

125. Ibid., 14. Gance, who also uses the Novalis quote in other texts, seems to be modifying an often-quoted fragment, "Every word is a word of incantation" (Gerhard Schulz, ed., *Novalis Werke* [Munich: C.H. Beck Verlag, 1969], 375).

126. "PROJECT de M. Abel GANCE sur une SOCIETE MONDIALE de FILMS," 13.

127. Interestingly, to justify the expense of the film to his backers, Gance cited the $1,103,736.38 figure Universal used in advertising for *Foolish Wives* ("The First Million Dollar Movie") in his own proposal, arguing that his film about Napoleon would be "the greatest film of modern times" (Brownlow, *Napoleon*, 40–45). The participation of Stinnes was a source of contention for some French nationalists, but these concerns were partially allayed when Pathé purchased thirty of the seventy parts sold via subscription. The death of Stinnes precipitated an eight-month break in production, which resumed once the finances were restructured around a new organization (also controlled by a White Russian, Jacques Grinieff), the Société Générale de Films.

128. Dimitri Vezyroglou, "Les Grandes Espérances: Abel Gance, la société des nations et le cinéma Européen à la fin des années vingt," *1895* 31 (October 2000), 133.

129. This idealistic faith in international solidarity found concrete political manifestation in the League of Nations. Zara Steiner discusses the formation and function of the League as "an experiment in internationalism at a time when the counterclaims of nationalism were running powerfully in the opposite of direction" in *The Lights That Failed: European International History, 1919–1933* (Oxford: Oxford University Press, 2005), 349–386.

130. The first part of Vertov's *One Sixth of the World* includes an elaborate list of different ethnic groups, rituals, and practices within the Soviet state (whose boundaries are elaborated in the second part of the film), each prefaced by "[I see] you . . ." This extends even to "you, the Black Sea," and "you, sitting in the movie theater." The strategy of

repetitive, exhaustive cataloging of lyrically rendered details as a way of emphasizing a larger totality is very similar to that employed by Whitman in the lengthy Book XII ("The Song of the Broken Axe") of *Leaves of Grass*, although the political implications in each case are, of course, very different.

Ruttmann's *Melody of the World* juxtaposes scenes taken in wildly different locations, organizing them thematically or conceptually around types of movement or activity (so that, for example, shots of rickshaws in South Asia and cars in Western Europe are linked together). The film is particularly notable for including sounds and voices from all over the world, sometimes juxtaposed with one another, and it includes a revealing scene in which George Bernard Shaw and Ivor Montagu "meet" on a road, speak together, and then walk off arm in arm. Shots of two men speaking Chinese are inserted at various points throughout the scene, suggesting not only shared understanding across cultural boundaries but also that sound technology could help facilitate international dialogue (ironically, it would do just the opposite, making it more difficult for films to travel across national borders).

131. Griffith, "Griffith to Film History." According to the article, Griffith hoped to produce eight to ten historical films, each approximately twelve reels long and made up of "dramatic incidents based on facts."

132. Quoted in Anton Kaes, *Shell Shock Cinema* (Berkeley: University of California Press, 2009), 193.

133. Hans Richter, "A History of the Avant-Garde," in *Art in Cinema*, edited by Frank Stauffacher (New York: Arno Press, 1971), 8–21.

134. Gance describes his plans in a letter (dated July 12, 1929) that is held in the Bibliothèque du film, GANCE 287-B77.

135. Icart, *Abel Gance ou Le Prométhée foudroyé*, 24.

136. In *Prisme*, Gance gives several characteristic examples of the synthetic approach to world mythology that informed his theatrical projects and film works:

> All the Greek myths with which I have wandered around, Homer and my *Victoire* [*de Samothrace*, a massive, never-performed play Gance wrote in 1912 and 1913 that was inspired by the famous Hellenistic statue in the Louvre], all the medieval myths—Brocéliande, Melusine and the Sirens. . . . Having judged the poetic value, so dissimilar, of these two civilizations, I can touch the two poles of poetry. Homer and Merlin, Orpheus and King Arthur, Helen of Troy and Viviane, are for me great Dionysian entities. (Gance, *Prisme*, 48)

137. A dossier on *La Fin du monde* can be found in the Bibliothèque du film, GANCE99-B43. Plans for *La Passion de Jésus*, which was abandoned in April 1929, can also be found in the Bibliothèque du film, GANCE413-B93.

138. Roger Régent, "*Napoléon* d'Abel Gance ressuscité, enrichi de la perspective sonore," *Pour Vous* 337 (May 2, 1935), 7.

139. Gance's original cut of *La Fin du monde* was at least 5,250 meters long and would have had a projection time of well over three hours. The version screened at the 1931 premiere had been reduced by almost 50 percent to approximately 2,800 meters (about one hundred minutes). The film currently exists in two even more fragmentary versions: a French version that lasts for approximately ninety-four minutes and an American version released in 1934 that lasts for fifty-four minutes and was retitled *Paris After Dark*.

According to Roger Icart, the ten-minute discrepancy between the current French print and the premiere version was at least partially caused by Gance's decision to excise some of the material for use in his 1937 sound version of *J'accuse* (Icart, *Abel Gance ou Le Prométhée foudroyé*, 221).

140. At an earlier stage, *La Fin du monde* was explicitly tied to *The Kingdom of the Earth* by featuring the same protagonist, Novalic (a probable play on Novalis).

141. Abel Gance, "Départ vers la polyvision," *Cahiers du cinéma* 41 (December 1954), 4–5.

142. The triple-screen version of the rising of the dead sequence from *J'accuse* was shown as part of a special presentation by Abel Gance intended to demonstrate the artistic potential of Polyvision in January 1957. Information on the screening and the response by the government ministers and press representatives in attendance can be found at the Bibliothèque du film, GANCE384-B90.

143. Abel Gance, "Je tournerai *Christophe Colomb* parce que le cinéma est une machine à ressusciter les héros," *Cinémonde* 12, no. 546 (April 5, 1939), 5.

144. The statement is from 1965 (in support of de Gaulle) and is quoted in Icart, *Abel Gance ou Le Prométhée foudroyé*, 403.

145. Ibid., 275.

146. Bibliothèque du film, GANCE400-B92.

147. Gance continued to believe that he would be able to make his great religions project throughout the 1930s and discussed this in several interviews. Script extracts from the Polyvision version of *The Kingdom of the Earth* were published in several journals (in English, see *Film Culture* 3, no. 5, issue 15 [December 1957], 10–13, and 4, no. 1, issue 16 [January 1958], 14–16). Gance's original scenario and filming notes for *La Divine Tragédie* are available at the Bibliothèque du film, GANCE35-B13. Significantly, the film moves back and forth between different periods, in the manner of *Intolerance* (it culminates in a visionary scene in which Jesus repeats "Love your enemies" over and over again).

Abel Gance's trip to China is discussed in Icart, *Abel Gance ou Le Prométhée foudroyé*, 398–399. Nelly Kaplan, Gance's partner and assistant in the 1950s and 1960s, provides her account of the meeting with Mao Zedong and Zhou Enlai in Nelly Kaplan, *Mon cygne, mon signe . . . Correspondances Abel Gance–Nelly Kaplan* (Paris: Éditions du Rocher, 2008), 58–63.

148. Friedrich Hölderlin, *Poems and Fragments*, translated by Michael Hamburger (London: Anvil Press, 2004), 505.

149. Albert Speer, *Inside the Third Reich*, translated by Richard Winston and Clara Winston (New York: Simon and Schuster, 1970), 58–59.

150. Bertolt Brecht, "The Modern Theatre Is the Epic Theatre," in *Brecht on Theatre: The Development of an Aesthetic*, edited and translated by John Willett (New York: Hill and Wang, 1964), 38.

151. *Mahogany* is referred to in part two ("A German Dream") of *Hitler, a Film from Germany*.

152. The phrase *"stählerne Romantik,"* which appears on the soundtrack in the first and last parts of *Hitler, a Film From Germany*, was used repeatedly by Joseph Goebbels, who defined it in 1933 as "a Romanticism . . . that has the courage to confront problems and look firmly into their pitiless eyes without flinching" (Rüdiger Safranski, *Romanticism: A German Affair*, translated by Robert E. Goodwin [Evanston, IL: Northwestern University Press, 2014], 243).

Jeffrey Herf argues that Nazi ideology can be characterized by a technopihilic resistance to the Enlightenment in *Reactionary Modernism: Technology, Culture, and Politics in Weimar and the Third Reich* (Cambridge: Cambridge University Press, 1984).

The book of photographs from the 1930s that Syberberg published the year *Hitler, a Film from Germany* was completed is also shaped by an attempt to rework the principles of Surrealist collage (Hans-Jürgen Syberberg, *Fotografie der 30er Jahre: Eine Anthologie* [Munich: Schirmer/Mosel Verlag, 1977]).

153. Syberberg acknowledges the influence of this "grand master" in "Quelques mots pour Bologne," a 1990 text reprinted in *Syberberg/Paris/Nossendorf*, edited by Christian Longchamp (Paris: Éditions Centre Pompidou, 2003), 81–82.

154. Hans Sedlmayr, "Toward a Rigorous Study of Art," translated by Mia Fineman in *The Vienna School Reader: Politics and Art Historical Method in the 1930s*, edited by Christopher S. Wood (New York: Zone Books, 2000), 145. Sedlmayr's arguments about cultural decline are summarized in his 1948 book *Art in Crisis: The Lost Center* (first translated into English in 1957).

155. Ibid., 155.

156. Sedlmayr refers to the "*Gesamtkunstwerk der Kathedrale*" several times in *Die Entstehung der Kathedrale* (Zurich: Atlantis Verlag, 1950), 156, 361, etc.

157. Hans-Jürgen Syberberg, *Hitler, a Film from Germany*, translated by Joachim Neugroschel (New York: Farrar, Straus and Giroux, 1982), 236. Syberberg's use of cutout figures suggests the influence of the cinema museum developed by Henri Langlois in the 1970s.

158. Hans-Jürgen Syberberg, "Seeing the Light," *New Republic* 199, no. 14 (October 3, 1988), 35.

159. Syberberg, *Hitler, a Film from Germany*, 19.

160. Ibid., 61.

161. Hans-Jürgen Syberberg, *Syberbergs Filmbuch* (Munich: Nymphenburger Verlagshandlung, 1976), 243–296. The concept of mourning work, derived from Freud's 1917 essay "Mourning and Melancholia" and Walter Benjamin's *The Origins of German Tragic Drama* (1928), has been invoked in many critical essays on the film, especially Susan Sontag, "Eye of the Storm," *New York Review of Books*, February 21, 1980, 36–43; Thomas Elsaesser, "Myth as the Phantasmagoria of History: H. J. Syberberg, Cinema, and Representation," *New German Critique* 24–25 (Autumn 1981–Winter 1982), 108–154; and Eric L. Santner, *Stranded Objects: Mourning, Memory, and Film in Postwar Germany* (Ithaca, NY: Cornell University Press, 1990), 103–149.

162. Sigmund Freud, "Mourning and Melancholia," in *The Standard Edition of the Complete Psychological Works of Sigmund Freud*, vol. 14 (London: Hogarth Press, 1974), 251.

163. Syberberg, *Hitler, a Film from Germany*, 251.

164. Esteban Buch, *Beethoven's Ninth: A Political History* (Chicago: University of Chicago Press, 2003), 209–210. Roger Hillman has also pointed out that the combination of Beethoven's Ninth Symphony and *Fidelio* was requested by Goebbels for "performances honoring Hitler's birthday in the last two prewar years" (Roger Hillman, *Unsettling Scores: German Film, Music, and Ideology* [Bloomington: Indiana University Press, 2005], 84).

165. Interestingly, *Hitler, a Film from Germany* does include a pair of structurally reversed zooms in the interior sections: a zoom out from a reproduction of the baby in Runge's *The Great Morning* at the beginning of part two ("A German Dream") is mirrored by a zoom in

on a craggy landscape at the beginning of part three ("The End of a Winter's Tale"). These reinforce the film's "melancholic" alternation between attraction and repulsion.

166. Syberberg, *Hitler, a Film from Germany*, 310.

167. Quoted in E. T. Kirby, ed., *Total Theatre* (New York: Dutton, 1969), 207–208.

168. Antoine de Baecque and Jacques Parsi, *Conversations avec Manoel de Oliveira* (Paris: Cahiers du cinéma, 1996), 76–77.

169. Gérard Lefort, "Godard et Oliveira sortent ensemble," in *Jean-Luc Godard par Jean-Luc Godard*, edited by Alain Bergala, vol. 2, *1984–1998* (Paris: Cahiers du cinéma, 1985), 270.

170. The artistic affinities shared by Gance and Claudel are discussed in Antoinette Weber-Caflisch, "Claudel, Gance, Valéry: 1919–1929," *Bulletin de la Société Paul Claudel* 92 (1983), 24–32.

171. In the notes for the beginning of Scene X of "The Fourth Day," for example, Claudel writes, "No music, but some well-spaced thumps of the big drum. The cinema may be used" (Paul Claudel, *The Satin Slipper, or The Worst Is Not the Surest*, translated by Fr. John O'Connor [New York: Sheed & Ward, 1945], 296).

172. The full version of the play was first performed publicly at the Festival d'Avignon in 1987.

173. Oliveira explores the impact of this messianic Sebastianism throughout Portuguese history in films such as *No, or the Vain Glory of Command* (1990) and *The Fifth Empire* (2004).

174. Rodrigo makes this explicit when he says, "I am fastened to the cross, but my cross is no longer fast to anything. It is floating on the sea, the free sea, away to that point where the limit of the known sky melts."

Chapter 2

1. Thomas Carlyle, *On Heroes and Hero Worship, and the Heroic in History* (London: World's Classics, 1920), 18. This quotation is included epigrammatically in Gregory Markopoulos' notes for *Eniaios* (Gregory Markopoulos, *Chiron Notes*, vol. 17, pages unnumbered). All references to *Chiron Notes, Cerberus, Ein Edelweiss*, and *The Sovereignty of the Filmmaker as Physician* refer to the bound volumes of the same names preserved at the Temenos Archive in Uster, Switzerland. Some of these volumes include page numbers, but most do not.

2. Charles Baudelaire, *The Flowers of Evil*, translated by James McGowan (Oxford: Oxford World's Classics, 1993), 151.

3. In 2004, the first two and a half cycles were screened over three consecutive evenings. The entirety of cycle three was shown along with cycles four and five, again over three consecutive evenings, four years later. Unfortunately, because of printing problems, the last three reels of the fourth cycle could not be screened during the 2008 Temenos projections, but they were publicly presented at Yale University along with an earlier version of this chapter in April 2009. Cycles six, seven, and eight were presented in 2012.

4. Stephen Koch, *Stargazer: The Life, World, and Films of Andy Warhol*, rev. ed. (New York: Marion Boyars, 2002), 61. Koch continues:

Empire is a massive, absurd act of attention, attention that nobody could possibly want to give or sit through. Indeed, nothing could possibly tolerate it—and here's the point—but a machine, something that sees but cannot possibly care. The film completes Warhol's Duchampian dehumanization of the cinematic eye.

5. Stan Brakhage, *Essential Brakhage* (Kingston, NY: McPherson, 2001), 213.

6. Markopoulos stayed with Brakhage at his home in Colorado during the period in which *The Art of Vision* was being edited and later dedicated *Ming Green* (1966) to him. They continued a warm and lengthy correspondence until at least 1974, often discussing their current projects in great detail.

7. P. Adams Sitney, *Eyes Upside Down: Visionary Filmmakers and the Heritage of Emerson* (Oxford: Oxford University Press, 2008), 76.

8. Frampton's "For a Metahistory of Film: Commonplace Notes and Hypotheses" was first printed in the September 1971 issue of *Artforum* (32–35). It was subsequently reprinted in Hollis Frampton, *Circles of Confusion: Film-Photography-Video Texts, 1968–1980* (Rochester, NY: Visual Studies Workshop Press, 1983), 109–116. Frampton refers to this text as the start of *Magellan* in Bill Simon, "Talking about Magellan: An Interview with Hollis Frampton," *Millennium Film Journal* 7–9 (Fall–Winter 1980–1981), 15.

9. Frampton, *Circles of Confusion*, 116.

10. Simon, "Talking about Magellan," 9.

11. Ibid., 11–15.

12. Jonas Mekas called *Twice a Man* the greatest film of 1963 in "An Interview with Markopoulos," *Village Voice*, October 10, 1963, 17–18. He later wrote with equal enthusiasm about *Galaxie* (1966), *The Illiac Passion* (1967), and *Himself as Herself* (1967), which he called "a perfect one-character novel . . . as perfect stylistically, as, say, Flaubert or Stendhal was" ("An Interview with Gregory Markopoulos on *Himself as Herself*," *Village Voice*, February 2, 1967, 15).

13. Nietzsche's letter is from January 21, 1887, and is quoted in Bryan Magee, *The Tristan Chord* (New York: Henry Holt, 2000), 325.

14. That Mekas also used this same piece of music in the section of his autobiographical "odyssey" *Lost, Lost, Lost* (1976) entitled "On the Outskirts of New York," as he is completing his journey into the United States, reinforces these implications. Mekas returns almost obsessively to *Parsifal* in his post-1960s work; the overture is also used at both the beginning and near the end of *He Stands in a Desert Counting the Seconds of His Life* (1985). In the latter instance, it is tellingly accompanied by the text, "It's not lost yet . . ."

15. Gregory Markopoulos, *Boustrophedon* (Florence: Temenos, 1977), 22. Markopoulos' comments in an unpublished letter to Robert Freeman on November 26, 1972, are typical of his thoughts on this subject: "The foundations are simply interested in a form of urban development in which an artist's work becomes a commodity for the spectator, become the consumer. One need only think of Lincoln Center, and other disasters. No interest is taken in the structure and what it should contain—it is simply made gigantic, and does not serve the art form it must contain" (Markopoulos, *Cerberus*, vol. 19).

16. Markopoulos, *Boustrophedon*, 60.

17. Ibid., 74.

18. Markopoulos speaks of his decision to select Greece as the site of his Temenos in *Boustrophedon*, 100. The goals of the Temenos presentations are outlined in a 1980 grant application included in *Cerberus*, vol. 25.

19. Markopoulos first begins discussing the idea of his own projection space in 1967 and mentions the Temenos in his diaries in 1969 (*Ein Edelweiss*, vol. 22). The word first

appears in print in one of his essays, "The Redeeming of the Contrary," written in 1971 and first published in *Film Culture* 52 (Spring 1971), 13–19.

20. The letter to Clara Hoover (dated March 2, 1968) is included in *Cerberus*, 7:2304. The operas are also mentioned in a letter to Brakhage from Brussels dated March 8, 1968 (*Cerberus*, 7:2324).

21. In a letter to Robert Freeman dated November 8, 1967, Markopoulos remarks that one of the things that struck him most during his first attendance at a performance of a Wagner opera was the fact that the "orchestra was hidden" (Markopoulos, *Cerberus*, 6:1765). He repeatedly expresses his belief that the projector should be invisible in subsequent letters.

22. "Gregory Markopoulos: A Solemn Pause . . . ," in *New York Filmmakers Newsletter* 5, no. 3 (January 1972), 58. Markopoulos mentions the Doge's Palazzo to Robert Freeman in a letter from October 7, 1973, writing, "It may be part design for the projection space of the Temenos—though Temenos where? Where? Who will do it?" (*Cerberus*, vol. 21).

23. Goethe, "On German Architecture," in *Goethe's Literary Essays*, edited and translated by J. E. Springarn (New York: Frederick Ungar, 1964), 7. In *The Genius of Christianity* (1802), Chateaubriand developed similar ideas in a French context:

> The forests were the first temples of the Divinity, and in them men acquired the first idea of architecture. . . . The forests of Gaul were, in their turn, introduced into the temples of our ancestors, and those celebrated woods of oaks thus maintained their sacred character. Those ceilings sculptured into foliage of different kinds, those buttresses which prop the walls and terminate abruptly like the broken trunks of trees, the coolness of the vaults, the darkness of the sanctuary, the dim twilight of the aisles, the secret passages, the low doorways,—in a word, every thing in a Gothic church reminds you of the labyrinths of a wood; every thing excited a feeling of religious awe, of mystery, and of the Divinity. (Chateaubriand, *The Genius of Christianity*, translated by Charles I. White [Baltimore: John Murphy, 1875], 386)

24. Sergei Eisenstein, *Nonindifferent Nature*, translated by Herbert Marshall (Cambridge: Cambridge University Press, 1987), 355–357.

25. Ibid., 216–217.

26. In his collected writings, Markopoulos repeatedly tries to distance himself from Eisenstein, but does admit to a grudging respect for *Ivan the Terrible* (see, for example, Markopoulos, *Boustrophedon*, 18). He denies the influence of Eisenstein in at least two interviews: "Question-and-Answer Session with Gregory Markopoulos Following a Screening of *The Illiac Passion* in Brussels, Early 1968," in *Gregory J. Markopoulos: Mythic Themes, Portraiture, and Films of Place*, edited by John G. Hanhardt and Matthew Yokobosky (New York: Whitney Museum of American Art, 1996), 98–106; and "Special Events Program: Interview with Gregory J. Markopoulos," Radio Free Europe, May 10, 1966 (transcript held at Anthology Film Archives). The emphatic nature of Markopoulos' statements suggests the possibility of an "anxiety of influence" on his part.

27. Markopoulos attributes many of his formal experiments to his enthusiasm for von Sternberg's work, writing:

> It is significant to set down that during the final production days of *Psyche* I was fortunate in arranging a private projection at Paramount Studios of Josef von Sternberg's masterworks, *The Scarlett Empress* [1934] and *The Devil is a Woman*

[1935]. My unbounded and ardent zeal for these works permitted me to stray farther afield from the conventional unspontaneous manners of narrative description for the film spectator. (Gregory Markopoulos, *Chaos Phaos* [Florence: Temenos, 1971], 2:14–15)

Although he does not mention it, the use of multiple superimpositions and mirror reversals at the end of *The Scarlett Empress* creates a sensory effect very similar to Markopoulos' work of the 1960s (the interlacing of religious paintings, for example, anticipates some of the visual strategies of *Bliss*).

28. According to P. Adams Sitney, the images in *Psyche* are onscreen for around one second; in *Swain*, they last for between one-eighth and one-third of a second (three to eight frames). In *Twice a Man*, by contrast, each of the seventy-seven shots included in the final recapitulation is only two frames long (P. Adams Sitney, *Visionary Film*, 3rd ed. [Oxford: Oxford University Press, 2001], 130–134).

29. In "Special Events Program: Interview with Gregory Markopoulos," Markopoulos said that he was interested in Resnais' films, especially *Last Year at Marienbad* (1961), but had not been influenced by them.

30. Markopoulos, *Chaos Phaos*, 2:7.

31. Ibid., 75.

32. Markopoulos, *Boustrophedon*, 81.

33. Markopoulos, *Chaos Phaos*, 2:18.

34. Markopoulos includes a detailed diagram of this process along with a transcription of the first twenty shots of *Twice a Man* (including frame counts) in ibid., 15–16. In this, the structure of his writing resembles that of Eisenstein, who frequently provided frame-by-frame analyses of his films in his theoretical essays.

35. Ibid.

36. Markopoulos' screening notes for the premiere of the film (a copy of which is in the collection of Anthology Film Archives) include his observation that "*The Illiac Passion* retells the passions of one man, the figure who crosses Brooklyn Bridge at the beginning of the film, comes to the Mother Muse, then proceeds to the forest in the tradition of, say, all heroes, perhaps, Zarathustra, and there under an apple tree communes with his selves." He then provides a detailed cast list associating actors and deities.

37. Ibid.

38. The Markopoulos quote is from Gregory Markopoulos, *Quest for Serenity: Journey of a Film-Maker* (New York: Filmmakers Cinematheque, 1965), 31. The Shelley quote is from act 3, line 195 of *Prometheus Unbound*.

39. Markopoulos held a steady job at Brentano's Books in New York until 1962, after which he decided to devote himself entirely to his filmmaking. Although he tried repeatedly to secure the long-term support of various patrons, he was frequently without money, and his turn toward in-camera editing, small-scale filmmaking, and the separation of figure and ground was also a move away from the costly, epic form of *The Illiac Passion*. A similar confluence of personal, financial, and aesthetic factors informed Brakhage's contemporaneous decision to begin making his 8mm *Songs* (1965–1969) immediately after completing *The Art of Vision*.

40. Markopoulos, *Chaos Phaos*, 3:98–99.

41. For *The Divine Damnation* (1968), Markopoulos went so far as to shoot the locations and the human subjects separately.

42. Portraiture had become a major focus of American avant-garde filmmaking at precisely this moment, when Andy Warhol was continuing his ongoing series of ironic, single-shot portraits taken from a fixed camera position and Stan Brakhage was beginning work on his *Songs*. The differences in the treatment of portraiture by Markopoulos and Brakhage are evident by comparing their respective portraits of Jonas Mekas, completed at almost the same time (Brakhage's is included in *Fifteen Song Traits*, 1965). Characteristically, Brakhage attempts to convey a sense of the dynamism of the subject by cutting rapidly between brief shots of Mekas' hands and face, and alternating these with cropped shots of him on the phone. Whereas Brakhage's emphasis is on the fluidity of vision and selfhood, the combination of precisely composed, lushly lit images and the inclusion of symbolic objects turns Markopoulos' portrait films into studies of psychological essences (an interest he shared with von Stroheim).

43. Gregory J. Markopoulos, "Adventures with *Bliss* in Roma," *Prisma* 2, no. 4 (1969), 35.

44. St. Demetrius is remembered as a military martyr who, according to tradition, protected the city of Thessaloniki from invasion by pagan forces in the fourth century. He later became, along with St. George, one of the patron saints of the Crusades. Markopoulos identifies one of the paintings as depicting "the Virgin Mary embracing St. Anne" (ibid.).

45. The "local" elements are signified, above all, by the braying goats shown outside the church in the early part of the film and on the soundtrack at several crucial junctures. Through Markopoulos' editing, these sounds are linked to the light passing through the church above the altar at the end of the film, which has clear religious implications.

46. Rainer Maria Rilke, *The Notebooks of Malte Laurids Brigge*, translated by M. D. Herter Norton (New York: W.W. Norton, 1964), 209.

47. Markopoulos, *Ein Edelweiss*, vol. 19, entry dated May 19, 1967. Decades later, during the final stages of work on *Eniaios* in 1988, Markopoulos reads Charles Sherrington's landmark psychology text, *The Integrative Action of the Nervous System* (Cambridge: Cambridge University Press, 1952), and argues that the insertion of white leader provides a "catharsis" for the viewer whose nerves have been stimulated by the flashes of imagery (*Chiron Notes*, vol. 20, entry dated February 8, 1988).

48. In a letter to Stan Brakhage on March 24, 1968, Markopoulos explains that *The Mysteries* was made "Inbetween [*sic*]" the difficult production of his two operas (*Cerberus*, 7:2386).

49. A plan for each of the cycles of *Eniaios*, with the sequencing of the films delineated, is available at the Temenos Archive. Sections from the original *Twice a Man* were incorporated into cycles four, eight, fifteen, and nineteen.

50. Markopoulos, *Boustrophedon*, 83.

51. In the essay "Institutions, Customs, Landscapes," Markopoulos wrote, "Today, one is tempted to admit that the future of civilization rests simply upon the conveyance of images similar to the Egyptian hieroglyphics" (*Chaos Phaos*, 3:71). He then includes a definition, taken from the *Columbia Encyclopedia*, of "hieroglyphics" as "conventionalized pictures used chiefly to represent meanings that seem arbitrary and are seldom obvious" and describes their three functions as those of the "ideogram," "phonogram," and "determinant." Certain images in *Eniaios* suggest each of these categories, and his use of these terms is related to his insistence that picture narratives ontologically precede verbal ones.

Markopoulos was not alone in reviving the idea of the cinematic hieroglyph in this period. Experimental animator Harry Smith declared in 1971 that film frames "are hieroglyphs, even when they look like actuality. You should think of the individual film frame, always, as a glyph, and then you'll understand what cinema is about" (quoted in Sitney, *Visionary Film*, 257).

52. Markopoulos, *Cerberus*, vol. 16.

53. These similarities extend even to some of their compulsive habits. Both Markopoulos and Gance were prolific self-chroniclers, filling volume after volume with precisely dated (and sometimes even timed) entries containing philosophical ideas as well as personal details.

54. Diagrams of a double- and triple-screen version of *Psyche* are included in *Chiron Notes*, vol. 3.

55. Letter to Robert Freeman from Gregory Markopoulos, dated March 19, 1973 (*Cerberus*, vol. 20).

56. Markopoulos, *Chiron Notes*, vol. 2, dated October 4, 1983.

57. As Markopoulos writes in a 1986 prose poem entitled "Fundamen" in *The Sovereignty of the Filmmaker as Physician*, vol. 7: "Image, what Image is heard? In or within the image; spoken images" (11). This is echoed on the following page: "Silence, what silence is heard? In or within the image, spoken silence" (12).

58. Gregory Markopoulos, "Unification of the Frame," in *The Sovereignty of the Filmmaker as Physician*, 7:3. The title of the text alludes, among other things, to the reunification of Germany, which Markopoulos refers to in the opening sentence: "The beginning of the motion picture was like the unification of Germany, today; *today*, for I write on the day of the unification" (1).

59. Markopoulos, *Cerberus*, 7:2336.

60. Markopoulos, *Boustrophedon*, 49.

61. Markopoulos, *Chaos Phaos*, 3:92.

62. Markopoulos, *Boustrophedon*, 77–93.

63. Karl Kerenyi, *Prometheus: Archetypal Image of Human Existence* (New York: Pantheon Books, 1963).

64. For example, in a 1957 diary entry included in the book *Quest for Serenity*, Markopoulos writes, "Prometheus, like the Buddhisattva [sic], appears and a miraculous Lotus springs out of the earth, and he seats himself thereon, and takes in all the world at a glance" (31). Similarly, in an unpublished 1964 notebook (*Prometheus*, vol. 1), Markopoulos writes that in introducing Prometheus, who had taken on "all the world's disorders, so he may mirror them himself, so see himself—all his contours," he should "use Mudra Patterns and [the] gestures of Japanese Buddhist sculptures." There are also references to passages from the Koran as well as countless sourcebooks on Greek mythology.

It is difficult to determine whether or not Markopoulos read the Graves or Campbell books upon their initial publication because the notes from that period no longer exist. He did, however, refer to Graves in the *Prometheus* notebooks.

65. In his 1841 essay "History," Emerson interpreted Prometheus as the symbol of intellectual independence and self-actualization:

The beautiful fables of the Greeks, being proper creations of the imagination and not of the fancy, are universal verities. What a range of meanings and what perpetual pertinence has the story of Prometheus! . . . Prometheus is the Jesus of the old mythology. He is the friend of man; stands between the unjust "justice" of the Eternal Father and the race of mortals, and readily suffers all things on their account. But where it departs from the Calvinistic Christianity and exhibits him as the defier of Jove, it represents a state of mind which readily appears wherever the doctrine of Theism is taught in a crude, objective form, and which seeks the self-defence of man against this untruth, namely a discontent with the believed fact that a God exists, and a feeling that the obligation of reverence is onerous. It would steal if it could the fire of the Creator, and live apart from him and independent of him. The Prometheus Vinctus is the romance of skepticism. (Ralph Waldo Emerson, *Essays and Lectures* [New York: Library of America, 1983], 251)

On the progressive Prometheanism of Shelley, see the analysis of *Prometheus Unbound* in David S. Ferris, *Silent Urns: Hellenism, Romanticism, Modernity* (Stanford: Stanford University Press, 2000), 134–157.

66. Markopoulos, *Boustrophedon*, 63.

67. Narcissus assumes a prominent role in much of the poetry of Valéry, and he wrote about the myth explicitly in at least three poems: "Narcisse parle" (1890), "Fragments du Narcisse" (1922), and finally the "Cantate de Narcisse" (1938). In these works, Narcissus is portrayed as the embodiment of absolute beauty, and his self-regard is considered in wholly aesthetic terms. Mallarmé's unfinished *Hérodiade* uses the Narcissus myth in a similar fashion. In conversation with a nurse, for example, Herodias responds to the question, "For whom would you, consumed by pangs, keep the unknown splendor and the vain mystery of your being?" by saying simply, "For myself alone" ("Herodias—Scene," in Stéphane Mallarmé, *Collected Poems and Other Verse*, translated by E. H. Blackmore and A. M. Blackmore [Oxford: Oxford University Press, 2006], 34–35). André Gide's *Le Traité du narcisse* (1891) is also in this tradition, and a copy is visible on Markopoulos' bookshelf in *Ming Green*.

68. The homoerotic and "queer" underpinnings of this treatment of Narcissus are addressed in Steven Bruhm, ed., *Reflecting Narcissus: A Queer Aesthetic* (Minneapolis: University of Minnesota Press, 2001).

69. Friedrich Schlegel, *Philosophical Fragments*, translated by Peter Firchow (Minneapolis: University of Minnesota Press, 1991), 35.

70. For authors like Plotinus (and St. Augustine), images are perceived when rays projected by the eyes intersect with external objects.

Markopoulos appears to have had limited knowledge of Heidegger's work at the time he wrote this essay. His interest deepened considerably after reading John Sallis' *Delimitations: Phenomenology and the End of Metaphysics* (Bloomington: Indiana University Press, 1986), a book he heavily annotated. On a page in which Sallis discusses "the thematization of understanding as projection (*Entwurf*)," he quotes Heidegger's *Being and Time* (1927): "*Dasein* ["being-in-the-world"] has, as *Dasein*, always already projected itself: and as long as it is, it is projecting. As long as it is, *Dasein* always has understood itself and always will understand itself from possibilities" (123). In the margins, Markopoulos wrote "use for film orchestration." When Sallis writes, elsewhere on the page, "*From* these possibilities *Dasein* is, in turn, given back to itself, disclosed to itself," Markopoulos again makes a comparison with his film work, "as in film from end to beginning" (123). Later, in *Chiron Notes*, vol. 24, Markopoulos links Heidegger's 1935 essay "The Origin of the Work of Art" to "The origins of the *Eniaios*."

In this sense, the triangulation in Markopoulos' essay could be related to the idea of *Dasein* as a thrown projection onto the external surface of the world that extends out from the self and is then reflected back upon it (as if it bounced off of a screen).

71. Markopoulos refers to line 121 of Euripides' *Hippolytus*, and the Asclepius Rock is mentioned in line 1209.

72. Euripides, *Hippolytus*, lines 131–140.

73. Robin Mitchell-Boyask, *Plague and the Athenian Imagination: Drama, History, and the Cult of Asclepius* (Cambridge: Cambridge University Press, 2008), 45–55.

74. J. J. Pollitt, *Art and Experience in Classical Greece* (Cambridge: Cambridge University Press, 1972), 124–126.

75. Karl Kerenyi, *Asklepios: Archetypal Image of the Physician's Existence* (Princeton, NJ: Princeton University Press, 1959), 29–32. In a tradition not alluded to in the Euripides play, Asclepius eventually brings about the resurrection of Hippolytus. It is this legend that informs Markopoulos' *Twice a Man* (the title stems from the fact that the resurrected Hippolytus is referred to as "Twice Born"). It may also be relevant in this context that Aeschylus attributes the origins of Greek medicine to Prometheus in *Prometheus Bound* (lines 691–702 in the James Scully and C. John Herington translation [Oxford: Oxford University Press, 1975]).

76. The number of bright white flashes between images apparently represents a corresponding letter in the Greek alphabet (with one flash equaling alpha, two equaling beta, etc.). According to Robert Beavers, the dedication spelled out by these flashes would translate into English as "The Soul of the Eyes."

77. Ovid, *Metamorphoses*, Book IX, lines 338–406.

78. Oswald Spengler, *The Decline of the West*, translated by Charles Francis Atkinson, vol. 1 (New York: Alfred A. Knopf, 1966), 61. This passage is marked in Markopoulos' copy of the book, which he read in 1966 (as indicated in the frontispiece).

79. While editing *Eniaios*, Markopoulos highlighted a passage in Carl Dalhaus' *Richard Wagner's Music Dramas* in which Dalhaus writes that "the *Leitmotiv* technique emerges not simply to send narrative signals to the audience, but as a means of musical organization that replaces periodic structure" (*Richard Wagner's Music Dramas* [Cambridge: Cambridge University Press, 1979], 224).

80. According to his work notebooks, Markopoulos decided to treat *Eniaios* as a series of cycles rather than a single film on May 10, 1983 (*Chiron Notes*, vol. 2). In a subsequent entry, on the evening of October 4, 1983, he wrote, "A projection should be devoted (a) to 1 day, or, if necessary, to many days" (*Chiron Notes*, vol. 2). The eighty-hour length of the film he finished nearly a decade later obviously dictated that the cycles be broken up over many days.

81. A subsequent generation of ambitious avant-garde filmmakers has followed this model, producing extensive series films over the course of several decades that are loosely linked to their own autobiographies. Andrew Noren, for example, has described his ongoing *Adventures of the Exquisite Corpse* series as

an extended visual music, by now many hours long. Themes and variations, first stated long ago in the first parts of the work, continue on through the work as a whole. With each part these themes are refined and transmuted, gathering depth and complexity as the work goes on. They appear, disappear, echo, and reverberate from part to part, in both rhyme and disjuncture. New themes and variations are added all the time, as mind goes through life and life goes through mind, adding to the complexity. (Laurence Kardish, "An Interview with Andrew Noren," distributed by the Museum of Modern Art to accompany the retrospective program "What the Light Was Like," October 21–25, 2009)

Much of what Noren says here is particular to his own project, but his description of the process of making an ever-expanding series film is paradigmatic. Canadian filmmaker R. Bruce Elder's Poundian film cycle, *The Book of All the Dead* (1975–1994, approximately forty-two hours long), is one of the few contemporary projects that could be compared with the extended structural form Markopoulos developed in *Eniaios*, although its overall design is closer to that of Frampton's *Magellan*.

82. Kahnweiler, who was eighty-six when the film was shot, was the most important patron of Picasso and Braque and was the subject of two major portraits by the former. Édouard Roditi was an American poet and translator who also conducted interviews with a number of major modernist artists that were collected into *Dialogues on Art* (London: Secker and Warburg, 1960). Barbara Hepworth was one of the preeminent modernist sculptors of her generation.

83. "Gregory Markopoulos: A Solemn Pause," 58.

84. This series of paintings is discussed in detail in Michael R. Taylor, ed., *Giorgio de Chirico and the Myth of Ariadne* (London: Merrell, 2002).

85. The connection between Ariadne and Arachne in Ruskin's work is discussed in J. Hillis Miller, "Ariadne's Thread: Repetition and the Narrative Line," *Critical Inquiry* 3, no. 1 (Autumn 1976), 56–77 (Markopoulos appears to have read this article; see *Chiron Notes*, vol. 25).

86. Jeffrey Stout, "All Mean Egotism Vanishes," lecture delivered at Princeton University, November 16, 2007.

87. Pavel Florensky, *Iconostasis*, translated by Olga Andrejev (Crestwood, NY: Oakwood Publications, 1996), 63. My treatment of these issues is informed by conversations with Jeffrey Stout after the 2008 Temenos screenings.

88. In Markopoulos' production notebooks, *Eniaios* is defined as meaning "single, unitary," and it is used elsewhere to refer to a sort of all-encompassing wholeness (*Chiron Notes*, vol. 6).

89. "Gregory Markopoulos: A Solemn Pause," 59.

90. Kerenyi, *Asklepios*, 61.

91. The Greek title is *TO ΜΕΓΑ ΧΑΣΜΑ*. The title is probably an allusion to a passage in Heidegger's *Introduction to Metaphysics*:

Only with the sophists and Plato was seeming explained as, and thus reduced to, mere seeming. At the same time, Being as *idea* was elevated to a supersensory realm. The chasm, *khorismos*, was torn open between the merely apparent beings here below and the real Being somewhere up there. (Martin Heidegger, *Introduction to Metaphysics*, translated by Gregory Fried and Richard Polt [New Haven: Yale Nota Bene, 2000], 111)

92. J. J. Pollitt links the sculptures used to decorate the temple built for Asclepius at Epidaurus to the shift from an aesthetic of *ethos* to one of *pathos* (Pollitt, *Art and Experience*, 143–146). My interpretation of the excerpts of *The Mysteries* used at this juncture is at least indirectly supported by Markopoulos' comments on the film. In his notes on C. M. Woodhouse's book *George Gemistos Plethon: The Last of the Hellenes* (Oxford: Oxford University Press, 1986), Markopoulos compares "'the doctrine of the immortality of the soul' through the [Eleusinian] Mysteries" to *"The Mysteries*, with its particular ending/ meaning," and also alludes to an "Eleusinian Mysteries" grouping elsewhere in *Eniaios* (*Chiron Notes*, vol. 22).

Chapter 3

1. Jacques Aumont, Jean-Louis Comolli, Jean Narboni, and Sylvie Pierre, "Time Overflowing," translated by Amy Gateff, in *Rivette: Texts and Interviews*, edited by Jonathan Rosenbaum (London: British Film Institute, 1977), 37.

2. This issue, no. 153, was one of the first edited by Jacques Rivette.

3. Aumont et al., "Time Overflowing," 34.

4. Jonathan Rosenbaum, Rivette's most steadfast partisan in the English language, is also the foremost advocate for this interpretation of his work, in pieces such as "Work and Play in the House of Fiction: On Jacques Rivette," *Sight and Sound* 43, no. 4 (Autumn 1974), 190–194, and "*Tih-Minh, Out 1*: On the Nonreception of Two French Serials," *Velvet Light Trap* 37 (Spring 1996), 58–65. More recently, B. Kite has referred to "the liberating potentials and revolutionary energies of play" in "Jacques Rivette and the Other Place, Track One," *Cinema Scope* 30 (Spring 2007), 17.

5. Robin Wood, "Narrative Pleasure: Two Films of Jacques Rivette," *Film Quarterly* 35, no. 1 (Autumn 1981), 3.

6. See, for example, the chapter "*La Règle du jeu*: Games and Play," in Douglas Morrey and Alison Smith, *Jacques Rivette* (Manchester: Manchester University Press, 2009), 117–146.

7. Bernard Eisenschitz, Jean-André Fieschi, and Eduardo de Gregorio, "Interview on *Out*," translated by Tom Milne in Rosenbaum, *Rivette: Texts and Interviews*, 49. In an interview included in the documentary *The Mysteries of Paris* (Robert Fischer and Wilfried Reichart, 2015), cinematographer Pierre-William Glenn, who shot *Out 1*, made similar comments: "All the scenes where the characters are on their own remind me of being in church. I felt as if I was at Mass, watching the actors express themselves. It was as if we were filming some sort of ritual. . . . Rivette holds great store by ritual. He's always held great store by it."

8. *Pericles* is the central play in *Paris Belongs to Us, Andromaque* is rehearsed in *L'Amour fou*, and the two Aeschylus plays are performed by rival theater troupes in both the thirteen-hour (1971) and the five-hour (*Spectre*, 1974) versions of *Out 1*.

9. In "The Genius of Howard Hawks," Rivette wrote that in these comedies, there is a repetition of "the same actions, endlessly recurring, which Hawks builds up with the persistence of a maniac and the patience of a man obsessed, suddenly whirl madly about, as if at the mercy of a capricious maelstrom" (Jacques Rivette, "The Genius of Howard Hawks," in *Cahiers du cinéma: The 1950s*, edited by Jim Hillier [Cambridge, MA: Harvard University Press, 1985], 129). *Monkey Business* (Hawks, 1952) is the best postwar example,

although it is equally true of *Gentlemen Prefer Blondes* (Hawks, 1953) and *I Was a Male War Bride* (Hawks, 1949).

10. Jacques Rivette, in conversation with Serge Daney in *Jacques Rivette, le veilleur* (Claire Denis, 1990). The title of this section comes from part of Jacques Rivette's contribution to "Bio-filmographie de Jean Renoir," edited by André Bazin, *Cahiers du cinéma* 78 (Christmas 1957), 82.

11. Jacques Rivette, "The Hand," translated by Tom Milne, in Rosenbaum, *Rivette: Texts and Interviews*, 65–68.

12. Jacques Rivette, "Letter on Rossellini," translated by Tom Milne in ibid., 64.

13. Jacques Rivette, "L'Art de la fugue," *Cahiers du cinéma* 27 (August–September 1953), 50; Jacques Rivette, "De l'invention," *Cahiers du cinéma* 27 (October 1953), 60.

14. Rivette's most explicit comments in this vein are in the "Letter on Rossellini":

Rossellini, however, is not merely Christian, but Catholic; in other words, carnal to the point of scandal; one recalls the outrage over *The Miracle* [included in the two-part film *L'Amore*, Roberto Rossellini, 1948]; but Catholicism is by vocation a scandalous religion; the fact that our body, like Christ's, also plays its part in the divine mystery is something hardly to everyone's taste, and in this creed which makes the presence of the flesh one of its dogmas, there is a concrete meaning, weighty, almost sensual, to flesh and matter that is highly repugnant to chaste spirits: their "intellectual evolution" no longer permits them to participate in mysteries as gross as this. . . . Rossellini has the eye of a modern, but also the spirit; he is more modern than any of us; and Catholicism is still as modern as anything. (Rivette, "Letter on Rossellini," 63)

Rivette would briefly be censured by the church for making *The Nun*, but there is little in that film, or any of Rivette's subsequent works, to indicate that he would retract these claims about the nature of Catholicism.

15. Ibid., 54.

16. Jacques Rivette, "Notes on a Revolution," in Hillier, *Cahiers du cinéma*, 95.

17. Ibid., 96. The Triangle Film Corporation was an early American studio founded in the summer of 1915 by D. W. Griffith's partner Harry Aitken and his brother Roy. Griffith was one of the key producer-directors, along with Thomas Ince and Mack Sennett, and the stars under contract included Douglas Fairbanks, Lillian Gish, Mary Pickford, and "Fatty" Arbuckle. By the end of the 1910s, the studios were purchased by Samuel Goldwyn as part of the Goldwyn Pictures Corporation, one of the rising "Hollywood" powers (in 1924, the Goldwyn Pictures Corporation merged with the Metro Pictures Corporation and Louis B. Mayer Pictures to form MGM).

18. Jacques Rivette, "Nous ne sommes plus innocents," in Hélene Frappat, *Jacques Rivette, secret compris* (Paris: Cahiers du cinéma, 2001), 67.

19. Ibid., 68.

20. Louis Marcorelles, "Interview: Roger Leenhardt with Jacques Rivette," *Sight and Sound* 32, no. 4 (Autumn 1963), 173.

21. Although it was not completed until 1960, Rivette began actively planning *Paris Belongs to Us* in 1956 (in "Time Overflowing," he attributes its origins to "the Budapest crisis," Aumont et al., "Time Overflowing," 26) and shot it piecemeal from the summer of 1958 through 1959, largely using borrowed film stock. By the time *Paris Belongs to Us*

was released, important films by Claude Chabrol, Éric Rohmer, François Truffaut, Jean-Luc Godard, and others had already announced the emergence of the "New Wave," but it was nevertheless one of the first features by any of the critics associated with *Cahiers du cinéma* to begin production.

22. Rivette reflexively addresses aspects of his method when Gérard explains his motivations for trying to direct *Pericles*:

> Everyone says I'm crazy . . . but the reason I want to stage it is because it's "unplayable." It's shreds and patches, yet it hangs together over all. Pericles may traverse kingdoms, the heroes are dispersed, yet they can't escape, they're all reunited in act five. I want to show that. . . . But we must try to make people understand it. It shows a chaotic but not absurd world, rather like our own, flying off in all directions, but with a purpose. Only we do not know what. . . . I'm counting on the music [to make that clear].

23. "Conférence de presse (extraits): Jacques Rivette," *Cahiers du cinéma* 445 (June 1991), 34.

24. Rivette continues:

> Stravinsky systematically uses contrasts and simultaneously, at the very point where they are used, he brings into relief what it is that unites them. The principle of Stravinsky's music is the perpetual rupture of the rhythm. The great novelty of *The Rite of Spring* [1913] was its being the first musical work where the rhythm was systematically varied. Within the field of rhythm, not tone, it was already almost serial music, made up of rhythmical oppositions, structures and series. And I get the impression that this is what Resnais is aiming at when he cuts together four tracking shots, then suddenly a static shot, two static shots and back to a tracking shot. Within the juxtaposition of static and tracking shots he tries to find what unites them. In other words he is seeking simultaneously an effect of opposition and an effect of profound unity. (Jean Domarchi, Jacques Doniol-Valcroze, Jean-Luc Godard, Pierre Kast, Jacques Rivette, and Éric Rohmer, "Hiroshima, notre amour," in Hillier, *Cahiers du cinéma*, 66)

25. André S. Labarthe, "Comment peut-on être moderne?" in *La Nouvelle Vague*, edited by Antoine de Baecque and Charles Tesson (Paris: Cahiers du cinéma, 1999), 14.

26. Jacques Rivette, "Revoir Verdoux," *Cahiers du cinéma* 146 (January 1963), 43. Rivette regularly attended concerts by Boulez in this period, and his interview was published in 1964: Jacques Rivette and François Weyergans, "Entretien avec Pierre Boulez," *Cahiers du cinéma* 152 (February 1964), 19–29.

27. The comments about Mizoguchi are in Jonathan Rosenbaum, Lauren Sedofsky, and Gilbert Adair, "Phantom Interviewers over Rivette," *Film Comment* 10, no. 5 (September–October 1974), 24. His claims about Boulez are in Aumont et al., "Time Overflowing," 29.

28. *The Nun* premiered at the Cannes Film Festival in 1966 but was then banned for over a year. The film was finally released commercially in July 1967.

29. Rosenbaum, Sedofsky, and Adair, "Phantom Interviewers over Rivette," 24. Cinematographer Charles Bitsch described Rivette's enthusiasm for *The Golden Coach* in Frappat, *Jacques Rivette, secret compris*, 57.

30. Carlos Clarens and Edgardo Cozarinsky, "Jacques Rivette," *Sight and Sound* 43, no. 4 (Autumn 1974), 195. Paulhan's "Braque le patron" is translated by Éric Trudel in *George*

Braque and the Cubist Still Life: 1928–1945, edited by Karen K. Butler (Munich: Prestel, 2013), 201–216.

31. Edgar Morin, "Pour un nouveau cinéma vérité," *France observateur* 506 (January 14, 1960), 23.

32. Richard Leacock, "For an Uncontrolled Cinema," *Film Culture* 22–23 (Summer 1961), 25.

33. Rivette has argued on several occasions that the seeds for the New Wave were contained within Rouch's work:

> Rouch is the force behind all French cinema of the past ten years, although few people realize it. Jean-Luc Godard came from Rouch. In a way, Rouch is more important than Godard in the evolution of the French cinema. Godard goes in a direction that is only valid for himself, which doesn't set an example, in my opinion. Whereas all Rouch's films are exemplary, even those where he failed, even *Les Veuves de quinze ans* [1965], Jean-Luc doesn't set an example, he provokes. He provokes reactions, either of imitation or of contradiction or of rejection, but he can't strictly be taken as an example. While Rouch or Renoir can be. (Aumont et al., "Time Overflowing," 35)

In a 1980 lecture at the Centre Georges Pompidou, Edgar Morin described the difference between "Direct Cinema" and cinéma vérité as follows: "There are two ways to conceive of the cinema of the Real: the first is to pretend that you can present reality to be seen; the second is to pose the problem of reality. In the same way, there were two ways to conceive cinéma vérité. The first was to pretend that you brought truth. The second was to pose the problem of truth" (quoted in Isabelle Veyrat-Masson, *Télévision et histoire, la confusion des genres: Docudramas, docufictions et fictions du réel* [Brussels: Éditions De Boecke Université, 2008], 208).

34. Aumont et al., "Time Overflowing," 43.

35. In "Time Overflowing," Rivette said:

> Of course the choice of *Andromaque* was not completely naive. The possibilities of analogy—if I may say so—between *Andromaque* and *L'Amour fou* were so striking even when we reread the play that Jean-Pierre [Kalfon] and I decided from the start to avoid any terribly obvious comparisons between Racine and what we were doing. It was really too facile and was becoming rather annoying. During all the filming and then again during the editing, we didn't force ourselves constantly to eliminate every juxtaposition which appeared, but we never looked for them and when they seemed really too obvious or too much of a cop-out, we always tried to break them up. They had to remain two parallel entities, with even the echoes from one to the other remaining accidental. (Aumont et al., "Time Overflowing," 11)

36. Jean Racine, *Andromache*, translated by Richard Wilbur (New York: Harcourt Brace, 1980), 93.

37. Rivette explained that initially the actors were "still under the illusion that they will get to play *Andromaque* at the end of the week; while three or four days later, they know very well that they never will" (Aumont et al., "Time Overflowing," 12).

38. Ibid., 11.

39. Peter Lloyd, "Jacques Rivette and *L'Amour fou*," *Monogram* 2 (Summer 1971), 14.

40. The domestic scenes also highlight the fundamental contradiction between Sébastien's public persona and his private life, by depicting him as domineering toward his wife and largely indifferent to her feelings of isolation.

41. Aumont et al., "Time Overflowing," 26. It is likely that Rivette's interest in, and awareness of, Stockhausen stems from his friendship with Jean-Claude Éloy, a student of Stockhausen who composed original scores for *L'Amour fou* and *The Nun*.

42. Karlheinz Stockhausen, ". . . How Time Passes," *Die Reihe* 3 (1959), 10–39.

43. Penderecki's comments are from a 1993 presentation quoted by Mieczysław Tomaszewski in "Krzysztof Penderecki: Orchestral Works," translated by Jan Rybicki and Richard Whitehouse in *Penderecki: Orchestral Works*, vol. 1 (Hong Kong: Naxos, 2000), 3.

44. Rivette claims that this structure is "a sort of homage to Stravinsky, since it's the beginning and ending of lots of Stravinsky, especially *The Flood* or *Canticum*, with the beginning and the end being mirror images of each other" (Aumont et al., "Time Overflowing," 28). Significantly, *Canticum Sacrum ad honorem Sancti Marci nominis* (1955) and *The Flood* (1962) are among Stravinsky's most explicitly religious works, the latter an oratorio derived from Genesis.

45. Mizoguchi converted to Nichiren Buddhism in the early 1950s. For more information on Mizoguchi's attitude to religion, see Shindō Kaneto's documentary *The Life of a Film Director* (1975).

46. Rivette claimed that the sound of the child crying was "completely accidental and not at all premeditated, recorded in synch with the last shot" (Aumont et al., "Time Overflowing," 25). To create the circular effect used in the film, this same sound, captured fortuitously at the end of shooting, must then have been edited into the soundtrack at the beginning of the film. Tom Milne argued that this sound helps to explain two (appropriately) paired, but otherwise incongruous scenes, when Claire tries to buy a puppy and Sébastien attempts to buy a kitten (Tom Milne, "Ah! Je l'ai trop aimé pour ne le point hair," *Sight and Sound* 38, no. 2 [Spring 1969], 66).

47. *Cahiers du cinéma* 163 (February 1965).

48. Edmund Burke, *A Philosophical Enquiry into the Sublime and Beautiful* (London: Penguin Classics, 1998), 86.

49. Gilles Jacob, "Letter from Paris," *Sight and Sound* 38, no. 1 (Winter 1968–1969), 23.

50. This same pattern was followed by another controversial film completed in 1968, Marcel Ophuls' four-and-a-half-hour documentary about the French Occupation, *The Sorrow and the Pity*. Denied television broadcast or general release, it opened in a single art house in the fall of 1969 and played for several years without interruption.

51. Nicole Lubtchansky, who has edited nearly all of Rivette's films since *L'Amour fou*, reports that Rivette made this remark to Truffaut in Frappat, *Jacques Rivette, secret compris*, 178.

52. Ibid., 146. Tchalgadjieff was a major patron of some of the most radical (and least commercially minded) filmmakers of the period; in addition to Rivette, he also produced challenging films by Robert Bresson, Marguerite Duras, and Jean-Marie Straub and Danièle Huillet.

53. Martin Even, "'Out 1' Voyage au-delà du cinéma," *Le Monde*, October 14, 1971, 13. A screening report, on the same page and also by Martin Even, was called "Un film de 12 h

40." Even mentions the weak colors of the work print in his article and says that the audience was told ahead of time that there might be stoppage between reels. The work print was also missing credits and titles.

54. John 20:17.

55. Yvonne Baby, "Entretien avec Jacques Rivette," *Le Monde*, October 14, 1971, 13.

56. Rosenbaum, Sedofsky, and Adair, "Phantom Interviewers over Rivette," 22.

57. Eisenschitz, Fieschi, and de Gregorio, "Interview on *Out*," 48. The 16mm format was also used for most documentaries and avant-garde films in this period.

58. It was, of course, possible to go in and out during projection. Martin Even mentions seeing several people do precisely that, but Rivette also felt that anyone truly engaged by the film should fully commit to it:

> It should be like in the theatre, where you can leave in the middle—which I do, very often. On the other hand, I would like those who stay to stay right through to the end; I even think the doors ought to be locked. Going to see a film must be a contract—an act and a contract. And one of the clauses of the contract is that they have the right to leave during the interval but not at any other time. (Aumont et al., "Time Overflowing," 28)

59. Eisenschitz, Fieschi, and de Gregorio, "Interview on *Out*," 48.

60. Like his argument that silent films should be shown silent, rather than with the musical accompaniment they would have had in the 1910s or 1920s, Langlois' decision to strip the serials of intertitles was almost certainly a way of treating material deficiencies (the incompleteness of prints) productively.

61. Louis Delluc, *Paris-Midi*, July 5, 1919, reprinted in Pierre Lherminier, *Louis Delluc et le cinéma français* (Paris: Ramsay, 2008), 301–302.

62. Francis Lacassin has written numerous essays and books on Feuillade, such as *Maître des lions et des vampires, Louis Feuillade* (Paris: P. Bordas, 1995).

63. Rivette described the Cinémathèque as

> both the Louvre and the Museum of Modern Art of film as they should be and not as they are. It is also the Galerie Maeght and the Galerie Sonnabend. One could see there successively at 6:30 PM [D. W.] Griffith's *Broken Blossoms* [1919] and at 8:30 Andy Warhol's *The Chelsea Girls* [1966]. And it was fabulous precisely because one could see Griffith and Warhol together on the same night. Because it was then that one realized that there are not two or three kinds of cinema, there is only one cinema. It was the perpetual interaction of the present and the past of the cinema that was so exciting. (Richard Roud, *A Passion for Films: Henri Langlois and the Cinémathèque Française* [Baltimore: Johns Hopkins University Press, 1999], xxiv)

Although Langlois did not often show experimental films, Godard also recalled seeing *Chelsea Girls* there (Gene Youngblood, "No Difference between Life and Cinema," in *Jean-Luc Godard Interviews*, edited by David Sterritt [Jackson, MI: University Press of Mississippi, 1998], 11). Rivette later said that it made "a strong impression" (Jean-Marc Lalanne and Jean-Baptiste Morain, "Entretien Jacques Rivette: L'Art secret," *Les Inrockuptibles*, March 30, 2007, 34).

64. Rivette describes the importance of Hitchcock's *Marnie* to *L'Amour fou* in Aumont et al., "Time Overflowing," 12. His comments about "American Underground Films" are in Rosenbaum, Sedofsky, and Adair, "Phantom Interviewers over Rivette," 24. It is extremely unlikely that Rivette saw any of Markopoulos' films because they were rarely screened in France.

65. The various versions of *Jaguar* are described in Jean-André Fieschi and André Téchiné, "Jean Rouch, 'Jaguar,'" *Cahiers du cinéma* 195 (November 1967), 17–20. Jean-Luc Godard mentions *Jaguar*, "as yet not shown publicly," in several pieces in the late 1950s, especially "L'Afrique vous parle de la fin et des moyens," *Cahiers du cinéma* 94 (April 1959), 19. *Jaguar* was an early example of a 16mm feature shot with a battery-powered Nagra tape recorder, which greatly expanded the possibilities for location filming.

66. Fieschi and Téchiné, "Jean Rouch, 'Jaguar,'" 20.

67. Clarens and Cozarinsky, "Jacques Rivette," 196.

68. The longest shots in *Out 1* are devoted to the theater rehearsals, and the longest is in the first episode; the scene appears to be more than forty minutes long, but it is interrupted at multiple points by cuts to Colin playing cards in his room, and shots are continuous for no more than eleven minutes. Extended rehearsal sequences in the third and seventh episodes also feature interrupted long takes.

69. Eisenschitz, Fieschi, and de Gregorio, "Interview on *Out*," 41.

70. Frappat, *Jacques Rivette, secret compris*, 140.

71. Ibid., 142.

72. When asked for his views on the utopian ideals of "collective cinema around the time of 1968, [such as] Godard's Groupe Dziga Vertov," Rivette responded, "The films that you are speaking about were collective in the same way that the regime in Peking was a democracy!" (Lalanne and Morain, "Entretien Jacques Rivette," 35).

73. In a conversation on March 3, 2015, Bernard Eisenschitz said that Rivette had nevertheless expressed fascination with Gance's conception of films as "Cathedrals of Light."

74. Aeschylus, *Prometheus Bound*, translated by James Scully and C. John Herington (Oxford: Oxford University Press, 1975), line 738.

75. Johann Gottfried von Herder, "Essay on the Origin of Language," in *On the Origin of Language: Two Essays*, edited by John H. Moran and Alexander Gode (Chicago: University of Chicago Press, 1966), 128.

76. In 2002, Rivette explained that the Rousseau film was "a project that began before *L'Amour fou*. In the beginning, it concerned an idea of [Georges de] Beauregard and of Gruault, which consisted in taking Rousseau at the end of his life, after the *Confessions* [1782] . . . and there would have been flashbacks of the young Rousseau, played by Jean-Pierre Léaud" (Hélène Frappat and Jacques Rivette, *Trois films fantômes de Jacques Rivette* [Paris: Cahiers du cinéma, 2002], 9). In *Jacques Rivette, secret compris*, Frappat notes that "*Out 1* bears the traces of the last joint project of Rivette and Jean Gruault, interrupted by May '68" and mentions "Essay on the Origin of Languages" as a possible influence (138). The project fell through because of lack of financing.

Rousseau, as the avatar of French Romanticism, had also featured prominently in two films made by Godard (then quite close to Rivette) at the same time, both featuring the same actor: Rousseau's ideas inform passages read by a man (Jean-Pierre Léaud) dressed in Revolutionary costumes and standing in a field in *Weekend* (1967); and its follow-up, *Le Gai Savoir* (1968), is a very loose adaptation of *Émile, or On Education* (1762). The conspicuous presence of Rousseau in these films may be related to the 1967 publication of Jacques Derrida's *On Grammatology*, which includes a lengthy discussion of Rousseau's "Essay on the Origin of Languages" and is visible in one shot of *Le Gai Savoir*.

77. Jean-Jacques Rousseau, "Essay on the Origin of Languages," in Moran and Gode, *Origin of Language*, 41, 51.

78. Actors Michael Lonsdale and Hermine Karagheuz were actively involved in the theater world in these years, and, beginning in 1966, Rivette could have seen work by Brook and Grotowski at the annual Théâtre des Nations festival in Paris. Rivette acknowledged that Brook was among "the most obvious" theatrical points of reference decades later ("An Interview with Jacques Rivette," in Mary Wiles, *Jacques Rivette* [Urbana: University of Illinois Press, 2012], 140).

79. The comments about Brook and Grotowski are from Christopher Innes, *Avant-Garde Theatre, 1892–1992* (New York: Routledge, 1993), 127. Rivette's observations are in Eisenschitz, Fieschi, and de Gregorio, "Interview on *Out*," 53.

80. Innes, *Avant-Garde Theatre*, 127.

81. Innes describes *Orghast* in the following way:

"Orghast" itself was the name [Ted] Hughes invented for the fire of being—in metaphoric terms the sun (from ORG for "life/being," and GHAST for "spirit/flame")—and the material for the play was a myth of creation compiled from the legends of Prometheus, Chronos devouring his children, and the sun-worshipping cults of Helios and Zoroaster. It included passages from Aeschylus' *Prometheus Bound* and *The Persians* [472 BCE], and Seneca's *Thyestes* [62 CE] and *Hercules Furens* [54 CE] in the original Greek and Latin as well as sections in Avesti; and in the same way that Hughes sought to return to the source of language, this collage of mythical material was an attempt to rediscover the universal root myth buried under a wide range of archetypes. (Ibid., 138)

82. Jerzy Grotowski, *Towards a Poor Theatre* (New York: Simon and Schuster, 1968), 257. Grotowski's conception of the actor's body as a hieroglyph recapitulates ideas developed by Antonin Artaud in his book *The Theater and Its Double* (1936).

83. In the sixth episode, for example, Thomas meets with Pierre to talk about the group, asking if it is really dormant and explaining, "We said we'd leave it for two years. We'd let it mature, we'd wait and see." In 2007, Rivette confirmed the political implications of these dates:

I shot two years after '68 and, without ever making reference to the events [of that year], the characters never stop referring to what happened two years prior. As for Jean-Pierre [Léaud]'s and Juliet [Berto]'s characters, they absolutely do not comprehend the world in which they are evolving. But around them, the secret society of the Thirteen ([Michael] Lonsdale, [Bulle] Ogier, Bernadette Lafont) never stops commenting upon what's happened. For me, it's clear, the film speaks of '68, or rather the immediate post-'68. (Lalanne and Morain, "Entretien Jacques Rivette," 34)

84. Here, for example, is Balzac's way of introducing the group:

In Paris under the Empire thirteen men came together. They were all struck with the same idea and all endowed with sufficient energy to remain faithful to a single purpose. They were all honest enough to be loyal to one another even when their interests were opposed, and sufficiently versed in guile to conceal the inviolable bonds which united them. They were strong enough to put themselves above all law, bold enough to flinch at no undertaking; lucky enough to have almost always succeeded in their designs, having run the greatest hazards, but remaining silent about their defeats. (Honoré de Balzac, *History of the Thirteen*, translated by Herbert J. Hunt [London: Penguin Classics, 1974], 21)

85. Ibid.

86. Jacques Rivette, "Mizoguchi Viewed from Here," in Hillier, *Cahiers du cinéma*, 265.

87. Marie is visible standing behind the window of the café where Colin receives the note that initiates the central "plot" of *Out 1*. This image appears inconspicuous on a first viewing but, seen in light of the final shot, it suggests that the "minor character" Marie may have been the agent behind the notes, whose true function remains mysterious.

88. "'To be continued' is a formula that I would like to put at the end of all films," Rivette claimed in Jacques Rivette and Marguerite Duras, "Le Nouveau Film de Jacques Rivette: sur le pont du nord un bal y est donné—dialogue avec Marguerite Duras," *Le Monde*, March 25, 1982, 15. Toward the end of the film, the viewer is made aware of the existence of another group, appropriately called "The Devourers" (another organization mentioned in Balzac's *History of the Thirteen*).

89. *Cahiers du cinéma* 159 (October 1964).

90. John Hughes, "The Director as Psychoanalyst: An Interview with Jacques Rivette," *Rear Window* 1 (Spring 1975), reprinted as part of "John Hughes On (and With) Jacques Rivette," edited by Jonathan Rosenbaum, *Rouge* 4 (2004), available online at http://www.rouge.com.au/4/hughes.html.

91. Rosenbaum, Sedofsky, and Adair, "Phantom Interviewers over Rivette," 22.

92. Even, "'Out 1' Voyage," 13.

93. Jean Durançon, "Le Guetteur du rêve," *Études cinématographiques* 63 (1998), 8.

94. Rivette claims to "start to see the film" during editing in Frédéric Bonnaud, "Jacques Rivette: La Séquence du spectateur," *Les Inrockuptibles*, March 25, 1998, translated by Kent Jones and reprinted as "The Captive Lover," *Senses of Cinema* 16 (September–October 2001), available online at http://archive.sensesofcinema.com/contents/01/16/rivette.html. The comments about Dziga Vertov are in Clarens and Cozarinsky, "Jacques Rivette," 196.

95. Clarens and Cozarinsky, "Jacques Rivette," 197. Denise de Casabianca was the editor for *Paris Belongs to Us*, *The Nun*, and Rivette's early short *Le Coup du berger* (1956).

96. Soviet filmmaker Lev Kuleshov conducted a series of experiments into the perception of sequential film images in the late 1910s and early 1920s. The most famous experiment involved the creation of a montage film in which a repeated shot of the actor Ivan Mosjoukine was juxtaposed with three different shots (a bowl of soup, a dead child, and a woman). Viewers are said to have interpreted Mosjoukine's face differently depending on which of the other shots was juxtaposed.

97. Chris Darke, "Films of Ruin and Rapture: In Search of Jean-Daniel Pollet," *Film Comment* 43, no. 3 (May–June 2007), 58.

98. Jean Narboni, Sylvie Pierre, and Jacques Rivette, "Montage," translated by Tom Milne in Rosenbaum, *Rivette: Texts and Interviews*, 82. Rivette would have known Pollet's film, which also influenced Godard's *Contempt* (1963), before this event, but the 1969 screening may have given him a fresh perspective on it.

99. Hughes, "The Director as Psychoanalyst."

100. In a 1935 discussion with *Cahiers d'art* editor Christian Zervos, Picasso famously stated, "In my case, a picture is a sum of destructions" (Alfred H. Barr Jr., *Picasso: Fifty Years of His Art* [New York: Museum of Modern Art, 1946], 272).

101. Denis, *Jacques Rivette, le veilleur* (1990).

102. Frappat and Rivette, *Trois films fantômes*, 19.

103. Rivette told interviewers from *Film Comment* that the main motivation for *Céline and Julie Go Boating* was "simply the desire to make a film. To get out of the dumps that we all felt we were in, make a film for as little money as possible, and, we hoped, amuse people. Because the adventure of *Out* didn't turn out very well, from the point of view of public reception—there was no reception. It was almost impossible to show the film" (Rosenbaum, Sedofsky, and Adair, "Phantom Interviewers over Rivette," 20).

104. Ibid., 22.

105. Rivette retrospectively identified the "scandalous" support for the group of four films by the Centre national de la cinématographie in early 1975 as a "grand finale" for a "five- to six-year period" in which the "advance on receipts" system was "very open" (Serge Daney and Jean Narboni, "Entretien avec Jacques Rivette," *Cahiers du cinéma* 323–324 [May 1981], 44–45).

106. The phrase "house of fiction" comes from the 1908 preface to Henry James' novel *The Portrait of a Lady* (1881). James was an influence on a number of Rivette films, especially *Céline and Julie Go Boating*, which literalizes the metaphor in the image of the mansion that the characters must pass through in order to experience their imaginative projections.

107. *Noroît* was withheld from release after *Duelle* failed at the box office, although it was screened sporadically at specialized festivals and events.

108. Jacques Rivette, "For the Shooting of *Les Filles du Feu*," translated by Tom Milne in Rosenbaum, *Rivette: Texts and Interviews*, 89.

109. Ibid.

110. "Igor Stravinsky on Film Music," *Musical Digest*, September 1946, reprinted in *The Hollywood Film Music Reader*, edited by Mervyn Cooke (Oxford: Oxford University Press, 2010), 278. The quotation in the title of this section comes from Igor Stravinsky and was used as the epigraph to *Cahiers du cinéma* 152 (February 1964).

111. A file of newspaper clippings on these scandals is included, along with a coded map of Paris, in a black valise that the two women steal from Marie's lover Julien, and this map leads them wandering around the city in an attempt to decipher its hidden meanings.

112. Rainer Maria Rilke, *Letters to a Young Poet*, translated by M. D. Herter Norton, rev. ed. (New York: W.W. Norton, 1993), 69.

113. Dore Ashton, *A Fable of Modern Art* (New York: W.W. Norton, 1980).

114. *Le Chef-d'oeuvre inconnu: Eaux-fortes originales et dessins gravés sur bois de Pablo Picasso* (Paris: Ambroise Vollard, 1931).

115. Balzac may also have been thinking of Victor Hugo, the central figure in debates over French literary Romanticism at the time he wrote the first version of *The Unknown Masterpiece* in 1831. The year before, he had written a review of Hugo's *Hernani* in which he declared Hugo's name "a standard, his work the expression of a doctrine, and he himself a sovereign" (Honoré de Balzac, "Victor Hugo: *Hernani*," in *The Works of Honoré de Balzac*, vol. 20, translated by Katherine Prescott Wormeley [New York: Athenaeum Club, 1899], 141).

116. Honoré de Balzac, *The Unknown Masterpiece*, translated by Richard Howard (New York: New York Review of Books Classics, 2000), 35–36.

117. Sigmund Freud uses very similar terms to describe Prometheus and his phallic torch in the 1932 essay "The Acquisition of Fire," *Psychoanalytic Quarterly* 1, no. 1 (1932), 210–215.

118. Jacques Rivette, "De l'abjection," *Cahiers du cinéma* 120 (June 1961), 54. In *La Belle Noiseuse*, Frenhofer describes the way erotic desire is transformed into art when he tells Marianne about his work with his wife Liz:

> At first, I wanted her, before wanting to paint her. For the first time, I was scared. The fear became the driving force behind what I did . . . I became blind. A tactile painting. As if it were . . . as if it were my fingers that saw and commanded themselves. That's what I'm looking for. That's what I want. . . . It was then, maybe, that I became a real painter.

119. Quoted in Michel Estève, "*La Belle Noiseuse* ou la recherche de l'absolu," *Études cinématographiques* 63 (1998), 125.

120. Denis, *Jacques Rivette, le veilleur*.

121. Between 1932 and 1935, Balthus made nearly fifty studies based on Emily Brontë's *Wuthering Heights* (1847), and he eventually selected fourteen of them for lithographic reproduction in book form, although the project fell through and the drawings were not shown together until the major retrospective exhibition at the Centre Georges Pompidou in 1983. It is likely that Rivette's interest in Balthus was heightened by this exhibition, which was the most extensive Balthus show held anywhere up to that point and took place two years before *Wuthering Heights* was released.

Eight of the images were first exhibited in 1935 in the important Surrealist journal *Minotaure* (no. 7). Several years earlier, Luis Buñuel, another person associated with the Surrealists in this period, had written a screenplay based on *Wuthering Heights* with Pierre Unik. As he explained in his autobiography: "In 1930, Pierre Unik and I had written a screenplay based on *Wuthering Heights*. Like all the Surrealists, I was deeply moved by this novel, and I had always wanted to try the movie. The opportunity finally came, in Mexico in 1953" (Luis Buñuel, *My Last Sigh*, translated by Abigail Israel [New York: Knopf, 1983], 205–206). The fact that Brontë's book was finally translated into French in 1929 undoubtedly contributed to the sudden interest of the Surrealists in the early 1930s (*Les Hauts de hurle-vent*, translated by Frédéric Delebecque [Paris: Éditions Payot, 1929]).

122. On the influence of German Romanticism, Jean Clair observes, "Romanticism for instance, the attraction for Novalis and Jean Paul—which for [André] Breton and his disciples, who had scant knowledge of Goethe's language, was a mere dandy's affectation— was for Balthus the natural milieu in which he had been immersed since his very first words" (Jean Clair, "From the *Rue* to the *Chambre*: A Mythology of the *Passage*," in

Balthus, edited by Jean Clair [New York: Rizzoli, 2001], 19). Clair traces these influences in "Balthus and Rilke: A Childhood" (*Balthus*, 35–42).

123. Tony Pipolo, *Robert Bresson: A Passion for Film* (Oxford: Oxford University Press, 2010), 7–8.

124. Rivette describes this sequence in his interview with John Hughes:

There is a sequence where we see Colin near madness, banging his head against the wall. Then he recovers mysteriously and visits his old friend, Warok (Jean Bouise). He says that he has understood and transcended the story of the thirteen, that it doesn't bother him anymore. He says that he intends to lead a happy life in the future, but after he leaves Warok we see him dancing madly about in the streets with his harmonica. Then we see him begging, posing as a deaf mute as in the beginning of the film. (Hughes, "Director as Psychoanalyst")

Jonathan Rosenbaum, who was in attendance, confirms that the scene was still present when the film was projected at the 1989 Rotterdam Film Festival:

Based on my notes taken at the Rotterdam screening, the sequence, punctuated by a few patches of black leader, shows [Léaud] crying, screaming, howling like an animal, banging his head against the wall, busting a closet door, writhing on the floor, then calming down and picking up his harmonica. After throwing away all three of the secret messages he has been trying for most of the serial to decode, he starts playing his harmonica ecstatically, throws his clothes and other belongings out into the hall, dances about manically, and then plays the harmonica some more. (Rosenbaum, "*Tih-Minh, Out 1*," 65)

The scene is not in any available print or video of the film.

125. Frappat, *Jacques Rivette, secret compris*, 178.

126. In an interview commissioned for the Artificial Eye DVD release of *La Belle Noiseuse*, Rivette says, "Since I was fourteen, I have been a huge fan of Igor Stravinsky. When I heard *The Rite of Spring* on the radio for the first time in my life during the Occupation … it was a shock, and I never recovered from it." The title of the shorter cut of Rivette's film, *Divertimento*, is also the name of a reduced 1934 concert version of Stravinsky's ballet *Le Baiser de la fée* (1928).

127. Luke 22:44.

Chapter 4

1. Ezra Pound, *The Cantos of Ezra Pound* (New York: New Directions, 1996), 807.

2. Hermann Broch, *The Death of Virgil*, translated by Jean Starr Untermeyer (New York: Vintage Books, 1995), 282. Godard quotes extensively from this novel, a fictional meditation on Virgil's desire to destroy his own work begun while Broch was in a concentration camp, in *Keep Your Right Up* (1987) and *Histoire(s) du cinema* (1988–1998).

3. A character says this at the very beginning of *Détective* (1985), and it later became the focus of *Une catastrophe* (2008), a one-minute film made as the official "trailer" for the Vienna Film Festival.

4. Pound, *Cantos*, 4.

5. Near the end of Canto I, Pound refers quasi-bibliographically to Andreas Divus' translation of 1538:

> Lie quiet Divus. I mean, that is Andreas Divus,
> In officinal Wecheli, 1538, out of Homer. (Ibid., 5)

Godard has suggested that cinema is subject to this same process of historical layering:

> It is necessary to have the sense of the history of cinema, a little like [James] Joyce, who had a profound sense of the history of literature, and who knew that, when he wrote a phrase, some of the words had been invented in the time of the Latins, some in the Middle Ages. At the moment when Joyce wrote that word, with all its baggage and all the history that it contains, it was the modern age of literature, its adult age, so to speak. (Gérard Lefort, "Godard et Oliveira sortent ensemble," in *Jean-Luc Godard par Jean-Luc Godard*, edited by Alain Bergala, vol. 2, *1984–1998* [Paris: Cahiers du cinéma, 1985], 267; hereafter "*Godard par Godard*, 2")

Just as it is possible to read Joyce (or Pound) without recognizing the etymological roots of the words used or the meaning of the embedded references, it is possible to watch *Histoire(s) du cinéma* without identifying the sources of the onscreen material or the art historical traditions that inform them, but these layers are nevertheless the fabric with which the works are woven together.

6. Godard does not simply transpose a few words here. Cuny's speech is constructed from a long extract of the fourth volume of Faure's *Histoire de l'art* (*L'Art moderne* [Paris: Les Éditions G. Crès et Cie, 1921], 70–79), with several sections elided and a number of words replaced. In restructuring these excerpts, Godard shifts the discussion of motifs from ones prominent in Rembrandt's work ("open books," "lanterns," "sheets") to ones prominent within his films ("open windows," "car lights," "screens"), while also making Faure's prose harmonize with the aesthetic paradigms—"the continual and indifferent interchange between everything that is born and everything that dies"—that, originating in Romanticism, underlie *Histoire(s) du cinéma*. Ferdinand reads a passage from the same Faure book at the beginning of *Pierrot le fou* (1965), and the four historical categories adopted by Faure ("Classical," "Medieval," "Renaissance," and "Modern") are used to structure the postcard sequence in *Les Carabiniers* (1963).

7. MacCabe argues that "there is good reason to compare [*Histoire(s) du cinéma*] to James Joyce's *Finnegans Wake. Finnegans Wake* takes the whole of history and language for its subject and uses montage as its basic creative principle, but a montage which operates within the individual word" (Colin MacCabe, *Godard: A Portrait of the Artist at Seventy* [New York: Farrar, Straus and Giroux, 2003], 315). Jonathan Rosenbaum makes his arguments in "Trailer for Godard's *Histoire(s) du cinéma*," reprinted in *Goodbye Cinema, Hello Cinephilia: Film Culture in Transition* (Chicago: University of Chicago Press, 2010), 305–319.

Godard's comments in one of his Montreal lectures make it clear that although the Belmondo character in *Pierrot le fou* refers to Joyce, he is parroting Élie Faure:

> I came upon a book I was familiar with, by Élie Faure, which talked about Velázquez and said that at the end of his career—which I did at the beginning

of mine, although I didn't know it—at the end of his career Velázquez painted the things that lie between things. And gradually I realised that cinema is what lies between things. It isn't a thing, it's what is between one person and another. (Jean-Luc Godard, *Introduction to a True History of Cinema and Television* [Montreal: caboose, 2014], 182)

8. Pound became increasingly convinced that "*usura*" (greed) was the principle underlying democratic government throughout the 1920s and 1930s; it was the focus of an entire Canto (Canto LXV) and the basis for the speeches he gave on the radio in fascist Italy between January 1935 and April 1945. These speeches would eventually result in his imprisonment, initially in an open-air cage, during which time he began working on the "Pisan Cantos" (first published in 1948). A copy of *Le Travail et l'usure*, a French translation of some of Pound's speeches that was first published in 1968, is shown on a table in Godard's *Adieu au langage* (2014).

In the final Pisan Canto, Pound remembers artistic compatriots who have passed away (like Béla Bartok, referred to in Pound, *Cantos*, Canto LXXXIV, 558), a strategy he continues in subsequent cantos, where he mentions friends like W. B. Yeats and "Old Wyndham [Lewis]" (Canto XCVIII, 705) or adopts a memorial tone:

> Yseult [Gonne MacBride] is dead, and Walter [Morse Rummel],
> and Fordie [Ford Maddox Ford],
> familiares (Canto CIV, 761–762)

Godard employs similar language at the end of *Une vague nouvelle* (3B): a girl asks him, "[Jacques] Becker, [Roberto] Rossellini, [Jean-Pierre] Melville, [Georges] Franju, Jacques Demy, [François] Truffaut, you knew them?" and he closes the section by responding, "Yes, they were my friends." As with Pound's Vortex group (which splintered shortly after World War I), Godard and his New Wave companions were close for only a few short years in the late 1950s and early 1960s. These and other (related) "friends" are referred to throughout *Histoire(s) du cinéma* through clips of their films, footage of them at work, or, most frequently, photographs.

9. Pound introduced the term in his 1914 essay "Vortex" and later elaborated his ideas in language that resonates strongly with Godard's practice in *Histoire(s) du cinéma*: "The image is not an idea. It is a radiant node or cluster; it is what I can, and must perforce, call a VORTEX, from which, and through which, and into which, ideas are constantly rushing" (Ezra Pound, *Gaudier-Brzeska: A Memoir* [New York: New Directions, 1970], 92).

10. In his 1934 essay "Date Line," Pound wrote, "An epic is a poem including history" (Ezra Pound, *Literary Essays of Ezra Pound* [New York: New Directions, 1968], 86). On the comparison of the *Commedia* to a cathedral, see Hugh Kenner, *The Pound Era* (Berkeley: University of California Press, 1971), 355. As symbolic structures, temples are alluded to throughout the *Cantos*; like epic poems, they are "holy" because they are "not for sale" (Pound, *Cantos*, Canto XCVII, 696).

11. Reflecting Pound's Vicoian sense of historical cyclicity, the lost city toward which the Odyssean protagonist of his narrative journeys varies over the course of the *Cantos*, moving from Ithaca (Canto I) to Venice (first mentioned in Canto III), Troy ("but a heap of smouldering boundary stones," Canto IV, 13), and even Wagadu (Canto LXXXIX), before finally becoming the Byzantium of Yeats (Canto XCVI).

In *Les Signes parmi nous* (4B), Godard defines *Histoire(s) du cinéma* through two phrases presented back to back as text: *"odyssée de l'utopie"* ("odyssey of utopia") and *"vertige de l'histoire"* ("vertigo of history"). As in the *Cantos*, utopia is accessible only beyond the veils of time and myth, and the interdependence of the two phrases, whose recurrence reconnects the early and late phases of the work, is paradigmatic.

12. Hugh Kenner argues that Pound "had always wanted . . . to write a long poem" and traces its origin to a conversation with Professor Ibbotson "circa 1904–5" (Kenner, *The Pound Era*, 354). Kenner also claimed that while "Joyce saw *Ulysses* [1922] as a whole and worked at opening and closing episodes simultaneously; Pound hoped to become, while writing the poem in public, the poet capable of ending the *Cantos*" (377). The final cantos were first published in 1969.

13. Godard identifies *Les Enfants jouent à la Russie* and *2 fois 50 ans de cinéma français* (1995) as "annexes" in Frédéric Bonnaud and Arnaud Viviant, "La Légende du siècle," *Les Inrockuptibles* 170 (October 1998), 26. The footage, paintings, and musical extracts used in *Histoire(s) du cinéma* are often given new contexts in these "annexes."

14. In the forty-nine-page proposal completed in January 1973 for the unmade film *Moi, je*, Godard asks, "Who will write one day a true history of cinema and of television?" (Jean-Luc Godard, *"Moi, je*, projet de film," in Nicole Brenez et al., *Jean-Luc Godard, Documents* [Paris: Éditions du Centre Pompidou, 2006], 238).

15. Antoine de Baecque, *Godard, biographie* (Paris: Bernard Grasset, 2010), 678–679. For a firsthand account of Langlois' endeavors, see Richard Roud, *A Passion for Films: Henri Langlois and the Cinémathèque Française* (Baltimore: Johns Hopkins University Press, 1999), 192–198.

16. In a 1983 interview, Godard referred to Langlois' film work, observing, "Cameras have always been commissioned by filmmakers, including Lumière, who was a painter, as you can see from Langlois' documentary" (Jean-Pierre Beauviala and Jean-Luc Godard, "Genesis of a Camera (First Episode)," in *Jean-Luc Godard Interviews*, edited by David Sterritt [Jackson, MI: University Press of Mississippi, 1998], 145). He refers to the project named after Malraux's *La Métamorphose des dieux* (a three-volume study of the relationship between the human and the sacred published between 1957 and 1976) in Michel Ciment and Stéphane Goudet, "Entretien Jean-Luc Godard: Des traces du cinéma," *Positif* 456 (February 1999), 50.

17. Friedrich Schlegel, *Philosophical Fragments*, translated by Peter Firchow (Minneapolis: University of Minnesota Press, 1991), 50–51. The words in the title of this section—a reworking of René Descartes' *cogito ergo sum* ("I think therefore I am") that puns on both the format used for *Histoire(s) du cinéma* ("video") and its Latin meaning ("I see," making the revised phrase, "I think therefore I see")—are used at the very beginning of *Une histoire seule* (1B). The title of the 1637 book from which this phrase originates, *Le Discours de la méthode*, is read out by Godard later in *Une histoire seule* (1B).

18. Roud, *A Passion for Films*, 199. In a 1998 interview, Godard claimed that "around 1975–1976," he proposed the idea to Langlois (Bonnaud and Viviant, "La Légende du siècle," 26). Comments in 1978 also make it clear that, as both a set of videos and a film, this was already envisioned as a project that would run for at least four hours (Godard, *True History*, 216). In fact, the idea of length was built into the genesis of his "history of cinema" project, which would explore

how [films came to last] for an hour and a half, an hour and a half to two hours, which is a completely idiotic length. And I think that the history of cinema should be able to recount how, suddenly, because films started out at two or three minutes, how little by little they arrived at a certain standard length. . . . This business of length is interesting. Soccer games too for example, a soccer game lasts around an hour and a half to two hours, about the same time as a film. . . . I'd like the games to go on for eight or nine hours. (*True History*, 225)

19. This is how Godard describes the origin of the talks in his preface to the published version (Jean-Luc Godard, *Introduction à une véritable histoire du cinéma* [Paris: Éditions Albatros, 1980], 15). A more detailed description is provided by Timothy Barnard in his English-language translation (which makes a number of adjustments based on a new transcription of the original recordings): "A Note on the Text," in Godard, *True History*, lxxi–lxxxviii. Hereafter, all references are to the Barnard translation.

20. The plan was to have ten "Voyages," but Godard only completed seven. In the fourth "Voyage," Godard explained that when he agreed to take on the lectures, it "wasn't a question of taking over from Henri Langlois, it was a question of continuing in another way a job he had begun," by treating the lectures "as a film production" (Godard, *True History*, 209–210). The relationship to the *Histoire(s) du cinéma* is acknowledged in a page, just before the table of contents, in all four volumes of the book version of *Histoire(s) du cinéma* (Paris: Gallimard, 1998), that reads "*introduction/à/une/véritable/histoire/du/cinéma/la/seule/la/vraie.*"

21. Claire Devarrieux, "Se vivre, se voir," in *Godard par Godard: Des années Mao aux années 80*, edited by Alain Bergala (Paris: Flammarion, 1991), 161. A transcript of the FIAF meeting is included in Brenez et al., *Jean-Luc Godard, Documents*, 286–291.

22. Michael Witt, *Jean-Luc Godard, Cinema Historian* (Bloomington: Indiana University Press, 2013), 29–31.

23. Todd McCarthy, "Jean-Luc Godard Segues into Yank Filmmaking via Zoetrope," *Variety*, January 12, 1981, 36.

24. De Baecque, *Godard, biographie*, 677. Canal Plus was launched in November 1984.

25. INA was a new organization intended for research and development after the state-controlled (and strongly Gaullist) ORTF was broken up during the rule of President Valéry Giscard d'Estaing. Colin MacCabe, who helped produce some of Godard's later television work through the British Film Institute, discusses the arrangements that made it possible for Godard and his company Sonimage to create these programs (*Godard*, 253–260).

26. Significantly, Rolle is located in the same canton (Vaud) of Switzerland as Nyon, the town where Godard—whose parents frequently moved back and forth between Switzerland and France—was raised. In this sense, the 1977 move represented a sort of homecoming, a return to Godard's roots, which could certainly be related to the retrospective turn that culminated in *Histoire(s) du cinéma* and manifests itself in the autobiographical tenor of many of Godard's later films (especially *Nouvelle vague* and *JLG/JLG—Self-Portrait in December*).

27. Alain Bergala, Serge Daney, and Serge Toubiana, "Le Chemin vers la parole," in *Jean-Luc Godard par Jean-Luc Godard*, edited by Alain Bergala, vol. 1, *1950–1984*, 2nd ed. (Paris: Cahiers du cinéma, 1998), 504; hereafter "*Godard par Godard*, 1."

28. Godard's description of *Détective* is in a letter to Alain Cuny included in Bergala, *Godard par Godard*, 2:71. In an interview with Régis Debray during the making of

Histoire(s) du cinéma, Godard expressed this even more strongly: "As a filmmaker, television is, for me, the occupier that cinema does not want to upset, except under American influence" (Régis Debray, "Jean-Luc Godard rencontre Régis Debray," in Bergala, *Godard par Godard*, 2:426).

29. In 1990, Godard put this succinctly: "Television diffuses, it does not produce" (Léon Mercadet and Christian Perrot, "Le Télévision fabrique de l'oubli," in Bergala, *Godard par Godard*, 2:239). On another occasion, he observed:

> It is only at the movies that everybody sees more or less the same thing. They darkened the theaters and widened the screen for that, so that everybody is on an equal footing. That was projection's strength, which is precisely what television killed. Projection has disappeared on television, hence the "project" has disappeared. Now there is only broadcasting, diffusion, that is, something diffuse. (Jean-Luc Godard, *The Future(s) of Film: Three Interviews 2000/01* [Bern: Verlag Gachnang & Springer AG, 2002], 73–74)

30. In a text entitled "Each Art Has a Verb" produced to accompany the first two sections of *Histoire(s) du cinéma*, Godard writes:

> To film, that is, to record a sight and project it, is the act of cinema of the makers of films. It's always freedom speaking. Only television has no creative act or verb to authenticate it. That's because the act of television both falls short of communication and goes beyond it. It doesn't create any goods, in fact, what is worse, it distributes them without their ever having been created. To program is the only verb of television. That implies suffering rather than release. (Raymond Bellour with Mary Lea Bandy, eds., *Jean-Luc Godard: Son + Image, 1974–1991* [New York: Museum of Modern Art, 1992], 158)

Godard has elsewhere argued that while arts like cinema are "the domain of creation," television is wholly an instrument of "culture . . . the domain of diffusion and distribution," a distinction he makes in several interviews (see, for example, Frédéric Bonnaud and Serge Kaganski, "Le Cinéma est toujours une opération de deuil et de reconquête de la vie," in Bergala, *Godard par Godard*, 2:390; Alain Bergala and Serge Toubiana, "L'Art de (dé)montrer," in Bergala, *Godard par Godard*, 2:138; Serge Daney, "Godard Makes [Hi] stories," translated by Georgia Gurrieri in Bellour and Bandy, *Jean-Luc Godard*, 161; or Olivier Péretié, "Quand Godard raconte deux ou trois choses qu'il sait de tout, ABCD . . . JLG," *Le Nouvel Observateur*, December 18–24, 1987, 51).

31. Marie Rambert, "Parti de Chase . . ." in Bergala, *Godard par Godard*, 2:95. On "Apparatus Theory," see, for example, Jean-Louis Baudry, "The Apparatus: Metapsychological Approaches to the Impression of Reality in Cinema," in *Film Theory and Criticism*, edited by Leo Braudy and Marshall Cohen, 7th ed. (Oxford: Oxford University Press, 2009), 171–188.

32. Claire Devarrieux, "Entretien Godard/Pialat," in Bergala, *Godard par Godard*, 2:91.

33. Clearly, for Godard, this metaphor of the cave and the imaginary does not have the same connotations that it has for Plato. In 2000, for example, Godard said:

> The New Wave was a relationship with the imaginary, taking that word as it is commonly understood. We were closer to cavemen, to the myth of the cave in any case. The relationship with reality came later, at the same time as the idea that the real imaginary requires you to proceed via reality, to put it naively: shoot out in the

street, film your girlfriend, or your girlfriend's story, etc. (Godard, *The Future(s) of Film*, 15)

He also explains that with technologies, like video, that lack the tactile positive/negative structure of the photographic image, "the phenomenon of the cave is no more" (23). The crucial factor, however, lies in what Godard sees as a triangulating structure of projection that involves the viewer in a way that digital technologies "invented [not] for production, but for distribution" do not (23). As Godard explained to Gavin Smith, "I like not to have the light in the back, because the light in the back belongs to the projector, the camera must have the light in front like we have ourselves in life. We receive and [then] we project" (Gavin Smith, "Jean-Luc Godard," in Sterritt, *Jean-Luc Godard Interviews*, 193). Godard's appropriation of Plato's philosophical ideas for his own poetic purposes is similar to Markopoulos' treatment of Heidegger.

34. As Godard explained in 2000, "I am always sensitive to, not the form, but rather the pictorial value of a certain type of projected image, which is not painting, can be in VHS or 35mm and belongs to large-screen projection alone, although it does indeed spring from painting" (Godard, *The Future(s) of Film*, 14). Godard has repeatedly called video "an adjacent wing of cinema," "a child, a natural daughter of cinema," a material perfect for "making 'studies'" (Jean-Luc Godard and Youssef Ishaghpour, *Cinema: The Archaeology of Film and the Memory of a Century*, translated by John Howe [New York: Berg, 2005], 36). Nevertheless, he also recognizes its limitations: "No one has worked as hard as I have to bring video into the pictorial tradition, and I haven't really succeeded" (Godard, *The Future(s) of Film*, 24).

35. In *Keep Your Right Up*, made while the first two sections of *Histoire(s) du cinéma* were being developed, Godard is shown collapsing under the weight of film reels, crying out, "They're not videos! It's a real movie. You'll see—the toughest thing in movies is carrying the cans."

36. Godard, *True History*, 10.

37. Godard sometimes requested that people interviewing him bring copies of particular tapes he wanted to use with them (see, for example, Godard's insistence that an interviewer bring a tape of Stanley Kubrick's *The Shining*, 1980, in Godard, *The Future(s) of Film*, 11–12). He has also frequently expressed his discomfort with watching videos, telling Andrew Sarris in 1994 that while he has "a large number of [video] cassettes," they are used "mainly for reference purposes … about every two or three years I like to see an old John Ford movie, and even on video you get some idea of what it was, but if you look too closely you begin to miss the real thing" (Andrew Sarris, "Jean-Luc Godard Now," *Interview* 24 [July 1994], 5). In 2002, Godard observed that his dependence on video has encouraged him to privilege the accumulation historical documents over fictional features, explaining, "They are the same thing. I do not make the distinction … an extract of the Nuremberg trials and a shot of Hitchcock both tell us what we have been. Both are cinema" (Antoine de Baecque, "Entretien avec Jean-Luc Godard: Le Cinéma a été l'art des âmes qui ont vécu intimement dans l'Histoire," *Libération*, April 6–7, 2002, 45).

38. Ciment and Goudet, "Entretien Jean-Luc Godard," 52. Godard also argued that what "video permits, as in music, is the fluidity of superimpositions" (52).

39. As Godard explained to Youssef Ishaghpour:

Technically it was textbook stuff, very simple things. Of the forty possibilities in the list I used one or two, mostly overprinting to help retain the original cinema image, while if I'd tried to do the same thing with film I'd have had to use reverse negative copies and that causes a loss of quality, above all you can alter the image easily with video, while with film all variation has to be preplanned. Incidentally, there was no huge console, no team with twenty-five video screens, I didn't even have a video librarian: it was an act of painting. The overprints, all that comes from cinema, they were tricks Méliès used . . . (Godard and Ishaghpour, *Cinema*, 32–33)

As he observed in another interview, "All of that was done very simply, with very old equipment. I have a studio that is not very sophisticated, neither George Lucas nor Le Fresnoy, maybe Méliès" (Godard, *The Future(s) of Film*, 26).

40. "The Joy of Celluloid," *Guardian*, October 10, 2011, available online at http://www.theguardian.com/artanddesign/2011/oct/10/steven-spielberg-martin-scorsese-celluloid. Another version of this quotation is used in *Notre musique*, where it is attributed to French philosopher Claude Lefort.

41. Godard and Ishaghpour, *Cinema*, 32. Later in the interview, Godard elaborates:

Somewhere between the video game and the CD-ROM there could be another way of making films, which would be a lot closer to [Jorge Luis] Borges and people like him. But it'll never be done, we needn't worry . . . Perhaps one day there will be someone, a Chris [Marker] or a [Johan] Van der Keuken, who will make that sort of film. . . . I find though that Van der Keuken for example doesn't dominate the stuff at all, it's either very cinema or too video-arcade and you lose the thread, it needs a comprehensive key. In my case, with *Histoire(s)*, no key is needed. (39)

In 1985, Godard declared, "Today, the cinema is still being made, but the cinema will disappear when it is no longer projected. It will become something else" (Alain Bergala, "L'Art à partir de la vie: entretien avec Jean-Luc Godard," in Bergala, *Godard par Godard*, 1:16). He maintained this distinction when speaking more specifically about *Histoire(s) du cinéma*, arguing that while the image may look "better on TV, if your TV set is properly adjusted and [you have] fairly good stereo equipment," you do not have the feeling of projection, which is "peculiar to cinema" (Smith, "Jean-Luc Godard," 192).

42. At the press conference held at the 1997 Cannes Film Festival, Godard explained that although "it was a small video at the beginning . . . it was transferred to 35mm with digital techniques, which are more precise. Therefore, one could say that I also make special effects" (Paul Amar, "Godard/Amar: Cannes 97," in Bergala, *Godard par Godard*, 2:414).

43. Although they are, by design, more episodic, both of the multipart television series Godard completed in the 1970s employ techniques that anticipate *Histoire(s) du cinéma*, such as the use of slow overlapping dissolves and superimposition to create a montage between still images in *France/tour/détour/deux/enfants*. The final section of "Movement 2," for instance, demonstrates this process for the viewer by first showing an image being developed and then juxtaposing black-and-white and color images from different periods (often with words like "*histoire*" or "*lumière*" overlaid), generating a historical montage by interrelating images of Nazi rallies, concentration camps, and suffering in Vietnam

with images of athletes, political leaders, and film stars. *Six fois deux (Sur et sous la communication)* has fewer technical links to *Histoire(s) du cinéma*, but, like the later work, it is arranged into dialectically paired sections labeled 1A, 1B, 2A, 2B, etc.

44. Individual sections of *Histoire(s) du cinéma* were shown at special events, festivals, and retrospectives in France, Germany, England, Canada, and the United States during the period the project was being developed. The work was shown as a complete unit at the Ciné Lumière (Institut français) in London on September 27, 1997, and it was subsequently shown that way in Paris (in 1998) and at the Museum of Modern Art (in 2004). Godard does not appear to have given any guidelines on where to place intermissions.

45. Quoted in David Sterritt, *The Films of Jean-Luc Godard: Seeing the Invisible* (Cambridge: Cambridge University Press, 1999), 20.

46. In a 1998 interview, for example, Godard observed, "I tried several times to put the eight programs on course. They already had the same titles without my knowing what I would put in each one, but the titles remained, which helped with classification: eight folders [for sorting images, clips, and sounds] for eight programs" (Bonnaud and Viviant, "La Légende du siècle," 26). Similar comments were made to Alain Bergala in 1997 and to Youssef Ishaghpour in 2000:

> I had a plan that I never changed, which is the name of the eight programs. I knew that the first episode, *Toutes les histoires*, would show that the cinema was immediately seized by all. (Bergala, "Une boucle bouclée: Nouvel entretien avec Jean-Luc Godard par Alain Bergala," in Bergala, *Godard par Godard*, 2:16)
>
> [*Histoire(s) du cinéma* is] eight films combined in one, both together. It came like that.... It's a big book with eight chapters, and that layout didn't budge in ten years. (Godard and Ishaghpour, *Cinema*, 5)

Godard has also suggested that at one stage he conceived a work much longer than the one he eventually made: "The most interesting [aspect] is the notes. [To fully develop these ideas] would require a film lasting one hundred hours. This is what I naively thought of making at the time" (Bergala, "Une boucle bouclée," 15).

The title of the project also changed several times while it was in production. In a lecture to the students of La Fémis on April 26, 1989, for example, Godard referred to "the history of cinema that I am preparing, *Quelques histoires à propos du cinéma*" (Jean-Luc Godard, "Le Montage, la solitude et la liberté," in Bergala, *Godard par Godard*, 2:242).

47. René Bonnell told Richard Brody, "We had great press [for the initial broadcast of *Toutes les histoires*, 1A and *Une histoire seule*, 1B], but nobody watched. It was practically a grant—the films hardly had an audience, they had an audience too small to be measured—but we had extraordinary press, and Canal Plus doesn't live on viewership alone, but also on its image" (Richard Brody, *Everything Is Cinema: The Working Life of Jean-Luc Godard* [New York: Metropolitan Books, 2008], 517). In return for their cosponsorship, *Toutes les histoires* (1A) and *Une histoire seule* (1B) were broadcast on FR3 a year after their Canal Plus premieres (on May 7 and 14, 1989, according to Jacques Siclier, "Les 'Histoires' de Jean-Luc Godard: Si fort est son amour," *Le Monde*, May 6, 1989, 16).

48. In 2000, Godard described his new agreement with Gaumont as marking a major shift in his approach:

When *Histoire(s) du cinéma* was first taken up by Gaumont, it had been on hold for three or four years. I hadn't completed my plan, I had only made the first two chapters although there were eight in preparation. At the time Canal+ and a lot of other institutions didn't want to make them. Then Gaumont took the project on, and all of a sudden I found myself wondering how I was going to go about it, where to restart the thing. (Godard and Ishaghpour, *Cinema*, 8–9)

49. A press document released by JLG Films and the catalog accompanying the 1992 exhibition at the Museum of Modern Art, *Jean-Luc Godard: Son + Image, 1974–1991*, list the titles and dedications of the ten-part version (with each part listed as a "chapter") as follows:

Chapitre 1A—*Toutes les histoires*—Mary Meerson
Chapitre 1B—*Une histoire seule*—John Cassavetes
Chapitre 2A—*Seul le cinéma*—Gideon Bachmann
Chapitre 2B—*Fatale beauté*—Nicole Ladmiral
Chapitre 3A—*La Monnaie de l'absolu*—André Malraux
Chapitre 3B—*La Réponse des ténèbres*—Michèle Fink
Chapitre 4A—*Une vague nouvelle*—Frédéric C. Froeschel and Armand Caulier
Chapitre 4B—*Montage, mon beau souci*—Jacques Rivette and Anne-Marie Miéville
Chapitre 5A—*Le Contrôle de l'univers*—Albert Einstein
Chapitre 5B—*Les Signes parmi nous*—Charles F. Ramuz (Bellour and Bandy, *Jean-Luc Godard*, 123)

In the completed, eight-part version, *La Réponse des ténèbres* and *Montage, mon beau souci* dropped out. However, the words do still appear in a sequential list of titles that appears onscreen in the final versions of *Seul le cinéma* (2A), *Fatale beauté* (2B), and *La Monnaie de l'absolu* (3A). In all three of these sections, the titles appear in a slightly different order from the above: *Seul le cinéma, Fatale beauté, La Monnaie de l'absolu, La Réponse des ténèbres, Montage, mon beau souci, Une vague nouvelle, Le Contrôle de l'univers, Les Signes parmi nous*, finally ending with the words *Histoire(s) du cinéma*. The order is scrambled further in the final versions of *Une vague nouvelle* (3B), *Le Contrôle de l'univers* (4A), and *Les Signes parmi nous* (4B), suggesting that Godard continued to restructure this template up until the final moment.

Godard described the intended plan for *La Réponse des ténèbres*, listed as 3B, in his interview with Daney:

I think that, until the camps, cinema was the identity of nations and peoples (who were more or less organized into nations) and that after the camps, it sort of disappeared. I deal with this in a program, program 3B, *La Réponse des ténèbres*, which talks about war films and says, more or less, that cinema is primarily a Western art form, made by white guys. And when I talk with Anne-Marie [Miéville], whose family wouldn't let her watch films, except for Westerns, which she hated . . . still does today, even John Ford's, she has trouble with all those men on horses, all those guys. (Daney, "Godard Makes [Hi]stories," 165)

Montage, mon beau souci is described as coming "from an article I had written in all innocence but that I don't understand very well today. The idea is that, just as painting succeeded in reproducing perspective, cinema should have succeeded in something, too, but was unable to, due to the application of the invention of sound. But there are traces of it . . ." (Daney, "Godard Makes [Hi]stories," 167).

50. Godard explained, "It could go on forever. . . . But at some point, it is necessary to reach the conclusion; if not, it would last thirty years, with a series of annexes, the genre *Nouvelles histoire(s) du cinéma*. It would never end" (Bonnaud and Viviant, "La Légende du siècle," 26). Godard implies here and elsewhere that the project was ended because he felt he had found the right point. Biographer Antoine de Baecque argues instead, "Without doubt . . . Godard would have liked to leave his series incomplete, as a film without an ending, so that he could always come back to it, change elements, integrate extracts, metamorphose ideas. . . . But the main sponsor of the work, Gaumont, wished to close the loop by presenting the last two sections at Cannes in 1997" (de Baecque, *Godard, biographie*, 751). It is likely that Gaumont, which had been subsidizing the work with no possibility of recouping costs for several years, was putting pressure on Godard to finish it, which would help explain why the ten-part plan was reduced to eight parts at some point between 1992 and 1997. Nevertheless, given the tone of Godard's many statements about the *Histoire(s) du cinéma* throughout the 1990s and the existence of outlines like the one included in the files of the Museum of Modern Art, there is also no reason to accept the contention that it was ultimately meant to be left unfinished (however invested Godard was, and remains, in keeping it "open").

51. During conversations on March 3 and 4, 2015, Bernard Eisenschitz, who had been commissioned to create an inventory of the material quoted by Godard, explained that the most serious issues were with the Nicolas de Staël paintings. Godard made his own copies for the broadcast/release version of *Histoire(s) du cinéma*.

52. This treatment of music is very similar to Godard's use of texts. Although there are important examples of quotations from the middle of a book, a large percentage of the quotations in Godard's work are from the very beginning or very end of a work, sometimes from the first or last page. According to Colin MacCabe, Godard's sister Véronique recalled "her elder brother often telling both her and Claude that you needed to read only the first and the last page of any book" (MacCabe, *Godard*, 399).

53. *Two or Three Things I Know About Her* contains eleven linked musical extracts from Beethoven's String Quartet Number 16 (opus 135), gradually moving from the first to the third movement. Although it is interwoven with passages from other Beethoven string quartets (in particular, opuses 59, 74, and 132) and is repeatedly interrupted, *First Name: Carmen* includes all four movements of opus 135 and ends with the conclusion of the final movement.

54. MacCabe, *Godard*, 212. The commercially released version with the song at the end is called *Sympathy for the Devil* (the title of a song originally included on the 1968 Rolling Stones album, *Beggars Banquet*); *One + One* is the title of Godard's original cut.

55. In addition to subscribing to the notion articulated in Athenaeum Fragment 116 of a Romantic art that is "still in the state of becoming . . . that should forever be becoming and never be perfected," Godard's approach is also very much in line with Schlegel's idea of contradiction and fragments, as the following parallel passages demonstrate (Schlegel, *Philosophical Fragments*, 32):

Athenaeum Fragment 24: Many of the works of the ancients have become fragments. Many modern works are fragments as soon as they are written. (*Philosophical
Fragments*, 21)

Godard: At the time [the mid-1960s] there began to be a quite clear sense of fragments. . . . I even accentuated this to the point of making an entire film out of a
fragment. (*True History*, 174)

Athenaeum Fragment 103: The fact that one can annihilate a philosophy—whereas
a careless person can easily accidentally annihilate himself as well—or that one
can prove that a philosophy annihilates itself is of little consequence. If it's really
philosophy, then, like the phoenix, it will always rise again from its own ashes.
(Schlegel, *Philosophical Fragments*, 30)

Godard: [I'm] always interested in the moment when something is destroyed,
either destruction or construction, and the moment between the two. I think this
is where the most interesting moments are always found. A film should start at the
end of something—that's why all films are the end of something, or the beginning.
(*True History*, 338)

Athenaeum Fragment 121: An idea is a concept perfected to the point of irony, an
absolute synthesis of absolute antitheses, the continual self-creating interchange of
two conflicting thoughts. (Schlegel, *Philosophical Fragments*, 33)

Godard: I'm trying to destroy what is preventing me from being what I believe
myself to be inside, and at the same time . . . to reconstruct it in a different manner.
(*True History*, 377)

The ethical union Schlegel postulated between a classical unity predicated on homo-
geneous assemblage and a Romantic totality ("*Ganzheit*") founded on the always provisional weaving together of "extremely heterogeneous components" could also be
related to Godard's approach in *Histoire(s) du cinéma* (quoted in Schlegel, *Philosophical
Fragments*, 20).

56. Brody, *Everything Is Cinema*, 39. One notable exception to the critical neglect of this
aspect of Godard's work is Raymond Bellour, who has invoked the Romantics in general
and Schlegel in particular in analyzing Godard's treatment of love:

It remains to write on Godard's behalf this "letter to the beloved," which he so elo-
quently claims lives in every work (see *Changer d'image* [1981]), and indeed is every
work. We've known this since Rousseau, since the Romantics, since Schlegel and
his "Letter" *On Philosophy (to Dorothea)* [1798]—Dorothea-Lucinda, the woman-
light, she who gives form and life to light, when she stands behind both the man
and the work. (Raymond Bellour, "(Not) Just an Other Filmmaker," in Bellour and
Bandy, *Jean-Luc Godard*, 228)

Jacques Aumont also described Godard as "heir to the Romantics" in *Amnésies: Fictions
du cinéma d'après Jean-Luc Godard* (Paris: P.O.L., 1999), 30.

57. Jean-Luc Godard, "*Hollywood or Bust*," translated by Tom Milne in *Godard on
Godard*, edited by Tom Milne (New York: Da Capo Press, 1972), 58.

58. Jean-Louis Comolli, Michel Delahaye, Jean-André Fieschi, and Gérard Guégan, "Let's Talk about Pierrot," translated by Tom Milne in Milne, *Godard on Godard*, 219.

59. Ibid., 216.

60. Jean-Luc Godard and Michel Delahaye, "The Question," in *Robert Bresson (Revised)*, edited by James Quandt (Bloomington: Indiana University Press, 2011), 650–652.

61. The text, spread out over several minutes, reads "*La Vocation théâtrale de Guillaume Meister et ses apprentisages et ses années de voyage*," the French titles of the first (*Wilhelm Meister's Apprenticeship*, 1796) and the second (*Wilhelm Meister's Travels*, 1829) parts of Goethe's novel. The allusion to the protagonist's "theatrical vocation" is connected to his revolutionary aspirations by the montage strategies Godard employs and by text scrawled on a dilapidated building reading "*théâtre année zéro*." Schlegel describes the Goethe novel as one of the three great "tendencies of the age" in Athenaeum Fragment 216 (Schlegel, *Philosophical Fragments*, 46).

62. In 1793, a Revolutionary Calendar was introduced that began with the autumnal equinox and changed the names of the months (the first month, "Vendémiaire," began in late September, the second, "Brumaire," began approximately thirty days later, etc.). This calendar remained in use until 1805, and Godard uses the names of the months as chapter headings in both *Weekend* and *JLG/JLG—Self-Portrait in December*. In the latter film, the names of the months appear on the pages of Godard's notebook as breaks within the sections of the film, but they appear out of order and sometimes in reverse (proceeding, for example, from the third month, "Frimaire," to "Brumaire," and then finally "Vendémiaire"), another way Godard links them to an idea of continual renewal.

63. Godard and Gorin made similar claims (see, for example, Michael Goodwin, Tom Luddy, and Naomi Wise, "The Dziga Vertov Group in America: An Interview with Jean-Luc Godard and Jean-Pierre Gorin," *The Georgia Straight* 5, no. 67, May 18, 1971).

64. Despite the absence of formal credits, Godard's voice can be clearly made out in *Un film comme les autres* (1968), and a dialogue between Godard and Gorin makes up most of the soundtrack to *Letter to Jane* (1972). In a lecture at Bard College on June 24, 2014, Gorin explained that although he and Godard "were accused of following the Maoist catechism to the nth degree," they "were trying to unfurl things in a constantly provisional way." Unlike the works produced by other radical organizations in the period, Gorin argued, the Groupe Dziga Vertov films were "intended to absolutely infuriate [and wake up] the Left."

65. It could, of course, be reasonably objected that this is part of historical dialectics (the French Revolution was a key reference point for both Karl Marx and Vladimir Lenin), but what is unusual here is the manner in which these ideas are articulated. For all Godard's pretense to objectivity, the fixation on landscapes and on an emotionally extravagant style of political rhetoric suggests the treatment of Revolutionary fervor in novels like Victor Hugo's *Ninety-Three* (1874) more than cold, rational analysis. In *Pravda*, for example, Godard paraphrases Friedrich Engels' *Dialectics of Nature* (1883) and declares, "Don't say 'nature,' say 'dialectic of nature,'" but although this may apply to the montage style of the film, it is hard to see what is dialectical about the symbolically charged use of red, a color motif that runs throughout the film and culminates in a heavily saturated image of a rose. In the Groupe Dziga Vertov films, as in his other work, Godard's Marxist politics and his Romantic imagination are interrelated and, in many cases, mutually reinforcing.

66. Alan Riding, "What's in a Name If the Name Is Godard?" *New York Times*, October 25, 1992, 11. Godard has reiterated this on other occasions. In 1996, for example, he argues that it was cinema that led him to re-evaluate his political commitments:

> When I made *Histoire(s) du cinema*, the ensemble of history was seen better. At one moment, in a section on the New Wave, I say that our only error was to believe that the New Wave was a beginning. Just as in May '68, one said: "This is only a beginning." My films are part of a current of the European Left that flies from defeat into defeat, in a beautiful romantic spirit. The cinema limited my militantism and permitted me to see its romanticism better. (Bonnaud and Kaganski, "Le Cinéma," 384)

67. The passage Godard uses is this:

> In this simple form of assent [after Jim says, "Let them go" and people said they "believed" him] to his will lies the whole gist of the situation; their creed, his truth; and the testimony to that faithfulness which made him in his own eyes the equal of the impeccable men who never fall out of the ranks. Stein's words, "Romantic!—Romantic!" seem to ring over those distances that will never give him up now to a world indifferent to his failings and his virtues, and to that ardent and clinging affection that refuses him the dole of tears in the bewilderment of a great grief and of eternal separation. (Joseph Conrad, *Lord Jim* [New York: W.W. Norton, 1996], 233)

In *Hélas pour moi*, "Madame Monod" (the name of Godard's maternal family) recites parts of this passage after two students repeatedly ask her to tell them what Romanticism is, explaining that "it is really important." The protagonist of *Détective* says that he was given Conrad's book by his mother, who told him that he should open it, to any page, at a turning point in his life and he would find something useful.

68. Péguy's arguments are laid out most clearly in *Notre jeunesse* (1910). His posthumously published book about the spirit of history, *Clio* (1917), is discussed in *Les Signes parmi nous* (4B).

69. *Blind Love* (Alexander Kluge, 2001). Godard was equally explicit at the Cannes press conference for the film in May 1991: "Although I am of French origin, and very French, [Germany] is a country that formed me a bit—by its literature, especially Romanticism—during my adolescence" (Jean-Luc Godard, "Ne raconte pas d'histoires," in Bergala, *Godard par Godard*, 2:224). Similar comments were made in Ciment and Goudet, "Entretien Jean-Luc Godard," 55.

70. Jean-Luc Godard and André S. Labarthe, "Le Cinéma est fait pour penser l'impensable," in Bergala, *Godard par Godard*, 2:296.

71. Jean-Luc Godard, "*JLG/JLG, autoportrait de décembre*," in Bergala, *Godard par Godard*, 2:288. The end of Godard's statement is a paraphrase of the humanistic final line of Sartre's autobiography: "A whole man, composed of all men and as good as all of them and no better than any" (Jean-Paul Sartre, *The Words*, translated by Bernard Frechtman [New York: George Braziller, 1964], 255). The actual line used in *JLG/JLG—Self-Portrait in December* is slightly different: "A man, nothing but a man, no better than any other … [pause] but no other better than him." This revised version may also include an allusion to the opening of Rousseau's *Confessions*:

Myself alone. I feel my heart and I know men. I am not made like any that I have seen; I venture to believe that I was not made like any that exist. If I am not more deserving, at least I am different. . . . "Assemble about me, Eternal Being, the numberless host of my fellow-men; let them hear my confessions, let them groan at my unworthiness, let them blush at my wretchedness. Let each of them, here on the steps of your throne, in turn reveal his heart with the same sincerity; and then let one of them say to you, if he dares: *I was better than that man*." (Jean-Jacques Rousseau, *Confessions*, translated by Angela Scholar [Oxford: Oxford World's Classics, 2000], 5)

72. Malraux's *Psychologie de l'art* was originally published in three volumes between 1947 and 1949. The text was subsequently revised and expanded into a single-volume edition, *Les Voix du silence* (Paris: Gallimard, 1951). *La Monnaie de l'absolu*, the title of the 3A section of *Histoire(s) du cinéma*, is also the French title of the final section of Malraux's work (it was translated by Stuart Gilbert as *The Triumph of the Absolute* when it was published as the third volume of *The Psychology of Art* [New York: Pantheon Books, 1951] and as "Aftermath of the Absolute" in *The Voices of Silence* [Garden City, NY: Doubleday, 1953]). Malraux's idea of an imaginary museum also informs a scene in *Les Carabiniers* in which the two male leads rifle through a series of postcard representations of famous places and artworks (a scene that also functions as an ironic commentary on the commodification of experience).

73. The French phrase as it appears in *Toutes les histoires* (1A) and, with slight variations, in *Fatale beauté* (2B), *Scénario du film Passion* (1982), and *JLG/JLG—Self-Portrait in December* is "*l'art, c'est-à-dire ce qui renaît dans ce qui a été brûlé*" ("Art is that which has been reborn from that which is burned"). Godard is alluding here to the final sentence of the first section of Malraux's *Les Voix du silence*: "*Car le génie est inséparable de ce dont il naît, mais comme l'incendie de ce qu'il brûle*" (144). This was translated into English as "For genius is inseparable from that which gives it birth as is a conflagration from that which it consumes" (Malraux, *The Voices of Silence*, 146). Godard appears to have publicly referred to this passage for the first time in a 1957 essay on Jean Renoir, in which he writes, "Genius, Malraux wrote somewhere, is born like fire. *Of what it consumes*" (Jean-Luc Godard, "Jean Renoir," translated by Tom Milne in Milne, *Godard on Godard*, 63).

74. To the best of my knowledge, Godard has never spoken directly about *Nostalghia* (which attracted considerable attention after its 1983 Cannes premiere), but it is highly likely he saw it, especially since he cast the otherwise obscure lead actress Domiziana Giordano as the female protagonist in *Nouvelle vague*. The use of Andrei Rublev's *Archangel Michael* (ca. 1410s) at the end of *Seul le cinéma* (2A) is a likely reference to Tarkovsky's film about the artist (*Archangel Michael* is one of the final icons shown in the epilogue).

75. The relationship between objects and illumination is an abiding interest in Godard's work. Candles and lighters also feature prominently in films like *Détective*, and Hasumi Shigehiko has persuasively identified Godard as one of the great creators of "lamp films" (see, for example, "Who Can Put Out the Flame?" in *Hou Hsiao-hsien*, edited by Richard I. Suchenski [Vienna: Österreichisches Filmmuseum; New York: Columbia University Press, 2014], 111–112).

76. Tarkovsky attached mystical significance to the idea of making this particular shot, lasting for nearly eight minutes, work in a single take. Lead actor Oleg Yankovsky later explained the meaning this had for Tarkovsky in a text entitled "How We Shot the

'Inextinguishable Candle' Episode for *Nostalghia*," available online at http://people.ucal-gary.ca/~tstronds/nostalghia.com/TheTopics/Yankovsky.html). According to Yankovsky, Tarkovsky started the shoot with this shot, telling the actor that he "chose this scene without words for you, an entire human life, from birth to death. In fact the leading character promises a deranged man he will carry a burning candle through the waters of the St. Catherine pool, and in so doing heal him." When asked why he placed such importance on the candle, Tarkovsky responded: "Because of the flame, the unprotected fire. Remember the candles in Orthodox churches, how they flicker. The very essence of things, the spirit, the spirit of fire."

77. Godard and Labarthe, "Le Cinéma," 297.

78. Godard, "Le Montage," 244. Several months earlier, Godard said, even more directly, "Cinema is montage" (Michèle Halberstadt, "Godard arrêt sur images: Le Cinéaste commente quelques photos de SOIGNE TA DROITE," *Première* 130 [1988], 59).

79. Jean-Luc Godard, "Montage, mon beau souci," *Cahiers du cinéma* 65 (December 1956), 30–31; translated by Tom Milne as "Montage, My Fine Care" in Milne, *Godard on Godard*, 39–41.

80. Ibid., 39; Godard, "Le Montage," 245.

81. Godard, "Montage, My Fine Care," 40.

82. Ibid., 39.

83. Jean-Luc Godard, "*The Wrong Man*," translated by Tom Milne in Milne, *Godard on Godard*, 49.

84. Ibid., 50. The phrase that Godard uses in the original essay (Jean-Luc Godard, "Le Cinéma et son double," in *Godard par Godard: Les Années cahiers (1950 à 1959)*, edited by Alain Bergala [Paris: Flammarion, 1989], 93), "*les données immédiates de la conscience*," is a reference to the title of Henri Bergson's first book, *Essai sur les données immédiates de la conscience* (1889).

85. Godard's montage of art historical images in *La Monnaie de l'absolu* (3A) suggests that this tradition does have precursors earlier with works like Johannes Vermeer's *Girl with a Pearl Earring* (1665), but the fact that seven separate Manet paintings are included reinforces his centrality.

86. At the very end of *La Monnaie de l'absolu* (3A), Godard inserts onscreen text reading "a thought / which forms / a form / which thinks," accompanied by a photograph of Pier Paolo Pasolini and the cropped face of a man from Piero della Francesca's *The Legend of the True Cross* (1453–1455).

87. Godard, "Le Montage," 245.

88. Serge July, "Alfred Hitchcock est mort," in Bergala, *Godard par Godard: Des années Mao aux années 80*, 179.

89. Godard, "Le Montage," 242.

90. Ibid., 245.

91. Jean-Luc Godard, "*Histoire(s) du cinéma*: À propos de cinéma et d'histoire," in Bergala, *Godard par Godard*, 2:403. Godard has been arguing that Eisenstein's main achievement was the discovery of angles rather than montage since the 1970s (see, for example, Godard, "*Moi, je*, projet de film," 237, or Godard, *True History*, 223–224).

92. Breton writes, "If one accepts, as I do, Reverdy's definition [of the image] it does not seem possible to bring together, voluntarily, what he calls 'two distant realities.'" For Breton, "*the light of the image*" can be "sprung" only from "the fortuitous juxtaposition of

the two [realities]" (André Breton, *Manifestoes of Surrealism*, translated by Richard Seaver and Helen R. Lane [Ann Arbor: University of Michigan Press, 1969], 36–37).

93. The poem was first published in *Nord-Sud* 2, no. 13 (March 1918). It was reprinted in Pierre Reverdy, *Le Gant de crin* (Paris: Flammarion, 1968), 30–32.

94. In 1967, Godard explained the importance of this in the following terms:

> If you didn't base yourself on realism you wouldn't be able to do anything any more, you couldn't even step into a taxi in the street, always assuming you dared to go out in the first place. But I believe everything. It isn't about two separate things—one "real" and the other a "dream." It's all just one thing. *Belle de jour* [Luis Buñuel, 1967] is fantastic. (Jean-Luc Godard, "Struggling on Two Fronts," translated by Diana Matias in *Cahiers du cinéma: The 1960s*, edited by Jim Hillier [Cambridge, MA: Harvard University Press, 1986], 298)

95. Louis Aragon, *Paris Peasant*, translated by Simon Watson Taylor (Boston: Exact Change, 1994), 204. In his book *Compulsive Beauty* (Cambridge, MA: MIT Press, 1993, 20), Hal Foster explains that Aragon first elucidated this key Surrealist concept in 1924. The poems Louis Aragon wrote during the Occupation of France, particularly those collected in the 1941 book *Le Crève-coeur*, are used frequently in Godard's work of the 1980s and 1990s and had been quoted as early as *Breathless*. In addition to references in *JLG/JLG—Self-Portrait in December*, the book is alluded to or quoted in *Toutes les histoires* (1A) and *La Monnaie de l'absolu* (3A), where Aragon's photo also appears. A poem from one of Aragon's postwar collections, 1946's *La Diane française*, is used in the following section (*Une vague nouvelle*, 3B).

96. Godard conducted a conversation with Pelechian that was published in *Le Monde* shortly after the launch of the Armenian director's first Paris retrospective at the Galerie Nationale du Jeu de Paume in March 1992 (Jean-Luc Godard, "Un langage d'avant Babel," *Le Monde*, April 2, 1992, 28). In it, Pelechian, modifying ideas from the silent era, describes the "language of cinema" not as a "synthesis of the other arts," but as "dating from the tower of Babel, from before the division into different languages." Godard agrees, incorporating his often-repeated comments linking the coming of sound to the rise of nationalism:

> Sound technology came at the moment of the rise of fascism in Europe, which is also the period of the advent of the speaker. Hitler was a magnificent speaker, and also Mussolini, Churchill, de Gaulle, Stalin. Talkies were the triumph of the theatrical scenario against the language that you referred to, from before the curse of Babel.

Yet while Pelechian shares much with Godard—both filmmakers blur the boundaries between documentary and fiction and transform found footage into montage material, interweaving different historical periods into a complex matrix—the execution and ultimate goals of their montage approaches differ in a way that highlights the importance of German Romanticism to Godard's thinking. For Pelechian, distance montage would substitute for the "explosive" collisions of Eisenstein or Lev Kuleshov, "a retroaction, the effect of returning, which loops the sequence or the film itself. Flux and reflux. Movement from birth to death but also from death to birth: growth-degradation, death-resurrection" (François Niney, "Entretien avec Artavazd Pelechian," *Cahiers du cinéma*

454 [April 1992], 35). In Pelechian's films, this occurs primarily through the repeated returns to clusters of imagery in which actions are filmed from a number of vantage points (often through the use of mirror printing). *The Seasons* (1975), for example, begins with a cluster of shots showing a man pulling a goat down a mountain and ends with the inverse of the first image; at three separate points in between, the smooth flow of the film is broken up by the rapid cutting around actions in a way that is homologous to this opening scene, creating a form of rhythmic structure that harmonizes with that of Vivaldi's *The Four Seasons* (opus 8, 1723, which is used throughout on the soundtrack). Thus, the final images that often occur after Pelechian's films seem to end lock everything into a continuous loop, thereby overcoming the dictates of ordinary time. As Pelechian explains:

> Distance montage creates a magnetic field around the film. It's like when a light is turned on and generates a magnetic field around the lamp. In distance montage when the two ends are excited, the whole thing glows. Sometimes I don't call my method "montage." I'm involved in a process of creating unity. In a sense I've eliminated montage: by creating the film through montage, I have destroyed montage. In the totality, in the wholeness of one of my films, there is no montage, no collision, so as a result montage has been destroyed. In Eisenstein, every element *means* something. For me, the individual fragments don't mean anything anymore. Only the *whole* film has the meaning. (Scott MacDonald, *A Critical Cinema 3* [Berkeley: University of California Press, 1998], 102)

Godard too strives to use montage to link birth and death, but, crucially, he does *not* attempt to create a sense of wholeness in which the constituent elements are all blended together into a perfect unity. In the 1992 interview, he responds to Pelechian's claim that he is searching for "a montage that would create around itself an emotional magnetic charge" by saying, "Since I am quite pessimistic, I see the end of things rather than their beginning" (Godard, "Un langage d'avant Babel").

97. Godard reads a modified version of the following passage from "For a Metahistory of Film: Commonplace Notes and Hypothesis" (words removed from the original text in brackets and italics): "As one era slowly dissolves into the next, some individuals metabolize the former means for [*physical*] survival into new means [*for psychic survival*]. These latter we call art ... no activity can become an art until its proper epoch has ended" (Hollis Frampton, *Circles of Confusion: Film-Photography-Video Texts, 1968–1980* [Rochester, NY: Visual Studies Workshop Press, 1983], 114). This essay was reprinted, with Jonathan Rosenbaum's "Trailer for Godard's *Histoire(s) du cinéma*," in a special issue of *Trafic*, 21 (Spring 1997), timed to coincide with the premiere of most of *Histoire(s) du cinéma* at the Cannes Film Festival in 1997. In an article published later that year, Godard again referenced this text:

> I am inclined moreover to think like Hollis Frampton that the twentieth century barely existed ... it had events, certainly, but few proper creations. The twentieth century was, and still is, under the influence of inventions that came before it, and I imagine that the nineteenth is ending these days. (Nicolas Truong, "Résistance de l'art," in Bergala, *Godard par Godard*, 2:445)

98. Stan Brakhage, *Essential Brakhage* (Kingston, NY: McPherson, 2001), 14. Similar comments are made in other Godard films: Carmen in *First Name: Carmen* asks, "What comes before the name?" while in *King Lear*, Professor Pluggy (Godard) insists, "I ain't interested in names. What if we made a mistake at the very beginning and we called 'red' 'green'? How would we know today?" Another variant of this had been used earlier in *Two or Three Things I Know About Her*, "What if blue had been called green by mistake," a probable reference to the discussion of color naming in Part II of Ludwig Wittgenstein's *Brown Book* (the *Blue and Brown Books*, 1958, are shown onscreen elsewhere in the film). The long section from Hermann Broch's *The Death of Virgil* read out by Sabine Azéma in *Fatale beauté* (2B), in which the poet Virgil yearns to return to the "natal country . . . the universal time where nothing was silent for the silent eyes of a child and everything was a new creation," also reflects these preoccupations (and resonates with Brakhage's text).

99. In a 1983 interview, Godard explained:

> People always want to know what things are called. Do things always have to be called by a name? . . . I think that the cinema should show things before they receive a name. . . . Today we live in an epoch of total power being given to all forms of rhetoric, a time of terrorism of language which is further accentuated by television. I, as a modest employee of the cinema, have an interest to speak of things before words and names take over, to speak of the child before daddy and mummy give it a name. (Gideon Bachmann, "The Carrots Are Cooked: A Conversation with Jean-Luc Godard," in Sterritt, *Jean-Luc Godard Interviews*, 129)

The search for the origins of images is worked into both Godard's films—the protagonist of *King Lear* endeavors to find a word that will accompany "the dawn of the first image"—and his public comments. Tellingly, his most recent "last film" is a 3D feature entitled *Adieu au langage* (2014).

100. The similarities and differences come out most clearly through the two filmmakers' frequent use of shots through car windows: in Brakhage films like *Scenes from Under Childhood* (1967–1970) or *Visions in Meditation* (1989–1990), these shots articulate a distinctly American sense of vast space and a consciousness in the process of becoming; in Godard's films, on the other hand, motion inside cars is more often linked to existential journeys (*Contempt, Alphaville, Pierrot le fou*) or to the structure of memory (*In Praise of Love*). A similar comparison could be made using Godard's and Brakhage's treatment of arena-like spaces (e.g., the basketball courts in Brakhage's *Western History*, 1971, and Godard's *Hail Mary*, 1985) or their use of film negative (in Brakhage's *Dog Star Man*, 1961–1964, and Godard's contemporaneous films *Une femme mariée: Fragments d'un film tourné en 1964 en noir et blanc* and *Alphaville*).

101. Brakhage's use of the back-and-forth fluttering of two frame extracts of Vietnam War footage in *23rd Psalm Branch* (1967) could be productively compared to the opening "Hell" montage of *Notre musique*, the use of very brief shots in the video short *On s'est tous défilé* (1988), or the rapid intercutting of disparate sources in several sections of *Histoire(s) du cinéma*. At the same time, many of the stills used in *Histoire(s) du cinéma* are connected via lap dissolves with the full image held only for a beat or two (a few frames) before hard cuts to black. As with Brakhage's step-printing, the effect is of an image that is

only partially apprehended before it disappears, but while both filmmakers use it to keep perception active, Godard makes stronger use of the mnemonic effect of these images (Brakhage places a greater emphasis on the suspended present of the moment of seeing).

102. In both *The Dante Quartet* and *Night Mulch*, Brakhage paints over preexisting film material (a print of Billy Wilder's 1964 *Irma La Douce* in the former and a trailer for Philip Kaufman's 2001 film *Quills* in the latter). Brakhage's ironic use of onscreen text, like quotes from the *New York Times*, in the latter film (and in *23rd Psalm Branch*) is similar to Godard's more systematic transformation of preexisting phrases throughout *Histoire(s) du cinéma*. By contrast, Brakhage's open declaration of love for his family through hand-scratched text in *Untitled: For Marilyn* is startlingly sincere.

103. Brakhage was asked to introduce Godard at the Telluride Film Festival in 1989 (the same festival where he met Tarkovsky several years earlier) and their encounter is recounted in Jerry Johnson, "Film at Wit's End," *Austin Chronicle*, September 12, 1997 (available online at http://weeklywire.com/ww/09-15-97/austin_screens_feature1. html). Godard expressed his admiration for Brakhage in a 1996 interview with Gavin Smith: "When I read recently that an American critic wrote that *Hélas pour moi* looked like a Brakhage picture, I was very pleased" (Smith, "Jean-Luc Godard," 181).

104. In 1968, Godard told an American audience, "I'm aware of the existence of the underground cinema, but unfortunately I haven't seen many. The French National Cinematheque is the only place in France where one may see the American underground" (Gene Youngblood, "No Difference between Life and Cinema," in Sterritt, *Jean-Luc Godard Interviews*, 11). The French company Re:Voir has made several Brakhage films available on videotape, but they only began releasing these in 1995, as *Histoire(s) du cinéma* was nearing completion.

105. Godard told Gavin Smith that he "was friends with Gregory Markopoulos long before I joined *Cahiers du cinéma*. Later I don't think his pictures were good but I remember him and other people who were for a candid cinema. It was democracy. We didn't realize that the United States doesn't like democracy any more than the communist government of Russia" (Smith, "Jean-Luc Godard," 181). Both Godard and Markopoulos shared an obsessive fascination with Jean Cocteau in this period.

106. In *Struggle in Italy*, the sections of leader intercut with imagery are used to represent the gaps in bourgeois vision, and they gradually become "filled in" as the film progresses and the protagonist comes to understand the principles of the 1970 Louis Althusser text, "Ideology and the State," that the film attempts to adapt cinematically. Godard's experiments with a black screen are roughly contemporaneous with Markopoulos' attempts to develop the visual language employed throughout *Eniaios*.

By the time he made *Histoire(s) du cinéma*, Godard had clearly reconceived the empty screen as primarily a rhythmic device: "It's cinema, in other words not like literature which is more closely bound to meaning, in film there's rhythm, it's more like music, that's how I came to use black for rhythm" (Godard and Ishaghpour, *Cinema*, 24). The most substantive change made to the versions of *Toutes les histoires* (1A) and *Une histoire seule* (1B) included in the final 1998 version of *Histoire(s) du cinéma* was the addition of passages of black, giving the whole work a more explicitly musical structure. Godard would continue to insert passages of black in many of the films and videos initiated after *Histoire(s) du cinéma* was underway (they are especially prominent in *Hélas pour moi, The Old Place*, and *In Praise of Love*).

107. As Godard explained:

It's the duty to say in the course of a patient's treatment, the duty to look into the recovery that is extremely painful. Even though I'm the son of a doctor, it's hard for me to go to the doctor because then you have to say and look, and you have to confront that with seeing and speaking. . . . [*Les Signes parmi nous*, 4B] says if you film a traffic jam in the streets of Paris and if you know how to see it (not just me, but [Nobel Prize–winning bacteriologist] François Jacob and I), we discover—if we know how to see—a vaccine for AIDS. (Daney, "Godard Makes [Hi]stories," 165–167)

Similar ideas are verbalized by Godard onscreen in *Fatale beauté* (2B):

The history of cinema is first linked to that of medicine. Eisenstein's tortured bodies, beyond Caravaggio and El Greco, speak to [Andreas] Vesalius' dissections. Joan Fontaine staring at the glass of milk [Godard here dissolves to Manet's *The Dead Christ with Angels* (1864)] does not correspond to a [Eugène] Delacroix heroine but to [Louis] Pasteur's dog. Kodak made its fortune with X-rays, not with Snow White. . . . Oh, how many screenplays about babies, about flowers . . . but how many about bursts of gunfire? [The onscreen text at the end reads, "*Vrai / fauxtographie.*"]

108. *An Extraordinary Woman: Selected Writings of Germaine de Staël*, edited and translated by Vivian Folkenflik (New York: Columbia University Press, 1987), 300. Napoleon suppressed *On Germany*, and Godard plays off of these associations by having the most widely quoted statement from that book directed to him in *Fatale beauté* (2B): "One must go into mourning, but forgetting about it, and Madame de Staël told us how she wrote to Napoleon: 'Glory, Sire, is the dazzling mourning of happiness'" (the passage Godard repurposed was in a chapter about "Love in Marriage," 318).

109. In each of these cases, the invocation of Orpheus hinges upon the use of the phrase "Don't look back." Lennox says this to Elena in *Nouvelle vague*, and Lemmy Caution says this to Natacha von Braun in *Alphaville*. The man in the café hearing telegraphic messages from beyond in *Two or Three Things I Know About Her* is also an allusion to Cocteau's *Orpheus* (1950).

The Orpheus myth is referred to in one way or another in *Une histoire seule* (1B, sound from Cocteau's *Orpheus* intermixed with music from Christoph Gluck's 1762 opera *Orfeo ed Euridice*; the image of the boatman first appears here), *Seul le cinéma* (2A, "the cinema authorizes Orpheus" is from here, paired with the image of the boatman), and *La Monnaie de l'absolu* (3A, an audio extract from Cocteau's *Testament of Orpheus*, 1960).

110. Dominique Païni and Guy Scarpetta, "Jean-Luc Godard; La Curiosité du sujet," *Art Press*, special issue 4 (December 1984–February 1985), 18. Godard made similar comments in his 1980 eulogy for Alfred Hitchcock:

For me, the cinema is Eurydice. Eurydice says to Orpheus: "Don't look back." And Orpheus turns around. Orpheus is the literature that kills Eurydice. And the rest of his life, he makes money by publishing a book on the death of Eurydice. (July, "Alfred Hitchcock est mort," 180)

111. In the first spoken dialogue after the long Victor Hugo recitation at the beginning of *La Monnaie de l'absolu* (3A), Godard playfully but significantly connects biblical narratives to the photochemical process by which an image is permanently imprinted on the film strip: "The Holy Scriptures tell us that before leaving for a voyage, the daughters of Lot [it is actually Lot's wife, Genesis 19:26] wanted to return one last time, and they were turned into pillars of salt. . . . One films only the past, I mean, what is happening, and there are silver salts that fix the light." See also Michael Witt's discussion of Godard's treatment of the Orphic myth "as an allegory for the activity of the historian" in *Jean-Luc Godard, Cinema Historian*, 70–76.

112. This quote—from the first of the *Duino Elegies* (lines 4–5), as translated by Stephen Mitchell in *Ahead of All Parting: The Selected Poetry and Prose of Rainer Maria Rilke*, edited by Stephen Mitchell (New York: Modern Library, 1995), 331—is used in several Godard works, most notably *First Name: Carmen* and *The Origins of the 21st Century*. Godard discovered it while shooting *Every Man for Himself* (Bergala, "L'Art," 18).

113. The reading from Hugo's text at the beginning of *La Monnaie de l'absolu* (3A) goes on for approximately four minutes, and a title card, "Victor Hugo / 29 août 1876," appears as soon as Godard finishes; the unusually bibliographic nature of this citation testifies to its special importance. Godard includes an equally political passage, this time about guerilla warfare, from Victor Hugo's *Ninety-Three* in *For Ever Mozart*: "One begins by attacking a republic and ends by robbing a stagecoach" (Victor Hugo, *Ninety-Three*, translated by Lowell Bair [Cresskill, NJ: Paper Tiger, 2002], 175). Godard's treatment of Hugo's politically charged Romanticism is very similar to his treatment of Delacroix's paintings from the same period, and the two are interconnected in his 1993 short *L'Enfance de l'art*, a video about children surrounded by revolutionary violence that includes the reading of a long extract from *Les Misérables* (1862) and postcard reproductions of Delacroix paintings like *Liberty Leading the People* (1830). Delacroix's 1837 *Pietà* is one of the images presented onscreen while Godard reads the Hugo text at the beginning of *La Monnaie de l'absolu* (3A) and its appearance had been anticipated by the use of another Delacroix canvas, *Young Orphan Girl at the Cemetery* (1824), at the end of the preceding section, *Fatale beauté* (2B).

114. *Seul le cinéma* (2A).

115. There is either footage of, an explicit verbal reference to, or an audio extract from Adolf Hitler in every section of *Histoire(s) du cinéma* except *Seul le cinéma* (2A). He "appears" most frequently in *Toutes les histoires* (1A) and *Les Signes parmi nous* (4B), the two bookends to the work.

116. In a public lecture in 1995, Godard explained:

My idea . . . which [Jules] Michelet did not have even when he finished his grandiose *Histoire de France*, that Sistine Chapel of history . . . is that history is alone, it is far from man . . . Fernand Braudel said something of this kind when he said that there are two histories: a close history that runs toward us with hurried steps—which is television or *Der Spiegel* and soon Goya and [Henri] Matisse on CD-ROM ("ROM" for Romans, no doubt, *pax romana, pax Americana*)—and a distant history that accompanies us in small steps, and that is Kafka, it is Pina Bausch, it is [Rainer Werner] Fassbinder, to speak only of [German-language] artists. (Godard, "*Histoire(s) du cinéma*: À propos de cinéma et d'histoire," 403)

Braudel's landmark 1949 history of the Mediterranean was a strong influence on *Film socialisme*, but as in *Histoire(s) du cinéma*, Godard's conception of history is inextricable from his aesthetic impulses:

> To me History is, so to speak, the work of works: it contains all of them. History is the family name, there are parents and children, literature, painting, philosophy . . . let's say History is the whole lot. . . . It seemed to me that History could be a work of art, something not generally admitted, except perhaps by Michelet. (Godard and Ishaghpour, *Cinema*, 28)

Godard underscored the Romanticism of his project when he told Ishaghpour, "History is stating something at a given moment, and [G. W. F.] Hegel puts it well when he says you're trying to paint gray on gray [a line, from the preface to the 1820 *Philosophy of Right*, that is quoted in *Germany Year 90 Nine Zero*]. From what little I know of Hegel, what I like about his work is that . . . he's a novelist of philosophy, there's a lot of romantic in him" (*Cinema*, 27).

117. Bonnaud and Viviant, "La Légende du siècle," 25.

118. The implied associations include the use of the same reference points in earlier Godard films. The cavalry poem, for example, had previously been quoted in *Le Petit Soldat* (1960/1963) and *Germany Year 90 Nine Zero* (the source of the audio extract in *Fatale beauté*, 2B).

119. Daney, "Godard Makes [Hi]stories," 161.

120. Jean-Pierre Lavoignat and Christophe d'Yvoire, "Le Cinéma n'a pas su remplir son rôle," in Bergala, *Godard par Godard*, 2:336. Godard made similar comments in a television interview with Marguerite Duras on December 28, 1987, and in his encounter with Régis Debray ten years later:

> In the cinema, one does not want to see, one prefers to speak of evil. I always take the example of the concentration camps: one prefers to say "never again" than to show [them]. A year ago, students were marching around with this slogan ["never again"]; we do not tell them that it has already been used. ("Marguerite Duras et Jean-Luc Godard: entretien télévisé," in Bergala, *Godard par Godard*, 2:144)

> The documentary function of cinema had been so anesthetized since 1900 that it was incapable of acting. When [George] Stevens made his first documentary in color on Auschwitz, he buried it within himself. Now, one shows it only on the occasion of commemorations. The Americans showed the concentration camps to the Germans and the population near the camps, but not to the French. It is at that moment that the cinema definitively lost its documentary function, and television began. (Debray, "Jean-Luc Godard rencontre Régis Debray," 425–426)

121. Godard has been openly referencing the Holocaust in his work since at least 1964 (when the protagonist of *Une femme mariée: Fragments d'un film tourné en 1964 en noir et blanc* goes to a theater showing Alain Resnais' *Night and Fog*, 1955), often in a deliberately jarring way, as in the appearance of people with numbers embedded on their skin in *Alphaville* or the discussion of concentration camps in *Numéro deux*. In his Montreal lectures, Godard expressed his interest in making a film about the day-to-day life of a secretary at a concentration camp (Godard, *True History*, 402). Nevertheless, Godard's

criticism of *Shoah* has resulted in a French cultural climate in which, as Bernard-Henri Lévy has observed, his "anti-Semitism" is simply assumed in a flippant and dismissive way (see Bernard-Henri Lévy, "Godard et l'antisémitisme: pieces additionnelles et inédites," *La Règle du jeu*, April 6, 2010, available online at http://laregledujeu.org/2010/04/06/1210/godard-et-lantisemitisme-pieces-additionnelles-et-inedites/). Lévy has tried to facilitate several proposed collaborations between Godard and Lanzmann, most recently a joint project entitled *Promised Land*, which apparently fell apart because of Godard's insistence that Swiss-born Islamic scholar Tariq Ramadan be invited to participate.

Godard has long been a vocal critic of imperialism in all its forms, and he has repeatedly focused on mirroring dialectics, attempts to see contemporary events as repetitive iterations of intractable patterns. This leads, on the one hand, to claims that contemporary Israel projects onto the Palestinians the sorts of attitudes that the Nazis projected onto the Jewish population (ideas that come out most vividly in the discussion of the "Legend of Stereo" in *JLG/JLG—Self-Portrait in December*) and, on the other, to the insistent characterization of cinema as "under occupation" by the hegemony of American capitalism, "Hollywood," and the deadening banality of televisuality. To treat these as simple analogies or to claim that Godard's arguments reflect a latent anti-Jewish (or anti-American) bias is to conflate vociferous criticism of Israeli state policy with anti-Semitism and to ignore the fundamentally dialectical aspect of the comparisons. Like the paralleling of collective and individual trauma in *Hiroshima mon amour* (Alain Resnais, 1959), Godard's intellectual "montages" are predicated on the structural concordances as well as the incommensurability of different historical experiences; the suffering of a young girl in occupied Nevers is of a fundamentally different order from the bombing of Hiroshima, but their association generates a more complex understanding of events (like the war) that cannot adequately be represented through conventional narratives. It is in this sense that Godard's description, in films like *JLG/JLG—Self-Portrait in December* and *Notre musique*, of the way the term *musulman* ("Muslim") was attached by the internees of concentration camps to those sentenced to death needs to be understood. Although it is not clear where Godard read about this appellation, Primo Levi mentions the use of the equivalent German term, *Muselmann*, in his 1947 memoir *If This Is a Man*.

122. Claude Lanzmann, "La Question n'est pas celle du document, mais celle de la vérité," *Le Monde*, January 19, 2001, 29. In a 1998 essay, Lanzmann argued:

> There is indeed an absolute obscenity in the project of understanding. Not to understand was my ironclad rule during all the years *Shoah* was in the making: I braced myself on this refusal as on the only possible attitude, at once ethical and operative. Keeping my guard high up, wearing these blinkers, and this blindness itself, were the vital conditions of creation. (Claude Lanzmann, "Hier ist kein Warum," in *Claude Lanzmann's Shoah: Key Essays*, edited by Stuart Liebman [Oxford: Oxford University Press, 2007], 51)

Godard criticized this aspect of *Shoah* in his television interview with Marguerite Duras, declaring, "It showed nothing, it showed the Germans" ("Marguerite Duras et Jean-Luc Godard," 146).

123. Siegfried Kracauer, *Theory of Film: The Redemption of Physical Reality* (Princeton, NJ: Princeton University Press, 1997), 306.

124. Godard is exercising poetic license in his description of Stevens' wartime documentary work. Although Stevens and his Signal Corps unit may have been the first to use 16mm color film stock in Europe, the Field Photographic Branch of the Office of Strategic Services, run by John Ford, had been using it in the Pacific since at least 1942. *The Battle of Midway* (John Ford, 1942) was made up entirely of 16mm color footage, and it shared the first Academy Award for Best Documentary years before the camps were liberated.

125. In "La Sainte et l'héritière: À propos des *Histoire(s) du cinéma*" (*Cahiers du cinéma* 557 [July–August 1999], 58–61), Jacques Rancière argued:

> By cutting the profile of Mary Magdalene, Godard has not only intended, following others, to deliver the pictorial image from the original sin of perspective and history. He has released the figure of the saint from a plastic dramaturgy whose proper sense was absence, the irremediable separation of the empty tomb that was, for Hegel, the heart of Romantic art. Instead of the *Noli me tangere* stands the absolute image, the promise that descends from the heavens, raising the rich heiress—and with her the cinema—from the tomb, just as the speech of the visionary Johannes brought the young mother of *Ordet* [Carl Theodor Dreyer, 1955] back to life. . . .
>
> Undoubtedly, I had believed it possible to honor Godard in this way while discreetly saving him from the surrounding neospiritualism. These two laudable intentions were equally misplaced. Godard's art is resolutely anti-Mallarméan. What he opposes to fiction is . . . the image as the imprint of presence. It is these icons of presence that the cinema "projects." (61)

Although I agree with Rancière that *Histoire(s) du cinéma* challenges "the great contemporary *doxa* that accuses the fatal screen, the reign of spectacle and the simulacrum" ("La Sainte et l'héritière," 61), to attribute notions of iconicity to his images or image-clusters seems to me very ill-advised. Rancière is not alone in this. Raymond Bellour, for example, also compares Godard's treatment of the image to that of icons:

> Godard is, in a sense, quite close to old Nicephorus, who believed in the image, and thought that the evangelical message of the icon was not only equal but superior to that of the Gospel itself. The image is all the more universal and absolute in that, unlike words, it is without contradiction—there is no counter-image—and its presence is whole and immediate, without delay. (Bellour, "(Not) Just an Other Filmmaker," 227)

The repeated religious metaphors in *Toutes les histoires* (1A), and throughout *Histoire(s) du cinéma*, do connect visual ideas to sacred ones, but the facile slippage of "image" into "icon" in critical discourses like these belies the irony of Godard's juxtapositions and ignores the question of whether such images can ever be experienced in their totality. Whatever sacred presence images may have had in an earlier period, there is never an absolute, static image within Godard's work. Everything is always presented in a fragmented, partial way, and this is especially true in projects like *Histoire(s) du cinéma* where images—painted or photographed—can only be viewed through the skein of a perpetually shifting montage. As Godard put it:

We use the word "image" even though that's not what they are anymore. One image leads to another, an image is never alone, contrary to what we call "images" today, which are sets of solitudes connected by speech that, at worst, is Hitler's, but that will never be [Françoise] Dolto's, Freud's, or Wittgenstein's. (Daney, "Godard Makes [Hi]stories," 167)

In another interview, and in *Les Enfants jouent à la Russie*, Godard speaks of icons as if they are divorced from the (Western) notion of the image coursing through his work: "There is painting, and then there are icons. Eisenstein was closer to icons. It is a thought relatively Eastern. Only the Russians have brought something from the East into the cinema" (François Albéra and Mikhail Iampolski, "Le Briquet du Capitaine Cook," *Les Lettres françaises* 19 [April 1992], 21). In these terms, Godard is on the side of "painting" (a metaphor he has frequently employed), and the "image" he advocates emerges only out of comparisons, collisions, and contradictions. As he explained in another interview, "This is not an image, it's a picture. The image is the relation with me looking at it dreaming up a relation at someone else. An image is an association" (Smith, "Jean-Luc Godard," 190).

126. John 20:17. The *Noli me tangere* is virtually unique in being a direct representation of one of the statements attributed to Christ in the Bible. In the context of the montage in this section of the *Histoire(s) du cinéma*, it may also be relevant that Titian's depiction of this scene, held by the National Gallery in London, was selected by the British public in 1942 as the first "picture of the month" to be retrieved from emergency storage in Wales (Neil MacGregor with Erika Langmuir, *Seeing Salvation: Images of Christ in Art* [New Haven: Yale University Press, 2000], 191).

127. This too is a quote, from a line in Georges Bernanos' *Diary of a Country Priest* (1936) that was included in Robert Bresson's 1951 film adaptation of the same name. In the interview with Daney (and the précis for *Histoire(s) du cinéma* released by his company), Godard explicitly compares himself to the protagonist of these works:

My [hi]story of cinema begins with a chapter called *Toutes les histoires* [1A], lots of short [hi]stories where you can see signs. It goes on to say that this [hi]story stands alone, the only [hi]story there has ever been. So—you know how unbounded my ambition is—I say it's not only alone, but also the only one there ever will be or that there ever was (later, it won't be a [hi]story, but something else). It's my mission to tell it. It's my [country priest; *curé de campagne* in the original] side coming out, if you will; this is what I preach. (Daney, "Godard Makes [Hi]stories," 167)

Godard has Elena in *Nouvelle vague* cite another line from *Diary of a Country Priest* to Lennox in *Nouvelle vague*: "How wonderful to give what you don't have." Lennox responds: "Miracle of empty hands." The soundtrack from this part of Bresson's film can be heard in *JLG/JLG—Self-Portrait in December*.

128. Rossellini defined Neorealism in ethical terms, describing it as "a moral approach which then becomes an aesthetic fact" (Roberto Rossellini, "Ten Years of Cinema," in *My Method: Roberto Rossellini Writings and Interviews*, edited by Adriano Aprà [New York: Marsilio Publishers, 1995], 66). He also strongly opposed what he saw as the excesses of cinéma vérité and its idea of direct recording, arguing in 1963 that there is "a myth about the camera as though we were on Mars. The camera's a ball-point pen, an imbecile, it's not worth anything if you don't have anything to say" (quoted in Tag

Gallagher, *The Adventures of Roberto Rossellini* [New York: Da Capo Press, 1998], 558).
Godard mounted a similar critique in his 1964 short, *Le Grand Escroq*, where a character named Patricia Leacock (played by Jean Seberg of *Breathless*) goes to Marrakech and begins constructing a documentary-style portrait only to have her methods turned against her by a swindler. The film ends with Godard, in voiceover, quoting Shakespeare ("All the world's a stage"), and solidifying what the film has already suggested, that there is no way of wholly removing subjectivity from filming, no way of attaining naked, wholly unmediated vision with photographic equipment.

When asked in a recent interview about the democratization of filmmaking via digital technologies (the contemporary equivalent of the 16mm cameras that had helped spark the debate over cinéma vérité), Godard reiterated a version of these same ideas:

> Yes, but the pencil is also available to all. Yet not everybody writes like Shakespeare. Most people still do not know how to use a camera. They just do not want to understand that a camera has two openings. You look at something and it is reflected as an image. The camera should be a way of thinking. (Florian Keller and Christoph Schneider, "Das Kino ist heute wie eine ägyptiche Mumie," *Tages Anzeiger*, November 30, 2010, available online at http://www.tagesanzeiger.ch/kultur/kino/ Das-Kino-ist-heute-wie-eine-aegyptische-Mumie-/story/17930831)

129. The actual origins of this passage are obscure, but it has been quoted repeatedly in subsequent centuries. Most relevant for Godard, it was used in several important texts of the 1960s, such as Dag Hammarskjöld's *Markings* (1963; it is used as the epigraph for the book) and Marshall McLuhan's *The Medium Is the Massage* (1967).

130. Bresson is also used to embody the purity of true (European) cinema in *In Praise of Love*, where a poster from *Pickpocket* (1959) is contrasted with one for *The Matrix* (Andy and Larry Wachowski, 1999). One of the characters waiting in line quotes the famous ending of *Pickpocket*, "What a strange road I had to take to reach you," a line that is also used by Joseph in Godard's *Hail Mary*.

131. The title of Bresson's film also shows up several minutes later, superimposed over an image of concentration camp victims.

132. Like *Les Anges du péché*, *Les Dames du Bois de Boulogne* was made during the Nazi Occupation of Paris and begun before the Liberation. Production was frequently halted due to air raids and electricity shortages (Paul Guth elaborates in *Autour des Dames du Bois de Boulogne: Journal d'un film* [Paris: René Julliard, 1945]). Godard is almost certainly also playing off Bresson's widely assumed status as a member of the Resistance during these years. That the phrase "*échec à la Gestapo*" is the French title of *All Through the Night* (Vincent Sherman, 1941), a Warner Brothers thriller about Nazi fifth columnists released the week before Pearl Harbor, adds another layer to this wartime context.

133. Godard provided a surprisingly explicit description of this in 1992 (at a point when only *Toutes les histoires*, 1A, and *Une histoire seule*, 1B, were complete):

> It was the only moment where there was a true relationship, for one hears the voice of de Gaulle, who said that it was necessary to resist the enemy—he had a terrible formula, "This despicable, hated enemy, this dishonorable enemy"—and you see a shot of Siegfried in the forest [from *Siegfried*, Fritz Lang, 1924], trying to understand from where the voice is coming. Just before that, I put the last shot of *Les Dames du Bois de Boulogne*, which was shot in 1943. For me, the historical justice of

the montage is that it was a film of '43, which was finished under the British bombardments of '44, and which corresponds to a speech by de Gaulle from '43 to '44. It is a shot with Paul Bernard and Elina Labourdette, who is a courtesan or who is accused of being one, and who is therefore, in political terms, a *Munichoise* [a supporter of the 1938 Munich Agreements]. As France was a courtesan. Paul Bernard says: "Struggle!" and she responds, "I struggle." In this sense, it is a true political film, but nobody takes it in that sense today. (Albéra and Iampolski, "Le Briquet du Capitaine Cook," 17)

As both complex histories and as metaphors, Occupation and Resistance have assumed a central role in Godard's thought and work over the past several decades. After describing his childhood memories of the war period (in a family that he suggests was mildly collaborationist), he went so far as to claim that this was the defining experience of his life: "It is in this sense that I say [*Histoire(s) du cinéma*] is my story rather than the fact that I made a film in 1960 [*Breathless*]" (François Albéra, "Cultivons notre jardin," *CinémAction* 52 [July 1989], 87). In an interview with *Le Nouvel Observateur* two months earlier, Godard said, "I had to politicize during the war. My other family [his father's side] collaborated . . . or almost; like, say, Robert Brasillach [an author, and film historian, who was the only person to be executed entirely for his writings; a version of his final words is read out in *In Praise of Love*]. When he died, my grandfather was very moved" (Jean Daniel and Nicole Boulanger, "Week-end avec Godard," in Bergala, *Godard par Godard*, 2:176). Similar comments are made in the radio interview, "Le Bon Plaisir de Jean-Luc Godard" (in Bergala, *Godard par Godard*, 2:307).

Significantly, the wartime Resistance network in *In Praise of Love* is named Tristan and Isolde.

134. Mercadet and Perrot, "Le Télévision fabrique de l'oubli," 240. Perret's film is surprisingly reflexive for its period and depicts the attempt by doctors to construct a cinematic reenactment of the traumatic death of a woman's husband; she faints when the footage is projected for her, but when she awakens, her memory has returned. Godard uses the image of the woman fainting when encountering projections of her own suppressed past in *Toutes les histoires* (1A), immediately after a section in which the voices of de Gaulle and Hitler are interlaced, and then again during the discussion with Daney in *Seul le cinéma* (2A).

135. Godard is here alluding to a conversation between Vidor and Selznick that is mentioned in Vidor's autobiography *A Tree Is a Tree* (Hollywood, CA: Samuel French, 1981, 193). In the original text, Vidor refers to Joel McCrea rather than Tyrone Power.

136. In 1959, Godard described this scene using mythic language that resonates strongly with its use in *Histoire(s) du cinéma*: "In *The Searchers*, when John Wayne finds Natalie Wood and suddenly holds her up at arm's length, we pass from stylized gesture to feeling, from John Wayne suddenly petrified to Ulysses being reunited with Telemachus" (Jean-Luc Godard, "Supermann," translated by Tom Milne in Milne, *Godard on Godard*, 117). The scene is used to suggest similar ideas of mythic reconciliation in *Toutes les histoires* (1A), *Fatale beauté* (2B), *Le Contrôle de l'univers* (4A), and *Les Signes parmi nous* (4B); shots of riders on horseback entering the camp where Natalie Wood's character is being held captive were also used at the end of *La Monnaie de l'absolu* (3A). In three instances, shots from *The Searchers* are directly linked to the sensation of memory: right

after text reading "Time Regained" in *Fatale beauté* (2B); and in connection to Fernand Braudel's ideas of history in both *Le Contrôle de l'univers* (4A, where the scene is accompanied by an excerpt from the 1963 book *Le Monde actuel* in which Braudel speaks of "a recent past and a past more or less distant" intermingling in "the multiplicity of the present") and *Les Signes parmi nous* (4B, the same images appear onscreen when Godard says Braudel's name).

In the midst of the escalating war in Vietnam, Godard summarized his complex relationship to this part of Ford's film in terms that connect strongly with its appearance in *Toutes les histoires* (1A):

> Rewatched *Fallen Angel* [Otto Preminger, 1945]. Mystery and fascination of the American cinema. How can I hate [Robert] Mac Namara [*sic*] and adore [the Korean War drama *Take the High Ground*, Richard Brooks, 1953], hate John Wayne when he supports [Barry] Goldwater and love him tenderly when he suddenly takes Natalie Wood in his arms in the second to last reel of *The Searchers*? (Jean-Luc Godard, "Trois mille heures de cinéma," in Bergala, *Godard par Godard: Les Années Karina (1960 à 1967)*, 157)

137. Kristin Thompson has traced the origins of the widely repeated phrase back to Frank J. Marion (director of the Kalem film company), who in 1918 declared, "Trade follows the film. The projection of industrial pictures, backed by distribution of the product advertised, will create an immediate outlet for goods of American manufacture" (Kristin Thompson, *Exporting Entertainment: America in the World Film Market, 1907–1934* [London: British Film Institute, 1986], 122). Although the United States government did not begin considering these issues in earnest until Herbert Hoover became secretary of commerce in 1921, Janet Staiger has convincingly argued that the seeds of the "trade follows film" idea were being discussed in the trade press as early as 1911 (Janet Staiger, "Combination and Litigation: Structures of U.S. Film Distribution, 1896–1917," *Cinema Journal* 23, no. 2 [Winter 1983], 52).

In *JLG/JLG—Self-Portrait in December*, this same quote is attributed to the chimerical Senator MacBridge, when Godard's housemaid Cassandra says, "In 1914, Senator MacBridge declared to Congress, 'Trade follows films.' Only JLG noted this in his *Histoire(s) du cinéma*, 1A, where he recounts that Méliès had offices in New York and that they were stolen by Paramount during the Verdun offensive." Godard seems conscious of his manipulation of historical data here. In *In Praise of Love*, an American businessman attributes this to a different senator in a different year: "It's okay, sir, trade follows films. Senator McBride said that way back in 1910." As if in explanation, just before the businessman makes this declaration, the protagonist, quoting the most famous line in *The Man Who Shot Liberty Valance* (John Ford, 1962), says, "When the fact becomes legend, print the legend." Godard also playfully "corrects" his own attributions throughout *La Monnaie de l'absolu* (3A) by inserting a series of titles reading "error" (in this way, for example, he belatedly acknowledges that Carl Laemmle, not Erich Pommer, founded Universal Studios).

From 1957 to 1959, just before he began directing features, Godard worked in the publicity department of Fox's Paris office. As he described it later, "It was a way of being in Hollywood. Since Hollywood has always been like that, it may have spared me the desire to go there" (Godard, *True History*, 138).

138. The still image from *La Strada* recurs throughout the sequence (and a heavily pixelated clip from another part of the same film had been used earlier in *Toutes les histoires*, 1A). In the Montreal lectures, Godard makes similar arguments about post–World War II film policy, suggesting that cinema fully became an instrument of culture that "gives safe conduct to the rest of capitalist industry" when quotas were formalized through international agreements like the Marshall Plan and the Blum-Byrnes accords (Godard, *True History*, 336).

139. Godard quotes epigram 125 of *On Certainty* (he reads the same text in *JLG/JLG— Self-Portrait in December*).

140. "*Cabiria*: The Voyage to the End of Neorealism," in André Bazin, *What Is Cinema?*, translated by Hugh Gray, vol. 2 (Berkeley: University of California Press, 1971), 83–92. Bazin's article is focused on *Nights of Cabiria* (1957), but he discusses Fellini's development more generally, arguing that the director "drives on" past the "boundaries of realism" and "takes us beyond them" (88).

141. These same methods were tremendously influential on the New Wave, and Godard cements this association by titling the section of *Histoire(s) du cinéma* that immediately follows the Neorealist montage, *Une vague nouvelle* (3B).

142. None of these are translated or subtitled into French. Throughout the late work, and especially in *Histoire(s) du cinéma*, Godard puns in those European languages that were dominant in the 1930s and 1940s (French, German, English, Russian, Italian, and occasionally Spanish).

143. In the order cited, these are lines 648–649 of Ovid's *Cures for Love* (here rendered in the Peter Green translation from Ovid, *The Erotic Poems* [London: Penguin Classics, 1982], 258), lines 663–664 of Book XV of Ovid's *Metamorphoses* (here rendered in the Mary M. Innes translation [London: Penguin Classics, 1955], 352), and lines 770–772 from Book IV of Lucretius' *On the Nature of Things* (here rendered in the Ronald Melville translation [Oxford: Oxford World's Classics, 1997], 122). In an intriguing concordance with the work of Markopoulos, the passage from the *Metamorphoses* is about Asclepius and sleep healing, ideas that also resonate with the sleep/dream imagery in the Lucretius passage, both of which Godard clearly aligns with the nature of film viewing.

144. Élie Faure, *The Spirit of the Forms*, translated by Walter Pach (New York: Garden City, 1937), 425.

145. Truong, "Résistance de l'art," 444.

146. As Godard explained in a 1989 interview, "When I read in St. Paul that the image will come at the time of the resurrection, I thought: 'There, something that, as a director, I can begin to understand'" (Daniel and Boulanger, "Week-end avec Godard," 179). In an interview conducted while Godard was preparing *Hail Mary*, he argued that what truly interests him is not religion per se, but the structure of faith:

> Probably [this interest] came from my education, from the culture of my family. And then I discovered religion in politics, distorted in a way, but still religion. Actually, it's not religion that interests me, but faith. Like my own faith in movies. What is faith? Why do people have faith in themselves? And then you have to deal with the subject of faith. (Colin MacCabe, "'Politics Is Only a Movie Made in Russia,'" *American Film* 10 [June 1984], 34)

This phrase Godard attributes to St. Paul was used for the first time in *King Lear* (1987), and it appears (ironically) as onscreen text four times in *Une histoire seule* (1B).

147. Bachmann, "The Carrots Are Cooked," 132. Godard was referring to his planned use of the screen in *Hail Mary*, but the same metaphor had appeared in *Scénario du film Passion*. *Histoire(s) du cinéma* was being fully conceptualized at precisely this moment. Toward the end of *Toutes les histoires* (1A), just before his discussion of the neglect of cinema's documentary responsibilities, Godard uses similar language (which is reiterated again in *Les Enfants jouent à la Russie*):

> The *cinématographe* never meant to create an event, but a vision. Because the screen is the same white canvas as the Samaritan's shirt. What [August] Arnold and [Robert] Richter's cameras preserve, so as not to be undone by nightmares and dreams, will not be shown on a screen, but on a shroud.

Godard's comments are strongly informed by the critical work of André Bazin, who notes "in passing that the Holy Shroud of Turin combines the features alike of relic and photograph" in his most celebrated essay ("The Ontology of the Photographic Image"), and who observes that "the camera is there like the veil of Veronica pressed to the face of human suffering" in another (André Bazin, *What Is Cinema?*, translated by Hugh Gray, vol. 1 [Berkeley: University of California Press, 1967], 14, 163).

148. Roud, *A Passion for Films*, xxiv.

149. In a discussion with Manoel de Oliveira, Godard observed:

> Great artists, honest artists, make their first prayer and then there is the Mass, with the public, more or less faithful. The Americans have regulated the Mass. What is important for them in the Mass is the collection: a good Mass is the Mass where the church is full or the collection is big. (Lefort, "Godard et Oliveira," 267)

150. Discussion with Caroline Champetier at the Festival International du Film de La Roche-sur-Yon in October 2012, available online at http://www.fif-85.com/conference/caroline-champetier.html. Champetier also argued that Godard's approach to framing may be influenced by his near-sightedness, which causes one to "see volumes, not lines; one sees light before forms."

151. In a speech delivered at the Cinémathèque française on the occasion of a 1966 Lumière retrospective, Godard claims that he learned of this statement in school:

> At school I learned in school that Goethe on his death-bed called for more light. It was therefore only logical that some years later Auguste and Louis [Lumière] should invent what we know today as the cinema, and that they should have first demonstrated it in Paris, since that city had long borne their name ["city of light"]. (Jean-Luc Godard, "Thanks to Henri Langlois," translated by Tom Milne in Milne, *Godard on Godard*, 234)

In interviews, *Germany Year 90 Nine Zero*, and *Histoire(s) du cinéma*, Godard has argued that the German cinema is defined not by montage, but by light:

> The Germans, they were something else. They constructed sets first, then they arranged the light. They have always spoken of light: the "century of lights" [the eighteenth century], Goethe who asked for more light, they always start with light; they put the projector before it. (Albéra and Iampolski, "Le Briquet du Capitaine Cook," 19)

Daniel Morgan has suggested that the use of the phrase in *Germany Year 90 Nine Zero* may also be a reference to a story by Thomas Bernhard (Daniel Morgan, *Late Godard and the Possibilities of Cinema* [Berkeley: University of California Press, 2013], 239).

152. Toward the end of *Germany Year 90 Nine Zero*, protagonist Lemmy Caution says, "Even Philips globes could no longer light the streets of Karlgrüne [Karl Grüne was a German director in the Weimar period best known for the pioneering 1923 film *The Street*] with the brilliance of the lights of Karlheim [Karl Heim was a Lutheran theologian, whose student Dietrich Bonhoeffer is often said to have been involved in the failed assassination attempt on Hitler in 1944]." This comment comes almost immediately after a scene in which the phrase "the light that is always turned on" makes Caution think of Nazi resistant Sophie Scholl (a member of the "White Rose" who, as the narrator tells us, was "decapitated with an ax" for putting up posters). Earlier in the film, an unidentified female character alludes to Goethe's *Theory of Colors* (1810): "One thing was clear for Goethe: different shades of darkness can never produce light."

In *Histoire(s) du cinéma*, Godard frequently plays with the French titles of books and films—*Lumière d'août* (William Faulkner's *Light in August*, 1932), *Les Trois Lumières* (*Der müde Tod*, Fritz Lang, 1921), *Lumière d'été* (Jean Grémillon, 1944)—and in *Une histoire seule* (1B), he even puns on the name of the "two brothers"—"they could have been called lampshade [*abat-jour*], but they were called light [Lumière]." The sections of Broch's *The Death of Virgil* read out by François Périer (in *Une histoire seule*, 1B, and *Une vague nouvelle*, 3B) and by Sabine Azéma (in *Fatale beauté*, 2B) all concern light, as does the long text by Élie Faure in *Le Contrôle de l'univers* (4A).

153. Godard is, of course, alluding to Genesis 1:3: "And God said, Let there be light: and there was light." Godard used the same metaphor in a contemporaneous interview:

> The New Wave was . . . like the Christians who were converted without ever having seen either Jesus or St. Paul. . . . For us, the good cinema, the true, was that which could not be seen because it was not released. The other, one could see every Saturday, but the true, Griffith, Eisenstein . . . one had great difficulty seeing it; it was forbidden, not released, badly distributed. . . . Therefore, for us, it was the true cinema. One could swear allegiance. (Lavoignat and d'Yvoire, Le Cinéma," 336–337)

At the press conference for *Histoire(s) du cinéma* at the 1997 Cannes Film Festival, Godard made an even more direct declaration: "The cinema baptized me, in a certain fashion, with the real" (Amar, "Godard/Amar: Cannes 97," 422).

154. Devarrieux, "Se vivre, se voir," 162.

155. As Godard explained in 1989, "My grandfather was at the summit of Olympus, my father was a demi-god, and I was a boy. Now, I do not consider myself the equal of Hitchcock nor of Shakespeare. I am two levels below . . . sometimes making things that I find good also" (Daniel and Boulanger, "Week-end avec Godard," 174). Similar comments were made at the 1997 Cannes Film Festival press conference: "Someone spoke of John Ford and me. For me, John Ford is like Moses for an Israeli citizen. At his side, I remain small" (Amar, "Godard/Amar: Cannes 97," 418).

156. Godard was apparently inspired to make this connection by seeing a TV program entitled *La Leçon d'histoire de Fernand Braudel* (which originally aired in October 1985):

> When an emission called *La Leçon d'histoire de Fernand Braudel* showed on television, I recorded it and came upon a clip. [Braudel] spoke of the siege of Toulon. Therefore, in my *Histoire(s)*, you see a shot of Napoleon leaving on his ship in

the film of Gance and, at the same time, one says, "That's how we went to the Cinémathèque of Langlois." It seems to me better than saying, "One day, X or Y went to the Cinémathèque [at the] Avenue de Messine." (Bonnaud and Viviant, "La Légende du siècle," 25)

In *Les Enfants jouent à la Russie*, a video "annex" to *Histoire(s) du cinéma*, Godard stresses Gance's relationship to the Romantic tradition in a similar way by cutting from an image of one of the women signing "La Marseillaise" in *Napoléon* to an image of Delacroix's *Liberty Leading the People*. Godard reinforces this in *Liberté et patrie* by cutting from the same Delacroix painting to a superimposition of a shot from Gance's *Austerlitz* (1960) and a shot of Saint-Just (Jean-Pierre Léaud) reciting speeches from his own *Weekend*.

157. Godard frequently characterizes Gance as one of the key exceptions to the commercial dictates of French cinema (see, for example, de Baecque, "Entretien avec Jean-Luc Godard"). Although his portrait never appears in any of his films or videos, in the *Cinéma de notre temps* episode, *Le Dinosaure et le bébé: Dialogue en huit parties entre Fritz Lang et Jean-Luc Godard* (André S. Labarthe, 1967), Godard calls *Napoléon* one of the enduring masterpieces of cinema—along with Dreyer's *The Passion of Joan of Arc* (1928) and Lang's *M*—and says, "What strikes me about Abel Gance . . . is an incredible sense of youth, always being interested in things at the point at which they are born as if they are happening for the first time." Godard also declares that *Napoléon* is "one of the pictures I like best" in Youngblood, "No Difference," 41.

Photographs of Erich von Stroheim appear several times in *Toutes les histoires* (1A, a photograph of him at work appears after the MGM logo and precedes its pairing with the Moreau painting by several minutes), once in *Une histoire seule* (1B, where a photograph of von Stroheim at work on *Greed*, 1924, is irised in to a long extract from Orson Welles' similarly mutilated *The Magnificent Ambersons*, 1942), and once in *Les Signes parmi nous* (4B, a portrait photograph accompanied by an image of a hand). In *Toutes les histoires* (1A), shots taken from *Greed* and *The Merry Widow* (1925) are juxtaposed with images of producer Irving Thalberg, while an image of von Stroheim performing as a vicious Hun in the World War I propaganda film *The Heart of Humanity* (Allen Holubar, 1918) appears along with onscreen text declaring "trade follows films" and then again at the end of the section. Images or stills from films directed by von Stroheim also appear in *Une histoire seule* (1B, an image of Trina from *Greed*), *Seul le cinéma* (2A, an image of McTeague in *Greed* accompanies Godard declaration that there are at most ten truly great films; an image from *The Merry Widow* appears two minutes earlier), and *Les Signes parmi nous* (4B, images of von Stroheim's characters in *Foolish Wives*, 1922, and *The Wedding March*, 1928).

Near the end of *Une vague nouvelle* (3B), Godard declares, "Our sole error was to believe that it [the New Wave] was a beginning, that Stroheim had not been murdered, that [Jean] Vigo had not been covered in mud, that *The 400 Blows* [François Truffaut, 1959] would continue." He then interjects a clip, taken from an obscure 1932 film called *The Lost Squadron* (George Archainbaud), of von Stroheim, cast as a parody of himself, shouting, "I'm making this picture for the theater, not for the actors." This same section of *The Lost Squadron* also appears, as an ironic commentary on the position of cinema in the contemporary world, on a television screen in *Détective*. Godard identifies Thalberg's confrontation with von Stroheim over the making of *Greed* as a decisive shift in the history of cinema as an art:

And then there came a time when the big corporations—like the great feudal lords—commanded the great poets. As if Thalberg had spoken to Stroheim the same way Julius II spoke to Michelangelo: No, paint this angel's wings like this, not like that! (Daney, "Godard Makes [Hi]stories," 162)

158. Ovid, *Metamorphoses*, Book III, lines 259–315.

159. The Picasso etching originally appeared as plate three in Ovid, *Les Métamorphoses* (Lausanne: Albert Skira, 1931, 71). The 1545 painting, traditionally attributed to Jacopo Tintoretto, is held in London's National Gallery.

160. Jean Paladilhe and José Pierre, *Gustave Moreau*, translated by Bettina Wadia (New York: Praeger, 1972), 128.

161. Since Orpheus is traditionally considered the founder of the Dionysian (Bacchic) mysteries and the forty-third Orphic Hymn is dedicated to Semele, the image is also implicitly linked to the mythic exploration of memory and poetry throughout *Histoire(s) du cinéma*.

162. Images of the final scene of *Duel in the Sun* appear in *Une histoire seule* (1B), *Fatale beauté* (2B), and *Le Contrôle de l'univers* (4A). *Alexander Nevsky* shows up in *Toutes les histoires* (1A), *Une histoire seule* (1B), and *Le Contrôle de l'univers* (4A). Other films cited at least this frequently include *Battleship Potemkin*, *The Searchers*, *M*, *Metropolis* (Fritz Lang, 1927), and *Mr. Arkadin*. Godard also uses particular sounds to link films together; for example, the sound of a crow recurs frequently in *King Lear* and also appears several times, as a sort of indirect authorial signature, in *Nouvelle vague* and *Une histoire seule* (1B).

163. In addition to praising it as a model of expressionism, Tillich also links it to El Greco's *Crucifixion* (1596–1600), "an expression of the esthetic form of the counter-reformation" (Michael Palmer, ed., *Paul Tillich: Writings in the Philosophy of Culture* [Berlin: Walter de Gruyter, 1990], 277). Karl Barth refers to the *Isenheim Altarpiece* repeatedly (see, for example, his discussion of the hand of John the Baptist in *The Word of God and the Word of Man* [Boston: Pilgrim Press, 1928], 65–76), and his various discussions of the work are the focus of an entire German-language book: Reiner Marquard, *Karl Barth und der Isenheimer Altar* (Stuttgart: Calwer Verlag, 1995).

Godard has mentioned in several interviews that, on his mother's side, he belongs to "a true Protestant tribe, the Monods" (Daniel and Boulanger, "Week-end avec Godard," 175). However, while he "had a Protestant education, it didn't take," and what fascinates him within Christianity is more in line with Catholicism, in particular its tradition of image-making (Godard, *The Future(s) of Film*, 34):

> I am Franco-Swiss. I am from a Protestant family, and it is true that I am always surprised by the ornaments in Catholic churches. . . . It took me a long time to return, in my way, to what I had learned in Sunday School. (Païni and Scarpetta, "Jean-Luc Godard," 16)

Godard also described himself as a nonpracticing Protestant interested in Catholicism in Katherine Dieckmann, "Godard in His 'Fifth Period:' An Interview," in Sterritt, *Jean-Luc Godard Interviews*, 169. In the same interview, Godard explains that he used Bach throughout *Hail Mary* because "historically Bach was the music of Martin Luther. And as I was saying before, Martin Luther was attacking the Catholic church, specifically the way the Catholic church makes images" (171). In the conversation with Daney at the beginning of *Seul le cinéma* (2A), Godard says he is "like a Calvinist or a Lutheran . . . always guilty or cursed" (the reference to Calvin and Luther is elided from the very incomplete English subtitles in the Gaumont DVD release of *Histoire(s) du cinéma*). These ideas are explored in *Hélas pour moi*.

Given Godard's historical concerns, it may also be relevant that the monastery housing the altarpiece is located in the frequently contested French-German border region of Alsace.

164. Significantly, this image first appears in *La Monnaie de l'absolu* (3A), in a superimposition with the title of the work, *Histoire(s) du cinéma*. It reappears in *The Old Place, The Origins of the 21st Century*, and *Notre musique*. Other scenes from the *Isenheim Altarpiece* appear in *Toutes les histoire(s)* (1A, the Madonna and Child from the "Concert of Angels and Nativity" panel) and *La Monnaie de l'absolu* (3A, "The Temptation of St. Anthony"). Sections of the "Temptation of St. Anthony" panel appear twice in *Germany Year 90 Nine Zero* (once over the cover of a French translation of Hans Jakob Christoffel von Grimmelshausen's picaresque novel *The Adventures of Simplicius Simplicissimus*, 1668), as does the Crucifixion from Grünewald's *Tauberbischofsheim Altarpiece* (1523–1525).

165. 2 Corinthians 3:6. As Godard explained to Youssef Ishaghpour:

Texts come from longer ago, and, anyway, the first texts were about money, the earliest tablets . . . it was accountancy. By contrast, the earliest images had nothing to do with bookkeeping. . . . An image is peaceable. An image of the Virgin and her baby on a donkey doesn't cause a war; its interpretation by a text is what will lead to war and cause Luther's soldiers to go and deface Raphael canvases. I have a strong feeling that the image enables us to talk less and say more. (Godard and Ishaghpour, *Cinema*, 103)

166. Mercadet and Perrot, "Le Télévision fabrique de l'oubli," 238. Godard makes similar comments in other interviews:

My thesis is that the speech of silent films was greater than the speech of talkies. It was therefore necessary to reduce them. This happened at the time of the New Deal, of Roosevelt, and of Hitler. From the first projections of silent film, talkies were ready. Gaumont had its equipment. But the public chose silence over speech. In Paris, at the first projections of talkies, nobody came. (Péretié, "Quand Godard raconte," 52)

Cinema started out silent, and was very successful. Sound, just like color, had always been an option. They had their own processes, even if they weren't technically perfect—which they still aren't. . . . But they didn't want sound. [Jean] Mitry and [Georges] Sadoul described how [Thomas] Edison came to demonstrate his talking cinema, but it was already under way at the Grand Café [where the Lumières showed their first films]. First, there were twelve disciples, then thirty, forty, then four hundred million. It wasn't until *later* that we wanted talkies, which is, moreover, fairly well explained by social circumstances. Talkies came at a historical moment, when Roosevelt spoke up, democracy spoke up and said: New Deal. And after a few stock market crashes, Fascism spoke up, and Hitler said what he said. It's "saying," but a *wrong* saying that took over. (Daney, "Godard Makes [Hi]stories," 165)

Similar sentiments are expressed in *Notre musique*, when a character says that in 1936 "the field of text had already covered the field of vision." In the Montreal lectures, Godard suggested that silent cinema opened up the possibility of using speech differently: "If I look at my own trajectory I have the impression that I am trying to go back through silent film in order to find my own talking film style" (Godard, *True History*, 333).

167. These connections did not escape the eye of Joseph Goebbels. The symphonic version was premiered by conductor Wilhelm Furtwängler in Berlin in February 1934 to much controversy. By the end of that year, Hindemith's works had been banned. Furtwängler wrote a public declaration of support in the November 25, 1934, edition of the *Deutsche allgemeine Zeitung*, partially with the hopes of making a public performance of the operatic version possible in early 1935, but the work was not premiered until 1938 (in Zurich). Despite eventually signing a personal loyalty oath to Hitler, Hindemith was included in the "degenerate music" exhibition of 1938 and eventually fled to the United States, where he took up a professorship at Yale University. A detailed account of the production and Nazi-era exhibition history of *Mathis der Maler* can be found in Michael Kater, *Composers of the Nazi Era* (Oxford: Oxford University Press, 2000), 34–43. This complicated history—shared by many of the films, artworks, texts, and pieces of music cited in *Histoire(s) du cinéma* (Godard's frequent use of the opening movement of Arthur Honegger's 1946 Third Symphony, for example, has comparable historical weight)—was surely one of the factors motivating Godard to employ the piece as he does.

168. Godard uses the third, and final, movement of the *Mathis der Maler* symphony in *Toutes les histoires* (1A, accompanying the montage fusion of *Germany Year Zero*, *La Strada*, and Wittgenstein's *On Certainty*), *Une histoire seule* (1B; the movement is used repeatedly here, first with images of Cocteau's *Orpheus* and then with extracts from *M*), and *La Monnaie de l'absolu* (3A, where it is used ironically in connection with a discussion of Selznick's memo on *Bird of Paradise*). All three movements from the symphony are used in *Nouvelle vague*, and the implied allusions to the *Isenheim Altarpiece* are enriched when shoelaces are tied at the very end of the film in an iconographic nod to St. John the Baptist (the reference is in all four Gospels: Matthew 3:11, Mark 1:7, Luke 3:16, and John 1:27).

169. Robert Bresson, *Notes on the Cinematographer*, translated by Jonathan Griffin (Copenhagen: Green Integer, 1997), 44. Bresson is here alluding to the ideas of a "hidden" God developed throughout Blaise Pascal's *Pensées* (the model for his epigrammatic "Notes"), particularly in the fragments numbered 13, 275, 644, and 690 in the Philippe Sellier edition.

170. Ludwig Wittgenstein, *Culture and Value*, edited by G. H. von Wright and translated by Peter Winch (Chicago: University of Chicago Press, 1980), 32e.

171. Godard has mentioned this same passage in interviews: "This philosophic base, which is that cinema is that which cannot be seen, is anchored in an honest and secular Christianity. This made me think of that phrase of Wittgenstein: 'You have there a story; you should believe it, whatever happens'" (Debray, "Jean-Luc Godard rencontre Régis Debray," 429).

172. *M* is universally recognized as one of the definitive early sound films, and Godard's use of it here reinforces the implicit subtext that sound introduced a new,

linguistic divisiveness into cinema (which, Godard suggests, had in the silent era been characterized by an image-driven universality).

173. *The Trial of Joan of Arc* appears in *Une histoire seule* (1B), *Seul le cinéma* (2A), *Fatale beauté* (2B), *Une vague nouvelle* (3B), and *Les Signes parmi nous* (4B). By contrast, images or clips from more well-known Bresson films like *Pickpocket* (1959) and *Au hasard Balthazar* (1966) appear only once (in *Une histoire seule*, 1B, and *Seul le cinéma*, 2A, respectively).

174. The final section of *Ordet* plays a similar role in three post-*Histoire(s) du cinéma* works: *The Origins of the 21st Century* (a clip of the young girl standing with Johannes appears near the midpoint of the film, with overlay text reading "Rise, I command"), *Liberté et patrie* (a still image of Inger's body during her funeral appears toward the end), and *Notre musique* (a still reproduction of *Ordet*'s final shot—the embrace of the resurrected Inger and her husband Mikkel—is visible on a wall just after Godard's lecture to the students in Sarajevo ends).

175. Godard, "Le Montage," 246.

176. Wittgenstein, *Culture and Value*, 50e (dated 1946). The category of gesture has special importance for Wittgenstein. "Not every purposive movement of the human body is a gesture," he writes; it must be something that "insinuates itself into my life" and is then adopted as one's own (42e, 1942; 73e, 1948).

177. Although these connections are overt with the Caravaggio and *The Anatomy Lesson of Dr. Deyman*, which shows the action of surgical slicing far more explicitly than Rembrandt's famous *Anatomy Lesson of Dr. Nicolaes Tulp* (1632), they are also present in the more obscure painting depicting the third of Daniel's five visions. Daniel's third vision finds him by the Ulai River watching an allegorical confrontation between a ram with two horns and a he-goat who "was moved with choler against him, and smote the ram, and brake his two horns" (Daniel 8:7). Rembrandt's painting shows Gabriel explaining this vision to Daniel, who looks at the he-goat from the other side of a darkened ravine that bisects the painting through the middle; characteristically, Godard crops the painting to emphasize the hand gestures of the two figures, leaving the object of the vision entirely offscreen.

178. Godard, *True History*, 353. He used similar language when distinguishing his creative practice from media-generated auteurship in 1992: "It's society, the producer, the distributor. They're the auteur. I am just the worker, the builder" (Riding, "What's in a Name," 11).

179. In a 1989 lecture, for example, Godard observes, "At the moment [of cutting], there is an ensemble of things that is closer to architecture or to an art that I have never understood and that I am only beginning to understand: sculpture" (Godard, "Le Montage," 242). In an interview several years earlier, Godard declared that he used only two tracks of sound because he has "two hands to manipulate them . . . if I had only one arm, maybe I'd have only a single sound track" (Bachmann, "The Carrots Are Cooked," 134).

180. Beauviala and Godard, "Genesis of a Camera," 141. It is likely that the availability of palm-sized 3D cameras helped to inspire Godard's move into 3D filmmaking (with *Les Trois Désastres*, 2013).

181. The Swiss writer Denis de Rougemont—most famous for his 1938 book *Love in the Western World* and for his involvement with the "nonconformist" personalist movement of the interwar period—went to Germany to teach in 1935 and became an ardent anti-Nazi (he escaped to the United States once the war began). After the war, he founded the Centre

européen de la culture (CEC), which he ran until his death in 1985 and which became one of the strongest advocates for a left-leaning pan-Europeanism unified not by technical-industrial progress but by a shared culture. De Rougemont saw himself as continuing the ideas developed at the first 1926 Pan-European Congress in Vienna and strongly argued against nation-states and in favor of an organization of federated, regional enti-ties. Although the post-Maoist Godard of the 1980s and 1990s—who has frequently used the statement "The dream of the state is to be one, the dream of individuals is to be two" in his films—would reject the quasi-imperial underpinnings of some of de Rougemont's proposals, he shares his utopian conception of a Europe defined, above all, by its cultural heritage ("Apart from her culture, Europe is just a promontory of Asia, with few natu-ral resources," de Rougemont argued in *The Meaning of Europe* [London: Sidgwick and Jackson, 1963], 54).

182. Malraux, *The Voices of Silence*, 642. Similar language was used at the end of *The Creative Act*, the second volume of *The Psychology of Art*, but the final sentence ends with the less theologically charged phrase, "forms which testify to the might and the honour of being a man" (translated by Stuart Gilbert [New York: Pantheon, 1949], 220).

183. Godard, "Le Montage," 242.

184. Although Godard had utilized shifts in focus for artistic purposes in earlier films (such as *Weekend*), they were used much more markedly in the films made after *Histoire(s) du cinéma* commenced. They are particularly noticeable in *Hélas pour moi*, which, like *Nouvelle vague* and *In Praise of Love*, also uses high-contrast imagery shot using natural light sources to emphasize the act of perception and to set different zones of space in relation to one another. The frequent use of multiplanar composition-in-depth—which is adopted even in lateral tracking shots like the long take accompanied by Arnold Schoenberg's *Transfigured Night* (opus 6, 1899) in *Nouvelle vague*—makes shots focusing on hands stand out more distinctly.

185. Godard frequently plays with the theological idea of a Trinity, or as he puts it, "the three persons" in his late work. In *The Old Place*, for example, Godard says, "That reminds me of my old philosophy teacher, Mr. Brunschwig: 'One is in the other and the other is in the one, and those are the three persons.'" Variations of this line are used in *Hélas pour moi* and *Film socialisme*.

186. Martin Heidegger, "What Are Poets For?" in *Poetry, Language, Thought*, translated by Alfred Hofstadter (New York: Harper Perennial, 2001), 92. In France, this essay was first published in a 1950 collection of Heidegger's writings called *Chemins qui ne mènent nulle part*, the title of which Godard reads out three times in *Toutes les histoires* (1A). This title also appears as intertitle text in *Germany Year 90 Nine Zero* and on the page of a note-book in *JLG/JLG—Self-Portrait in December*. Excerpts from "What Are Poets For?" were used earlier in *Une histoire seule* (1B), and when the words "not only have the gods and the god fled, but the divine radiance has become extinguished" are spoken, intertitles read-ing "*le cinéma*" and then "Hail Mary" appear, a triple reference to Godard's 1985 film of the same name, Mary Pickford, and traditional Christian prayers ("What Are Poets For?" 89). In this context, it should also be noted that the woman reading out the text, Maria Casarès, is best known for her roles in Bresson's *Les Dames du Bois de Boulogne*, Marcel Carné's *Children of Paradise* (1945), and Cocteau's *Orpheus*.

In "What are Poets For?" Heidegger contrasts the authentically disclosed Being artic-ulated by Friedrich Hölderlin with the struggle by poets like Rilke to recapture that sen-sibility in works such as the *Sonnets to Orpheus* (1922). For Heidegger:

"The poet in the time of the world's night utters the holy," while "poets in a destitute time" must especially gather in poetry the nature of poetry. Where that happens we may assume poets to exist who are on the way to the destiny of the world's age. We others must learn to listen to what *these* poets say—assuming that, in regard to the time that conceals Being because it shelters it, we do not deceive ourselves through reckoning time merely in terms of that which is by dissecting that which is. (92)

Godard consciously assumes this prophetic role in *Histoire(s) du cinéma*, struggling to gather "the nature of [cinema]" within his work in an attempt to recapture its lost purity, which is presumably why this text is invoked as frequently as it is. As he explained in 1988:

I am sure that Fra Angelico or Giotto did not say, "Yes, but painting . . ." However, with respect to Delacroix, they said: "painting." The painter thinks that he is the representative of painting, that he is an extraterrestrial, that he is painting in the form of the painter. . . . [After the interviewers argue that artists like this "save" painting, Godard continues:] It is a sentiment that Manet had, not Renoir because he was very open, that Nicolas de Staël, Matisse, and [Georges] Braque had, that Bresson had always. Me also, completely. (Bergala and Toubiana, "L'Art de (dé) montrer," 135)

According to Godard, these same ideas also informed *Hélas pour moi*, an ambitious attempt to rework the legend of Alcmene and Amphitryon (the subject of important plays by Heinrich von Kleist—*Amphitryon*, 1807—and Jean Giraudoux—*Amphitryon 38*, 1929—as well as a poem by Leopardi) in a modern context that was completely restructured after star Gérard Depardieu walked off the set:

[*Hélas pour moi*] was made on the absence of God. If the film had succeeded, one would have realized that God was not there. There was this idea, very Heideggerian (when he speaks of Hölderlin), that the gods have fled and that in times of distress, the poets should show the traces of the vanished gods. Then the inverse happened: it became a film on the presence of God. ("Le Bon Plaisir," 321)

187. In his original outline for *Nouvelle vague*, Godard aligns these two drownings with a shift from the Old to the New Testament:

In a first time—the Old Testament—a human being (a man) is saved from drowning by another human being (a woman).

In a second time—the New Testament—a human being (a woman) (the same) is saved from drowning by a human being (the man) (another). (Jean-Luc Godard, "*Nouvelle vague*, genèse," in Bergala, *Godard par Godard*, 2:189)

188. The onscreen text alludes to a scene in the Acts of the Apostles in which a prayer in prison leads to an earthquake, but the prisoners stay. St. Paul reassures their jailor: "Do thyself no harm: for we are all here" (Acts 16:28). The same text appears in *Germany Year 90 Nine Zero*, and Anne-Marie Miéville used the phrase as the title of a film she made in 1997, with Godard cast in a comic role (*Nous sommes tous encore ici*, 1997).

189. Carl Theodor Dreyer, "The Real Talking Film," in *Dreyer in Double Reflection*, edited by Donald Skoller (New York: Da Capo Press, 1973), 53.

190. Precisely because they were used so rarely, Godard attributes great power to the use of superimpositions in Classical Hollywood films:

> Personally, I loved superimpositions, especially in the work of Stevens, who made very long ones in *A Place in the Sun*. When you make them into a principal material, they permit you to go directly from one thing to another without forgetting where you have come from and without realizing where you are going, knowing that in the middle or three-quarters of the way through, the unexpected may arise. (Ciment and Goudet, "Entretien Jean-Luc Godard," 52)

Godard also partially blames the New Wave, and especially the great success of *Breathless*, with bringing this form of superimposition to an end:

> Around the time of *Breathless*, I helped put an end to superimpositions in film narrative. [French film lab] GTC had a special department at the time. Twenty years later, someone stopped me in the street to say, "You put me out of work." I've always felt a certain debt. (Godard, *The Future(s) of Film*, 25)

Virtually identical comments are in Albéra, "Cultivons notre jardin," 88.

191. Alain Bergala and Serge Toubiana, "Parler du manque," in Bergala, *Godard par Godard*, 2:361–364.

192. Ibid., 360.

193. Since Hugo's four-hundred-page *Cromwell* from 1827 was considered unperformable in the nineteenth century, it was the premiere of his follow-up, *Hernani*, that announced the emergence of Romantic drama to the French public. As Peter Brooks put it:

> The premiere of *Hernani*, on 25 February 1830, marked the public triumph of Romantic doctrine: it planted the Romantic banner in the bastion of institutional artistic conservatism, the Comédie-Française. So great was the prestige of the theater, as a public, sociable genre and institution, one that had been a center of life for good society for two centuries, that a victory in its most illustrious house carried great symbolic value. (Peter Brooks, "1830: An Oedipal Crisis," in *A New History of French Literature*, edited by Denis Hollier [Cambridge, MA: Harvard University Press, 1989], 651)

Although it is unclear how invested Godard is in Hugo's plays, they are certainly relevant to the arguments developed in *Histoire(s) du cinéma* insofar as they privilege sensations developed through primarily visual means (costuming, set design, gestures) over traditional dramaturgy.

194. Bonnaud and Viviant, "La Légende du siècle," 28. Most of the Hitchcock films excerpted in *Histoire(s) du cinéma* are made in the transitional period immediately preceding or just following the explosion of New Wave styles around 1960. In a press conference for a special screening of *JLG/JLG—Self-Portrait in December*, Godard stressed that it was this period of Hitchcock's career that impressed him most:

> Hitchcock is the only one who succeeded in controlling the universe. That is what I say in my second to last *Histoire(s) du cinéma*. . . . There was a period of ten years, the time of *Rear Window* (1954) and *Psycho* (1960), of a richness that one could compare to that of certain painters of the Renaissance, who did not have that sort of range, excepting possibly Michelangelo. . . . It is something very unique, not a

film every ten years like Dreyer, not impossibilities like Eisenstein who could make only bits of things. (Jean-Luc Godard, "J'ai toujours pensé que le cinéma était un instrument de pensée," in Bergala, *Godard par Godard*, 2:304)

195. Chateaubriand, *The Memoirs of François René, Vicomte de Chateaubriand*, translated by Alexander Teixera de Mattos (New York: G.P. Putnam's Sons, 1902), 2:154. Another section from Chateaubriand's memoirs is quoted at the end of *In Praise of Love*: "Thus is nought left me save pictures of what has passed so quickly: I shall descend to the Elysian Fields with more shades than mortal man has ever taken with him" (1:245). Significantly, this passage implicitly refers to the underworld encounters of Book XI of *The Odyssey* and Book VI of Virgil's *The Aeneid*.

Chateaubriand's most celebrated book, *The Genius of Christianity* (1802), was a key progenitor of French Romanticism.

196. Marcel Proust, *In Search of Lost Time*, vol. 6, *Time Regained*, translated by Andreas Mayor and Terence Kilmartin (New York: Modern Library, 1999), 261.

197. July, "Alfred Hitchcock est mort," 181. In *Le Contrôle de l'univers* (4A), Godard includes an excerpt in which Hitchcock talks about the hypnotic power of montage. Godard responds, in voiceover, "Images first, but the ones St. Paul mentions, which are a death, therefore a resurrection." Godard had been discussing the relationship between images and "Gutenberg, what he invented" since at least the late 1960s (transcription of an interview shot for ORTF on March 19, 1969, included in the Jean-Luc Godard files held in the Celeste Bartos Film Study Center of the Museum of Modern Art). In 2000, he argued that despite the rhetoric of the digital, the contemporary world remains defined by the "Gutenberg" paradigm:

Today's cinema is a script-oriented cinema. Since Gutenberg, the text has triumphed. There was a long struggle, marriage or liaison between painting and text. Then the text carried the day. Film is the last art in the pictorial tradition. People talk a lot about images but there is only the text nowadays. On computers, there is more text than image. It's advertising copy and commentary that dominate. (Godard, *The Future(s) of Film*, 19)

198. Malraux, *The Voices of Silence*, 516.

199. Jean-Luc Godard, "Textes pour servir aux *Histoire(s) du cinéma*," in Bergala, *Godard par Godard*, 2:183–184.

200. André Malraux, "Sketch for a Psychology of the Moving Pictures," in *Reflections on Art*, edited by Susanne Langer (Oxford: Oxford University Press, 1958), 326. This same text was included on the wall of the first room ("Salle 1: Le Mythe") of Godard's 2006 exhibition at the Centre Georges Pompidou, *Voyage(s) en utopie, Jean-Luc Godard, 1946–2006: À la recherche d'un théorème perdu*.

201. This statement in *Toutes les histoires* (1A) is a slight variation on another passage from Malraux's text: "The myth begins with [British detective] Sexton Blake, but it ends with Christ" (Malraux, "Sketch for a Psychology," 327).

202. In his discussion with Régis Debray, Godard uses cathedral imagery to link art and religion, implicitly tying both to his idea of the collective, communal experience of cinema:

I said that art was the morality of the West. Today, art has disappeared, because this notion of art has disappeared. The notion of religion, very close to art (that of the cathedrals, that of Michelangelo), is no more. The dead become something else. (Debray, "Jean-Luc Godard rencontre Régis Debray," 423–424)

203. Ciment and Goudet, "Entretien Jean-Luc Godard," 57.

204. Godard continues, by repeating the first line of *Swann's Way* (the first volume in Marcel Proust's *In Search of Lost Time*, 1927): "For a long time, I went to bed early, for a long time I went to bed early, I say that and suddenly Albertine disappears and time is regained [a reference to the title of the last volume of Proust's seven-volume work]."

205. The phrase "*Histoire(s) du cinémoi*" appears in *Fatale beauté* (2B), but Godard first highlights the autobiographical subtext of the work at the very beginning of *Une histoire seule* (1B), when, just before the dedication, he says, "But concerning me, first of all, concerning my story, what do I have to do with all of this? All this light?" An intertitle reading "*c'est moi*" appears in the middle of the discussion with Daney at the beginning of *Seul le cinéma* (2A), just after Godard announces that literary historians would concentrate on only a few authors—"Homer, Cervantes, Joyce"—one of several acknowledgments of his artistic lineage.

This element of Godard's work seems to have surprised some of his critics. In 1992, Jacques Aumont wrote, "Godard differs from his contemporaries in his extraordinary lack of pretensions to the autobiographical, in fact, in a lack of any noticeable interest in himself. He is not his own biographer, either in the here and now or in the long term" (Jacques Aumont, "The Medium," in Bellour and Bandy, *Jean-Luc Godard*, 206). Although neither project came to fruition, Godard had attempted to publicly analyze himself in two projects of the mid-1970s that anticipate certain elements of *Histoire(s) du cinéma*. In January 1973, Godard completed a forty-nine-page proposal for *Moi, je*, which would have been divided into two fifty-six-minute parts entitled *Moi, je suis un homme politique* and *Moi, je suis une machine*. Structured around the juxtaposition of different materials organized according to the principles of dialectical montage, *Moi, je* was conceived as an exploration of a politically and historically aware form of subjectivity, one that could

> dare to say "I," dare to say that the phantoms that one sees on the screen are mine, dare to say in '41 that eighty million of my countrymen loved *juif-susser* Hitler [a reference to the French title of the notorious Nazi propaganda film *Jüd Suss*, Veit Harlan, 1940], dare to say in '72 that the Americans force the Vietnamese to die for nothing . . . because I am connected to the representation of these phantoms, because there is a direct relationship between "I" and the "it" which is objective, because "I" am another . . . I can finally really criticize this "it" of which I am a part. (Pages -6 and -6′ in Godard, "*Moi, je*, projet de film," 212–213)

Some of these same ideas were worked out in *Numéro deux* two years later. In the Montreal lectures, Godard also mentions trying to make a film called *Mes films* that would "simply talk about the films I haven't made and will never make" (Godard, *True History*, 402). Godard claims to have worked on this project for three years and explains that he abandoned it because "it had become a 200,000-hour film and there wasn't enough time left in my life to shoot it" (202).

206. In "Le Bon Plaisir de Jean-Luc Godard," Godard said that he "would prefer that *JLG/JLG* be shown at the same time as *Histoire(s) du cinéma*. One could see at the same time the work and one way that the author has signed the work, by making [his] self-portrait" (312).

207. Godard insists on the distinction between self-portrait and autobiography late in the film, declaring that this is an "*Autoportrait, pas autobiographie*," before moving to shots of himself playing tennis (a frequent metaphor for montage in the late work). Godard elaborates in an interview:

That's why I call *JLG/JLG Self Portrait.* A self-portrait has no "me." It has a meaning only in painting, nowhere else. I was interested to find out if it could exist in [motion] pictures and not only in paintings. . . . A self-portrait is only a face in a mirror basically, or in the camera. (Smith, "Jean-Luc Godard," 183)

208. As the narration continues, Godard describes the boy in the photograph as follows:

He possessed hope, but the boy did not know that what counts is to know by whom he was possessed, what dark powers were entitled to lay claim to him. Usually, it begins like this: death arrives, then we put on mourning. I don't know exactly why, but I did the opposite [A title appears reading "Dark Room"]. I first put on mourning, but death never came, neither on the streets of Paris nor on the shores of Lake Geneva. Even later, I didn't have to go to any far off Samarkand. The obstacles came themselves: that is, life . . . which may explain my distressed look in the picture. Not because I was bent out of shape, but because I had bent the rules at some imagined Last Judgment. The sole purpose of this film should be to determine that.

Godard may have adopted an oblique approach to self-portraiture to help direct the viewer's attention to the work itself. His celebrity status in France has made it possible to secure financing for his films, but it has also prevented full engagement with them. Godard has repeatedly expressed frustration at the fact that "one speaks of Godard, but not of his films!" and in both *JLG/JLG—Self-Portrait in December* and *Histoire(s) du cinéma*, he remains focused on the ways in which selfhood is shaped by external relationships and manifested through creative work, rather than on a notion of the artist as a wholly autonomous entity (Daniel and Boulanger, "Week-end avec Godard," 178):

That which interests me is more to speak of things and only after of the person who made them. This is what I did a bit in the last part of *Histoire(s)*: I could then say, "I was that man." I could not have said it at the beginning; I did not know it. It was necessary to make the work first. (Bergala, "Une boucle bouclée," 14)

In the dialogue with Serge Daney at the beginning of *Seul le cinéma* (2A), Godard similarly observes, "Had it not been for cinema, I wouldn't have known that I had a history of my own. It was the only way [to understand that], and I owe it to the cinema."

209. "History, Stephen [Dedalus] said, is a nightmare from which I am trying to awake" (James Joyce, *Ulysses*, edited by Hans Walter Gabler [New York: Vintage Books, 1986], 28).

210. Godard's rhetorical use of *toi* evokes the final section ("For Thine is the Kingdom") of T. S. Eliot's 1925 poem, "The Hollow Men."

211. De Baecque, "Entretien avec Jean-Luc Godard."

212. The fact that this footage depicts the French Liberation, the same events linked (nearly two hours earlier) to the self-portrait in *La Monnaie de l'absolu* (3A), further strengthens this echoing effect. Footage of and/or audio extracts of speeches by de Gaulle also appear in *Toutes les histoires* (1A), *La Monnaie de l'absolu* (3A), *Le Contrôle de l'univers* (4A), and *Les Signes parmi nous* (4B).

213. Ovid *Metamorphoses*, Book XV, lines 871–879 (these are the final lines of the work, here rendered in the Mary M. Innes translation, 357). Interestingly, in a phone conversation about the difference between culture and art earlier in the film, Godard said, "If only I knew Latin to make everything clear." In an interview for the fiftieth anniversary

issue of *Télérama*, Godard claims that, in his youth, he received Latin lessons from family friend Paul Valéry (quoted in Brody, *Everything Is Cinema*, 5).

214. The relevant passage is:

> Man of Troy, the descent to the Underworld is easy.
> Night and day the gates of shadowy Death stand open wide,
> but to retrace your steps, to climb back to the air—
> there the struggle, there the labor lies. (Virgil, *The Aeneid*, translated
> by Robert Fagles [London: Penguin Classics, 2006], Book VI, lines 149–152)

The final section of this text is quoted even before the first image, a still from *Rear Window* with protagonist L. B. Jeffries looking out his window with a camera, appears.

Virgil's "*omnia vincit amor*" ("Love conquers all," Eclogue X, line 69) had been used as the penultimate title card of *Nouvelle vague*, the final one reading "*consummatum est*" (the Latin version of "It is finished," the last words of Jesus in John 19:30). In *Germany Year 90 Nine Zero*, released the following year, Godard includes a Latin title reading "If I cannot sway the heavens, I will wake the powers of hell," a line from *The Aeneid* (Book VII, line 365, Fagles translation) that was also famously quoted on the first page of Sigmund Freud's *The Interpretation of Dreams* (1899).

In addition to Virgil, Ovid is also cited in *Histoire(s) du cinéma*: at the very end of *Seul le cinéma* (2A), after the credits are finished, the following Latin words appear onscreen: "*Aurea prima sata est aetas, quae vindice nullo, sponte sua, sine lege fidem rectumque colebat.*" This is a quote from the *Metamorphoses*: "In the beginning was the Golden Age, when men of their own accord, without threat of punishment, without laws, maintained good faith and did what was right" (Book I, lines 89–90, here rendered in the Mary M. Innes translation, 31).

Godard has continued to cite passages in Latin in more recent films, including title cards that read "*clarum per obscurum*" ("the clear by the obscure") and "*abii ne viderem*" ("I turned away so as not to see") in *Film socialisme*. The latter is the title of a piece of music by the contemporary composer Giya Kancheli that was written during the 1991–1992 Georgian civil war, released by ECM in 2000, and used in several Godard works (including *Le Contrôle de l'univers*, 4A).

215. After traveling to "the Kimmerian lands, and peopled cities / Covered with close-webbed mist, unpierced ever / With glitter of sun-rays / Nor with stars stretched, nor looking back from heaven / Swartest night stretched over wretched men there," Odysseus' crew begins performing rites to the god of Hades, "Pluto the strong," while the hero pulls out his sword and sits "to keep off the impetuous impotent dead / Till I should hear Tiresias" (Pound, *Cantos*, Canto I, 3–4). It is then, poised in between the dead civilization they have just past (the Kimmerian lands) and the home to which they yearn to return (Ithaca) that Odysseus encounters Elpenor in the passage read out in *Histoire(s) du cinéma*.

216. Odysseus speaks with "Tiresias Thebae" in Canto I (Pound, *Cantos*, 4) and Pound refers to having "speech with Tiresias, Thebae" in Canto LXXXIII (553).

217. The implied connection of Odysseus' encounter with Elpenor and the neglect of the cinema is heightened by its proximity (less than fifteen minutes earlier in the same section) to Godard's recounting of Charles F. Ramuz's story of a colporteur who arrived in a village along the Rhône and befriended everyone "because he knew how to tell a thousand and one stories; and now a storm breaks and lasts for days and days and the peddler says, 'This is the end of the world.' But the sun finally came out and the

inhabitants of the village chased the poor colporteur out. The colporteur, it was the cinema." Significantly, the colporteur in Ramuz's novel *Les Signes parmi nous* (1919), which Godard used as the title for this section of *Histoire(s) du cinéma*, sold religious books and images. The later novel *La Séparation des races* (1922) includes a colporteur who provides the main link between two communities divided along religious and ethnic lines. It was the basis for the most important Swiss film made before World War II, *Rapt* (Dimitri Kirsanoff, 1934).

Godard at one point intended to dedicate the final section of his work, then identified as 5B, to Ramuz (Bellour and Bandy, *Jean-Luc Godard*, 123). In addition to biographical connections to the Swiss canton of Vaud, Godard and Ramuz share what Denis de Rougemont has described as the "incarnation of myth" expressed in terms of concrete details and a sense of imminent catastrophe (see Denis de Rougemont, "Vues sur C.F. Ramuz," *Esprit* 44 [May 1936], 161, and the introduction to C. F. Ramuz, *The End of All Men* [New York: Pantheon, 1944], xv–xvi).

The closest analog within *Histoire(s) du cinéma* to the Tiresias imagery in the *Cantos* is the shot of L. B. Jeffries with his elongated camera in *Rear Window*; when it reappears in *Une vague nouvelle* (3B), it reminds the viewer of the very first image shown in *Toutes les histoires* (1A). Images of the famous lions in *Battleship Potemkin*, which also appear in both *Toutes les histoires* (1A) and *Une vague nouvelle* (3B), have a similar linking function.

218. Pound, *Cantos*, 794. With these words, Pound announces his intention to shift into the *Paradiso* section of the *Cantos* while simultaneously referring back to the beginning of the quest by echoing the Italian passage—"*O voi che siete in piccioletta barca*"—from Canto VII (26). The Italian phrase in Canto VII is a verbatim quotation of the first line of Canto II in Dante's *Paradiso*. A variant is included, in English, in another late Canto (XCIII): "'Oh you,' as Dante says 'in the dinghy astern there'" (651). Pound frequently alluded to the influence of the *Commedia* on the *Cantos*, writing in 1944:

> For forty years I have schooled myself, not to write an economic history of the U.S. or any other country, but to write an epic poem which begins "In the Dark Forest," crosses the Purgatory of human error, and ends in the light, and "*fra i maestri di color che sanno*" (Ezra Pound, "An Introduction to the Economic Nature of the United States," in *Ezra Pound, Selected Prose: 1909–1965*, edited by William Cookson [New York: New Directions, 1973], 167).

219. This passage is included in Canto CXVI (Pound, *Cantos*, 815–816). Canto CXVII was never completed, but in one of his published notes for it, Pound wrote, "I tried to make a paradiso—terrestre / I have tried to write Paradise" (822).

In the early stages of the *Cantos*, Pound had stressed the Neoplatonic perfection of the *Paradiso*, observing, "One hears far too much about Dante's Hell, and far too little about the poetry of the *Purgatorio* and the *Paradiso*," and arguing, "The beauty of the *Paradiso* hardly suffers one to transplant it in fragments, as I here attempt" (Ezra Pound, *The Spirit of Romance* [New York: New Directions, 1968], 128, 143). It is only later—after the war, the camps, "The Cage"—that Pound reconciled himself to a more fractured, provisional approach to representing paradise.

220. A little more than halfway through *Nouvelle vague*, the opening lines of *Inferno* (Canto I, lines 1–9, with a short gap separating 1–6 and 7–9) are recited in Italian by lead actress Domiziana Giordano (Elena), structurally echoing Dante's celebrated opening:

"Midway in the journey of our life / I came to myself in a dark wood, / for the straight way was lost" (Robert and Jean Hollander translation [New York: Doubleday, 2000], lines 1–3). Lines 19–27 from the same canto are used after the protagonists have been reunited. This excerpt culminates in "so my mind, still in flight, / turned back to look once more upon the pass / no mortal being ever left alive." Lennox then says (in French), "Don't look back!" explicitly connecting the reunited lovers to Orpheus and Eurydice. Lines 1–7 from Canto III of the *Purgatorio* appear several minutes later, followed shortly thereafter by lines 12–15 (intermediate lines seem to be recited in between, but they are drowned out by other parts of the soundtrack).

The quotations in *La Monnaie de l'absolu* (3A) are from lines 119–120 of Canto XXIV of *Inferno* ("O how stern it is, the power of God, / hurling such blows as it takes vengeance!") and line 26 of Canto XX in *Purgatorio* ("you chose poverty with virtue," Robert and Jean Hollander translation [New York: Doubleday, 2003]).

Dante's discussion of Ulysses' attempt to journey beyond mortal limits in Canto XXVI of *Inferno* is referred to in *Contempt* during the scene in which Fritz Lang presents the footage from his adaptation of *The Odyssey*. He recites lines 112–120 in German, and the character played by Michel Piccoli responds in French by pairing the openings of two stanzas, lines 127 and 136, with the final line of the canto (line 142). A discussion of Hölderlin's "The Poet's Vocation" follows several minutes later.

221. The United States Marine Corps hymn, also known as "The Halls of Montezuma," had been used in Hollywood films like *Gung Ho!* (Ray Enright, 1943), *The Sands of Iwo Jima* (Allan Dwan, 1949), and *The Halls of Montezuma* (Lewis Milestone, 1951), making this yet another instance of Godard playing off of collective memories of World War II.

222. Daney, "Godard Makes [Hi]stories," 159. The version presented onscreen differs slightly from the published transcription, especially because of verbal repetitions and the complexity of the soundtrack. Godard's use of the Brecht quotation also evokes the Lang character's (ultimately unrealized) ambition in *Contempt*: to find a way of translating Odysseus' quest into cinema.

223. Godard had expressed a desire to mount an exhibition that would complement *Histoire(s) du cinéma* to Youssef Ishaghpour during their interview (first published in France in 2000): "I wanted to put on a small exhibition or something of that sort in a gallery, assemble something that would show the different modes of entering and leaving what one can call History" (Godard and Ishaghpour, *Cinema*, 48).

224. A detailed account of the production of both exhibitions is given by curator and initiator Dominique Païni in "D'après JLG . . . ," in Brenez et al., *Jean-Luc Godard, Documents*, 420–426. See also the parallel assessments of *Voyage(s) en utopie, Jean-Luc Godard, 1946–2006: À la recherche d'un théorème perdu* by James Quandt and John Kelsey in *Artforum* 45, no. 1 (September 2006), 73–78, 397.

225. This is the final sentence of Henri Bergson's *Matter and Memory* (translated by N. M. Paul and W. S. Palmer [New York: Zone Books, 1991], 249). It was intended to appear on the floor of the final room ("Salle 9: Le Tombeau") of the original exhibition, *Collage(s) de France, archéologie du cinema d'après JLG*.

226. The title of Bergson's book is one of the first things Godard says in *Toutes les histoire(s)* (1A), another instance of ends being connected to beginnings. Godard also reads out the title of the book onscreen midway through *Fatale beauté* (2B), in conjunction with an image of the burning car from *Weekend* and a voiceover, by Godard, declaring, "Films

are merchandise and we must burn films, I told Langlois, but be careful with the fire within [The Godard onscreen, looking at an offscreen book in his library says, "*Matière et mémoire*"]. Art is like fire, it is born from what it burns." This brief cluster brings together the Bergsonian idea of memory as an active process with the poetics of phoenix-like creative destruction derived, by way of Malraux, from the German Romantics.

The same quote used on the floor of the exhibition is also used in three short works that extend the principles of *Histoire(s) du cinéma*: *The Old Place*, *The Origins of the 21st Century*, and *Liberté et patrie*. In *In Praise of Love*, the first feature film Godard completed after *Histoire(s) du cinéma*, one character highlights this aspect of Godard's late work by saying, "Memory has no obligations. Read Bergson" (Godard made a similar statement himself in Truong, "Résistance de l'art," 446).

227. As Godard explained in an interview with Alain Bergala conducted just after *Histoire(s) du cinéma* was completed, in closing the loop as he does with the story of the flower, "There is a true montage. There were four hours of film which permitted me to make a montage" (Bergala, "Une boucle bouclée," 41).

228. In a letter demonstrating Godard's layered use of cultural references in *Germany Year 90 Nine Zero*, he draws out some of the other associations implicitly contained within the image of the white rose: the white dress in Goethe's *The Sorrows of Young Werther*, Goethe's argument that white is not an intermediate color, and finally, "the white rose, the only unknown of Rilke" (Jean-Luc Godard, "Lettre à Louis Seguin sur *Allemagne neuf zéro*," in Brenez et al., *Jean-Luc Godard, Documents*, 340). Rilke wrote a series of poems on roses, including one intended to be his epitaph, but Godard is probably thinking here of the vision of total but ever-mysterious perfection in the 1907 poem, "The Rose Bowl."

The Sanctus from Beethoven's *Missa solemnis* is also used in *Une vague nouvelle* (3B), accompanying a montage of hands and Godard's discussion of the "fraternity of metaphors."

229. Dante, *Paradiso*, Canto XXX, line 124 (Robert and Jean Hollander translation, New York: Doubleday, 2007). The rose is the allegorical image of the heavens, and once Dante enters the empyrean at the beginning of the next canto, it is depicted "in form, then, of a luminous white rose" (Canto XXXI, line 1). Crucially, in the final canto, Dante repeatedly reminds the reader that his image of the "eternal Light," which cannot be penetrated "with such unblinking eyes," is constrained by his particular limit of vision. He describes the perfect circling of the celestial spheres, "the universal form of this dense knot," as appearing "in you as light's reflection" (Canto XXXIII, lines 43–45, 91–92, 128). In this, Dante is following the Pauline tradition (often cited by Godard), which also informs the key section toward the end of the *Paradiso* in which Dante shifts tenses to remind the reader that this experience is being narrated retrospectively:

> From that time on my power of sight exceeded
> that of speech, which fails at such a vision,
> as memory fails at such abundance
>
> . . . .
>
> O Light exalted beyond mortal thought,
> grant that in memory I see again
> but one small part of how you then appeared
> And grant my tongue sufficient power

that it may leave behind a single spark
of glory for the people yet to come. (lines 55–57, 67–72)

While it clearly articulates the partiality of human knowledge, this passage also reinforces the crystalline structural cohesion of the *Divine Comedy* by referring (via the phrase "my memory") back to both the beginning of the *Paradiso* and, through the idea of dreaming, to Canto I of *Inferno* (lines 10–12). By linking the various sections of his epic together like this, Dante is deepening the sense that it attempts, however incompletely, to map out the perfect schema of the universe, which exists even if humans cannot fully perceive or represent it. For Godard, on the contrary, this circularity reflects the instability of history, the difficulty of processing cataclysmic events without recourse to a larger theological or metaphysical order.

Beatrice, who replaces the pagan Virgil and guides Dante into Paradise, plays a central role in the *Paradiso* that is prefigured by her appearance in the final four cantos of the *Purgatorio* and sporadic references earlier. The surprise appearance of Anne-Marie Miéville's name in the dedication to the final section of *Histoire(s) du cinéma* is similarly anticipated by the inclusion of her photograph at the beginning of the preceding section *Le Contrôle de l'univers* (4A) and the use of excerpts from her films *Mon cher sujet* (1988), in *Une histoire seule* (1B), and *Après la reconciliation* (codirected with and starring Godard, 2000), in *Fatale beauté* (2B).

230. The rose also evokes memories of images in two earlier *Histoire(s) du cinéma* sections. Near the end of *Fatale beauté* (2B), Godard irises an image of the Tramp at the end of *City Lights* (Charles Chaplin, 1931) on top of an image of roses made with an early color process. Charlie Chaplin is later shown holding a white rose to his mouth (an image from *Limelight*, 1952) near the end of *Une vague nouvelle* (3B). Roses had also shown up in at least two earlier Godard films: a white rose was symbolically associated with Claire and a red rose with Carmen in *First Name: Carmen*; and the Romantic underpinnings of Godard's Marxism are epitomized by the red rose shown in close-up in *Pravda*.

In *Scénario du film Passion*, Godard discusses Delacroix's decision, in the twilight years of his life, to devote himself to flower paintings and declares, "Someday I would like to paint flowers too," a perfect metaphor for what he does sixteen years later, in the final moments of the work that he saw as a late-period summation of his career.

231. In one of his notebook entries, Coleridge wrote:

If a man could pass thro' Paradise in a Dream, & have a flower presented to him as a pledge that his Soul had really been there, & found that flower in his hand when he awoke—Aye? And what then? (Kathleen Coburn, ed., *The Notebooks of Samuel Taylor Coleridge*, Text, vol. 3, *1808–1819* [Princeton, NJ: Princeton University Press, 1973], 4287)

Kathleen Coburn points out that this derives from Jean Paul's *Geist* (an unauthorized compendium of excerpts from the author's other texts):

Oh, if a mortal man were to wander in a dream through Elysium, if vast unfamiliar flowers were to close above him; if one of the blessed were to offer him one of these flowers, saying: "Let this remind you when you awake that you have not been dreaming"—how he would yearn for that Elysian land, whenever he looked at the flower. (Kathleen Coburn, ed., *The Notebooks of Samuel Taylor Coleridge*, Notes, vol. 3, *1808–1819* [Princeton, NJ: Princeton University Press, 1973], 4287)

Jean Paul's frequent quotations, like Godard's, are often inexact paraphrases.

The onscreen reference to Borges at the end of *Les Signes parmi nous* (4B) is probably due to a passage in his 1960 story "The Yellow Rose":

> In a goblet, a woman has set a yellow rose; the man murmurs the inevitable lines of poetry that even he, to tell the truth, is a bit tired of by now. . . . Then the revelation occurred. Marino *saw* the rose, as Adam had seen it in Paradise, and he realized that it lay within its own eternity, not within his words, and that we might speak about the rose, allude to it, but never truly express it, and that the tall, haughty volumes that made a golden dimness in the corner of his room were not (as his vanity had dreamed them) a mirror of the world, but just another thing added to the world's contents. . . . Marino achieved that epiphany on the eve of his death, and Homer and Dante may have achieved it as well. (Jorge Luis Borges, *Collected Fictions*, translated by Andrew Hurley [London: Penguin Classics, 1998], 310)

The imagery of the Coleridge story also appears in a more explicitly Dantean story by Borges, "*Paradiso, XXXI*, 108": "Who knows but that tonight we may see [paradise] in the labyrinth of dreams, and not know tomorrow that we saw it" (*Collected Fictions*, 316). That, in both of these cases, Borges' appropriation of Coleridge carries strong echoes of Dante's *Paradiso* implicitly strengthens these associations in *Histoire(s) du cinéma*.

The idea of a flower caught in a dream was developed in the same period by Novalis in his unfinished novel *Heinrich von Ofterdingen* (1802), where the protagonist longs to retrieve a symbolically charged "Blue Rose." In a 1964 article on Cocteau's *Orpheus*, Godard had paraphrased a famous passage from the second part of the novel ("World turns to dream and dream to world" in the Palmer Hilty translation [Long Grove, IL: Waveland Press, 1990], 152): "The German Novalis tells us . . . that if the world becomes a dream, the dream in its turn becomes a world" (Jean-Luc Godard, "*Orphée*," translated by Tom Milne in Milne, *Godard on Godard*, 205). In *Band of Outsiders*, released the same year this review was written, Godard, as offscreen narrator, says that the character Franz wonders whether "the world is becoming a dream or a dream is becoming the world."

232. Much of Jean Paul's work was preoccupied with questions of belief and the tenuous boundary between hope and despair. The section "On the Desert and the Promised Land of the Human Race" in the 1795 novel *Hesperus*, for example, ends:

> A veiled eye behind Time, an eternal heart beyond the world. There is a higher order of things than we can demonstrate—there is a Providence in the history of the world and in the life of each one of us, stoutly denied by reason, stoutly believed by the heart—there must be a Providence following other rules than those we had applied heretofore, linking this muddled earth as a satellite town to a loftier City of God—there must be a God, a virtue, an eternity. (Translated by Erika Casey in *Jean Paul: A Reader*, edited by Timothy J. Casey [Baltimore: Johns Hopkins University Press, 1992], 119)

Conclusion

1. Henry James, "The Middle Years," in *Selected Tales* (London: Penguin Classics, 2001), 254.

2. Godard told Régis Debray that he is "a child of the museum. But, contrary to [André] Malraux, I think that the museum can be living. The cinema immediately

became the museum of the real, but it did not fulfill this function" (Régis Debray, "Jean-Luc Godard rencontre Régis Debray," in *Jean-Luc Godard par Jean-Luc Godard,* edited by Alain Bergala, vol. 2, *1984–1998* [Paris: Cahiers du cinéma, 1998], 428).

3. The premiere screening was held on November 28, 2001. *In the Darkness of Time* was subsequently included as part of the 2002 anthology film, *Ten Minutes Older: The Cello.* Although *The Old Place* had been commissioned by the Museum of Modern Art in 1998 and was completed in 1999, it was not publicly shown there until 2001.

4. As Godard explains in a 1998 interview, for someone like Warhol, "The image signified nothing ... there was no longer either faith or law in the use he made of it: it was already publicity and it terminated in the image of Marilyn [Monroe] on cigarette packs" (Frédéric Bonnaud and Arnaud Viviant, "La Légende du siècle," *Les Inrockuptibles* 170 [October 1998], 27).

5. In *The Old Place,* Anne-Marie Miéville declares, "Art wasn't protected from time. It was what protected time." Godard uses similar language in his voiceover at the end of the final section of *Histoire(s) du cinéma* (*Les Signes parmi nous,* 4B).

6. The manifesto was reproduced in Barry Bergdoll and Leah Dickerman, eds., *Bauhaus: Workshops for Modernity, 1919–1933* (New York: Museum of Modern Art, 2009), 64–67.

7. This is also true of Godard's almost willfully self-destructive exhibition at the Centre Georges Pompidou; whereas the first, unmade, version (*Collage(s) de France, archéologie du cinema d'après JLG*) was designed to simulate the effects of cinematic viewing, the one he completed (*Voyage(s) en utopie, Jean-Luc Godard, 1946–2006: À la recherche d'un théorème perdu,* 2006) employs countless LCD screens of varying shapes and sizes, an ironic reflection of the distracted viewing characteristic of the post-cinematic world.

8. In a 2007 interview, for example, Lav Diaz explained his approach to making and viewing his films:

[They] can be shown anywhere. I can show these films in cinemas or on DVD or in galleries. In Toronto, they will show this film in a gallery as part of a performance. Some people will interact, so it is evolving into something else. I am seeing a different kind of cinema, where we destroy the concept of audience. So many things are possible. Art is really free now.

I don't believe in the concept that you have to sit in the cinema for two hours and watch a story that is compressed in this period of time. Cinema can be anything. My films are not purposely done for the cinema anymore. You can watch them there, or in the streets, or ... on a plane! ... You can watch it at home, you can make love with your girlfriend for two hours, and when you come back, the film is still running. (Lav Diaz, "Digital Is Liberation Theology," interview with Tilman Baumgärtel, *Greencine,* September 7, 2007, available online at http://www.greencine.com/central/lavdiaz)

9. Markopoulos' framing was largely dictated by the 16mm equipment that he was using, although he considered many other exhibition possibilities before finally concluding that the single projected image would have more power (Gregory Markopoulos, "Unification of the Frame," in *The Sovereignty of the Filmmaker as Physician,* 7:3). Godard had come to a similar conclusion after watching Gance's Magirama projections in the 1950s:

So the triple screen, whether associated with the variable screen or not, may in certain scenes provoke supplementary effects in the sphere of pure sensation, but no more; and I admire [Jean] Renoir, [Orson] Welles, or [Roberto] Rossellini precisely because they achieve a similar or even superior result by more logical means, breaking the frame but not destroying it. (Jean-Luc Godard, "Future, Present, Past: Magirama," translated by Tom Milne in *Godard on Godard*, edited by Tom Milne [New York: Da Capo Press, 1972], 42)

Most of the films Godard made after *Weekend* are designed for "Academy ratio" (1.37:1) projection, while Rivette has used it more selectively—in the features shot in 16mm (*Out 1; Out 1: Spectre*, 1972; *Céline and Julie Go Boating*, 1974; *Le Pont du nord*, 1981) and in both versions of *La Belle Noiseuse* (*La Belle Noiseuse*, 1991, and *Divertimento*, 1992, both shot with 35mm film). This ratio, standard for 16mm films and for twentieth-century television, originates in the silent era, which is undoubtedly one of the reason these three filmmakers employ it as they do.

10. Godard is certainly not oblivious to the often dark history of the Soviet Union; in his discussion with Serge Daney, he expresses his admiration for "absolutely fantastic books that are quite forgotten today, like David Rousset's" (Serge Daney, "Godard Makes [Hi]stories," translated by Georgia Gurrieri in *Jean-Luc Godard: Son + Image, 1974–1991*, edited by Raymond Bellour with Mary Lea Bandy [New York: Museum of Modern Art, 1992], 165). Rousset was a survivor of Buchenwald—his 1946 book, *The Other Kingdom*, is an important analysis of the Nazi concentration camps—who openly criticized the camps still in use in the Soviet Union and was among the first to use the French word for "Gulag" in print (see Tzvetan Todorov, *Hope and Memory: Lessons from the Twentieth Century* [Princeton, NJ: Princeton University Press, 2003], 148–158). Godard emphasizes this process in the final section of *The Origins of the 21st Century* (2000) by overlaying the word sequence "*konec-goulag-lager*" ("end" in Russian, "Gulag" in French, "camp" in German) on dialectically paired shots of trains, immediately after a montage that uses the color red to interlink clips depicting euphoric celebration from a number of different Soviet films.

11. Excluding films made by Godard or Miéville, archival footage compilations, and Agnès Varda's documentary about her husband Jacques Demy's 1967 musical *The Young Girls of Rochefort* (*Les Demoiselles ont eu 25 ans*, 1993), the works from the 1990s that are cited or included in *Histoire(s) du cinéma* are Chris Marker's 1993 documentary about Aleksandr Medvedkin, *The Last Bolshevik* (referred to in *Une vague nouvelle*, 3B, and *Le Contrôle de l'univers*, 4A); *Corridor* (Šarūnas Bartas, 1995, Lithuania, referred to in *Le Contrôle de l'univers*, 4A); *Three Days* (Šarūnas Bartas, 1992, Lithuania, referred to in *Le Contrôle de l'univers*, 4A); and *Whispering Pages* (Aleksandr Sokurov, 1993, Russia, referred to in *Les Signes parmi nous*, 4B).

12. Among other factors, the decreasing demand for celluloid processing and the closure of many labs has driven the cost of shooting, editing, and printing a film of this length far beyond the reach of most directors.

13. Untitled speech prepared by Tarr and distributed to the audience at the Museum of Modern Art on October 23, 2009, when the director was unable to appear (the text is dated October 2009). Tarr also observes, in another comment that applies equally to his own work, that Bódy "was clear about regional history having come to an end, and cosmic history having taken its place."

14. Like many Hungarian films made during the Soviet period, the first three films Tarr made in collaboration with László Krasznahorkai (*Damnation*, 1987; *Sátántangó*; and *Werckmeister Harmonies*, 2000) seem initially to encourage allegorical readings, only to confound those same readings by preventing the symbolic allusions (to things like

"Maya's veil" or a passage from the Old Testament) from mapping into an exhaustive schema, thereby allowing them to resonate on multiple levels at once. In all three films, Tarr uses these sorts of visual and textual references to create a foreboding atmosphere that has metaphysical connotations, but remains grounded within a concrete material reality.

15. No Hungarian feature film had been shot using real black-and-white film stock (as opposed to desaturated color stock) for fifteen years when Tarr decided to use it on *Damnation*; he has continued to employ it on all of his subsequent films, including the work he insists will be his last, *The Turin Horse* (2011). Tarr arranges the length of his shots around the 300-meter (eleven-minute) limit of the 35mm camera battery, which he has jokingly referred to as a type of censorship imposed by Kodak (Eric Schlosser, "Interview with Béla Tarr," *Bright Lights Film Journal* 30 [October 2000], available online at http://www.brightlightsfilm.com/30/belatarr1.html).

16. This structure is derived from László Krasznahorkai's novel *Sátántangó* (1985).

17. These ideas are further elaborated in *The Turin Horse*, which includes a scene in which a young girl reads a long passage from a book given to her by Gypsies. In a conversation at the New York Film Festival on October 9, 2011, Tarr described the book as being about "the disintegration of churches and what is lost." The book appears to include the Code of Canon Law because the girl reads sections devoted to "Sacred Places" almost verbatim (Book IV, Part III, Title I, Canons 1210 and 1211 in the 1983 code).

18. Tarr shares with Jancsó an abstract choreography of bodies and relationships, very long takes, and an inventive use of framing that creates a sense of pervasive confinement even in exterior shots. Bódy's influence is evident primarily in a mythic treatment of history (pushed furthest in Bódy's four-and-a-half-hour film *Narcissus and Psyche*, 1980), an obsessive interest in facial physiognomy, an experimental approach to film sound (more disjunctive in Bódy's work than Tarr's), and a desire to interrogate the structure of vision (the gun turret perspectives and onscreen maps in Bódy's *American Torso*, 1975; the persistent use of binocular framings in *Sátántangó*). Tarr mentions his interest in Bruegel and also expresses his belief that *Andrei Rublev* is Tarkovsky's best film in Fergus Daly and Maximilian Le Cain, "Waiting for the Prince: An Interview with Béla Tarr," *Senses of Cinema* 11 (December 2000–January 2001), available online at http://sensesofcinema.com/2001/feature-articles/tarr-2/.

19. The final words of the film, read out haltingly and accompanied by grunts over a dark screen, as if the doctor were writing them down as they are spoken, are

> not long before . . . the long drops . . . of the insufferably long . . . autumn rains . . . fell . . . on the parched . . . sodic ground . . . on the western side of the yard . . . for . . . the stinking bog . . . to make the tracks . . . until the first frosts . . . impassable . . . and the town cut off . . . Futaki was woken . . . by the sound of bells. Closest . . . eight kilometers to the south-west . . . on the old Hochmeiss field . . . was a solitary chapel . . . but not only no bell there . . . even its tower collapsed . . . during the war.

INDEX